NATO in the 1990s

Edited by

STANLEY R. SLOAN

With a foreword by

SENATOR WILLIAM V. ROTH, JR.

CHAIRMAN, NORTH ATLANTIC ASSEMBLY SPECIAL
PRESIDENTIAL COMMITTEE ON NATO IN THE 1990s

Published with the cooperation of
the North Atlantic Assembly

PERGAMON-BRASSEY'S
International Defense Publishers, Inc.

Washington · New York · London · Oxford
Beijing · Frankfurt · São Paulo · Sydney · Tokyo · Toronto

U.S.A. (Editorial)	Pergamon-Brassey's International Defense Publishers, Inc., 8000 Westpark Drive, 4th Floor, McLean, Virginia 22102, U.S.A.
(Orders)	Pergamon Press, Inc., Maxwell House, Fairview Park, Elmsford, New York 10523, U.S.A.
U.K. (Editorial)	Brassey's Defence Publishers, Ltd., 24 Gray's Inn Road, London WC1X 8HR, England
(Orders)	Brassey's Defence Publishers, Ltd., Headington Hill Hall, Oxford OX3 0BW, England
PEOPLE'S REPUBLIC OF CHINA	Pergamon Press, Room 4037, Qianmen Hotel, Beijing, People's Republic of China
FEDERAL REPUBLIC OF GERMANY	Pergamon Press GmbH, Hammerweg 6, D-6242 Kronberg, Federal Republic of Germany
BRAZIL	Pergamon Editora Ltda, Rua Eça de Queiros, 346, CEP 04011, Paraiso, São Paulo, Brazil
AUSTRALIA	Pergamon-Brassey's Defence Publishers Pty. Ltd., P.O. Box 544, Potts Point, N.S.W. 2011, Australia
JAPAN	Pergamon Press, 5th Floor, Matsuoka Central Building, 1-7-1 Nishishinjuku, Shinjuku-ku, Tokyo 160, Japan
CANADA	Pergamon Press Canada Ltd., Suite No. 271, 253 College Street, Toronto, Ontario, Canada M5T 1R5

First edition 1989

Library of Congress Cataloging in Publication Data

NATO in the 1990s.
"Published with the cooperation of the North Atlantic Assembly."
Includes index.
1. North Atlantic Treaty Organization. I. Sloan, Stanley R.
II. North Atlantic Assembly.
JX1393.N67N36 1989 341.7'2 88-25252

British Library Cataloguing in Publication Data

NATO in the 1990s.
1. North Atlantic Treaty Organization.
I. Sloan, Stanley R., *1943*-II. North Atlantic Assembly
355'.031'091821
ISBN 0-08-036722-4

Printed in Great Britain by A. Wheaton & Co. Ltd, Exeter

18-95

NATO in the 1990s

Titles of Related Interest

Related Periodicals

(Specimen copies available upon request)

Contents

Foreword

Few institutions can expect to remain unchanged for forty years while still fulfilling the tasks for which they were originally designed. We live in a rapidly developing global economic, political, and security situation. Institutions that aspire to long-term relevance and validity must change with changing times. Change moves hand in hand with continuity, and any attempt to isolate the two is doomed to failure.

Of all the human institutions established in the aftermath of World War II, the North Atlantic Treaty Organization must rank preeminent as worthy of preservation into the next century. Under its protection, Western Europe, the focus of two major conflicts in this century, has prospered politically and economically under open, democratic governments. The threat to Western Europe from across the Elbe has been held back, without resort to direct military force.

Moreover, the alliance appears likely to be as relevant in the 1990s as it was in the 1950s. Notwithstanding recent arms control agreements, the threat from the East remains, in the form of vast Warsaw Pact forces of tanks, artillery, and motorized infantry. In addition, new threats have arisen from outside NATO's geographic area. No NATO member can rationally conclude that it is better equipped to cope with these threats alone than it is in concert with fifteen other free, democratic nations.

Consultations within the alliance framework will continue to provide the best way for the NATO allies to coordinate their attempts to improve relations with the Warsaw Pact countries. Through early and detailed discussions among the allies, each can be certain that its policies promote East-West stability and peace, while not undermining the security interests of the alliance.

Having established NATO's continued relevance into the 1990s, we must ask ourselves how we can guarantee that the alliance will, in the coming years, prove capable of protecting the security of its member nations. Past successes cannot be presumed to constitute evidence of future effectiveness. Certainly, the global situation has changed radically since the formation of the alliance. Can we reasonably expect NATO to enjoy success in the future if it fails to adapt to these changes?

As U.S. critics of the alliance are all too fond of pointing out, the transatlantic economic relationship has changed radically over the past forty years. Economic power, the virtual monopoly of North

America in the postwar period, has now become dispersed throughout Western Europe and the Pacific Basin. The distribution of the economic burden of protecting Western Europe should reflect these economic developments with some degree of equity. Likewise, domestic economic developments within the United States point to the need for some enhanced defense contribution by Washington's allies. As the U.S. government struggles to balance its federal budget under the strictures of Gramm-Rudman-Hollings, Congress and the electorate appear highly unlikely to permit any further real increases in the national defense budget in the foreseeable future. Thus, U.S. armed forces may no longer boast the resources to maintain their heavy commitment to Western Europe while prosecuting their traditional global maritime role.

Economic changes within the alliance have been mirrored by political developments. The European members of the alliance and Canada are no longer the quiescent allies of the United States. On occasion they pursue economic and foreign policies directly contrary to those emanating from Washington, as one would expect of any independent nation-state. Frustrations over such differences have alienated some of Europe's younger generation from the alliance and caused them to place undue faith in the goodwill of the Eastern bloc.

Meanwhile, in the United States, confusion over a perplexing global situation has given rise to liberal isolationism, while frustration with state-sponsored terrorism and supposedly recalcitrant allies has engendered right wing unilateralism. Most ominously of all, we have witnessed the emergence of a new generation of Soviet political leaders. These new figures are infinitely more politically sophisticated than their predecessors and fully capable of using aggressive public diplomacy to play upon transatlantic differences and irritations in their continuing quest to achieve the denuclearization of Europe and the cutting of the transatlantic knot.

The growing unpopularity of the nuclear deterrent on both sides of the Atlantic could facilitate Moscow's ambitions. Traditionally, the alliance has not tried to counterbalance the Warsaw Pact's huge advantage in conventional forces with comparable conventional deployments, the expense being too great. Instead, it has opted for the cheaper "nuclear option" that threatens to escalate any conventional conflict to the nuclear level rather than risk defeat. However, the Soviet achievement of nuclear parity has cast some doubt upon this assertion, as, in some quarters, has the signing of the INF treaty. Meanwhile, the rising cost of conventional weaponry has debilitated NATO's ability to negate the Pact's conventional advantage with its own conventional deployments.

None of these problems is insoluble, and they will harm the alliance only if they are ignored. A coordinated allied approach to conventional arms negotiations could achieve an equitable agreement that obviates the need for a conventional build-up. In the absence of such an agreement, the resource problems of the United States can be adequately offset only by the strengthening of the "European Pillar" of the alliance. This strengthening, in turn, would "raise the nuclear threshold" to a point where manifestly NATO would resort to its nuclear deterrent force only in the direst emergency. Rising conventional weapons costs can be contained by enhanced intra-European and transatlantic arms cooperation. Disagreements over out-of-area problems can be mitigated through enhanced consultation and cooperation, as has been demonstrated recently in the Persian Gulf.

If these steps can be achieved, the product will be a renewed, healthy alliance fully capable both of coping with the diplomatic offensives of General Secretary Gorbachev and of defending the security and interests of the peoples of its sixteen member nations as successfully in the future as it has in the past.

WILLIAM V. ROTH, JR.
U.S. Senate and
Chairman, North Atlantic Assembly
Special Presidential Committee
on NATO in the 1990s

Preface

At a time of change and challenge in the transatlantic relationship, the North Atlantic Assembly formed a special presidential committee to conduct a study of NATO's future. The Committee on NATO in the 1990s has over the past two years pursued an in-depth survey of the challenges facing the North Atlantic Alliance. This survey has included hearings in Washington, London, and Rome, during which a wide range of American and European views on the alliance were presented. The Committee also commissioned a group of leading U.S. and European experts to analyze major issues in the alliance. Their findings, plus the conclusions and recommendations of the Committee, are the basis for this publication.

The Committee's overriding objective has been to map out a bold, comprehensive framework capable of commanding broad political support on both sides of the Atlantic to guide the alliance through what is likely to be one of the most challenging periods in its history. Clearly, the economic and political environment is evolving on both regional and global levels and requires a readjustment in burdens and responsibilities among the allies.

In order to manage this readjustment, the Committee calls for a new political mandate built on the principles of continued U.S. presence in Europe and increased burden relief provided by the European allies through the creation of a viable European pillar—a new transatlantic bargain.

In the Committee's view, a summit of NATO heads of government is needed to provide the necessary backing to implement this mandate. Our parliaments and publics must appreciate that NATO is the guarantor of Western security and the future of NATO depends on an equitable redistribution of the political and defense burden among all 16 allies.

All of the Committee's recommendations are aimed at promoting necessary changes in the alliance and its policies to ensure that NATO will continue to serve the needs of the member countries in the 1990s and beyond. Specific recommendations are offered concerning future NATO strategy, nuclear and conventional force posture and arms control, bases, out-of-area security, new defense technologies, economic relations, and overcoming the division of Europe. The Committee advocates an imaginative approach to the shaping of a real European pillar in the alliance, including among its building blocks an annual security assessment by the European allies, institutional reform to rationalize European defense cooperation efforts, the creation ultimately of a "European" division, development of a European-scale defense market, and increased task specialization among the allies.

The Committee's survey was conducted with an open mind to the differing views that exist on the alliance and its policies among NATO countries. The Committee believes that a spirit of open debate and dissent is the key not only to the functioning of our individual democracies but also to the alliance as a whole. This volume is presented in keeping with that spirit.

Finally, I would like to express my deep gratitude to Stan Sloan, Study Director for NATO in the 1990s; Peter Corterier, Secretary General of the North Atlantic Assembly; Martin McCusker, Director of the NAA Military Committee; John Borawski, Director of the NAA Political Committee; the remainder of the excellent staff of the North Atlantic Assembly; the experts and officials who presented views to the Committee; and the contributors to this volume, without whose combined efforts this project would not have been possible.

TON FRINKING
President,
North Atlantic Assembly
May 1988

North Atlantic Assembly Committee on
NATO in the 1990s

William V. ROTH Jr., Chairman (Member of the Senate, United States)

Manfred ABELEIN (Member of the *Bundestag*, Federal Republic of Germany)

Gianfranco ASTORI (Member of the Chamber of Deputies, Italy)

Douglas BEREUTER (Member of the House of Representatives, United States)

Lasse BUDTZ (Member of the *Folketing*, Denmark)

François FILLON (Member of the National Assembly, France)

Ton FRINKING (President of the North Atlantic Assembly and Member of the Second Chamber of the States-General, Netherlands)

Javier BARRERO LOPEZ (Member of the Chamber of Deputies, Spain)

Bruce GEORGE (Member of the House of Commons, United Kingdom)

Sir Geoffrey JOHNSON SMITH (Member of the House of Commons, United Kingdom)

Thor KNUDSEN (Member of the *Storting*, Norway)

Sam NUNN (Member of the Senate, United States)

Bill RICHARDSON (Member of the House of Representatives, United States)

Peter CORTERIER, Secretary General of the NAA

Stan SLOAN, Study Director and Consultant to the NAA, U.S. Congressional Research Service

Martin MCCUSKER, Director of the Military Committee, NAA

John BORAWSKI, Director of the Political Committee, NAA

I
NATO in the 1990s

1

Summary Conclusions and Recommendations

Having examined NATO's future in the wake of the agreement between the United States and the Soviet Union to eliminate their intermediate-range nuclear missiles, the North Atlantic Assembly's Committee on NATO in the 1990s submits to the governments, parliaments, and citizens of NATO member nations the following conclusions and recommendations:

NATO AND WESTERN INTERESTS

The NATO alliance remains the best way for the United States, Canada, and the West European NATO nations to ensure their national security and to seek a more stable, nonthreatening security structure in Europe.

A NEW POLITICAL MANDATE FOR NATO

A fundamental change has occurred in the U.S.–European relationship, reflecting the gradual relative increase in the economic strength and political potential of the West European members of the alliance. Because of this change, the West European allies should in the future share more effectively the political, economic, and military responsibilities of Western defense and alliance leadership. This need to adjust U.S. and European responsibilities in the alliance should be confirmed in a new transatlantic bargain between the United States, Canada, and the European members of the alliance.

The Committee therefore recommends that, early in the term of the new U.S. administration, building on the results of the NATO summit meeting in March 1988, a high-level meeting of the NATO allies should be convened to adopt a new political mandate for the alliance. The new mandate, to update the Harmel Report's current basis for NATO policies, should endorse the established policy of maintaining a strong defense while seeking dialogue, cooperation, and arms control with the East, devoting added attention to the need

1

to harmonize Western defense planning and arms control approaches. The allies should add to the Harmel formula their commitment to promote a real West European pillar in the alliance. To implement this approach, at such a meeting,

- the European members of the alliance should pledge that they will intensify defense cooperation among themselves while ensuring that such cooperation increases the West's security and political cohesion, and contributes to prospects for the improvement of East-West relations and arms control;
- the United States should welcome movement toward greater European defense cooperation and pledge that it will continue its active involvement in the maintenance of peace and stability in Europe, including a substantial troop presence in Europe and, as long as they remain necessary, nuclear forces structured and deployed in ways that strengthen deterrence for the entire alliance;
- the allies should jointly pledge that all future alliance decisions will take into consideration the need for the European allies progressively to assume a greater share of NATO responsibilities.

BUILDING BLOCKS FOR A WEST EUROPEAN PILLAR IN THE ALLIANCE

The Committee recommends that the European members of the alliance in the near future take the following steps toward creating a real European pillar:

- prepare on an annual basis a European security assessment identifying the threats to the Western democracies and detailing how they intend to respond to those threats;
- initiate a study of institutional changes that the establishment of a real European pillar in the alliance would imply, and especially the place and role that the Western European Union (WEU) and the European Economic Community (EEC) would have in building this pillar;
- seek to form a European division based on forces of a number of European countries that could serve as a special covering force for the alliance to provide flexibility in responding to a crisis;
- develop routine meetings of the military Chiefs of Staff of West European NATO governments and establish a computerized communications network linking planning staffs in European defense ministries to foster more thorough military cooperation at the European level;
- intensify efforts to create a European-scale defense market;
- encourage task specialization as a means of eliminating wasteful duplication and overlap among national military efforts.

RESPONDING TO THE CHALLENGES OF THE 1990s

NATO's Strategy

The heart of NATO's strategy rests in credible deterrence of threats to Western security.

The Committee has examined NATO's present deterrent strategy based on the doctrines of flexible response and forward defense and has considered the alternatives to this strategy that have been advanced. The Committee has concluded that in spite of any shortcomings, NATO's current strategy still provides the best available way for the alliance to ensure peace and encourage the development of a more stable East-West security environment in the 1990s. Alternatives that might imply breaking the spectrum of deterrence can only undermine the security and political cohesion of the alliance. To sustain an effective deterrence policy, the NATO allies cannot permit a potential aggressor to believe that it can choose the level of conflict and not risk a Western military response at a higher level of hostilities.

The Role of Nuclear Weapons

There is a strong and quite understandable desire throughout the alliance to escape the awesome shadow of nuclear weapons. Perhaps in the future, under much improved global political conditions, this will be possible.

In the 1990s, however, irrespective of hoped-for progress in conventional or nuclear arms control or in defensive technologies, nuclear weapons will continue to play a key role in deterrence. Under contemporary political circumstances, the nuclear component in the West's deterrent posture provides an indispensable element of military stability that conventional forces alone cannot provide.

As NATO considers modernizing its nuclear posture, the Committee suggests several guidelines to shape nuclear weapons policies within the parameters of the INF Treaty as U.S. and Soviet intermediate-range nuclear missiles are eliminated:

- the balance within NATO's nuclear posture should preferably evolve toward longer-range, deterrence-oriented systems in and around Europe and away from shorter-range, battlefield systems, albeit without creating gaps in the overall spectrum of deterrence;
- NATO should in the 1990s seek arms control agreements and conventional defense improvements that would make it possible to reduce the overall numbers of nuclear weapons in Europe, ensuring

that any changes in nuclear force deployments are consistent with NATO's strategy and that they enhance security and military stability;

- the nature and location of nuclear deployments should be designed to enhance the security, safety, reliability, and command and control of nuclear weapons;
- nuclear deployments should be designed to raise, not lower, the nuclear threshold;
- nuclear deployments should therefore complement and not complicate conventional defense improvements; and
- nuclear deployments should be judged in terms of their potential effect on alliance cohesion and political consensus as well as their military utility.

Conventional Defense Improvements

The alliance must improve its ability to defend conventionally against nonnuclear Warsaw Pact capabilities if it hopes to raise the threshold at which NATO would be forced to use nuclear weapons.

The allies should sustain their efforts to identify critical deficiencies and to make a more serious effort to ensure that national force goals take those deficiencies into account. The allies still need to work on shortfalls of ammunition and other supplies that affect the ability of allied forces to sustain combat.

Beyond the important sustainability issue, the allies must seek ways to exploit the West's advantage in technology to render Soviet tank armies obsolete. The development of better nonnuclear means to defend against Warsaw Pact armor must be a high priority for NATO planning, research and development, and funding.

Given likely constraints on resources available for defense in the 1990s, the allies will have to make careful allocations of their resources, depending more heavily on reserve forces and improved crisis decision-making and mobilization capabilities. If there is no substantial progress toward reductions in Warsaw Pact capabilities for offensive operations against NATO, additional resources may be required to maintain a stable security environment in Europe.

The problem of improving conventional defenses is one that should be approached with a sense of common purpose by all political forces in the alliance. There may continue to be some fundamental differences in NATO countries about the appropriate role for nuclear weapons, but there should be a general consensus on the need to improve the defensive capabilities of NATO's conventional forces. Political forces of varying persuasions should put ideology aside and look pragmatically at all possible ways of approaching this objective.

New Defense Technologies: Challenge and Opportunity

The allies must persist in their efforts to harmonize technology export controls to ensure that measures taken to block Soviet acquisition of militarily relevant technologies do not impede technology transfer within the alliance. Governments should involve industrial representatives in their consultations on this issue to benefit from the expertise and experience that resides in the commercial sector.

NATO should reassess its procurement philosophy to emphasize reliability and ease of maintenance to help control the cost of weapons systems as technological sophistication increases. The missions to be performed should in the future guide NATO procurement decisions, rather than simple weapons replacement strategies. Choices should be governed by cost-effectiveness as determined by realistic testing rather than by simulation.

All the NATO allies must fully exploit research and development resources. The European allies waste substantial funds in duplication of research and development efforts. NATO as a whole should, wherever possible, seek to rationalize research and development efforts and, in particular, the European allies should seek to develop a common research and development fund.

The Committee further recommends that interested NATO nations begin now to investigate appropriate mechanisms for harmonizing development and construction of intelligence-gathering, communications, and early warning non-American military space projects as a first step toward ultimate alliance-wide harmonization of such systems. The Committee also recommends that the NATO nations attempt in the 1990s to coordinate the operations of American and non-American intelligence-gathering satellites to ensure more comprehensive coverage of critical intelligence requirements and to ensure against loss of coverage through accidents and malfunctions.

Economic Relations

The NATO allies must ensure that trade and economic differences do not undermine defense cooperation. The Committee hopes that the ongoing global trade negotiations under the auspices of the General Agreement on Tariffs and Trade (GATT), known as the "Uruguay Round," will help significantly improve the normative and institutional framework for international, and therefore transatlantic, trade. Both in the context of the GATT Round and in their bilateral contacts, the NATO allies should seek to reinforce consultative procedures, establish a functioning dispute-settlement mechanism, create effective conciliatory procedures, and take other steps to maximize understanding and minimize friction in the management of international trade questions.

Security Challenges Outside NATO's Area

Differences over security problems arising outside the area covered by the North Atlantic Treaty have the potential to create major political problems in the alliance. Because disagreements among the allies over "out-of-area" issues will likely arise again in the future, it is important that such issues be kept in perspective to protect the core of NATO cooperation and cohesion from differences they may stimulate.

The allies should intensify their consultations and cooperation at every level to ensure that complementary approaches are taken to out-of-area security problems whenever possible. But NATO was not designed to deal with such problems, and other Western-style democracies should also be involved in the process. Therefore, a new consultative and contingency-planning framework—a "Western Working Group on Global Security Issues"—should be established, separate from NATO, with the participation of NATO countries and Japan, and open to other Western countries that might wish to join. Implementation of plans or actions should remain independent national choices, and cooperation should be organized among participating countries on a national basis.

Overcoming the Division of Europe

Today, as in the past, it is important for the allies to seek avenues of political, economic, and security cooperation with the East to try to minimize the threats to Western security, promote a more stable East-West relationship, and overcome the division of Europe.

In the 1990s, NATO must continue to seek as a top priority to overcome the division of Europe and of Germany. These divisions lie at the root of East-West political tensions and the military confrontation in Europe today and must be surmounted if a new and more stable security structure is to be achieved between East and West. Given Eastern Europe's economic, social, and cultural history, Soviet hegemony over the region is unnatural.

Western policy toward Eastern Europe must continue to center upon the diversity that distinguishes the East European countries from each other and from the Soviet Union. It should reward those countries that move in the direction of greater foreign policy and economic independence, internal liberalization, and respect for human rights, while withholding benefits from countries that do not do so. Western policy must continue to promote the self-determination of peoples and the full implementation of the Helsinki Final Act of the Conference on Security and Cooperation in Europe (CSCE).

Individually, as well as collectively, the NATO allies all can play a continuing role in working toward a more acceptable relationship with the Warsaw Pact countries. At the same time, NATO governments must redouble efforts to explain to public opinion and parliaments the necessity for maintaining a strong national defense even while relations with the East are improving. The North Atlantic Assembly provides an important consultative forum for enhancing such communication. A strong, united, and confident West will make the best negotiating partner for the East.

Nuclear Arms Control

Arms control approaches, as well as modernization and deployment policies, should seek to reduce NATO's reliance on short-range nuclear weapons while preserving a credible, survivable nuclear weapons capability to sustain NATO's deterrence posture.

Over the next several years, while the U.S.–Soviet agreement to eliminate their intermediate-range nuclear missiles is being implemented, the main focus of NATO arms control efforts should be on nonnuclear forces, particularly those located in central Europe. However, after careful consideration, the allies may conclude that further nuclear arms reductions in Europe could be taken while maintaining NATO's deterrent strategy and avoiding the denuclearization of Western Europe. In such future negotiations, the alliance should seek to eliminate the Warsaw Pact's current superiority in short-range nuclear missiles.

Conventional Arms Control and Stabilizing Measures

The Committee believes that the West's ultimate objective in the new conventional stability talks should be reductions in Warsaw Pact forces to rough parity with NATO forces. This need not mean yielding precise equality in all subcategories of forces, but reductions should yield a relationship between NATO and Warsaw Pact forces that is stable and nonthreatening.

In the new Atlantic-to-the-Urals conventional stability talks, the West should seek reduction of complete Warsaw Pact units. Ideally, Soviet forces should be disbanded rather than redeployed elsewhere in the Soviet Union. The West might also consider proposing the storage of reduced equipment within the reduction area on both sides in mutually supervised storage sites as a first step toward reductions.

The West should also propose limits on production of tanks, monitored by on-site inspection at tank-production facilities. Such production constraints could help build down the military confrontation between the two alliances.

The Western requirement for asymmetrical reductions and the Soviet Union's concept of its defensive requirements might lead the new negotiations toward impasse. The West therefore should employ a subnegotiating strategy that would allow negotiation of small steps toward increased military stability in the near term while working toward more substantial reductions in the long term.

Toward this end, the West could early in the new conventional stability talks initiate discussions concerning characteristics of the Warsaw Pact's doctrine, force structure, and deployments that give rise to concern. The Western countries then should seek agreement on stabilizing measures that would actually constrain the operations of forces and make surprise attack a less feasible option.

Another useful step in the direction of a more cooperative European security system could be the establishment of a NATO–Warsaw Pact crisis-avoidance center. Such a center could bring together NATO and Warsaw Pact member military officers, experts, and diplomats to exchange on a continuing basis information on military activities, to raise issues about those activities of concern to either side, and to discuss and seek to resolve low-level incidents involving NATO and Warsaw Pact military personnel.

Finally, the NATO governments should seek in the framework of the Conference on Confidence- and Security-Building Measures and Disarmament in Europe (CDE) to strengthen the confidence-building measures that were agreed to in 1986 in Stockholm. In addition, the NATO countries should propose that the CDE participating states make arrangements for publication of an annual report on compliance with the Stockholm measures and with further measures that may be negotiated.

2
Report on NATO in the 1990s

NATO'S RATIONALE

In the 1990s, the United States, Canada, and the West European members of NATO will continue to need a transatlantic alliance to assure their defense and to promote their political and economic as well as security interests. This continuity, however, cannot be ensured unless there is also change—to adjust the alliance to fundamental shifts in the international environment and in relationships among the allies themselves.

Two fundamental reasons led Western nations after World War II to sign the North Atlantic Treaty and subsequently develop the North Atlantic Treaty Organization (NATO). The first was to provide a political and military counterbalance to the power of the Soviet Union in Europe. The second was to create a structure within which the nations of Western Europe and their North American allies—the United States and Canada—could promote peaceful and productive relationships among themselves, bringing to an end the cycles of internal conflict that had produced two world wars in the twentieth century.

After four decades, the alliance still serves these two fundamental purposes. Western relations with the Soviet Union have improved substantially since the days of the cold war. The current Soviet leadership appears to hold the promise of changes that could improve East-West relations even further in the years to come. But the aspects of Soviet ideology, internal behavior, and security policy that challenge Western ideals and interests are likely to change slowly, and the process now apparently underway could be reversed by a future Soviet leadership.

Therefore, the Western countries must remain sufficiently strong militarily and united politically to ensure that the Soviet Union cannot threaten the Western democracies through use of its substantial military power.

Western Europe has for these four decades remained an island of peace in a turbulent world, and NATO has played a vital role in

9

ensuring continuation of that peace and stability. The alliance, in combination with the European Economic Community (EEC), the Western European Union (WEU), and other organizations, has provided a framework for the full integration of the Federal Republic of Germany in the Western community of nations.

Without the active participation of the United States, it is difficult to imagine how the degree of cooperation that exists today within the Western alliance could be maintained. This important unifying role played by the United States will likely remain essential in the foreseeable future.

NATO'S INTERNAL RELATIONSHIPS: CONTINUITY

Over the years, observers on both sides of the Atlantic have suggested a variety of alternative ways to defend Western interests other than through the North Atlantic Treaty Organization. None of these proposals has been sufficiently compelling to convince any of the postwar U.S. administrations, Democratic or Republican. This Committee has examined a number of alternatives to NATO and has found no alternative that would serve North American and West European interests as well. Even though Members of the U.S. Congress have frequently criticized aspects of the alliance and policies of the allies, an overwhelming majority of U.S. Senators and Representatives favor continued U.S. involvement in NATO. This congressional perspective is supported by a similar majority in U.S. public opinion.

The North Atlantic Treaty embodies the highest ideals on which the United States has sought to base its foreign policies: to promote and defend democracy, protect the rights of the individual, and ensure freedom from international tyranny. U.S. participation in forward defense in Europe provides a necessary balance to Soviet power on the continent and a security envelope for the United States that extends far beyond American shores. Furthermore, the alliance relationship gives the United States substantial influence in a region of the world that remains vital to U.S. interests.

Within the other NATO nations, there is strong governmental, parliamentary, and public support for membership in the alliance. The security of all the West European allies is enhanced through alliance with their North American partners. NATO provides a framework within which European democracies can flourish, with no fear of imminent attack or hostilities from neighboring states. The alliance gives each ally greater security than could be provided on a purely national basis. It also establishes a firm foundation upon which allies can base their national policies toward Warsaw Pact members, encouraging the positive and yet realistic development of East-West relations along bilateral as well as multilateral lines.

Among the members of NATO, a variety of approaches to alliance commitments has developed over the years. While these variances in contributions to and roles in the alliance occasionally make it difficult to produce common solutions for the challenges to Western security, the ability of NATO to accommodate differing approaches remains essential. The flexibility of the NATO arrangements will continue to be an important requirement for the alliance, making it possible for sovereign nations to pursue common aims in spite of natural diversity within and among the members. In this regard, the alliance has been strengthened in the 1980s by the membership of Spain and the closer cooperation that has developed between France and other allies.

In sum, there is currently no more desirable alternative to membership in NATO for any member of the alliance.

NATO'S INTERNAL RELATIONSHIPS: THE NEED FOR CHANGE

All NATO allies will be well served by continuing and intensifying their participation in the alliance. But throughout NATO's four decades much change has been required in the structure and policies of the alliance to ensure its continuing relevance and effectiveness. Today, as ever, it is clear that in NATO there can be no continuity without change.

Sharing of Risks and Burdens

Continued Importance of the U.S. Role

In the face of a potential enemy that can quite freely allocate resources to its armaments efforts, Western democracies, which by their very nature do not have the same flexibility, can achieve a balance of forces only by uniting their efforts within the framework of the alliance. The United States has always played a major role in this effort to maintain a counterbalance to the military strength of the Warsaw Pact nations. The alliance in the 1990s will require the continued and effective participation of the United States. There is, however, an intimate relationship between U.S. economic strength, its role as a global power, and its ability to sustain a strong contribution to NATO. The United States cannot indefinitely incur budget and trade deficits without jeopardizing the future of its own economy and perhaps that of the international economic system.

In seeking to reduce its budget deficit, the United States is looking carefully at its international security commitments. The NATO alliance must search for additional ways that would help the United States control the costs of its commitments to European defense while ensuring a continuing strong U.S. role in the alliance. Particularly at a time of great uncertainty about the future directions of East-West relations and arms control, the United States should continue to maintain a substantial presence in Western Europe. Any significant reductions should come only as part of a negotiated and substantial reduction in Soviet forces opposing NATO. The presence in Europe of U.S. conventional as well as nuclear forces provides the indispensable link with the U.S. strategic arsenal and a tangible expression of the U.S. political and military commitment to Western defense. The relatively small financial gains, if any, that might be realized from cutting the level of U.S. troops in Europe would be far outweighed by the political costs and security risks.

Burden Relief and Access to Bases

To help the United States maintain its troop presence in Europe, the European allies should examine further steps to give the United States added relief from the burdens of its military presence in Europe. Such steps could include supplementary host-nation support programs to reduce the overhead costs of stationing U.S. forces in Europe.

In this regard, NATO countries should view the provision of NATO base facilities for allied forces and equipment as a part of their sovereign national contributions to Western security. Alliance members that do not participate in NATO's integrated command structure should consider providing base facilities to allies in a time of crisis. No ally should expect compensation for providing facilities that the alliance decides are essential to implement its strategy. This principle should be explicitly endorsed by the alliance. All wealthier members of the alliance should seek to assist Portugal, Greece, and Turkey to ensure that the alliance remains politically, economically, and militarily strong in its southern region as well as in its central and northern regions.

Measuring Risks and Burdens

Participation in the alliance must be based on a generally acceptable sharing of the risks and burdens of Western defense. But there are no scientific formulas for determining what balances of risks and burdens should be judged "equitable." Allies can and do contribute to Western security in a variety of ways, including providing troops and equipment, permitting access to bases for allied forces and playing host to personnel of allied nations, providing assistance to less wealthy allied nations, and cooperating to deal with challenges to Western interests that arise outside the NATO area. In addition, both

France and Great Britain as well as the United States make important contributions by maintaining nuclear forces that strengthen Western deterrence. However, no ally should attempt to avoid its reasonable share of direct contributions to the defense of the alliance. The perception that risks and burdens are not being shared adequately can easily undermine political support for the alliance. The U.S. commitment to continue its contributions to the alliance should be matched by a European commitment to provide the necessary resources to create a strong European pillar in the alliance.

The alliance has attempted over the years to employ a variety of devices for measuring and comparing defense efforts. None of these approaches is entirely satisfactory, as statistical measures by themselves are insufficient indicators of contributions that an ally is making to the alliance. The alliance needs to move beyond an accountant's approach to burdensharing and take the fundamental political decisions that are required to adjust alliance relationships to new political and economic realities.

A New Political Mandate for the Alliance

A fundamental change has occurred in the U.S.-European relationship, reflecting the gradual relative increase in the economic strength and political potential of the West European members of the alliance. At the same time, the European allies have recovered much of the confidence in national judgment that was lost as a consequence of World War II, and most enjoy relatively high standards of living and stable, modern industrial economies. Under these circumstances, the allies should adjust NATO's general policy framework to reflect and strengthen existing trends toward a more cohesive European pillar in the alliance.

In 1967, at an earlier time of transition in the alliance and in East-West relations, the allies adopted the Harmel Report, which recommended that NATO's mandate include effective policies directed toward a greater relaxation of East-West tensions as well as the maintenance of a defense sufficiently strong to deter a Warsaw Pact attack. The Harmel exercise rejuvenated the alliance, bridging political gaps among a variety of constituencies in NATO nations. The step responded to public and political desires for Western policies that could open the way to a less confrontational East-West environment while at the same time defending Western interests. More fundamentally, it created the potential for unified Western political and diplomatic approaches to overcoming the East-West division of Europe and of Germany.

The policy framework established by the Harmel Report focused most clearly on the relationship between NATO and the Warsaw Pact countries. The general approach contained in the Harmel Report remains valid for current alliance policies toward the East. But today's political challenge comes from within the alliance as well as from outside. NATO's political mandate therefore needs to be expanded to reflect the emerging answer to that challenge.

After a full year of study and deliberation, the North Atlantic Assembly's Committee on NATO in the 1990s has concluded that the American and European members of the alliance should adopt a new political mandate. Under the revised guidelines for future NATO policies, the allies should aim to

- achieve sufficient military strength and political cohesion to deter challenges to Western democracies, and ensure a successful defense against such challenges if necessary;
- pursue an active and realistic policy seeking dialogue and mutually beneficial cooperation with the East, recognizing that Warsaw Pact and NATO countries share certain common interests in the security arena; and
- promote a real West European pillar in the alliance, to share more effectively the responsibilities of Western defense and alliance leadership in a new transatlantic bargain with the United States.

Such a new mandate would reaffirm the two basic tenets of the Harmel Report, which guide the West's approach to the East, while recording in a third and new tenet the commitment to reshape some basic relationships within the alliance.

To help provide momentum toward this new transatlantic bargain, NATO governments, during the first year of the administration that will take office in the United States in 1989, should agree to certain declarations that reflect their commitments to the blend of continuity and change that the alliance requires.

1. The European members of the alliance should pledge that they will intensify defense cooperation among themselves while ensuring that such cooperation increases the West's security and political cohesion and contributes to prospects for the improvement of East-West relations and arms control;
2. The United States should welcome the movement toward greater European defense cooperation and pledge that it will continue its active involvement in the maintenance of peace and stability in Europe, and as long as they remain necessary, will maintain nuclear forces structured and deployed in ways that strengthen deterrence for the entire alliance;
3. The allies should jointly pledge that all future alliance force-planning, infrastructure, programmatic, and arms control decisions will take into consideration the need for the European allies progressively to assume a greater share of NATO responsibilities.

The goal of a more cohesive European contribution to the alliance will not be easy to obtain. Given prevailing perceptions of the threat, economic growth expectations, and demographic trends in Europe, both money and manpower for defense will be in short supply for several years to come. American critics of "insufficient" West European efforts in the alliance, however, will not be satisfied with simple declarations of European intentions to improve their military capabilities. The future political and military viability of the alliance therefore clearly requires that the European allies intensify their defense cooperation efforts with both words and deeds to compensate for projected limits on resources available for defense.

Building Blocks for a West European Pillar in the Alliance

The alliance will require a continued strong and effective American contribution to European defense for the foreseeable future. But a condition for that continuity will be a more cohesive European contribution. The second pillar of the alliance must be constructed in order to keep the first from crumbling under the weight of political and financial pressure.

Both politically and economically, Western Europe is bound to become a much more cohesive and stronger entity. The twelve member countries of the European Economic Community are aiming to constitute, by the end of 1992, a truly unified market and establish closer political and economic ties within the Community.

The recent historic progress in several areas of Franco-German defense cooperation has been encouraging. Intensified Franco-German bilateral consultations on defense issues, combined exercises, and the plan to organize a joint brigade all give greater meaning to Western defense efforts.

Franco-British cooperation has also moved to a more active stage. The active involvement of Great Britain in the future evolution of European defense cooperation is essential politically and militarily.

Such bilateral efforts are necessary and should continue, but it is equally important to provide a broader base to involve as many European NATO countries as possible. The Western European Union (WEU) offers great promise as part of the future European pillar. The European security platform issued by the WEU members in October 1987 constitutes an impressive start toward the outlining of a European defense identity, while reaffirming the European desire for continuing U.S. involvement in European defense. The Committee believes that the WEU should include Spain, Portugal, and other NATO European members who agree to accept the obligations and goals of the Brussels Treaty on which the WEU is based.

The Western European Union, however, is not an exclusive arena in which European defense cooperation can be promoted. The studies, collaboration, and consultation within the framework of the European Economic Community (EEC), the Independent European Programme Group (IEPG), and the Eurogroup in NATO also make important contributions to the development of a more cohesive European role in the alliance. It will become necessary in the 1990s for the West European allies to arrive at some rational divisions of responsibilities to eliminate conflict and overlap between the range of European institutions involved in promoting such cooperation. But for the time being, the positive aspects of these diverse organizational frameworks should be nurtured and developed as contributions to a real European pillar in the alliance.

The Committee on NATO in the 1990s has considered a number of suggestions for giving substance to the new transatlantic bargain. It recommends the following steps within the general framework suggested above:

A European Security Assessment

To provide a stronger political foundation for intensified European defense cooperation, the European members of NATO should organize on an annual basis preparation of a European security assessment. This assessment should identify the threats to the Western democracies, including those associated with instability and conflict outside the European region. The statement should note how the European countries intend to respond to those threats. After stating what they are willing to do, individually and collectively, the European allies could specify what role they hope the United States and Canada will play in dealing with the threats to Western security. This exercise could be organized initially by the Western European Union, but participation should be broadened beyond current WEU membership to ensure the participation of all European NATO member governments. Such an assessment should subsequently be submitted to NATO as a basis for discussion with the United States and Canada.

Institutional Reform

The European allies should initiate a study of institutional changes that the establishment of a real European pillar in the alliance would imply, and especially the place and role that the Western European Union (WEU) and the European Economic Community (EEC) would have in building this pillar. The creation of a European pillar eventually requires rationalizing the efforts and location of the numerous European institutions that currently possess a degree of competence in coordinating political, economic, and military aspects of security policy.

A European Division

The European allies should also agree to form a European division. Building on the concept of the Franco-German brigade now being organized, other European countries should be invited to contribute military units to such a division. Creating a European division could enhance the potential for more extensive joint European forces in the future by intensifying joint planning, exercising joint-command arrangements, stimulating more extensive logistical cooperation, and requiring more thorough standardization and interoperability of equipment. Such a division could serve as a covering force to enhance NATO's flexibility in responding to a crisis.

Cooperation among European Military Establishments

In addition, the European allies should make every effort to encourage and facilitate closer cooperation of French and Spanish military forces with those of other NATO nations. For example, the allies should support joint exercises with the French Rapid Action Force and allied units in Germany. Closer and regularized contacts among the military staffs of the European allies will be necessary to overcome the many potential barriers to intensified defense cooperation. Such contacts could, for example, include annual meetings among Chiefs of Staff of West European NATO governments and the establishment of a computerized communications network linking European defense ministries for the purpose of sharing planning information.

A European-Scale Defense Market

The European allies should furthermore intensify efforts to create a European-scale defense market. Only with such a market will the defense industries of the various European allies achieve the efficiencies and specialization that will be required for European defense efforts in the 1990s and beyond. Steps in this direction have already been taken in the framework of the Independent European Programme Group. To strengthen this effort, the IEPG countries should consider: the establishment of a secretariat to coordinate military requirements; joint funding of longer-term research projects; and agreement on compatible rules governing competition for production contracts on the European level, including regular publication of requests for proposals.

Increased Task Specialization

Within such a framework of intensified defense cooperation, the European allies should seek to encourage task specialization among themselves as a way of eliminating wasteful duplication and overlap among national military efforts. There are substantial barriers to specialization deeply rooted in military history and contemporary political and economic priorities of member nations. But the limited resource base for sustaining necessary defense improvements would appear increasingly to demand that smaller allies in particular take on special tasks well suited to their geographic location and national resources as part of a tasking strategy organized on a European level and compatible with NATO planning requirements. The Eurogroup should undertake an in-depth study of the potential for greater role specialization in NATO.

It has become popular with some analysts to suggest that NATO in the future appoint a European instead of an American as the Supreme Allied Commander Europe (SACEUR). Perhaps at some point in the future such a step will appear logical and necessary. For at least the next decade, however, the Committee believes that U.S. nuclear weapons will continue to play an important role in NATO's deterrent strategy and that the appointment of a U.S. military officer to the position of SACEUR will remain an essential symbol of and practical link to the U.S. President's authority to order the use of nuclear weapons.

NATO—B

In sum, the alliance should welcome the progress made in all bilateral and multilateral forums that promotes European defense cooperation. While the core of such efforts clearly depends on the active involvement of France, the Federal Republic of Germany, and Great Britain, the process in the long run should involve all the West European NATO nations. All steps toward greater cooperation should ensure compatibility with general alliance obligations and purposes. The European pillar of the alliance must be constructed within the alliance and not as an alternative to it.

Dealing with the Challenge of Transition

Managing the transition to a more prominent European security identity and role in the alliance will not be an easy task. The United States has since the late 1940s supported the goal of European unification, including the defense field. But faced with such a development, the United States will be challenged to accept the consequences of greater West European influence in the alliance. Under these circumstances, it will be particularly important for the allies to keep open existing channels of communication and possibly to develop new ones to sustain transatlantic support for the concept of European defense cooperation. The allies will have to pay special attention to the relationship between European defense cooperation and ongoing cooperation within the NATO framework to avoid creating divisive splits among the allies.

In addition, the allies will have to defend the process against tendencies toward isolationism, unilateralism, and neutralism in North American or European policies. There is a danger that isolationist forces in the United States and Canada could interpret the progress toward European defense cooperation as an opportunity to extract their countries from involvement in European defense. There is an equal danger that some in Europe could seek to use the process of defining a European security identity as a vehicle for attacking the United States and its policies. Managing this evolutionary process will require that officials and politicians on both sides of the Atlantic guard against such tendencies.

Importance of Common Values

At this time of transition in relationships within the alliance, the allies will do well to recall the common values that they share, the defense of which the alliance is intended to promote. In the North Atlantic Treaty, the allies pledged to "safeguard the freedom, common heritage and civilization of their peoples, founded on the principles of democracy, individual liberty and the rule of law." These values are still not universally accepted and practiced in the broader international community. But they should continue to bind the members of NATO together and provide a common sense of purpose, even if the direct military threats to the alliance may appear less imminent.

Economic Relations

The allies also pledged in the Treaty to eliminate conflict in their international economic policies and to encourage economic collaboration among them. A degree of conflict is inevitable in relations among nations in the naturally competitive Western economic system.

The past 40 years have witnessed the economic recovery of Western Europe and the dispersion of economic power that, early in the postwar period, had reflected the preeminence of the United States in the international economic system. Economic parity between the United States and Western Europe inevitably has led to trade tensions. On both sides of the Atlantic, there is a growing realization that an intensification of trade tensions between North America and Western Europe would seriously affect the transatlantic partnership. Over the past decades, trade, like economics in general, has become so inextricably enmeshed with political relations that a deterioration of trade relations now almost automatically affects political relations, and vice versa. This situation is of particular concern to an organization like NATO, composed of 16 sovereign nations with collective political and defense goals, but whose economic relationships are based as much on cooperation as on competition.

Until now, even in those cases where diplomacy initially failed to resolve transatlantic trade tensions and retaliation followed, peace was eventually restored. Nevertheless, with each successive dispute, it has become more difficult to dismiss rhetoric as mere brinkmanship, and the danger of a crisis with far-reaching economic and political implications has become steadily more acute.

The agenda of outstanding U.S.-EEC issues is a long one, and many of the items on it will not be easy to resolve, as they affect vital economic and trade interests. Millions of jobs in the industrial, agricultural, and service sectors in the European NATO countries, the United States, and Canada directly depend on exports. In the foreseeable future, protectionism is likely to remain a tempting response to pleas for assistance from these sectors.

In the longer term, some positive effect on transatlantic trade may be expected from the current Uruguay GATT Round of multilateral trade negotiations, which, for the first time, is dealing with domestic farm-support programs and export subsidies. Eventually, the round should help construct a more adequate, normative and institutional famework for international and, consequently, transatlantic trade.

In the meantime, however, North American and European NATO countries should pursue efforts aimed specifically at improving transatlantic commercial contacts. Reinforcement of consultative procedures, the establishment of a functioning dispute-settlement mechanism, creation of effective conciliatory procedures, and other institutional improvements to be achieved both within the GATT and through bilateral pragmatic arrangements are devices that probably would not eliminate all sources of friction but would certainly contribute to more rapid and constructive management of transatlantic trade disputes.

In the 1990s, as in the past, the allies must guarantee that the benefits of competition are preserved while the dangers of conflict are avoided. This task is made more difficult when economic growth is marginal or nonexistent. It will be particularly important in the 1990s to resolve trade and economic difficulties equitably and to ensure that such problems do not interfere with the priority objective of sustaining a credible defense posture.

NATO's Social Fabric, Public Opinion, and Political Consensus

In an alliance among democratic nations where political parties and public opinion play a direct role in national decision making, defense policies must take into account the broad range of factors that impinge on national security. The health and welfare of the societies that the alliance is designed to protect depend on a fine balance between government programs for defense and those for other needs of society. Particularly in the East-West competition, peacetime success or failure is measured in large part by the quality of life enjoyed by the citizens of the competing systems. The NATO countries must not lose sight of the need to protect and enhance the quality of life provided its citizens as an important ingredient of national security policy.

A central component of the welfare and cohesion of our societies is the educational systems that we support. The future economic growth and social development of the NATO nations will depend in large part on the quality of education that we provide our youth.

Public and parliamentary support is essential for the effective functioning of the Atlantic alliance. The North Atlantic Assembly, for its part, has sought to bring congressional and parliamentary opinions to the attention of NATO governments and to strengthen the legislative base of support for the alliance. The heightened public awareness of and participation in security policy debates over the last decade is likely to continue into the 1990s, unless the current period of transition in alliance relations yields a new consensus on defense policies and arms control objectives. Ensuring effective channels of communication among public opinion, legislators, and NATO governments will therefore remain a high-priority task.

In the 1980s, the controversy over intermediate-range nuclear force (INF) missiles has produced deep political splits between political parties of the left and right in Western Europe. It also aggravated some differing perceptions between Americans and Europeans about the nature of the threat and minimum requirements for defense. With the INF debate moving into the background, and with further opportunities for arms control progress, it may be possible over the next several years to achieve a higher level of consensus on defense policy both within Europe and between Europe and the United States. This certainly should be the objective of all NATO governments.

Neither American nor European public opinion believes that the Soviet Union is willing to take the risks that, under current circumstances, an attack on Western Europe would entail. The perception of the "threat" has declined throughout Western publics, partly due to NATO's success in ensuring unbroken peace in Europe for nearly four decades. Necessary Western programs designed to offset the Warsaw Pact's military capabilities and to seek negotiated reductions in Warsaw Pact forces require political support. NATO's policies must therefore be understandable and credible to the public if they are to be effective in practice.

The need is particularly acute in the case of the so-called successor generations in NATO countries. These younger citizens must remain convinced that the alliance is relevant to their future and that of their country if the alliance is to continue to prosper.

The results of a European security assessment, proposed earlier in this report, should be published and disseminated widely throughout the alliance in a form that is accessible and credible to all segments of NATO electorates. NATO governments should devote additional resources to educating their electorates concerning the ways in which the alliance seeks to increase their security and promote international peace.

NATO'S STRATEGIC CONCEPT

The Challenges

Soviet Military Power

The challenges facing NATO's strategic concept are in many ways similar to those it has confronted throughout its history. The most fundamental continuity is provided by the Soviet Union's massive military presence, including nuclear, chemical, and conventional forces within striking distance of the West European countries.

There is no consensus in the West concerning how to interpret the balance between NATO and Warsaw Pact forces. By almost all measures, the forces of the Soviet Union and its Warsaw Pact allies outnumber those of NATO. Some observers in the alliance interpret these forces as the Soviet Union's way of preserving a defensive zone to the west of its borders. The Committee believes that interpreting the NATO–Warsaw Pact military balance requires taking into account political, economic, geographic, and other factors as well as adding up troops and equipment on both sides. But even with the most optimistic assessments taken into account, there is a conventional force imbalance, and Warsaw Pact forces still appear to exceed reasonable defensive needs of the Pact countries.

Soviet Diplomatic Initiatives

The Soviet Union, under the leadership of General Secretary Mikhail Gorbachev, has declared its interest in measures to reduce the military confrontation in Europe and has acknowledged that there are "asymmetries" in the European military balance. The suggestion that he may be more flexible in this area than were his predecessors has convinced many in Western Europe that the Soviet Union's intentions are benign and that Mr. Gorbachev can be taken at his word. This combination of still-formidable Soviet military power and a highly persuasive political and diplomatic approach to the West poses unique challenges to Western leadership.

Questions relating to nuclear weapons present special problems. To compensate for Warsaw Pact superiority in tank forces in particular, NATO for many years has relied on short-range nuclear weapons to help defend against a Warsaw Pact attack. However, a substantial change has taken place in the Western political and public will to sustain a credible nuclear posture. The debate over INF deployments undermined support for nuclear deployments in many alliance countries.

The Soviet Union understands the depths of Western public concern about nuclear weapons and for many years has sought the denuclearization of Europe as one of its priority national security objectives. The dilemma for the West will be to meet the diplomatic challenge and take advantage of real opportunities for East-West cooperation while maintaining a defense posture that still ensures Western security.

Challenges Beyond NATO's Area

Another challenge to Western security that has become more prominent in the last decade is the fact that Western interests are in many cases threatened by instability and hostilities outside the area covered by the North Atlantic Treaty. NATO was not designed to deal with such "out-of-area" problems, and divergent American and European perceptions of the roots of out-of-area security problems and the appropriate policy instruments for dealing with them complicate efforts to organize a unified Western approach to most such problems. The Middle Eastern region is particularly important for Western security because of its strategic importance and the West's dependence on the sources of energy in the region. Developments elsewhere—in Africa, Latin America, Asia and the Pacific, and the polar regions—also impinge on Western security interests.

NATO's Responses

Strategy and Doctrines

The heart of NATO's policy rests in deterrence of threats to Western security. This requires maintaining sufficient forces to convince a would-be aggressor that potential gains of aggression are not worth the likely costs. Deterrence also requires a sufficiently stable military balance to ensure that no unfriendly power is able to use excess military power to achieve political advantages. These principles must be applied to the situation in NATO's northern and southern regions as well as in the central region.

The NATO allies decided in 1967 that the best way to deter Warsaw Pact military and political challenges was through a doctrine of flexible response. According to the doctrine, the alliance would be prepared to meet any level of aggression with equivalent force, conventional or nuclear, and would increase the level of force if necessary to terminate the conflict. The adoption of flexible response recognized that it was no longer credible to threaten massive nuclear retaliation against the Soviet Union in response to a wide variety of potential Soviet challenges. With the adoption of flexible response, the commitment to mount a forward defense at NATO's borders with the Warsaw Pact countries remained an important symbol of the cohesion of the alliance and the intent to defend the territorial integrity of all its members.

Over the last twenty years, the flexible response and forward defense concepts have been criticized from many perspectives. NATO has never in those two decades been able to meet all possible military threats it might face with equivalent military forces. The allies have continued to rely heavily on short-range nuclear systems to compensate for NATO's inferior numbers of tanks and other weapons systems. The alliance has therefore failed to deploy all the forces implied by the flexible response doctrine.

In the last decade, American and European critics of NATO's strategy have offered a variety of alternative approaches. A number of observers in the United States have called for NATO to renounce the possible first use of nuclear weapons. In Europe, many Socialist and Social Democratic parties have supported alternatives to NATO's strategy that involve either fewer or no nuclear weapons located in Europe and that rely heavily on a variety of "defensive" or "non-provocative" force postures and tactics. Advocates of these approaches generally argue that the Soviet Union is largely motivated by the desire to protect its own borders, that Warsaw Pact forces are not as superior to those of NATO as is commonly assumed, and that nuclear weapons are destabilizing in European security relationships. Under these circumstances, they contend, flexible response is no longer acceptable as a Western defense doctrine.

Such criticisms certainly reflect the imperfect nature of the flexible response doctrine. The Committee has nonetheless concluded that, even with the shortcomings of flexible response, conceivable alternatives, such as nonnuclear "defensive-defense" and the so-called "discriminate deterrence" approach recently advocated in the United States, are not viable alternatives under the circumstances most likely to obtain in the 1990s. NATO's current strategy still provides the best available way for the alliance to ensure peace and encourage the development of a more stable East-West security environment in the 1990s. While there is much room for the alliance to improve its ability to implement its doctrine and to reduce the degree to which it relies on the early use of nuclear weapons, the allies will have to live with the ambiguities inherent in the flexible response doctrine for the indefinite future.

The great virtue of flexible response is the essential political role it plays in accommodating a variety of differing attitudes toward the requirements of deterrence and defense. Within the flexible response framework, a variety of differing national force postures and mixes of weapons can be reconciled.

Furthermore, the NATO allies must not permit a potential aggressor to believe that it can choose the level of conflict and not risk a response at a higher level of hostilities. The uncertainty planted in a potential aggressor's mind by the flexible response doctrine is a major factor in NATO's deterrence strategy. Any suggestion that there is not a spectrum of deterrence that includes the possibility for escalation undermines NATO's war prevention strategy.

In addition, the forward deployment of forces from many allied nations, particularly those of the United States, remains an important symbol of the political and strategic cohesion of the alliance. Forward deployment of allied units in the Federal Republic of Germany expressly rejects singularity for the Federal Republic and ensures linkage between the security of Western Europe and that of North America.

Nuclear Weapons Modernization

Nuclear weapons play an important role in the flexible response doctrine, and this role was brought to the forefront of public attention by the debate over the deployment of INF missiles and the subsequent U.S.-Soviet agreement to eliminate all such missiles.

There is a strong and quite understandable desire throughout the alliance to escape from the awesome shadow of nuclear weapons. Perhaps in the future, under much improved global political conditions, this will be possible. This is a goal that all NATO governments must keep in mind.

In the 1990s, however, irrespective of hoped-for progress in conventional or nuclear arms control or in defensive technologies, nuclear weapons will continue to play a key role in deterrence. Even if NATO and Warsaw Pact nonnuclear forces were in rough equilibrium, there would be a role for nuclear weapons to play. History has demonstrated that there is no such thing as absolute conventional deterrence, as in the prenuclear age many aggressions were initiated against superior forces. Under contemporary political circumstances, a stable nuclear component in the West's deterrent posture ensures an element of military stability that conventional forces alone cannot provide.

In October 1983 the allies agreed in the "Montebello Decision" to withdraw unilaterally from NATO's inventory some 1,400 warheads. They also agreed to study modernization of the remaining inventory to ensure that the warheads and delivery systems are "survivable, responsive and effective." By the end of 1987, NATO had completed the withdrawals called for in the Montebello Decision and continued to study options for modernizing the remaining inventory, within the parameters of the INF Treaty. The INF accord has led to some differing perspectives in the alliance about the next steps that should be taken to continue implementation of the Montebello Decision.

The most politically effective response in the near term to concerns raised by the INF accord will be strong U.S. reaffirmation of its commitment to European defense and deterrence, not new deployments of American nuclear weapons to compensate for the elimination of the

INF systems. Such reaffirmation should be one of the first acts of whatever new administration comes to power in the United States in 1989.

In the 1990s, the alliance will have to decide what further changes in its nuclear posture are required to sustain its strategy. The Committee suggests the following guidelines for subsequent decisions concerning nuclear weapons deployments in Europe:

1. The balance within NATO's nuclear posture should preferably evolve toward longer-range, deterrence-oriented systems in and around Europe and away from shorter-range, battlefield systems, albeit without creating gaps in the overall spectrum of deterrence;
2. NATO should in the 1990s seek arms control agreements and conventional defense improvements that would make it possible to reduce the overall numbers of nuclear weapons in Europe, ensuring that any changes in nuclear force deployments are consistent with NATO's strategy and that they enhance security and military stability;
3. The nature and location of nuclear deployments should be designed to enhance the security, safety, reliability, and command and control of nuclear weapons;
4. Nuclear deployments should be designed to raise, not lower, the nuclear threshold;
5. Nuclear deployments should therefore complement and not complicate conventional defense improvements; and
6. Nuclear deployments should be judged in terms of their potential effect on alliance cohesion and political consensus as well as their military utility.

These criteria have implications for the variety of modernization decisions facing the alliance. For example, to ensure the viability of NATO's long-range nuclear delivery capability through the 1990s, NATO should seriously consider the deployment to Europe of a limited number of air-launched cruise missiles on fighter/bomber aircraft. In addition, to ensure that nuclear risks continue to be shared within the alliance, NATO governments should consider dual basing of a number of such aircraft with home bases in the United States and forward deployment bases in Western Europe. The aircraft should exercise from their European forward deployment bases with sufficient frequency to ensure effective operational capabilities from those locations in a crisis.

As noted above, the Committee sees the need to move away from reliance on short-range nuclear weapons. To do so, the alliance would require either an arms control agreement reducing the Warsaw Pact's advantage in tank forces in central Europe or a technological breakthrough in Western nonnuclear antitank capabilities. In the absence of such developments, NATO's short-range nuclear capabilities should in the 1990s be modernized within the criteria discussed above.

The alliance should continue to study options for modernizing the Lance missile system, but this should not be the highest priority in the modernization program. The alliance should explore the potential willingness of the Soviet Union to reduce its short-range missiles and the imbalance in conventional forces before replacing the Lance system. Meanwhile, bearing in mind that the Lance was originally deployed to help counter the Pact's ability to mass tanks for an attack against NATO, the Lance system should be kept operational.

In sum, NATO needs to find ways to decrease reliance on short-range nuclear weapons while maintaining a credible and survivable longer-range nuclear capability for deterrence. The alliance should aim to arrive at a position by the mid-1990s where a decision to use nuclear weapons would be the product of deliberation, not desperation, and where the principal role of nuclear weapons would be that of deterring a Warsaw Pact attack rather than defending against one—a no-early-first-use posture.

In the more distant future, if the Soviet Union's potential for attacking Western Europe is substantially diminished, it may well be possible to contemplate a security system in Europe far less dependent on nuclear weapons as part of a less threatening common security relationship between NATO and Warsaw Pact nations. But the ability to move in this direction depends principally on the willingness of the Soviet Union and its allies to adopt a much more defensively oriented force posture in Europe.

Conventional Force Improvements

In the years immediately ahead, the alliance must improve its ability to defend conventionally against nonnuclear Warsaw Pact capabilities if it hopes to raise the threshold at which NATO would be forced to use nuclear weapons. The highest priority is to strengthen NATO's ability to engage and defeat the first echelon units of Warsaw Pact forces—a strong forward defense capability. The second priority is to be able to delay reinforcing Warsaw Pact forces so that they cannot turn the tide of battle. Crucial to both phases of this defensive strategy is the ability of NATO to neutralize Warsaw Pact armored forces and to maintain air superiority over the battlefield.

At the same time, the allies cannot neglect the need to improve the defense to the north and south of its central region. A credible defense posture in the north is essential to NATO's ability to defend the central region. In particular, NATO's ability to control the North Atlantic, Norwegian Sea, North Sea, and Baltic waterways would be decisive in determining whether or not North American reinforcements would arrive in time to influence the tide of battle in the central region. NATO's southern region is of equal strategic importance to the alliance, given the Soviet naval presence in the Mediterranean, the intimate military relationship between hostilities in the south and those in the central region, the proximity to the turbulent Middle East region, and the dependence of NATO allies on the energy sources in the Middle East and Persian Gulf areas.

NATO will not find it easy to improve its conventional force capabilities under projected constraints. Taken in combination, a diminished perception of the threat, fewer young men available for military service in many NATO countries, and constraints on defense spending mean that the alliance will have to find ways to improve its conventional defense capabilities without increasing active duty manpower and without substantial increases in defense spending. Under these circumstances, the alliance will require a strategy that emphasizes the most effective use of available resources.

If there is no substantial progress toward reductions in Warsaw Pact capabilities for offensive operations against NATO, additional resources may be required to maintain a stable security environment in Europe in spite of the sacrifices that might be required of allied nations.

The ongoing Conventional Defense Improvement (CDI) program in NATO points in the desired direction with its strong focus on "output" objectives. The allies should sustain their efforts to identify critical deficiencies and to make a more serious effort to ensure that national force goals take those deficiencies into account. The allies still need to work on shortfalls of ammunition and other supplies that affect the ability of allied forces to sustain combat. Beyond the important sustainability issue, the allies must seeks ways to exploit the West's advantage in technology to render Soviet tank armies obsolete. The development of better nonnuclear means to defend against Warsaw Pact armor must be a high priority for NATO planning, research and development, and funding. NATO should also continue its efforts to improve air and naval defenses throughout all the regions.

In addition, the allies should think creatively about ways to improve conventional defense capabilities with low- or no-cost improvements. A number of suggestions have already been studied extensively by alliance and private experts. Allied governments now must overcome bureaucratic, doctrinal, and political resistance to implementing ideas that make good military sense. For example, it appears that combined with properly trained and equipped forces, a variety of antitank barriers could enhance NATO's capability to defeat tank attacks with nonnuclear weapons. The allies should give careful consideration to terrain enhancements and other steps that could be taken to assist NATO forces defend against Warsaw Pact armor.

Because manpower shortages in the 1990s will force NATO to rely more heavily on reserve forces to implement its strategy, the allies must do everything possible to improve their ability to detect Warsaw Pact preparations for attack and to manage more effectively NATO's response to such indications. Toward this end, NATO nations should intensify their sharing of intelligence information concerning Warsaw Pact military activities. They should also review NATO's crisis-management system with an eye to improving both procedures and methodologies for communicating among NATO political authorities and between NATO civil and military authorities. NATO should also examine the possibility of creating a covering force to assure rapid response in crisis to offset current vulnerability to surprise attack.

Even while the European allies are intensifying their defense cooperation, as strongly recommended by this report, the very positive trends of recent years toward greater transatlantic cooperation in the development of weapons systems must be sustained. In fact, a more rational European defense production capability is a prerequisite for more efficient cooperation between the United States and Europe in the production of standardized or interoperable defense systems for NATO.

The problem of improving conventional defenses is one that should be approached with a sense of common purpose by all political forces in the alliance. There may continue to be some fundamental differences in NATO countries about the appropriate role for nuclear weapons, but there should be a general consensus on the need to improve the defensive capabilities of NATO's conventional forces. In this effort, political forces of varying persuasions should put ideology aside and look pragmatically at all possible ways of approaching this objective. This should include careful study of the many ideas that have been stimulated by alternative or defensive-defense experts in Western Europe. And, supporters of this school of thought should be prepared to modify their approaches to come to terms with the political, military, and resource realities facing all the NATO countries. A pragmatic approach by all political parties in the alliance would offer the best possibility of improving conventional defenses in the next decade.

New Defense Technologies: Challenge and Opportunity

To maintain a qualitative edge over Warsaw Pact forces in the 1990s and beyond, NATO must reform its approach to procuring high-technology weaponry. The Pact has maintained its quantitative advantages over NATO while narrowing the qualitative gap between its forces and those of the West. The Pact has benefited in particular from the fact that the Soviet Union, virtually its sole-source producer, can sustain long production runs, economies of scale, and a high degree of standardization. Soviet central planning accords defense procurement a high priority, and incremental weapons development reduces research and development costs and eases maintenance, training, reliability, interoperability, and logistics.

NATO, by contrast, suffers from relatively short production runs, little attention to standardization, the intrusion of domestic political and economic factors in the procurement process, and a procurement philosophy that emphasizes new capabilities rather than ease of maintenance, reliability, and interoperability.

To help deal with this systemic mismatch, NATO must ensure that militarily critical technologies are not transferred to the East. Unfortunately, the inability of the allies to harmonize effectively their export-control policies seriously inhibits the transfer of technology among them and produces an inefficient exploitation of technology throughout the alliance. The allies must persist in their efforts to harmonize technology export controls to ensure that measures taken to block Soviet acquisition of militarily relevant technologies do not impede technology transfer within the alliance. This will require more effective bilateral cooperation among the allies as well as under the auspices of the Coordinating Committee on Multilateral Export Controls (COCOM). Governments should involve North American and European industrial representatives in their consultations on this issue to benefit from the expertise and experience that resides in the commercial sector.

NATO should reassess its procurement philosophy to emphasize reliability and ease of maintenance to help control the cost of weapons systems as technological sophistication increases. These requirements should be given equal standing with those of range, speed, and technological sophistication. The missions to be performed should in the future guide NATO procurement decisions, rather than simple weapons-replacement strategies. Options should not be constrained, for example, by service pressure to substitute new systems for old when other, more cost-effective opportunities may be available. Choices should be governed by cost-effectiveness as determined by realistic testing rather than by simulation, at all phases of the procurement cycle.

Future constraints on defense resources make it all the more important for the allies to use available research and development resources more wisely. Ideally, all alliance research and development should be coordinated to avoid waste and duplication.

The Committee believes that it is particularly urgent that the European allies harmonize their research and development efforts in the 1990s, perhaps through the establishment of a common research and development fund, to ensure the continued viability of a European defense industry as well as to provide a more solid foundation for needed defense improvements.

During the 1990s, a number of NATO nations will develop military space systems to perform a variety of tasks, joining the United States in deploying intelligence-gathering satellites, early warning and communication systems, and other space-based non-weapons systems. European civilian space programs are now effectively coordinated by the European Space Agency, in which Canada also plays an active role. But the European defense application programs are largely uncoordinated.

This is another area in which rationalization of European efforts and expenditures would make good sense. The Committee therefore recommends that interested NATO nations begin now to investigate appropriate mechanisms for harmonizing development and construction of nonweapons, non-American military space projects as a first step toward ultimate alliance-wide harmonization. The Committee also recommends that the NATO nations attempt in the 1990s to coordinate the operations of American and non-American intelligence-gathering satellites to ensure more comprehensive coverage of critical intelligence requirements and to ensure against loss of coverage through accidents and malfunctions.

Out-of-Area Security Issues

With regard to security challenges arising outside NATO's area, pragmatism and realism are also advisable. Throughout NATO's history, security problems outside the NATO area have caused serious divisions among the allies. The differing historical experiences and military capabilities of NATO allies have produced a wide variety of perspectives on security problems arising outside NATO's area.

NATO has never had a mission outside the Treaty area, initially because the United States preferred that NATO obligations be defined within narrow geographic parameters and, in more recent years, because the European allies have not been willing to expand NATO's defense commitments beyond their own resources or their domestic political base for the alliance. Contrary to common belief, however, the alliance has not totally ignored problems outside the NATO area. The allies have used a variety of consultative opportunities provided by NATO committees and meetings to continue a dialogue on threats to Western security outside the NATO area. Those efforts have been intensified in reaction to Persian Gulf instability, the Soviet presence in Afghanistan, and the situation in Lebanon. Great Britain and France, for example, have for many years maintained naval forces in the Persian Gulf region.

In 1987, Great Britain, France, Italy, Belgium, and the Netherlands as well as the United States sent additional naval units to the Persian Gulf region to demonstrate that they appreciate the threat of instability in that region to Western interests. West Germany sent naval units to the Mediterranean to help offset the transfer of the Italian naval units from the Mediterranean to the Persian Gulf. This European effort was not coordinated within NATO but was in part organized through consultations in the Western European Union. The naval vessels remain under national command, with informal cooperation and communication among Western units operating in the same area. Such informal bilateral cooperation has worked for Western interests. This approach might be applied to other out-of-area security problems as well.

However, it is important to keep open as many channels of Western consultations on such problems as possible. Differences over security problems arising outside the NATO area can create major political problems in the alliance. Sharp differences among the allies can undermine allied cohesion and weaken popular support for the alliance in NATO countries. Because disagreements among the allies over out-of-area issues will likely arise again in the future, it is important that such differences be kept in perspective and that the core of NATO cooperation and cohesion be protected from differences over problems arising outside the NATO area.

The allies should intensify their consultations and cooperation at every level to ensure that complementary approaches are taken to out-of-area security problems whenever possible. But NATO was not designed to deal with such problems, and other Western-style democracies should also be involved in the process. Therefore, a new consultative and contingency-planning framework—a "Western Working Group on Global Security Issues"—should be established, separate from NATO, with the participation of NATO countries and Japan, and open to other Western countries that might wish to join.

The purpose of this working group would be primarily consultative: to discuss global security problems, including state-supported terrorism, in all their political, economic, and military dimensions, and to consider certain contingencies that might arise. Implementation of plans or actions should remain independent national choices, and cooperation should be organized among participating countries on a national basis.

Improving East-West Relations

NATO's pursuit of detente was severely tested in the late 1970s when the Soviet Union tried to take advantage of an improving political climate in Europe to challenge Western interests elsewhere around the globe. In response, the allies, with good reason, adopted a more skeptical approach to the East's willingness to pursue cooperation on terms favorable to Western interests.

Today, as in the past, it is nonetheless important for the allies to seek avenues of political, economic, and security cooperation with the East to try to minimize the threats to Western security, promote a more stable East-West relationship, and overcome the division of Europe. A satisfactory East-West relationship cannot be taken for granted; it remains a goal to be pursued in Western policies, not yet an accomplished fact.

It is particularly important that defense and arms control policies be effectively harmonized and seen as means toward the goal of enhanced security, not as ends in themselves. Neither arms buildups nor force reductions necessarily guarantee more security. In the 1990s, the allies should not make the mistake of overemphasizing one aspect to the detriment of the other. NATO will have to ensure that its defense policies do not undermine security by stimulating responses by the East that only perpetuate the arms race. On the other hand, the allies must ensure that they are not so anxious for improved East-West relations that they neglect fundamental defense requirements.

The Role of Arms Control

In the wake of the U.S.–Soviet INF elimination accord, and given the potential for a U.S.–Soviet treaty substantially reducing their strategic offensive nuclear forces, the alliance must decide what further nuclear arms control measures would be in its interest.

Over the next several years, while the U.S.–Soviet agreement to eliminate their intermediate-range nuclear missiles is being implemented, the main focus of NATO arms control efforts should be on nonnuclear forces, particularly those located in central Europe. However, after careful consideration, the allies may conclude that further nuclear arms reductions in Europe could be taken while maintaining NATO's deterrent strategy and avoiding the denuclearization of Western Europe. The guiding principle for NATO's approach to nuclear arms control should complement its deployment and modernization objectives, discussed earlier. NATO's arms control approach, as well as its modernization and deployment policies, should therefore seek to reduce NATO's reliance on short-range nuclear weapons while preserving a credible, survivable nuclear weapons capability to sustain NATO's deterrence posture.

Conventional arms control negotiations could hold the key to NATO's future ability to reduce its reliance on short-range nuclear weapons. The overall relationship between NATO and Warsaw Pact forces, including nuclear forces, in Europe is such that there is no incentive for the Pact to launch an attack against the West. However, the manner in which Warsaw Pact forces are deployed, equipped, and trained gives the Pact the potential to mount an attack on Western Europe with relatively little warning time. This "surprise attack" potential is militarily threatening and politically destabilizing. Further, even though the overall military situation is relatively stable at the moment, that stability cannot be guaranteed in the future so long as the Pact continues to enjoy such substantial numerical advantages in tanks and some other categories of offensive weaponry deployed against NATO.

The beginning of new conventional stability talks among NATO and Warsaw Pact nations covering an area "from the Atlantic to the Urals" provides an opportunity to redress imbalances in conventional military forces in Europe. From one perspective, the logic of current trends in relations between NATO and the Warsaw Pact and in their resource priorities suggests that both alliances should have reasons to seek negotiated reductions in their conventional forces located in Europe. But a number of other factors mitigate against easy solution.

A prominent immovable object complicating conventional arms control remains the fact that the Soviet Union, with its massive military power and impressive resource base, is part of and has relatively easy access to the European area. The United States, NATO's strongest member, lies an ocean away, its defense, population, and resource base far from the area of potential conflict. This geographic disparity between the two alliances requires NATO governments to ask the Warsaw Pact for asymmetrical reductions in and constraints on Eastern forces to establish a more stable balance between NATO and Warsaw Pact forces in Europe.

The Committee believes that the West's ultimate objective in the new conventional stability talks should be reductions in Warsaw Pact forces to rough parity with NATO forces. This need not mean precise equality in all subcategories of forces, but reductions should yield a relationship between NATO and Warsaw Pact forces that is stable and nonthreatening.

The West should seek reduction of complete Warsaw Pact units and net reductions in particular in Pact tank forces and artillery tubes. Ideally, Soviet forces should be disbanded rather than redeployed elsewhere in the Soviet Union. The West might also consider as a variation on this approach proposing the storage of reduced equipment within the reduction area on both sides in sites supervised by inspection teams from the other alliance. This storage approach could be one way of equalizing the time required by the two alliances to mobilize reduced equipment and could provide unambiguous warning of mobilization efforts.

The West might also usefully consider proposing limits on production of tanks, monitored by on-site inspection at tank-production facilities. Such production constraints could help build down the military confrontation between the two alliances and, over time, equalize NATO and Warsaw Pact tank inventories.

Because the Western desire for highly asymmetrical reductions and the Soviet Union's concept of its defensive requirements might lead the new negotiations toward impasse, the West needs to develop a subnegotiating strategy for the conventional stability talks that would allow the possibility of small steps toward increased military stability in the near term while working toward more substantial reductions in the long term. Toward this end, the West could early in the new conventional-stability talks initiate discussions concerning characteristics of the Warsaw Pact's doctrine, force structure, and deployments that give rise to concern. Such discussions might help identify possible components of a first-stage agreement designed to constrain offensive operations and the ability to mount an attack with little or no warning.

As part of this building-block strategy, the Western countries should seek agreement on stabilizing measures that would actually constrain the operations of forces and make a short-warning attack a less feasible option. For example, the West could seek to constrain the deployment and exercising of bridging equipment and the forward deployment of engineering units. The West could also seek constraints on the location of ammunition dumps, moving such facilities back from the East-West dividing line and arranging mutual observation of such facilities.

These types of constraints are best suited for the NATO–Warsaw Pact conventional stability talks, as they would not necessarily be applicable to all 35 states participating in the Conference on Confidence- and Security-Building Measures and Disarmament in Europe (CDE). However, much remains to be accomplished to follow on the 1986 Stockholm CDE agreement. In particular, information exchanges about all phases of notifiable military activity must be strengthened; consideration should be given to stationing permanent observers at major military facilities and transportation centers; notification should capture alerts as well as earlier phases of military activities in the field. In addition, the CDE participating states should make arrangements for publication of an annual report on compliance with the Stockholm measures and with further measures that may be negotiated.

Another useful step in the direction of a more cooperative European security system could be the establishment of a NATO–Warsaw Pact crisis-avoidance center. Such a center could bring together NATO and Warsaw Pact member military officers, experts, and diplomats. The purpose of the center would be to exchange on a continuing basis information on military activities, to raise issues about those activities of concern to either side, and to discuss and seek to resolve low-level incidents involving NATO and Warsaw Pact military personnel. The center could serve as a clearing house for information exchanges worked out under the auspices of the CDE and as the source of inspection teams to participate in the implementation of current confidence-building measures agreed in Stockholm and further measures that might be agreed in future negotiations. Center participants could also discuss compliance with agreed measures and ways to improve the effectiveness of such measures.

The West also needs to continue to seek controls on chemical and biological weapons. While controlling chemical weapons poses substantial verification problems, it is possible that the experience with intrusive inspection measures in the INF accord will open the way for a global ban on chemical weapons. Regional prohibitions on such weapons would contribute little to common security compared to the benefits of a global elimination accord.

Overcoming the Division of Europe

The basic structure of East-West relations involving two competing political and military groupings as well as two different economic systems, is unlikely to change substantially in the next few years, perhaps not for the rest of this century. The division of Europe has deep roots and at its heart lies the division of Germany, a problem whose ultimate resolution cannot be foreseen today. NATO's policies toward the East have aimed not only at improving Western security but also at overcoming this division.

NATO must continue to seek as a top priority to overcome the division of Europe and of Germany. These divisions lie at the root of East-West political tensions and the military confrontation in Europe today and must be surmounted if a new and more stable security structure is to be achieved between East and West.

The closed nature of the Soviet and East European governmental systems is a central contributing factor to tensions in East-West relations. Gradual improvement in these relations over the years will require evolution in the nature of these social and political systems. At a minimum, such change would require the emergence of a more secure, pragmatic Soviet Union, willing to tolerate greater diversity and openness and human rights in its own society as well as in its relations with other nations. The Soviet Union under its new leadership has made some tentative steps in this general direction. But even if the process continues, it will likely be a slow and fitful one.

Under these circumstances, the NATO nations must be prepared for a further extended period during which Europe remains "divided." Nevertheless, much progress has been made toward ameliorating that division, and more can be made even within the limits imposed by the Soviet Union's current perceptions of its security requirements.

The Western policy most likely to encourage positive change in this area would be one built on the use of explicit carrots and implicit sticks. The carrots would consist primarily of economic benefits—trade, with competitive terms and credits for East European regimes, within limits of their anticipated ability to repay, granted more freely to regimes that are attempting to open up their systems. Many forms of East-West contact, however, should be encouraged as ways of opening doors to political and social liberalization. Such an alliance approach could be modeled, at least in principle, on the *Deutschlandpolitik* of the Federal Republic of Germany, attempting to build a web of mutually beneficial ties increasingly linking NATO and Warsaw Pact countries in a variety of cooperative ventures.

As the West expands ties with the Warsaw Pact countries, great care must be taken not to jeopardize Western security interests. The allies should intensify their efforts to develop procedures for protecting important technologies with defense applications while promoting economic cooperation with the East. The West's desire to encourage more normal relations between NATO and Warsaw Pact countries should not result in special military advantages for the Warsaw Pact countries. Transfer of sensitive military technologies to Warsaw Pact countries can only result in future demands on Western defense efforts.

The framework established by the Conference on Security and Cooperation in Europe (CSCE) provides means to continue the process of gradually breaking down barriers to the freer movement of people and ideas between East and West. The CSCE process has become an essential tool of Western efforts to mitigate the effects of Europe's division and the risks of war. It provides a forum in which the true meaning and implications of Soviet *glasnost* and *perestroika* policies can be tested. The allies should continue to use the Conference on Security and Cooperation in Europe to fullest advantage.

Individually and collectively, all the NATO allies can play a continuing role in working toward a more acceptable relationship with the Warsaw Pact countries. The United States has a special responsibility in managing its superpower relationship with the Soviet Union because U.S.–Soviet relations generally establish the overall tone for East-West relations. The Federal Republic of

Germany also plays a unique role in managing its relationship with the German Democratic Republic in ways that break down barriers that divide the German nation. All the other allies can and should make their own unique contributions within the framework of Western objectives and solidarity.

At the same time, NATO governments must redouble their efforts to explain to public opinion and national parliaments the necessity for maintaining a strong national defense even while relations with the East are improving. A strong, united, and confident West will make the best negotiating partner for the East.

Finally, the strength of the West ultimately rests in the principles for which the Western alliance stands, and the cohesion and well-being of the societies that the alliance is designed to defend. NATO governments must continue to assure that alliance policies remain true to the ideals expressed in the North Atlantic Treaty and responsive to the needs of their citizens as well.

APPENDIX

Separate Views of Mr. Lasse Budtz
Social Democratic Member of the *Folketing*, Denmark

The chairman of the Presidential Committee, Senator William V. Roth, Jr., and the Study Director, Mr. Stanley R. Sloan, and all members of the Committee have been very forthcoming in their efforts to establish a consensus. It has nevertheless been impossible for me to consent to all that has been written and suggested in the policy paper, and I therefore feel it necessary to present some dissenting views.

The time we are living in should force us to consider alternatives to the security policy that has been followed by the alliance for the last several years. Seen from this perspective, the report is too conservative and does not reflect many of the political mainstreams in Europe.

For instance, the report does not concentrate enough on the possibilities for disarmament and does not give the highest priority possible to disarmament and detente. It is more or less taken for granted that the West under all circumstances will need nuclear weapons for many years to come. But nuclear weapons do not necessarily guarantee our security. They might even be a threat to security.

The report is mainly negative toward the various zonal arms control plans, among them a Nordic nuclear-weapon-free zone and a European zone free of chemical weapons. And it does not discuss in depth the constructive ideas behind "common security." The West can achieve real security only through some kind of cooperation with the East.

A new role for the European countries as a whole, and for the European members of the alliance in particular, is important and necessary. But a Western Working Group on Global Security Issues should at least be constructed in a way that does not split Western and European countries. By the same token, the proposals to give a stronger role and influence to the Western European Union should also be received with deep skepticism, as should the idea of the formation of a so-called European division. Why present an idea that probably never can be realized?

The report also, more or less automatically, accepts the theory that to achieve disarmament we must first arm in all areas and first of all in the area of conventional forces. But if it is possible to reach an agreement on asymmetrical reductions under strict control, that is far preferable, as is an agreement on new strategies based on non-threatening defensive systems.

Economic and other kinds of assistance to and cooperation with developing countries play an important part in security policy, and this should be more strongly emphasized.

Any modernization of nuclear systems along the lines of the so-called Montebello Decision may harm the prospects for more disarmament in Europe. And it is difficult to understand the necessity of such a modernization when it is doubtful that the East has superiority in all categories of conventional weapons and as long as we have not really investigated the possibility for asymmetrical reductions in conventional forces.

II
The Past as Prologue

3

The First Forty Years

By A. W. DEPORTE

THE "LESSONS" OF HISTORY

The North Atlantic Treaty was signed on April 4, 1949. The relevant circumstances in which that event took place were these:

1. The Red Army stood along a line in Eastern Europe "from Stettin [Szczecin] in the Baltic to Trieste in the Adriatic." As a result, the Soviet Union had ultimate power with respect to the organization of government and society and the foreign policies of the countries to the east of that line.
2. The countries of Western Europe were individually much weaker militarily than the Soviet Union and were divided among traditional national sovereign states. The leaders of most of them acted as if they felt threatened, more or less acutely and directly depending on their individual situations, by the proximity of Soviet power and their weakness in the face of it and as if they wanted a guarantee of their security by the only power able to provide it: the United States.
3. The United States, whose leaders acted as if they believed that the expansion of Soviet power or influence westward of the line that divided Europe would be harmful to American interests, provided that guarantee to the West European countries in the form of the Atlantic alliance. The guarantee included a declaratory commitment to and a substantial military presence in Western Europe and was proclaimed to be one manifestation among others of the U.S. policy of "containing" further Soviet expansion.

In many respects the world has changed more rapidly since the 1940s than in any comparable span of history. That so much of what has been written about the alliance has emphasized challenge and change rather than continuity and stability is not at all surprising. If an intelligent Martian should descend to this planet today, however, knowing nothing of what happened before its arrival, it might describe Europe in these terms:

1. The Red Army stands along a line in Eastern Europe from Szczecin almost to Trieste. As a result, the Soviet Union has ultimate power with respect to the organization of government and society and the foreign policies of the countries to the east of that line.
2. The countries of Western Europe are individually much weaker militarily than the Soviet Union and are divided among traditional national sovereign states. The leaders of most of them act as if they feel threatened, more or less acutely and directly depending on their individual situations, by the proximity of Soviet power and their weakness in the face of it and as if they want a guarantee of their security by the only power able to provide it: the United States.
3. The United States, whose leaders act as if they believe that the expansion of Soviet power or influence westward of the line that divides Europe would be harmful to American interests, provides that guarantee to the West European countries in the form of the Atlantic alliance. The guarantee includes a declaratory commitment to and a substantial military presence in Western Europe and is proclaimed to be one manifestation among others of the U.S. policy of "containing" further Soviet expansion.

The most salient historical fact about the alliance and its surrounding circumstances is, thus, their persistence. However, saying that the alliance has survived and even flourished for nearly 40 years because the essential circumstances affecting it did not change much does not take us very far toward explaining the facts. *Why* have those particular circumstances of the 1940s changed so little in a period when so much else has changed? *How* have individual human actors and groups of them called governments, motivated by diverse and often contradictory beliefs, wishes, and intentions, acted in such ways over 40 years as together to produce this unexpected and often overlooked structural stability?

These questions can be answered only very partially and tentatively because, when we look at the immense literature about the alliance, we find that remarkably little of it is history. Several reasons account for that lack of history. The first is the difficulty, inherent in all history writing, of deducing motivation and design from observed behavior. In the present case, interpretation has to deal not only with the deep obscurities of Soviet decision making but also with the complexities of policy making in the democratic countries of the alliance where multiple elites and many-layered public opinion interact with each other in changeable and bewildering constellations, distinctive in each country, to produce policy. With these limits in mind, I have phrased the "three constants" of the European landscape in terms of observed circumstances and of surmises about motives ("acted as if . . .") rather than definite assertions about causes.

A second problem in the way of writing alliance history has been the off-putting scope of the task, which cannot be limited to formal institutions but must address the multitudinous relations among all the member governments (and not only those of the larger states) on all levels, between them and the Soviet Union and its allies, and between them and much of the rest of the world, together with the internal decision-making process (political and bureaucratic) in each country.

A third difficulty arises from the very continuity of the system. Although the 40-year period in question seems long enough to allow some degree of distancing, the fact that the issues that historians of the alliance would analyze—strategic, economic, political, out-of-area — are precisely the issues of current debate makes historical work on them difficult to write and read with detachment.

Thus, although the Atlantic alliance has a past and the facts about it should be as susceptible to being grouped, analyzed, and interpreted as any other body of historical data, serious obstacles have stood in the way of writing and "using" its history. The point is important because most of the many books, articles, and commentaries about the alliance—and no doubt much thinking about it, too—make explicit or implicit comparisons between whatever is being discussed and some past state of affairs (for example, the degree of agreement or disagreement among the allies, then and now, concerning appraisal of the Soviet threat, or strategic doctrine, or the implications for European security of Third World developments). But where is the data base for such comparisons? Who has systematically tracked past policy trends through the internal political sinuousities and multiple interrelationships of many countries over many years? How have alliance cohesion and the degree of the members' satisfaction with it and with each other over time been measured so accurately that serious comparisons of "better" and "worse" can be convincingly made?

The answers to these questions are, with only slight exaggeration: nowhere, no one, and nohow.

This first lesson of alliance history should put us on our guard when we come across purported "lessons of history," particularly when, as is so often the case, they express the conventional wisdom of humankind that the good old days were better than our own (e.g., that dissatisfactions in one or another member country with the alliance's structure or policies or with the behavior of other allies are said to be increasing). Perhaps the alliance truly has steadily degenerated from an early age of golden harmony and effectiveness to our present leaden times, with worse to come. Much of the writing about the alliance almost since "the creation" has provided such a picture of decline. Yet the facts of the persistence of the alliance and of the security of Western Europe for nearly 40 years give reasons to think that this may not be true. We should at least be alert to avoid what Barbara Tuchman calls "overload of the negative," the tendency to focus on "news," that is, on bad news.

Fortunately, this is not the end of the matter. We *can* grasp, as we have seen, the broad historical topography of the alliance's time and place. Using this big picture—which is reasonably clear if habitually neglected in discussions of current problems—we can then outline the circumstances in which it was formed and those in which it has persisted. With that, we can venture some explanations of why its history has taken that course rather than another and even provide a basis for speculating about what that pattern suggests for the future.

THE SOVIET THREAT

What can we say then, first, about why the Red Army stands along the Elbe 43 years after reaching that place in the last weeks of World War II and why, therefore, the countries of Eastern Europe remain under its ultimate control and the continent, as a result, remains divided? Confining ourselves to the facts of the matter as far as we can and limiting as far as possible necessarily imprecise comments on the hearts and minds of the leaders of the Soviet Union from Stalin forward, several considerations with respect to their behavior present themselves as partial answers to our questions. Because the order of their importance to the Russians is debatable and probably changeable over time and because we do not need to determine the order for our purpose, none is assigned here.

1. The Soviet Union has kept its forces where they are in central and Eastern Europe because doing so served its national interests as perceived by successive leaderships—not *all* its interests, of course, but more of them, and emphatically not without costs, but at smaller cost than alternative policies could have been expected (by them) to do as, for example, withdrawing their forces to within their own frontiers.

2. One of those interests has been to preserve what are seen as the fruits of victory of World War II. What the Russians call "the great patriotic war" was the moment of maximum recent danger for both the regime and the nation, as well as the moment of maximum binding together of the two. The war has been made, and is, far

more central to Russians' self-perception as a nation than World War II is for Americans and, by now, for most Europeans. The fact that a war that began with German armies marching (not for the first time) deep into the heart of Russia ended with the Red Army in the capital of Germany must have seemed to many Russians over these 40 years a just compensation for their heavy losses of wealth and population. This consideration as a factor in Soviet policy has no doubt waned over time, but Soviet leaders would not have been likely to contemplate a withdrawal of Soviet forces from German territory purely as part of a calculus of immediate policy gains and losses. In this sense the Soviet Union's continued military presence in the former Reich, with all that follows from that, has rested to some extent on a "suprapolitical" consideration for which nothing is comparable on the U.S. side, the British, or even the French.

3. This motivation for Soviet policy since 1945 is linked to but distinguishable from the consideration that the withdrawal of the Soviet military presence from Germany would have always—at anytime it took place—seemed to be a long step toward the reunification of that country, whatever the circumstances in which such withdrawal occurred. The specter of a powerful united Germany as a historic threat to Russian security has also, no doubt, weakened as the years have passed and Soviet military strength has increased so enormously in comparison to West Germany's or any that might be created in a united Germany. However, the identification of threats is, as we know, not an entirely rational matter for any country. The fact that the Russians have used the scarecrow of German revanche tactically at times to try to manipulate West German or West European opinion or to add a quasi-popular element to their coercive control of Poland and other Eastern European countries does not mean that it has had no reality for themselves.

4. This consideration in turn, has been further reinforced by the Soviet belief that a Germany freed of Soviet military presence would be unified and, whatever the conditions of such unification, would be oriented toward the U.S.-led bloc of which the Federal Republic has been such an important member. Even if Soviet withdrawal from the German Democratic Republic were not followed by the inclusion of its territory in a German state that remained or became part of the Atlantic alliance, or even if Soviet withdrawal were accompanied by the withdrawal of the FRG from the alliance, the Soviet leaders have probably been Marxists enough to assume that any German state or states not under their control would almost surely be part of a U.S.-led economic—if not security—bloc. The

increasing globalization of the international economic system in recent years and the attraction to this system even of Communist or Marxist countries in Eastern Europe, Africa, and elsewhere have not led the Russians to underrate the threat to their interests raised by whatever German state or states would follow upon their withdrawal.

5. The Russians have also had a clear-cut advantage in remaining in the GDR insofar as others do not take their presence to be fixed, even if the Russians think that under no circumstances would they choose to negotiate themselves out of that area in exchange for other benefits. Retention of the territory in question gives the USSR permanent diplomatic and economic leverage vis-à-vis the Federal Republic, to be used in periods of both tension and relative detente. Its presence also gives it some degree of leverage with the next tier of countries beyond Germany. These too might be drawn into Soviet diplomatic maneuvering in the belief that a negotiation might yet take place concerning the Soviet presence in, and eventual withdrawal from, the GDR.

6. Soviet military presence and political ascendancy in the countries of Eastern Europe other than the GDR, however much that has varied in detail from country to country and from year to year, has also seemed to the Russians, probably, both one of the fruits of their victory in 1945 and a strategic buffer against a possible resurgent threat from Germany and a permanent threat from a U.S.-led bloc. We can dismiss entirely Soviet claims that their security system in Eastern Europe is a defensive one organized in response to the American threat and still recognize that their military planners and others prefer to see the territory between the Elbe and the Soviet border remain under their own control rather than under anyone else's.

7. For many years the Russians' international bloc consisted mainly of the six countries of Eastern Europe. If these ever achieved a more independent international status, whatever the nature of their internal regimes, the list of generally dependable Soviet "friends" in the United Nations and elsewhere would be reduced to a very small and uncertain number indeed, a development the Soviets might have found poorly compensated for by the fact that they have become less isolated than they used to be in international bodies because large numbers of uncontrolled Third World countries have views similar to their own on many issues. Indeed, the Russians may even have thought that the loss of their Eastern European bloc would call into question their status as a superpower.

8. The Russians also have had a sense of historic rightness about the control of Eastern Europe they established by force after World War II. Americans, in particular, but others too have not had a very clear

memory of the map of Europe of 1914, when the Russian Empire controlled Finland, the eastern shore of the Baltic, and most of Poland including Warsaw, and even less knowledge of the plans of the Russian imperial government for the day of victory over the Central Powers in World War I (which it did not survive to see), including extension of Russian power into German territory and control or hegemony over much of the dismembered Austro-Hungarian state, the Balkans, Constantinople, and the Straits. If the Romanovs had remained in power until the defeat of Germany in November 1918, Russian power might well have been planted in Prague and elsewhere then rather than 30 years later.

The Soviet Union had been semi-isolated during much of the interwar period. Its eruption into central Europe after the war seemed not only alarming (because dangerous) but startling (because strange) to Americans, above all, but to some Europeans too who had forgotten that Russian troops had occupied Berlin in 1760 and Paris in 1815 (as Stalin reminded Averell Harriman at Potsdam) and that generations of British statesmen had had many a bad dream about the real or anticipated extension of Russian power westward into Europe, southward toward the Straits and Persia, and eastward across the steppes and Siberia toward India and China. To say that imperial Russian policy had pursued such goals provides no moral or other justification for Soviet domination of Eastern Europe since 1945. But it is not surprising that Russians, Germans, and some other Europeans looked at the tier of states from Finland south into the Balkans as having enjoyed a precarious independence during the interwar period only because both Russia and Germany had been defeated in 1918; many saw these countries as likely to be returned to the control or hegemony of one or both of those states once Russia and Germany had recovered their strength. The Western architects of the 1919 settlement—Great Britain, France, and, let us not forget, the United States—proved first unwilling and then unable to defend it. That settlement was destroyed by German aggression in Eastern Europe from 1938 on, for a time in collaboration with the Soviet Union and then by war with it. Soviet Russia, when its turn came, did not reannex all the territory Russia had lost in 1918, but it established effective control over an area not so unlike what its imperial predecessor had controlled and aimed to control. Russian policy in Eastern Europe has not been regime-specific or ideology-specific, however much ideological ties have been used as underpinning since 1945.

Whatever may be said about the American presence in and relationship with Western Europe, it has been essentially a marriage of reason reinforced by powerful but ambivalent ideological and cultural ties (a point to which I will return). The Russian presence in Eastern Europe, quite apart from the coercive methods by which it was established and has been maintained, has had deeper, darker, and more abiding or compelling roots as perceived by Russians. People, of course, usually see their control of others in a light most favorable to themselves. To Russians, Eastern Europe must have looked like an area that had been fought over for centuries by Turks, Swedes, Austrians, and Germans, as well as by themselves and some of the indigenous peoples (notably the Poles, who occupied Moscow in 1610 and Kiev in 1920), in a protracted struggle in which Russia started as one of the weaker players and at last, but only after 1945, survived all the others to become the dominant force in the area. Perhaps in light of this history they have seen their position as historically justified yet also, even after more than 40 years, as still uncertain, challenged by Americans today, Germans again tomorrow, and—with good reason—the indigenous peoples always.

9. This attitude has been powerfully reinforced by a set of ideological and institutional ties that were elaborated to yoke the occupied countries to the Soviet Union but also, as events have turned out, bind the Soviet Union to them or, more precisely, to their regimes to an extent it may not always have welcomed.

The subject of how the Soviet Union converted its military control of the areas it took over from the retreating German armies in 1944–45 into a hegemonic bloc has been examined in a large literature. The debate continues about whether everything it did in this respect was "inevitable" or might have been susceptible to modification in some ways had other people (the Americans, the British, the "London Poles," etc.) done other than what they did. We do not have the data to determine just what the Soviet leadership—presumably Stalin himself—intended in all respects or might have done in all imaginable circumstances beyond the obvious goal of establishing paramount Soviet authority over most, if not all, of these countries. We do know, however, what the Russians did. They let Finland off quite lightly and did not impose a Soviet-style regime there; they did impose such regimes on Poland, Rumania, and Bulgaria in 1945–46 and on Hungary and Czechoslovakia in 1947–48; and in 1949 they created a Communist regime in the Soviet zone of occupation in Germany after the creation of the Federal Republic by the Western allies in their zones. (We have learned since the 1940s that the Russians did not control developments in Yugoslavia.) With some superficial variations, single-party police states on the Soviet model were established in all these countries.

Opposition to Soviet policy in these countries was ruthlessly suppressed in Stalin's time, and Soviet authority seemed total insofar as police terror and state control of all institutions could make it so. Apparently, however, it was never as complete as it appeared to be. Resistance survived, or possibilities for creating or reviving resistance persisted. It was first manifested within a few years and then repeatedly and continuously afterward. The workers' uprising in East Berlin in June 1953, only three months after Stalin's death, was the first of a succession of open and muted challenges to Soviet control or, at least, pressure exerted to modify it. Very considerable modifications have taken place, some in the direction of national particularities, others in the direction of loosening the weight of police controls on the population. We have only to imagine how Stalin would have made short work of Lech Walesa and Solidarity and of the Polish leaders who let these challengers go as far as they did to realize the very considerable scope of change in Eastern Europe since 1953. From satellite regimes to which orders were given by Moscow, the Communist systems of Eastern Europe have been allowed to evolve to the status of dependents with which dialogue takes place.

Those who had hoped that this process of change would be continuous or open-ended have been as wrong, up to now, as those who thought no change at all would occur. The limits to these changes have been definite, imposed by force whenever the Soviet leaders thought that was necessary (Berlin in 1953, Hungary in 1956, Czechoslovakia in 1968), and imposed by more subtle means when possible (in Poland since 1981).

Modern Soviet leaders must have been unnerved or at least distracted to live with the near certainty of periodic eruptions against their rule in one or another Eastern European country and almost chronic resistance to it in some of them. Some have asked why the Russians have not gone further than they have to put their relations with these countries on a less tense and less threatening basis by allowing regime changes of a kind that could win public support. Why also have they allowed their diplomacy to remain burdened with what has seemed to be a chronic need to secure and resecure Western confirmation of their position in Eastern Europe (for which sometimes, as at Helsinki in 1975, they have paid a certain price)? Above all, why have they shown a chronic inability, from 1945 on, to play their East German card in a properly *realpolitik* manner to try to draw the FRG away from the Western bloc, a development that would presumably mean its end? This has commonly been described as the Soviet Union's primary goal in Europe. In fact, however, this goal has always been subordinated to its determination to maintain its hegemonic position in Eastern Europe, whatever the cost in other respects.

Part of the answer can be found in the strategic and historical considerations outlined above. Perhaps these suffice to explain Soviet policy. But less attention has been paid to the fact that the Soviet Union, having set up Communist regimes in the countries under its control in Eastern Europe in what it claimed was a part of the inevitable and irreversible revolutionary historical process on which its own legitimacy was based, has found its policies toward them and toward the West inhibited ever after by the consideration that the "motherland of socialism" could not allow those regimes, created by it in its own image, to change in far-reaching ways without calling into question the workings and the foundations of the Communist system in Russia itself. For the same reasons, it could not contemplate bargaining away the very existence of such a regime (e.g., the GDR) no matter what compensating diplomatic and strategic advantages it might hope to obtain in return. If the prospect of losing international allies inhibited Soviet diplomacy, how could the Soviet Union permit and even more connive at the destruction of any of the few Communist regimes in the world? What Soviet leader has ever dared contemplate that the Great October Revolution might be again reduced to socialism in one country?

Soviet leaders over the years may have sometimes wished that Stalin had been content to Finlandize some of the other East European states, forbearing from imposing Soviet-style regimes on them and allowing Soviet strategic interests to be assured somewhat as the "Paasikivi-Kekkonen line" has assured them in Finland (e.g., by what might have been a "Beneš-Masaryk line" in Czechoslovakia and something similar in Hungary and perhaps elsewhere). But such Soviet leaders would have understood that establishing ideologically compatible satellite regimes by force was easier than giving them solid foundations, allowing them to change enough to build substantial domestic support for themselves, or, perhaps hardest of all, disengaging from protégés to which it has bound itself all too tightly by ideological and other ties. No Soviet leader, therefore, has ever dared allow an evolution toward "socialism with a human face" anywhere in the Eastern bloc because he knew that some at home would then have demanded the same for Russia and that many others would have resisted the initial concessions for that very reason.

No Soviet leadership has ever implemented the alternative scenario: to carry out relatively radical changes in the Soviet Union itself with respect to, for example, economic organization and/or personal rights and political structure, and then direct the eventual extension of such changes to the other members of the Communist bloc. The obstacle to this course, from the point of view of the Soviet leadership, has no doubt been their realization that economic and/or even political change in the East European countries would not eradicate the deepest objection of their peoples—*Russian* domination, which is deeper even than their objection to Communist domination. In fact, such change would make *that* grievance more easily expressed.

Mikhail Gorbachev has now led the Soviet Union for more than three years. His program for change in the USSR surely implies the "forbidden scenario" just described: parallel *glasnost* and *perestroika* for the other Communist countries of Eastern Europe, all of which are suffering from economic stagnation or worse, and the eventual political consequences of such changes. Gorbachev's policies have so far had no significant impact on the structure of the Soviet position in Eastern Europe. They are welcomed in some countries but feared in others, not only because they would upset vested interests but also because they might lead to popular demands that the Russians could not satisfy short of dismantling their hegemony. The historical record tells us nothing yet about how Gorbachev will try to manage this formidable and unavoidable side issue of his plans for reform at home. It underlines to him as well as to us, however, the risks even more than the possible benefits of extending these reforms to Eastern Europe —risks for the Soviet leadership itself as well as for the dependent countries.

By Sovietizing Eastern Europe the Soviet Union severely limited its own freedom of action to make changes affecting the area that, from the point of view of its own state interests, it might (but only might, in certain circumstances) have had reason to consider. With change have been violent demands for more and forceful repression of these outbreaks. In the past a little *glasnost* in these countries has incited an appetite for more, which the Russians could not contemplate and quelled by force rather than accepted.

Still, they have not paid so high a price for doing that. The notion at times so popular in the West that the Soviet Union would "have to" change its fundamental policies toward Eastern Europe one day because it could not live with the tensions, costs, and burdens of these policies has been repeatedly tested over 40 years and never validated. The diplomatic, political, and image costs of maintaining Soviet hegemony (which has included some degree of episodic liberalization) have so far seemed to Soviet leaders quite bearable and certainly less painful than doing otherwise. Soviet diplomacy has been inhibited by the rigidity of the position Stalin created after the war in Eastern Europe, but the maintenance of that rigidity, often by force and always by police repression and the threat of force, has not had such seriously adverse long-term effects on Soviet diplomacy as to lead the Soviet leaders to try to escape by taking unacceptable risks with respect to the management of affairs in their bloc. The repression of the Berlin uprising was followed two years later by the first summit meeting between Soviet and Western leaders since Potsdam; the repression of the Hungarian revolution was followed within three years by a visit to the United States by the same Soviet leader who had both provoked and repressed it; the Warsaw Pact's invasion of Czechoslovakia led straight to the *Ostpolitik* negotiations and a major phase of U.S.-Soviet detente; and the putting down of Solidarity in Poland has not stood in the way of summit meetings and serious negotiations between the Soviet Union and the United States.

Even the internal costs to the Soviet leaders of letting developments in Eastern Europe get out of hand seems to have been limited. Nikita Khrushchev did not lose his political head because of the Hungarian revolution, nor did Leonid Brezhnev lose his because he let the Prague spring flower too long.

Mikhail Gorbachev surely understands that the overflow of his domestic policies into the countries of Eastern Europe will require very careful management indeed if undesired upheavals and challenges there are to be avoided. Presumably he believes that he can implement needed change while limiting its political consequences, or perhaps he thinks he has no choice but to risk undesired side effects of reform in the Soviet Union and that, in the worst case, he can reimpose control over Eastern Europe by force, as his predecessors did, with little lasting cost to Soviet diplomacy or even to his own leadership position.

THE WEST EUROPEAN RESPONSE

Discussing in a few pages the behavior of the countries of Western Europe since 1949 is much more difficult than discussing that of the Soviet Union because there are so many of them. Because most have been democracies, moreover, the many voices of government and media, majorities and minorities, leaders and led, invite confusion if not distortion about what the United Kingdom, France, the Federal Republic of Germany, Italy, and each of the other countries have perceived, wanted, or done over a period of 40 years with respect to the matters discussed here. When we speak of a country or people acting in these matters, we really mean the government and the parties and forces that support it, in and outside formal institutions. These have not necessarily represented a majority of elite or media or popular opinion on every issue at every moment. Because the leaders of these mostly democratic countries were periodically judged by their electorates with respect to their record in office, including foreign policy, speaking of their behavior as British, French, or West German behavior seems just.

Similarly, we cannot avoid speaking at times of Europe or Western Europe, but we must remember, of course, that no West European defense system, West European foreign policy, West European government, or Western Europe exists or has existed. European members of the alliance have numbered 10, 12, 13 and now 14, and a number of other countries are West European by geographic and other definitions. Listing all of them whenever we want to refer to behavior or attitudes of all or most of the governments of these allies or these Western European countries is inconvenient. Even as we fall short of proper precision for the sake of convenient communication, however, we should be on guard against taking useful shorthand (Europe or Western Europe) as reality.

This is not merely a formal issue. Discussions of the alliance and its problems have been muddled for years, for example, by references to the population, wealth, and potential for defense efforts of Western Europe, an entity that, if it existed, would or could or should be a superpower on the scale of the United States and the Soviet Union. But it has not existed and does not now. What exists are only the Federal Republic, Great Britain, France, and others, none on the scale of a superpower, none of which has acted or should have been expected to act like a superpower. Here, as in other contexts of alliance discussion, imprecisions of language have interfered with precision of thought, sometimes with serious consequences for our understanding of reality.

Bearing in mind these problems and limitations, as well as those related to the scarcity of historical studies of the alliance, still, a good deal can be said about the response of the West European governments and peoples to the fixed Soviet presence in Eastern and central Europe since 1945.

The countries of Western Europe, I have said earlier, "acted as if they felt threatened" by their proximity to Soviet power. The perception of this threat has obviously varied enormously over a period as long as 40 years and among a diverse group of countries from Iceland to Turkey and from Norway to Portugal, each of them with populations of different outlooks on this as on other matters. We need, but do not have, detailed studies of threat perception for each member of the alliance from 1949 to the present. But even if such studies could be made, they would probably be of limited value because of the near impossibility of reading so many minds (even of leaders) and interpreting so many people's motivations over so long a period, especially since European leaders have at different times found many benefits in the alliance beyond security against the Soviet Union. Some selection and condensation of the subject matter would be necessary even if such national studies existed. And, since they do not, some authorial generalizing and dogmatism seem unavoidable.

It seems fair to say that many European countries in the 1940s and early 1950s were concerned that the Soviet Union, having forcibly and militarily occupied many countries, intended to extend its frontier to control farther to the West by force, threat, or subversion if, as many deemed possible, it could do so with a reasonable expectation of success (that is, in face of Western European military weakness and the high level of uncertainty that the United States would respond to such Soviet moves). Iceland and Portugal probably felt this threat to a slighter degree and joined the alliance in part to "dignify" existing bilateral security ties with the United States (and, in the case of Portugal, to "validate" abroad its nondemocratic regime). But in France and the Low Countries, just behind Germany and not far from the Elbe; Denmark and Norway, recent victims of aggression and also adjacent to Soviet forces; Italy, near such forces in Austria and Hungary and confronted by a militant Yugoslavia not yet clearly seen as under its own rather than Soviet control; then, in 1952, Turkey, faced by Soviet territorial demands; Greece, bordering Communist Bulgaria and only recently convulsed by a Communist-led civil war; in 1954 the Federal Republic of Germany, directly facing the Red Army; and in Great Britain, whose vulnerability to aggression from the continent had been so recently demonstrated, many people in these years must have feared westward movement by the Soviet armed forces—the well-remembered kind of crisis based on the threat of force that another totalitarian power, Nazi Germany, had made familiar in 1938–39—or at least a Soviet move to seize the highly vulnerable Western zones of Berlin, with the demoralization of Western Europe that would surely follow.

Not only Iceland and Portugal but also practically all the members of the alliance had motives for joining other than strictly security considerations. Most if not all found a structured relationship with the United States beneficial with respect to their need for American aid for economic reconstruction, on which depended, in turn, social and political stabilization. In some, the ruling political parties looked to their ties to the United States as elements of internal strength in their competition with Communist or sometimes Socialist opponents. Italy, then the Federal Republic, and much later Spain saw in their alliance membership a badge of democratic association with the other European and Atlantic democracies. Neither Greece nor Turkey was likely to let the other have a monopoly of American and alliance benefits. Norway and Denmark saw advantage to being members of an alliance that Finland could not and Sweden, partly for that reason, would not join.

Some of these considerations, such as those affecting Greece and

Turkey, remain important. Most have ceased to be operative. Some
political parties that had opposed their countries' membership in the
alliance (e.g., the German, Italian, and Spanish Socialists) have come
to accept it. Others that at first were partisans of membership (e.g.,
the British, Dutch, Belgian, Danish, and Norwegian Socialists) have at
times become more critical of it or at least of some of its policies and
programs. In many countries the tendency has been to identify the
alliance with the United States, so that criticism of aspects of
American policy with respect to, for example, the Soviet Union,
Vietnam, or Central America has often led to criticism of the alliance.

The alliance and its activities have been important issues in the
politics of almost all member countries at one time or another, but
those elements that have believed that their country's ties to the
alliance were on balance beneficial to it have almost always prevailed,
in political influence, over those who held the contrary view. The
elections held in the 1980s in the Federal Republic, Great Britain,
Italy, the Netherlands, and Belgium in which deployment of
intermediate-range nuclear forces in those countries was an issue—
among others, of course—are only the latest whose outcomes confirm
this fact. The conversion of parties and leaders who opposed the
alliance to pro-alliance views once they are in office also points to the
same conclusion.

Explaining this behavior in all these governments, and the parties
and groups that kept them in office over so many years in the face of
considerable opposition to their alliance policies is difficult without
assuming that an effective majority of both leaders and populations
felt that the alliance continued to represent a connection that was
useful to them on the international level. The one common factor that
seems to underlie *that* belief in such very diverse international and
domestic circumstances was apparently a fixed concern about the
implications of the fixed Soviet position in Eastern Europe.

The fact that so many have felt this concern for so long does not
signify, however, that their sense of threat, diverse to begin with, has
remained unchanged for all that time. I suspect that it continued in
something like its initial form at least until the end of the Korean War
(1953) and that it revived to some extent during the second and last
phase of tension about Berlin (1958–62), which ended with the Cuban
missile crisis. As for what followed, we do not need the questionable
evidence provided by the semidisengagement from alliance structures
of France and Greece (followed, however, by no other countries) to see
that the sense of direct threat of Soviet aggression is much diminished,
as is concern over pressure backed by the threat of force or the outbreak
of conflict by accident, miscalculation, or Soviet use of a proxy (i.e.,
East Germany) in some operation around Berlin or elsewhere on the

NATO—C*

East-West border. The sense of threat in its earlier acute form did not revive anywhere in Western Europe after the Soviet invasion of Afghanistan in 1979 or the phase of high U.S.-Soviet tension that followed.

Why then have the allies continued to feel sufficient concern about the Soviet position in Europe since the Cuban crisis to maintain much the same alliance structure and activity as before? Inertia seems to be a profoundly inadequate explanation for the policies pursued in this respect by so many governments, of such diverse political coloration, over so many years, and through so many crises, difficulties, and periods of relaxation of tension. The alliance, after all, has not been just a paper agreement that no one bothered to repudiate but a structure of day-to-day decision making that absorbs large quantities of material resources and policy energy. Can we avoid the conclusion that these many governments and their varied supporters perceived that the existence of the alliance had a considerable amount to do with maintaining the stability in Europe, even though this stability itself seemed to raise questions about the need for the alliance? Can we not go a step further and conclude that for most of this time most of the European allies directly facing the Soviet bloc—above all the FRG, the most exposed and the most central to the alliance's continuation—continued to believe that their security was still threatened by the Soviet presence in Eastern Europe: not by imminent attack, as in the 1940s, but by what might be called a residual or situational threat, and not a threat that needed to be met with the rigid policies of earlier years but one that yet required their continued participation in the alliance established then?

This judgment helps to explain a good deal that has seemed perplexing (particularly to Americans) about West European responses to shifts in Soviet policy. Thus, the European allies have been much less inclined than some people had expected to believe that episodes of East-West detente were signals for the dismantling of the alliance or its defense system. Too little attention has been given to the fact that the allies did *not* succumb to what was ominously called "detente fever" in the early 1970s, the alleged belief that U.S.-Soviet detente and the success of the FRG's *Ostpolitik* meant that the Soviet threat was no more and that the alliance was henceforth superfluous.

Then again, they have also been less inclined than the United States to think that the security of Western Europe was affected adversely by Soviet activities outside Europe or even—as with respect to Poland after 1981—in Eastern Europe. The restrained response of most of the European allies to the Soviet invasion of Afghanistan and the Iranian revolution and their tepid support for American policies devised to respond to those events invoked a bitter reaction in the United States and, with it, what many connoisseurs of alliance crises consider one of the three or four most serious in its history. The United States wondered how Europeans could fail to understand that their own interests as well as those of the United States were gravely affected by what was seen as a Soviet move toward the Persian Gulf, linked in its consequences if not its causes with the revolution in Iran. Europe wondered how the United States could talk about detente as being indivisible, as if tension in southwest Asia had to be matched by tension in, for example, Berlin, which in fact had no tension and they wanted none.

The lesson of this abridged history seems to be that most of the European allies have had a relatively unvarying sense of a Soviet threat to their security that has, remarkably, survived actual Soviet crisis making in Europe by more than a quarter-century. This steady perception must have been based not on successive episodes of better or worse Soviet behavior but on the fact of the permanent (up to now) Soviet military and political presence in central Europe, so near to so many West European countries during periods of less tension as well as of more. For that reason the perception has been affected very little either by the relaxation of tension in Europe or by Soviet actions *within* the Eastern bloc or outside Europe. West European perceptions of the Soviet threat *to them* have been largely immune to both detente and out-of-area tensions and even to periodic Soviet crackdowns in their own bloc. This steadiness has scarcely satisfied U.S. hopes for close cooperation with the European allies on global anti-Soviet strategies or out-of-area issues (a topic to which I shall return below). It has given rise, in fact, to repeated transatlantic clashes that have often been said—nothwithstanding the ever-lengthening record to the contrary—to be likely to impede alliance cooperation in Europe. In fact, the West Europeans' permanent perception of the permanent Soviet threat to their interests has provided an extraordinarily durable foundation for such cooperation.

The persistence of the alliance provides evidence for the persistence of a sense of threat on the part of the European allies not only during the period of high cold war tensions, which culminated in 1962, but even more for the period—*twice as long*—of variable but diminished tension in Europe since then. However, maintenance of the alliance is not the only imaginable response by the European allies to their continued perception of a Soviet threat. Few or none of the American and European founders of the alliance imagined in 1949 or in the years that followed that the system would still be in place 40 years later. On the contrary, the nearly universal assumption on both sides of the ocean was that the American "protectorate" of Europe would be a short-lived or at least temporary state of affairs until the European members could stabilize their societies, rebuild their economies, and thus be able to provide the essentials of their own defense.

The West European countries have long since stabilized their war-torn political systems and societies and developed their economic productions to hitherto unimagined levels. Two of the allies have nuclear forces of their own, and all of them together provide 90 percent of the alliance's military effort in Europe and much of its equipment. Yet, the alliance has remained dependent on, and characterized by, the contribution of the United States: an American guarantee (almost unique among the many U.S. commitments and involvements around the world) to use nuclear weapons if necessary to defend Western Europe from attack, a large American military presence in Europe, and an American supreme commander who both commands the alliance's integrated forces and symbolizes the American commitment to the alliance and the allies. The provisional defense structure seems to have become as permanent as the alliance itself and the threat to which it has responded.

Yet the West European allies have among them the population, the wealth, and the industrial and scientific capacity to maintain the forces and develop weapons needed for them, by themselves, to be able to meet and thus to deter attack from a Soviet Union that is less populous, less wealthy, and no more scientifically and technologically adept than they are. Such a Western Europe could spare itself the distress of having to rely for its ultimate security on a distant superpower whose decision making it neither controlled nor very well understood. It could also free the alliance from the inherently disturbing characteristics of a relationship among unequals, which provokes unilateralism on the part of the strong and an unhealthy sense of dependence and resentment among the weak, who suffer what they must but do not like it, and which no amount of "enhanced consultation" can overcome.

How does the record explain the nonrealization over so many years of so evidently desirable a state of things with so many supporters in Europe and America? Western Europe could have built up armies and armaments to resist and deter Soviet attack—if only such a thing as Western Europe existed. It does not exist, for the very good reason that the West European allies have remained a collection of larger and smaller nation states. The visiting Martian to whom I referred earlier could scarcely have found a less suitable group of countries on this planet to form a joint defense system in pursuit of what would have to be a joint foreign policy made by, in turn, a federal union with authority to do these things. Western Europe has been no group of Swiss cantons (which, in fact, took centuries to form their federation) or American states (which were not nations to begin with and even so took 75 years and a civil war to settle their federal union) but, rather, the prototype nation-states of the world.

Loose language and loose interpretations of history have contributed much to widespread misunderstanding about the possibilities of West European "union." I have noted that the convenient use of *Europe* or *Western Europe* to describe the group of European allies has led too many people to mistake these words for a real or realizable political entity. This error has been reinforced by the popular notion that the two world wars were really a European civil war, as if in 1914 and 1939 a political entity called *Europe* had existed rather than, as was the case, many individual sovereignties whose peoples recognized the nation-state as the highest level of legitimate authority, if not also of loyalty and devotion. Then, the accurate observation that the poisonous nationalisms of pre-1914 and pre-1939 Europe have not reappeared since 1945 in their old forms (perhaps because they have had no opportunity to do so in the new system of things?) has been stretched to the belief that political nationalism itself had disappeared and the old national states would soon follow. Observations of West European unity in the form of the European Communities suggest a different conclusion. Even the fact that the West European allies, or most of them, no longer claim to provide their own defense—once thought of as the hallmark of national sovereignty—but depend for that on an alliance system centered on a protecting superpower does not contradict the fact that the nations of Western Europe are still organized as nations, however interdependent they may be with each other and with non-European countries, and that any and all of them still have the sovereign right, and the means, to withdraw from a voluntary alliance system and seek to promote their security, if they chose, by other means. A West European union comprising defense and other functions could not have been organized on that basis.

Such notions have been amply considered, however, and have often been encouraged by the United States itself, which saw in them the means to reduce its own defense burden with respect to Europe, assure the American people that the allies were doing their part, and help smooth the constant and debilitating tensions of alliance imbalance to which I have referred. Still, the record suggests that most of the European allies have found U.S. leadership more beneficial to their interests than any imaginable alternative, not only because the United States has been effective in the role (to judge by what matters most, Soviet behavior) but also because it was *not* a European nation. For example, West Europeans have never called for one of their own to be named supreme commander as a first, at least symbolic step toward "Europeanizing" the defense system and have not welcomed suggestions to that end by prominent Americans. Why should they? The American SACEURs, after all, not only have provided an irreplaceable link to the American presidents who control the nuclear weapons on which alliance deterrence capability has depended (which has made them the ultimate element of transatlantic coupling, the primal tripwire) but also have appealed to most of the allies most of the time precisely because they are *not* German or French but an ideally non-European "president" of the company.

In 1954 the French National Assembly rejected a plan (proposed by a French government) to dissolve the French army into a European Defense Community in order to prevent the creation (then much feared) of a separate German army. We do not know what would have happened if the EDC had been implemented. We do know that neither France nor the Federal Republic nor Great Britain has ever offered since then to give up control of its armed forces in such a way. Consultation and some cooperation on defense issues has taken place among these and other countries in the Eurogroup in NATO, the Western European Union, the French-German defense arrangement, and in numerous and varied ad hoc groupings for the production of military equipment. However, armies must have commanders, strategic and weapons policies must be devised for them, and an authority must have the power to make these decisions, raise the money to pay for them, and order the forces into action. No such authority on the European level has been created, for very good reasons.

In the 1960s American policy tried to promote the creation of what was called a *two-pillar* or *dumbbell* alliance structure in which the United States would be able to deal with a single European authority on security and, more broadly, common foreign policy issues. The western side of the Atlantic officially hoped either that the European allies, or some of them including the most important, would establish directly some kind of unified security system (not, however, the French-led "European Europe" that General de Gaulle was trying to build) or that the decision-making system of the European Economic Community would be eventually extended to or spill over into foreign affairs and security. Neither, of course, has happened. The Economic Community itself, founded in 1957, is still struggling to establish a true economic community, now with a target date of 1992. The Western European Union, the Eurogroup in NATO, or other arrangements could have served the desired purpose had the will existed to proceed. It has not, probably because the European allies are not so dissatisfied with the existing structure of the alliance, notwithstanding their complaints of inequality, as to be willing to give up their still cherished *national* sovereignties in order to construct a *European* sovereignty that would be more powerful than any of them and a more nearly equal partner with the United States.

Further, they have feared that movement down this long road might impel the United States to withdraw its guarantee before they had put a replacement security system in place, if, in fact, they would ever be able to do so.

The outcome of the contradictory impulses at play here has been the maintenance of European military forces that are national in structure, financing, and orientation, yet committed (most of them) to a larger system, the alliance we have known. This arrangement has persisted because it seems to have created fewer and milder problems for the allies, serious and persistent as these have been, than any feasible alternative they could imagine.

For West Europeans of the 1940s, the 1980s, and the years between, the persistence of what seemed to most of them a permanent threat arising from their proximity to Soviet power (whatever Soviet behavior was at any given time) and their continued inability to deal with it effectively by themselves impelled them to seek guarantees and support outside Europe. They literally followed the example of Canning in calling the New World into being to redress the balance of the Old. In the 1940s and for many years after, the imbalance of power in Europe could be righted only by the United States. More recently, long-range thinkers have suggested that China and Japan might be able to supplement or even replace Western Europe's American alliance, but these have proved to be distant dreams. Up to the present the fundamental power alignment affecting Europe has remained what it was in the 1940s: a powerful Soviet Union confronts a group of states less powerful than itself that have no real alternative to providing for their security than by maintaining a guarantee from the United States. The neutrality a few small European countries have been able to preserve between the two blocs has offered no realistic model to others because it presupposes the existence of both blocs.

For the countries of Western Europe, their alliance with the United States has had obvious benefits in preserving their independence and security, but also their conveniences to which I referred of dependence on a distant power that has common interests with them but also other interests with which they do not always identify. The history of the alliance, when it comes to be written, will highlight a complex pattern of steady agreement among the allies about the existence of a Soviet threat and also constant disagreements between the United States and various European allies on a wide range of topics including how best to deal with that threat, how to manage relations overall with the Soviet Union and its allies, how to act in concert—or not—with respect to the innumerable problems created for them all by the historic process of decolonization and its sequels, and how to manage the free world economic system.

The European allies, like the United States, have at times invoked alliance solidarity to try to win others' support for their own particular interests in all these spheres of international policy. At other times they have tried to elude such solidarity when invoked by others. In the early years of the alliance, the European colonial powers tended to be *demandeurs* of support in these ways, and the United States tended to be reluctant to be drawn into their problems with restive or rebellious colonies. In more recent years, the United States, engaged with the Soviet Union throughout the world and with Third World nationalisms that it has considered (with more or less justification) to be creatures of or vulnerable to the Russians, has more often sought West European support for the protection of what it deemed to be not only its own but also alliance and Western interests outside Europe.

All of these matters, to which I will return in discussing American interests with respect to the alliance, have shown, overall, some degree of transatlantic cooperation and a considerable measure of transatlantic tension and friction. All that needs to be said here is that none of the West European allies has ever found itself so exasperated by U.S. nonsupport for its own policies or so unbearably coerced by the Americans to follow their lead on some issue or other as to call into question its commitment to the alliance or, presumably, its continued need for the U.S. guarantee that the alliance embodies. Various allies, of course, have used their alliance membership and the facilities they provide to it and/or the United States as means to coerce U.S. support for their own particular interests, but this familiar process too has never been pushed so far by the Europeans or resisted so far by the United States as a derogation of the principle of multilateral commitment and contribution on which the alliance is based as to provoke a lasting rupture. For many reasons, including the West Europeans' need for a security guarantee in the face of a permanent Soviet threat, the alliance has proved to be good business for most of the allies most of the time, the more so as no alternative alliance, or the prospect of no alliance at all, has up to now ever offered a more appealing calculus of benefits and costs, risks and burdens, to the West European members.

THE AMERICAN INTEREST

More historical research has been done on American foreign policy since World War II than on that of the Soviet Union or most West European countries, in part because more data have been available. The very wealth of material, the complexity, and sometimes the confusion of American decision making have provided ample grounds for debate among orthodox, revisionist, and counterrevisionist historians. Nevertheless, the main preoccupation of American policy since the late 1940s has been to contain the expansion of Soviet power, first in Europe and then elsewhere in the world as well. The main goals of American policy have been more consistently and successfully pursued in Europe than almost anywhere else, the proof being that the expansion of Soviet power or influence west of the dividing line of 1945 by force or the threat of force has been prevented. At the same time, this success with respect to the essential has been obscured by a series of contentions between the United States and other members of the alliance and among the latter, so numerous and often so acute as to give the impression (reflected in the literature) that the allies have expended more of their energy disputing with each other than addressing the Soviet threat.

How can we explain both the durability of this American commitment—now one-fifth as old as the Constitution itself—and the continuous ambivalence about its costs, risks, and usefulness that these disputes have both reflected and incited?

The United States government during World War II made many plans for the postwar period, but they did not include an intention to keep substantial armed forces in Europe for more than forty years after hostilities ended. Historians continue to debate about just when the government began to act consistently on the judgment that the wartime alliance with the Soviet Union could not be maintained and that the latter, having ruthlessly established control by force over the countries occupied by its army at war's end, was likely to take advantage of weakness and disorganization in the next tier of countries beyond the military dividing line to extend its power over them too, by taking sides in a civil war (as in Greece), supporting strong and subversive Communist parties (as in France and Italy), or even threatening or using force (against Turkey, Norway, West Berlin, or the Western zones of Germany, should the United States and Great Britain withdraw from them, or perhaps even if not). The American response to this perception was developed in a series of measures over a two-year period, starting with the Truman Doctrine (March 1947), passing through the initiation of the Marshall Plan aid program (June 1947) and its implementation, and culminating in the signing of the North Atlantic Treaty (April 1949).

In all this American policy aimed to contribute to the rebuilding of the West European economies, the stabilization of their political systems, and the solidifying of their domestic morale by providing material aid and a guarantee of their security against Soviet attack, threat, or subversion during the period of reconstruction. Once that had been accomplished, the containment of Soviet power in Europe was to become increasingly, and at some point predominantly or even exclusively, the business of the European allies.

Decades have now passed since the European countries achieved the domestic economic and political goals established by and for them in the 1940s. For the reasons I discussed, they have remained divided and therefore have failed to achieve self-sufficiency with respect to defense, however much that would have been in their own interest. The United States, faced by the lack of success of the subsidiary or instrumental aspect of its European policy, has nevertheless persevered with the primary aspect of it. All American administrations, because they have believed that the Soviet Union continued to threaten not only the West European countries but also the American interest in a secure Western Europe, have pursued containment and maintained the alliance to that end, notwithstanding disappointment with the allies in many areas, periods of relative relaxation of tension, and the displacement of the arena of major U.S.-Soviet confrontations after 1962 from Europe to other parts of the world.

Contrary to myth, American policy has *not*, however, been Eurocentric. Two bloody wars in Asia, a constant active presence in the Middle East and Latin America, and U.S. bases and alliances everywhere do not suggest U.S. inattention to its interests outside Europe. If containment has been less successful in those areas than in Europe and if SEATO and CENTO are forgotten shadows of NATO, that is because local conditions were in some cases less propitious to American efforts outside Europe. If the United States has been less "present" militarily in conflicts in the Persian Gulf or Latin America (to take two cases among many), that cannot be attributed to lack of attention or means arising from overcommitment to Europe and even less to lack of European cooperation, but, rather, to lack of consensus in the areas in question or, above all, at home about the usefulness and feasibility of American military presence or involvement. The charge of Eurocentrism has been a convenient alibi for those who did not recognize or want to admit these constraining factors, going back as far as the "great debate" in 1950–51 in the United States about whether or not to expand the Korean War into a full-scale conflict with China and leave Europe to its chances, a course of action eventually rejected.

Nevertheless, some policymakers and many elements of public opinion have often reacted to issues of defense burdensharing with outbursts of bitterness and resentment. Because of the failure of the European allies to achieve the long-awaited defense self-sufficiency, they have felt, the United States has continued to find itself bound to the commitments of an "entangling alliance" that were made at a time ever longer ago and were presented—at the start and often since—as finite rather than open-ended. The cumulative importance of these sentiments and the many disagreements that have fed them should not be exaggerated. American policy in Europe has been very successful, and it could not have been pursued over so long a period without a broad perception of this success in the United States. But these periodic quarrels and the feelings behind them are important if only because they have obscured the enduring effectiveness of the system in dealing with the Soviet threat.

Perhaps the most important, although not always the most divisive, issues have arisen from the constant need to adapt alliance security policy to changing conditions of military technology and strategic thinking. This need has been the source of a series of debates, usually initiated by the United States, about strategy (e.g., massive retaliation, flexible response) and military planning, spending, and deployments. These debates have often ended without a full meeting of minds among the allies about what was to be done and, to the exasperation of the United States, with less than full implementation of what had been agreed upon (e.g., an annual real increase of three percent in defense spending).

These difficulties, however, should have suprised no one. They reflected the profound differences among the allies with respect to their geographical locations (some confronting the enemy, some on the flank, some across the ocean) and their financial, demographic, and military means. Every country has not had the same view about planning to deter or fight a war, where to fight it, or with what weapons. Nor has each had a clear-cut view about its own interests because either conventional or nuclear conflict would have had devastating effects on Western Europe. The countries there have perceived problems in the development of alliance planning in either direction and even more in detailed public discussion of war-fighting scenarios, which has often alarmed public opinion and reminded the allies of their vulnerability to Soviet attack and their dependence on the United States. We should be surprised that so disparate a group of allies, even with the United States "in the chair," achieved so considerable a degree of agreement that the Soviet Union has never been tempted by the self-proclaimed deficiencies of the alliance to probe them by an attack, particularly in these latter years when the credibility of the U.S. guarantee has been so widely said to have been eroded if not destroyed.

Linked to this has been the necessarily *permanent* problem of whether and how West European faith in the credibility of the American guarantee of their security could be maintained as military technology and political circumstances changed. This issue has existed at least in principle since the United States chose not to take advantage of what was then its monopoly of nuclear weapons to break the Soviet blockade of West Berlin in 1948–49 or, later, to make use of its long-held predominance in nuclear weapons to deal with other crises in Europe. (This is not to say that the allies would have welcomed the use of nuclear weapons on these occasions.) The hard fact is that the European allies have had to live permanently with uncertainty, as those whose security has depended on the guarantees of others have always had to live. The allies could never be entirely sure of the U.S. commitment. They have consistently sought reassurance. They have always allowed themselves to be reassured but never fully and finally. This state of affairs did not begin with U.S.-Soviet nuclear parity or even with the first sputnik (1957). It is as old as the alliance and inherent in its very structure.

The European allies have inevitably found their situation disturbing. West Germany in particular is the most exposed, especially in periods of high U.S.-Soviet tension. Yet the record of their behavior suggests that they have found this situation preferable to any other they perceived as available to them and tolerable when measured, as the years passed, by the Soviet Union's apparent respect for the American guarantee, however much its credibility has been questioned in the West. The Germans and others have noticed that, although the Soviet threat to them persisted, no crisis in Europe has been comparable to those of the 1940s and 1950s since the United States *lost* its nuclear preponderance. Presumably the latter was not a sine qua non of Western deterrent capability and security.

Relations between the Western allies and the Soviet Union were very limited before the early 1960s, but since then they have developed considerably though unevenly. The allies have thus had to pay attention to trying to coordinate their dealings, individually and as a group, with the Eastern countries. On the whole they have done so with considerable success, notwithstanding diverse divisions among them on pace and sometimes direction. For example, they did not all move at once after the Cuban missile crisis toward "peaceful coexistence" or what General de Gaulle, a pioneer in the process, called "detente, entente, and cooperation" between Western and Eastern Europe. The United States was hostile to de Gaulle's initiatives yet signed the first major arms control agreement with the Soviet Union in 1963 (the Limited Test Ban treaty), soon after terminating the quasi- or pseudo-proliferation policy embodied in the so-called multilateral force—a turnabout poorly received by the Federal Republic, whose nuclear needs the MLF was supposed to have met.

The *Ostpolitik* launched by the German government in 1969 stirred concern in the United States lest the Germans weaken their alliance ties in pursuit of real or delusive Soviet enticements, but its own next steps toward detente stirred concern among some of the allies, which habitually are troubled by the prospect of a superpower deal over their heads and to their disadvantage. Yet a suitable degree of coordination was achieved in the complex negotiations that led to the four-power agreement on Berlin, West Germany's treaties with its eastern neighbors, the U.S.-Soviet agreements known as SALT I, the multilateral agreements that produced the Helsinki Conference on Security and Cooperation in Europe (CSCE), and the negotiations concerning mutual and balanced force reductions (MBFR).

As the United States moved away from detente in the later 1970s, signed and then failed to ratify a major new arms control agreement (SALT II), invoked sanctions, and intensified hostile rhetoric against the Soviet Union after its invasion of Afghanistan, most of the European allies moved in the same direction, though not always at the American pace. The increase of U.S.-Soviet tension stimulated fears that inevitably became political issues in many countries. Party leaders involved in complex coalition situations had to take account of these issues. In no case did pacifists or neutralists (however those terms may be defined from country to country) come to office or upset any country's adherence to the alliance, not even in the five countries in which intermediate-range nuclear forces were to be deployed (and were deployed), where debate was particularly intense. Many governments and parties nevertheless urged the United States and the alliance to move ahead with arms control negotiations as called for by NATO's original decision to deploy INF.

These issues were most sharply joined in the Federal Republic. There, the very active and visible opponents of INF deployment not only failed to come to power but also contributed to the return to office after 13 years of the parties most clearly committed to deployment, the Christian Democrat and Christian Social Union. The new government went ahead with deployment but showed that it was determined to maintain and even expand the advantages gained by the Federal Republic from the *Ostpolitik* agreements and subsequent understandings with the Eastern countries, including, above all, the "other German state."

The Reagan administration, for all the intensity of its anti-Soviet rhetoric, did not object very strongly to this West German policy or go very far in confronting the allies in order to confront the Russians. The main exception to this was the famous gas pipeline episode, which came to a climax in 1982 and ended with a cancellation of the economic sanctions the United States had invoked to try to coerce Great Britain, France, the Federal Republic, and Italy on this matter, in exchange for their agreeing to further study of the problems of limiting strategic exports to the East. The United States has not repeated this tactic, and the question of export controls has remained on the alliance agenda, where it has been since the 1950s. The European allies have made clear that they would not subscribe to policies aimed at crippling the Soviet economy or bringing about the collapse of the regime, objectives they thought were futile, provocative, and likely to prove more costly to themselves than to the Russians. The U.S. government itself has not pursued such objectives very systematically, nor has it even adhered to a fixed position on the permanently controversial issue of export policy toward the Eastern countries. The difficult early years of the 1980s were gotten through with much less damage to alliance solidarity from issues of this sort than many had anticipated.

The resumption of serious U.S.-Soviet arms negotiations and the signing of an agreement for the removal of medium-range missiles from Europe has opened a new phase in the cycle of alliance coordination of policy toward the East. As usual, and naturally enough, European allies that regretted what they considered the excesses and dangers of U.S.-Soviet confrontation have also found cause for concern in U.S.-Soviet rapprochement. So far, however, the problems created for alliance solidarity by what may (or may not) prove to be a period of neo-detente have been as adequately managed—not always to the satisfaction of every country on every issue, of course—as were those of the preceding cycles of relaxation and recrudescence of tension.

Divisions among the allies on how to deal with situations affecting the interests of some or all of them outside Europe have been numerous and constant. We have only to think—among many other episodes—of the Suez war, Quemoy and Matsu, the French war in Algeria, the Vietnam War, successive Arab-Israeli wars, Soviet activities in Africa, the Iranian revolution, the Soviet invasion of Afghanistan, and the U.S. bombing of Libya. In many of these and other cases, the United States was more inclined to use or consider using military force because it had more than the other allies (though France, in particular, has not hesitated to use force in matters relevant to its interests). Perhaps even more important than the disparity among the allies with respect to means of action have been differences of outlook about what was going on in the Third World and what the West needed and could do about it. From the American perspective, the European allies have often seemed too willing to stand aside and let Soviet or radical nationalist influence grow in Third World countries in the vague hope that somehow things would get better later. From the perspective of many Europeans—particularly Scandinavians and Dutch, and many on the left but not only the left, in many countries— the United States has been too reflexively hostile to Third World nationalism and too ready to take actions that seemed to be directed more at its own domestic opinion (the "loss of China" syndrome) or at the Soviet Union than at the realities of complex local situations. To these European critics, of whom General de Gaulle was an early spokesman, the United States risked slowing down what they believed would be the inevitable evolution of even the most hostile Third World countries, Marxist or not, such as Egypt, Iran, and China (was the most devastating defeat of the cold war so great a Soviet success in the long term?), toward the rebuilding of pragmatic ties with the West.

Since the 1950s the allies have often been said to be unable to maintain their cooperation in Europe if they differed strongly and often on major problems elsewhere. The record indicates, however, that that has not been true. These differences have never become so serious as to lead any of the European allies to call into question their alliance ties, however much they might have questioned American actions or feared that these might lead to conflicts involving them. Nor has the United States ever become so distressed by European nonsupport of actions it considered to be in their interest as well as its own as to cut back its commitment to what is, after all, an *Atlantic* alliance. Presumably the self-diminution of American influence in Europe must have seemed, on reflection, a strangely self-defeating way to punish recalcitrant allies. Nevertheless, divisions of this kind have on many occasions seriously strained relations between the United States and some of the European allies. The American side questioned, "Where are the allies when we need them?" The Europeans, for their part, implied that they were in Europe, helping maintain stability in that first and still very important theater of East-West conflict.

The Atlantic alliance has no economic functions, but the members have recognized from the start that their ability to maintain adequate forces to protect their security required strong economies, as did also their internal stability. In addition, parallel to the alliance has been an international economic system centered on the International Monetary Fund, the General Agreement on Tariffs and Trade, and an expanding network of public and private institutional relationships within which the postwar economic system has been developed. The United States was the main architect of this system and has been the most powerful member of it. The other main members have been members of the Atlantic alliance, plus Japan, and they have been able to deal with the United States on a more nearly equal basis on economic than on security affairs. Therefore, the relations among the governments that manage the alliance have been affected by the relations among those same governments with respect to the free world's economic system, and the reverse.

The global economic system has experienced unprecedented growth since the 1940s but has also undergone serious difficulties that have strained its cohesion and even threatened, some thought, to impede the ability of the leading members to cooperate in other ways. One of these crises culminated in the Nixon-Connally "shock" of August 1971—the beginning of the end of the Bretton Woods monetary system and at the same time one of the three or four most serious crises among the leading members of the alliance, although the issues in question had no direct relationship to NATO. The rise in oil prices after 1973, and again after 1979, led to problems even more divisive and prolonged, culminating in the recession of the early 1980s, increased protectionism, and threats of yet more, high American interest rates and budget, trade, and payments deficits, a higher dollar and then a lower dollar, and related difficulties.

Serious as these issues were and are for members of the alliance, the record indicates that they have never failed to bear in mind that the reasons that impelled them to remain united in the alliance retained their validity despite economic differences and that pursuing distinct policies in these separate spheres was both necessary and possible. In addition, the international capitalist system has shown a remarkable ability to solve or circumvent the very serious problems I have mentioned and many others and to maintain its unity while doing so. Its leading members have been able to compete fiercely for markets and sources of supply and to disagree on interest rates, trade practice, and much else while working together to maintain the system itself within which they were doing diverse and sometimes discordant things. This fundamental commitment to the system of those managing it—governments, central banks, and private players—has meant that the members of the alliance were more tightly bound together in the economic sphere than was sometimes realized and that therefore their alliance ties were strengthened rather than weakened by their common membership in the economic system, notwithstanding all their many and acrimonious differences. Certainly no member of the alliance imagined, even during the worst recession the West has experienced since the 1930s, that it could have either withdrawn from that system or brought about its replacement with something else. The behavior of the French Socialist Party in the years 1981–86 was eloquent on this point. No country seriously challenged the centrality of the United States and the dollar in the system, for all the complaints about many specific American policies. If the European countries did not move in such directions in the face of the American "provocations" of the 1980s, we may well ask when they would be likely to do so.

Even a short review of the problems that have drawn together and pushed apart the United States and the European allies would be incomplete without some reference to the fact that American-

European relations have not been a blank page filled in only by events since 1945. On the contrary, both Americans and Europeans have a deep store of attitudes about each other that have both reinforced and envenomed their relations in the alliance and otherwise. The ties of history, ideology, institutions, values, and culture that underlie the recent security and political relationship are well known. Less talked about is the part of the historical legacy that tends to estrange the peoples on the two sides of the North Atlantic and make their disagreements on specifics more bitter than they might have been if their relations were based only on mutual strategic interests.

In the last few years the United States has seemed rather more attractive to those supporting most of the governments of Western Europe than the reverse. That has not been, to say the least, a fixed part of the landscape. Since the early nineteenth century, many European intellectuals believed, as the historian Peter Gay has put it, that

> the United States . . . presented itself as the visible destination of a fateful voyage on which Europe has long been embarked. It demonstrated that the society of the future would be governed by bureaucracies under the sign of equality, with all the vulgarity, mediocrity, and contempt for intellect and excellence that this implied.

However, mass culture, which Europeans have long identified with the United States because it took form there earliest, has now come to Western Europe in so sweeping a manner as to have overridden or silenced much of the traditional opposition to mass culture and to the United States by intellectuals and nationalists anxious to defend their own and Europe's culture against this intruding presence.

This does not mean, of course, that the old European societies have ceased to be themselves or that the old doubts about the United States and its influence on them have vanished. Jack Lang, the French minister of culture, did not speak only for himself when he warned in 1982 that the United States seized not territory but consciousness (the "Dallas syndrome"). Something not very different came from a Vatican spokesman who said, in September 1987 just before Pope John Paul II visited the United States, that

> the United States is like a giant shop window that the whole world is staring at dreaming about the American life style, and the Pope is very much aware of America's ability to export ideas and attitudes, for better or worse.

Such thinking persists in Western Europe and is important, but it has contributed less in recent years than before to the impulse there in favor of closer Western European unity and to U.S.-West European quarrels as they have come along.

The existence of a parallel set of American attitudes about Europe has been equally or more important in the Atlantic relationship but is commonly overlooked. These views and feelings persistently color American perceptions of the allies and the alliance and provide sustenance to disagreements particularly when political or economic relations worsen. What on one level has been a remarkably natural association between peoples with profoundly deep common roots, values, and outlooks has also been peculiarly difficult for the United States to sustain, for two reasons. First, it has been an *alliance*, which George Washington warned his fellow citizens against—advice that is still capable of calling up (inaccurate) nostalgia for the arcadian days of the republic. Second, and even more important, this alliance has been with a group of *European* countries, the "old countries" on which the United States as a nation, and many of its citizens and their ancestors, turned their collective back in acts of national and individual self-creation. On the Western side of the ocean they have built something they see as new and better, more wholesome and virtuous, than existed on the other side. John Adams spoke for his generation and for many to come, up to this day, when, in a letter to his wife from Paris in 1780, he said that he found there

> every Thing . . . that can inform the Understanding, or refine the Taste, and indeed one would think that could purify the Heart. Yet it must be remembered that there is everything there too, which can seduce, betray, deceive, deprave, corrupt and debauch it.

Whether Paris or Europe still offers a greater variety of enchantment or dangerous enticement than New York or even Boston may be doubted. America is no longer a paradise of rural virtue and Americans are no longer innocents abroad, or even at home. Still, Europe has continued to arouse profoundly ambivalent feelings in the American people quite different from those they hold about the peoples of Asia, Latin America, and other places. "Every white American who wants to know who he is," Wallace Stegner has written, "must make his peace with Europe," and many of them do not like the idea, even if they are not quite aware of it.

Such considerations seem essential to understanding the outbursts of virulent hostility, often disproportionate to the occasion, with which much of American opinion responds to noncompliance with U.S. policies or outlooks by one or more European countries (e.g., the 1980 Olympic games, economic sanctions against the Soviet Union, support for U.S. policy in successive Middle East wars, the bombing of Libya). Why are the European allies threatened with a shift to a "Pacific strategy" because they invest only an average of 3.5 percent of their gross national product (GNP) in defense while wealthy Japan, presumably the beneficiary of such a switch, spends only one percent of its GNP on defense and is scarcely more supportive of U.S. policies around the world than the Europeans? This background of American ambivalence toward Europe has by no means prompted a permanent estrangement of the United States from its European allies who comprise most of the democratic nations of the world, but these considerations have had recurrent impact on particular issues even during the recent decades when U.S. relations with the countries of Western Europe have been intimate and productive. Ambivalences that have lasted for more than two centuries have not disappeared in a few decades. They form an important part of the background noise of the Atlantic relationship.

American disagreements with one or more of the allies about security policy in Europe or the other issues discussed above, reinforced by deeper sources of misunderstanding, have repeatedly invoked complaints in the United States that the allies, enjoying a "free ride" in the form of the American commitment to their security, should cooperate more than they do with U.S. policies with respect to East-West relations, out-of-area problems, or international trade and monetary issues. Above all Americans say that they should do more for their own defense. These complaints have sometimes reached the point of proposals that the United States should abandon its ungrateful and uncoopertive European allies altogether, cut back its commitment to them in proportion to the gravity of their noncooperation, or at least threaten to do these things in order to spur them to improve their performance on defense or whatever other matter was at issue at the moment.

The allies have responded to these sentiments with various arguments. Some assert that their understanding of the Third World, for example, is at least as good as that of Americans and that their judgments on problems in those countries are at least as valid. They say too that the West as a whole benefits because some European countries can maintain useful ties to Third World countries from which the United States is estranged. This argument ties in with the European contention that they are providing much more foreign aid to many African and other countries than the United States, that this aid helps stabilize the recipient countries and thus minimizes the prospect that Soviet or radical influence of various kinds will expand in them, and that this European effort should be taken account of along with defense expenditures when the division of labor among all the members of the alliance is examined. Similarly, most of them maintain that the extensive network of bases and other facilities they provide to American military forces is useful not only to themselves as members of the alliance but also to the United States as a global power pursuing containment against the Soviet Union.

At bottom the European allies reject the idea, which they think is implicit in American complaints about their contribution to the alliance, that the U.S. security commitment to them has been maintained for their sake more than its own and that its presence and guarantee could, if their behavior did not satisfy it, be cut back or withdrawn with little or no cost to American interests. Autopsies of successive alliance crises and quarrels convince the Europeans that American policymakers—if not always the public—have never failed to act, sometimes after an exchange of passionate recriminations, on the belief that their own continuing perceptions of a Soviet threat to American interests in Europe never allowed them seriously to threaten, and even less carry out, a significant diminution of the American security role there in order to force the allies to increase their own contributions, to do or abstain from doing other things, or to punish them for the same. In this never fully joined conflict of outlooks and wills, the Europeans might seem to have been in the weaker position because they have more to lose: their independence. But the American stake in the loss of Western Europe's independence has apparently seemed almost as serious to American policymakers: the possible loss of the U.S. position as a global power and the leader of a global policy of containing Soviet power that must necessarily include Europe as well as other places and that, if it ceased to include Europe, could not be taken very seriously anywhere else.

Neither the Americans nor the West Europeans have, of course, ever allowed their quarrels to reach this point. The allies have not hesitated to differ with the United States on many matters but have usually been willing to compromise on many things and leave others to be resolved or overtaken by the passage of time (an important element, in the preservation of essential alliance harmony over the years). On perhaps the most sensitive issue of all, military effort, the European allies have vastly increased their contributions since the 1940s even if they have never reached a level that would have allowed the United States to believe that it could, with safety to its own interests, seriously diminish its military involvement in Europe and even less to cancel as superfluous its guarantee to Western Europe's security. They have, in fact, done as much as they have in considerable part to allow the U.S. government to justify to Congress and the public the viability of the strategies and structures of which American forces are in and committed to Europe have been part.

Because of the importance of the burdensharing issue in itself and as a recurrent source of American resentment toward and purported leverage on the allies, why has the United States never ventured down the road of threatening to curtail or withdraw its commitment, whether to punish the allies, inspire them to do more or cooperate more, reallocate its own military resources, or save money?

Some have argued that the European allies would have been obliged to establish a common defense effort, with whatever political machinery was needed to make it effective and credible, if the United States had forthrightly cancelled its security commitment to them, laid down a definite timetable for doing so, or severely cut back its military presence. This concept cannot be disproved but it is improbable for several reasons in addition to the primordial problem, discussed earlier, of overcoming the ancient sovereignties of Europe. For one thing, American disengagement might have been harder to bring about than has sometimes been believed. An American withdrawal or threat to withdraw would have had to be far-reaching indeed to disengage the United States from so long-standing a commitment to so important an area of the world. The allies have had the habit, throughout the history of the alliance, of setting personnel and equipment goals that they have usually not met and yet managing to live in a state of reasonable contentment with their security situation because the Soviet Union has never chosen, for whatever reasons, to act as if it believed that the alliance's self-proclaimed shortfalls or doctrinal deficiencies would allow it to risk invading or pressuring one or more West European countries without running unacceptable risks to itself. In other words, deterrence has worked despite the inadequacies of the deterrent. The perpetuation of this situation for so many years has naturally contributed to its further perpetuation. In light of this, partial American disengagement would probably not have been enough.

A cutback of half the U.S. forces in Europe, for example, would have led to a "crisis" that might well have ended not with a European defense force or greatly increased military efforts but with the announcement that the alliance could still fulfill its missions (because of, e.g., enhanced fire power, equipment, support, training) and with the United States agreeing to that. *Any* forces it left in Europe, including even the small garrison in West Berlin whose mission is to embody the American commitment, older than the alliance, to the freedom of the city, would be perceived either as a tripwire to activate a still intact U.S. commitment or as indefensible victims doomed to capture or death in the event of attack.

To have a chance of shaking the European allies into union or substantially increased defense spending, the United States would have had to take away the supreme commander and all its forces, cancel its treaty guarantee and its pledges to West Berlin, or threaten convincingly to do all of this. The United States would also have to persuade the allies, against their self-interested inclination *not* to believe, that the cautious Russians were truly convinced that the Americans had so little interest in the area—not even economic interest, which Europeans would expect Soviet Marxists not to overlook—that they could be credibly depended on to stand aside in the face of Soviet aggression or threat, notwithstanding the heavy cost to its prestige and standing as a global power. Europe, after all, would still be a part of the planet.

Even then, the European allies might have concluded, if the U.S. cutback or withdrawal took place in a period of relative detente, that they really did not need to make the great effort, in treasury and statesmanship, to form the required European defense system. This was the case when the United States made a reduction of forces in Europe in the later 1960s. In time of tension, however, many Europeans might have seen trying to compensate for U.S. withdrawal as a hopeless task, considering the long time that would have been required to establish a defense system that might deter Soviet aggression or pressure in the clear absence of the United States from the scene. In either case, "Western Europe," if it could be created at all, would be seen to be entering the big boy's game of weapons production and force building too late from the technological standpoint to catch up with the superpowers (unless they considerately stopped their own arms buildups). Even if "Western Europe" could build a sufficient deterrent or was given one by the United States, its area is perhaps too exiguous to allow it credibly to deter Soviet attack. The Russians might believe that the United States would risk the destruction of half its vast territory in order to defend its vital interests. Would they believe that the governing authority of a West European union would be ready to use nuclear weapons with the prospect that the Soviet Union could destroy all of its small, crowded territory, particularly if such use was to be in response to a nonnuclear attack? Would the European publics have believed it or allowed it? If the West Europeans found any of these considerations persuasive, why would they have bothered at all to try to build up sufficient weaponry, unite, or spend great sums for that purpose?

The road to West European defense self-sufficiency has seemed so long, costly, and complex and the results still so problematical that the countries' failure to start pursuing it is scarcely surprising. The United States has not made their doing so a condition of its support. The existence of a U.S.-led alliance structure, familiar in its strengths and weaknesses, has perhaps helped them avoid examining the deeper reasons that might dissuade them from the effort. The range of difficulties, which have not much been discussed, may have been clear enough to European decision makers to persuade them to make the best of the existing system rather than to embark in search of another that might have called for material and political efforts beyond their reach and unacceptable risks along what would have had to be a very long road to an uncertain outcome.

The same line of thinking has also inhibited serious exploration of the idea that the United States might have phased out or phased down its commitment to Western Europe as the allies phased up their contribution to their own security, not only quantitatively (which, of course, they have done) but qualitatively (with respect to the fundamental question of who provides the backbone of credible deterrence). How could deterrence be shared in this way? Either the Soviet Union would have had reason to believe that the United States would respond to an attack on Western Europe or it would not. If the U.S. phasedown persuaded the Russians that the American protective deterrent had ceased to be operative, what assurance would the West Europeans have had, on that day zero, that the Russians would recognize the new deterrent as a credible replacement—assuming, as we should for all the years between 1949 and the present, that on that day a widely (if not universally) perceived Soviet threat to Western Europe still existed? If, however, the United States then prudently deferred or rephased the withdrawal of its deterrent guarantee and whatever forces supported it in light of the all too likely West European difficulties and delays in their armament program, the impetus for the allies to go ahead would have diminished.

Perhaps such immensely fine-tuned long-term policy developments would have been possible, but they have eluded the imaginations of both Americans and West Europeans for the many years that have gone by since the latter acquired the economic base needed for making them conceivable.

THE HISTORY OF THE FUTURE

One day the Atlantic alliance will break up or wear out, its functions fulfilled or no longer fulfillable by it. Because it has endured and done its job with reasonable effectiveness for far longer than its founders and many observers along the way expected does not prove that it will last one day longer. Still, this most basic lesson of the alliance's history draws our attention to the factors that together explain its longevity. What will happen with respect to each of these factors in the years to come? Things may happen for which the events of the alliance's first 40 years provide us no clue at all, but the continuities in the three factors which seem to me the premises of the alliance's durability may persist into the indefinite future and, with them, the alliance too. Opinions about that—guesses, really, more or less well informed—will differ. My own are these:

1. The Soviet Union has maintained control over its East European bloc since 1945, notwithstanding permanent latent resistance and outbreaks

of overt resistance on the part of the permanently aggrieved inhabitants of these countries. The Russians have had many and powerful reasons for maintaining this control. Looking at those reasons, I can hardly imagine that the most far-reaching possible reform of Soviet institutions will in the foreseeable future allow true national independence to the countries of the bloc—an independence defined, for the purposes of this discussion, as a reduction of Soviet control and presence in these countries to a point that will cause others, above all West Europeans, to believe that the Soviet threat they have perceived since the 1940s has disappeared.

2. If, then, the West Europeans, or the governments and a working majority of the political class in the principal countries, above all in the Federal Republic, continue to perceive a threat to their security in the *presence* of the Soviet Union in Eastern Europe, however ameliorated its methods of control, they must either provide the needed military deterrence by themselves or continue to rely on alliance with the United States to provide it. The obstacles that have up to now blocked the former solution seem to me likely to continue to do so, leaving the latter, with all its inherent and adventitious difficulties and divisive problems, as the only viable choice for the West European nations, or most of them.

3. The United States has pursued containment of the Soviet Union as its primary policy objective since World War II, and I cannot imagine that it will do otherwise in the foreseeable future, however much relations between the two superpowers may be improved and their competition limited (by arms control and otherwise) in the future. The unprecedented alliance between the United States and Western Europe has provided security and stability in a very important part of the world. For all the policy differences on major issues that have characterized the alliance and the subliminal doubts about it among Americans, I can scarcely imagine that they will either give up the policy objectives the alliance has served or find better means to implement them. Differences and discontents will continue, therefore, but so, I believe, will the fundamental structure of security in Western Europe that the alliance has provided for 40 years, provided, of course, that it is managed as well or no worse than it has been in the past. Utopian levels of concord are not to be expected, nor are they needed. A pragmatic understanding most of the time by most of the allies of the interests and needs of most of the others is a goal that should be both sufficient and attainable.

4

The United States and NATO: Enduring Interests and Negotiable Bargains*

By CATHERINE MCARDLE KELLEHER

U.S. INTERESTS IN THE ATLANTIC ALLIANCE

The simple answer to the question "Does the United States have compelling national interests involved in the North Atlantic Treaty and the special entangling alliance known as NATO?" is, of course, yes. By whatever measure, the reasons that impelled the formulation of an American tie to Western Europe in 1949 remain valid. The calculus involved three compelling interests. First was the American interest in preserving West European nations as independent power centers in the difficult relationship to the Soviet Union (as a matter of necessity). The second was the preservation of the rimland of the Eurasian land mass as a fully contributing, fully developed partner in an international economic system that the United States believed crucial for its own continued existence. Last was the moral or ethical commitment of the United States to those values embodied in the democratic tradition of Western Europe. After the horrors of World Wars I and II, those values were so compelling and significant to the life of the United States that the defense of similarly minded nations was of the highest moral priority.

More complex are the reasons for the present debate on this question. The sources in the United States are many and not always explicit. A certain type of forgetfulness is nourished by changes in domestic political structure and in the type of perpetual political competition the United States enjoys. There also is what some have called the *peace problem*. Forty years have passed with no serious interruption in the North Atlantic zone of peace. Peace is now

---

*Jill Jermano provided research assistance for the preparation of this chapter.
NATO—D

accepted as the norm. Moreover, the use of force in Europe has so many devastating implications that it is an image from which many shrink—in the United States, as in Europe.

The North Atlantic Treaty and the Atlantic alliance remain firmly and clearly in the U.S. interest and will remain so for the foreseeable future. No realistic or politically viable alternative structures exist for the protection of U.S. interests or the effective exercise of American influence in Europe. The United States has no possibility for a retreat to the fond memories of an isolationism that never was or for the rapid growth of equally satisfactory alternative structures. This statement holds true for East-West discussion in the field of arms control, for the creation of a new international political order in Europe, and for West-West negotiations leading to a new framework for Western political and military relationships.

What must be understood, however, is the many possibilities within the basic relationship. Many forms, processes, and structures have already changed; the patterns of American influence and communications have undergone numerous shifts and changes. One example is the importance and then the dissolution of the NATO Standing Group in the 1960s; another is the change in the role played by the Nuclear Planning Group within NATO, at a critical point in the early 1970s, to roles now played within bilateral "nuclear" relationships. Concepts for reform of NATO have always been a good cottage industry for aspiring politicians and ambitious academics. The time for some of these reform ideas may well now have come.

Basic U.S. interests dictate a number of simple assertions. First, the North Atlantic area, broadly conceived, remains the principal framework for the exchange of pledges of cooperation and involvement among the NATO partners. Second, the United States has an abiding interest in a visible, permanent national involvement in Europe that, for the foreseeable future, will be the physical presence of American military forces. Third, the U.S. interest is to ensure a high level of coordination and cooperation in economic and political affairs with and among principal West European states. Coordination and cooperation will not only support specific military arrangements but also are essential to the Western concept of individual and state security. Fourth, regardless of how political and social relationships may evolve, the United States must firmly recognize the commitments and values it shares with West European states. These commitments and values—protecting individual human rights and promoting peaceful relations among states—extend back to the finest of Western political traditions and must continue to inform and serve as the yardstick against which to judge the international behavior of the United States.

LOOKING BACKWARD: THE DEFINITION OF U.S. INTERESTS
IN THE NORTH ATLANTIC AREA

Looking back to the initial definition of U.S. interests in NATO from which the original Atlantic commitment sprang is appropriate. Here we see not only George Kennan's specific proposals on containment but also how these concepts changed, first during the hectic eighteen weeks of 1949 around NATO's creation and then in the first decade of NATO's development.[1] Viewed objectively, these fall into three specific categories.

Preserve American and West European Security from External Threat

This interest stemmed from decisions made during World War II about the nature of American international involvement and the reasons why the United States had been drawn into World Wars I and II. The consensus of American political leadership during and after the war was that the United States needed an international order with open access to the rimland of the eastern and western edges of the Eurasian land mass. Negatively defined, the rimland was not to be controlled by a hostile power. Postively defined, the United States was to be able to cooperate freely with those states and enjoy full interchange with them in straight market terms but more importantly in terms of political debate and coordination.

The American elite's perception of the Soviet threat proceeded from this definition. According to containment, erecting a barrier to any possibility of further Soviet expansionism was in the U.S. interest. The extension of Soviet influence into Eastern Europe—the least economically and democratically developed part of Europe—represented a tolerable (if regrettable) change in the geopolitical situation. Soviet expansion beyond the point of advance of the Red Army was viewed as a direct threat to the international order that the United States conceived as being of primary necessity. Outside of Berlin, the concern was not necessarily that the Soviet Union intended to invade Western Europe in the near future or that Soviet forces would constitute a constant threat to the economic and political security of Western Europe. The concern was rather than at any point Soviet forces might be used to exercise political-military influence on vulnerable West European politics and leadership and, in the short run at least, bring the process of recovery and access to a halt.

---

[1]For further discussion, see Catherine McArdle Kelleher, "Containment in Europe: The Critical Context," in Terry L. Deibel and John Lewis Gaddis, eds., Vol.II, *Containment: Concept and Policy* (Washington, D.C.: National Defense University Press, 1986), pp. 381–400.

A second concern grew out of events in Eastern and Western Europe in 1947 and 1948, as reinterpreted against the fears of the 1930s. The threat was the continuing instability, rapid governmental change, and basic ungovernability that had been the norm for European societies during the Depression and the political unrest of the 1930s. The Soviet Union, then committed to a strategy of political agitation, raised the prospect of constant vigilance against an internal threat generated by Moscow and the remaining unsolved problems of nineteenth-century class tensions. By the mid-1950s, these concerns about Moscow's attempt to manipulate internal politics within Western states had been reduced to little more than futuristic nightmares with little relationship to the present.

Preserve a Political Balance in Western Europe

As Raymond Aron reminds us, the key question for internal European stability was the balance to be struck between the emerging German state and its neighbors and close relations, the so-called German problem.[2] The United States had twice intervened in wars resulting from European failure to arrive at the necessary political balance. Intervention had come late; in the case of World Wars I and II, independent European actions had not secured the balance.

U.S. interests dictated a two-part strategy. The first was to create a German state subject to Western influence that would assure its neighbors not only of its peaceful intent but also of the creation of the necessary political and economic structures to guarantee the implementation of that intent. To do so, however, required a structure in which to embed the German problem, a structure with sufficient flexibility and a guarantee of external backing. The United States and its continued involvement was to be a critical part of that framework.

The second part of the bargain, however, was the guarantee to the Germans that the framework would allow the equitable reentry of the German state and its citizenry into the European international order. The harsh rigors foreseen by the Morgenthau plan of the late World War II years were followed by various schemes for pacification and neutralization that were dangled in front of survivors through the late 1950s. All proceeded from a series of punitive measures against the German population and the harsh implementation of the saying "never again." For U.S. interests, the solutions were not only too drastic but also precisely those done up in a different garb that had led to the revival of aggressive German nationalism in the 1920s and 1930s. The balancing act would be difficult but would ensure the

---

[2]See Raymond Aron, *Peace and War: A Theory of International Relations* (Garden City, NY: Doubleday and Company, 1966).

Germans both justice and their appropriate retribution for the horrors of the past.

To be the holder of the European-German balance meant that the United States took up guarantees against the emergence of fragmented, insecure political leadership in all the major European states. The continuing German problem, or more specifically the search for a viable balance in European political affairs, required sufficient time and security for the evolution of politically responsible and responsive leadership. What could not happen was the replay of many of the nineteenth century's divisive political agendas that combined fears of internal instability and external threat and led to the emergence on both the Left and Right of ideas inimical to continued democracy. The holder of the balance directly guaranteed time and sufficient discussion to prevent the kind of continuing crisis sketched out by the Leftist and Rightist architects of fear. Western Europe would have no need or requirement for drastic solutions to guard against internal revolt or external aggression.

Provide a Framework for Economic and Political Security

The interest of the United States in the development of democratic political and free market economic structures in Western Europe was clearly a primary consideration inspiring the North Atlantic Treaty. The lessons were drawn from the hectic memories of the 1930s and the collapse of the international trading system in the 1920s. Without open economic and political structures and individual sharing in state prosperity, the interests of the United States and its citizens would not be served. The Washington of the 1947–48 period viewed the development of a viable international economic order as dependent on a Western Europe committed to and capable of implementing these values. The question was more than one of the economic advantages of the United States as the dominant economic power in the world economy, but rather how the United States could prosper in a world in which its major partners were only somewhat removed from privation and economic devastation.

The simplistic argument of the revisionist historians about a master plan for U.S. economic domination thus misses the point. Rather, all but the small isolationist wing of the Republican Party in the postwar period displayed a widespread understanding that military security was only one way to safeguard the American way of life. *Economic security,* defined as the creation and envelopment of the United States in a viable economic order, was more important as a long-term consideration and for the prospects of particular industries and particular ecnomic functions of the United States. Economic security was significant, too, for the actual advancement of individuals within American society and beyond, on the basis of human considerations. The argument that economic development was the underpinning for both the evolution of political structures and the proper basis for military security preparations was a central factor in the development of American international entanglements after World War II.

At this center, this policy proceeded from a belief in the values regarding individual political and economic development—values American leaders shared with the broad European liberal political tradition. These values had been badly served by the political developments of the 1930s in most European countries. They had been obscured in the rush for totalitarian solutions on both the Right and the Left. Still, most Europeans and Americans believed that these were still values shared with most postwar Europeans. They were values that could and would be realized by the open democratic structures in Western Europe, given both time and security in which to reinforce the best of the past and shared traditions.

QUESTIONS AND CRITICS

The present debate turns on how much has changed since the initial definition of American interests in NATO. To examine the full scope of argument, this chapter focuses primarily on the present critics—those in public life who believe that the political context of the American commitment to Atlantic security has not fundamentally changed and those others who believe that American interests have undergone or must now undergo redefinition. In turn, the discussion focuses on three broad categories of critics: the new isolationists or unilateralists, the pragmatists, and the founding fathers or true believers. The aim is to discuss each set of criticisms in detail, to examine the major assumptions about American interests and the political context, and to present contrasting evidence.

The New Isolationists

The first group to discuss, the new isolationists, are perhaps the most articulate critics heard in Washington and at the whistlestops of the 1988 election campaign. They are only distantly related to the 1930s isolationists. The arguments then advanced by the "America First" group started from the premise that the United States could and should act on its own. The warning that George Washington had given about entangling alliances was to be an absolute maxim that could be breached only at peril to the nature of national political life and at risk to fundamental national interests. The prudent course avoided both permanent friends and permanent enemies. Best of all, the United States, according to this view, could create a Fortress America, secure from international entanglements or risks from any direction.

The new isolationists, in contrast, assume the primacy of the international involvement of the United States and describe the interests sought as essential to the survival of the American political system.

Critics as varied as Irving Kristol and Gary Hart state that the primary framework in which American interests are to be understood are in terms of global competiton with the Soviet Union. The Left and the Right partisans differ substantially. They differ over how much of this competition involves competitive and adversarial elements and how much could be absorbed in cooperative ventures. They differ, too, in their visions of the future, as to the validity of a long-range protracted conflict with the Soviet Union involving all-out mobilization of economic, social, and political resources as well as military preparedness and whether this competition involves the ultimate transformation of ever-growing Soviet military strength within a favorable international economic order.

One point on which all agree is that the Europeans are, at best, a secondary element in U.S. foreign policy. Europeans are counted in the primary category as long as they contribute directly to, or at least do not detract from, American efforts to grow and prosper. Europeans who are "too fat to fight" and too dependent on the United States for their continued defense and deterrence of outside evil (the direct Soviet threat or others, such as the threat posed by regional instability to Persian Gulf oil supplies) are not contributors. The United States can best stand aloof or explore freely other relationships—with the more economically vibrant nations of the Pacific Rim, for example. This will lead to overall growth.

A dramatic popular example of this argument is Melvin Krauss's *How NATO Weakens the West.*[3] Krauss argues that the Western alliance is based on a set of false assumptions, particularly in the last ten years. A strong and revived Europe was initially vital to the U.S. competitive strategy. With the advent of U.S.–Soviet nuclear parity, however, the United States became committed to the conventional

---

[3]Melvin Krauss, *How NATO Weakens the West* (New York: Simon and Schuster, 1986).

defense of Europe, a defense to which none of the West European states was willing to commit the necessary forces or time. U.S. action to secure conventional defense has discouraged West European allies from taking up the necessary burden. A U.S. withdrawal from its security commitment will restore the vibrancy and vitality of Europe and stem the outflow of U.S. resources.

Krauss's argument goes somewhat beyond this challenge to the convergence of U.S. and European interests. He argues that the United States has made Western Europe safe for economic growth and economic bribery. He says the Europeans have chosen the "detente as defense" route.[4] They have prevented Soviet invasion not by vigorous conventional defense but by bribing the Eastern bloc with economic incentives such as subsidies and trade. They also stand by passively while Soviet adventurism beyond Europe threatens their economic interests indirectly, such as in Afghanistan or the Middle East. Lastly, they complain about any vigorous U.S. program that might give the United States strategic nuclear superiority, such as the Strategic Defense Initiative (SDI). Krauss concludes by saying that the decline of faith in Western values led the Europeans to value their welfare state and their levels of economic prosperity in a way that sacrifices Western interests and that "has kept the world on the edge of the nuclear precipice."[5]

Krauss's solution is to define a set of U.S. interests that can only be served by the phased withdrawal of troops from Western Europe as well as from South Korea. Only in the case of withdrawal will the United States be able to assert its independent interests and provide better for Western security as a whole. Many of the other unilateralists are not as explicit as Krauss but do in fact reach the same point. The United States is being hampered by its alliances. It is hampered in ways in which it cannot realize its own potential, and it cannot induce or encourage others to reach theirs.

Two recent criticisms of the absolute primacy of NATO in U.S. strategic planning have come from the Commission on Integrated Long-Term Strategy (chaired by Fred Iklé and Albert Wohlstetter) in its report, *Discriminate Deterrence*[6] and from Navy Secretary James Webb.[7] Both called for a reassessment of U.S. strategic priorities and commitments, including its commitment to the defense of Europe.

---

[4] Ibid., p. 22.

[5] Ibid., p. 26.

[6] Commission on Integrated Long-Term Strategy, *Discriminate Deterrence* (Washington, D.C.: U.S. Government Printing Office, January 1988).

[7] "Remarks by James H. Webb, Jr., Secretary of the Navy," National Press Club, Washington D.C., January 13, 1988 (Washington, D.C.: Department of the Navy, 1988).

In *Discriminate Deterrence,* the Commission calls for the United States to plan for a wider range of contingencies beyond the two "extreme" contingencies that have driven U.S. force planning since World War II: a Soviet conventional attack on Western Europe and a strategic nuclear attack on the United States. The Commission argued that excessive emphasis on these two extreme but most unlikely scenarios has left the United States insufficiently prepared to deal with other, more likely forms of Soviet aggression and has provided an inadequate conceptual framework for strategic planning. The Commission did not explicitly propose that the United States abandon the strategy of forward deployment in Europe and the threat of nuclear retaliation but did propose that it modify this strategy significantly to emphasize a wider range of contingencies.

In his controversial remarks before the National Press Club on January 13, 1988, then Secretary Webb called for a reassessment of U.S. commitments. The United States must no longer view the Soviet threat primarily in regional terms (i.e., in terms of a conventional attack on Europe), but rather in global terms. Webb (and the Commission) conceded that such a major shift in priorities would be difficult, given limited budgetary resources, and that, at a minimum, it would require greater contributions by U.S. allies to the common defense and greater efficiency in using resources.

In the face of such criticisms, and the drumbeats of the 1988 election campaign, President Reagan and Secretary of Defense Frank Carlucci made numerous statements reaffirming the U.S. commitment to NATO.[8] Yet the Commission and Webb represent only the most visible forms of a critique that is attracting growing support in Congress.

What is striking in these critiques is measurement almost exclusively in military terms of the Western failure to recognize its potential. The favorite area of complaint is the well-documented failure of the allies to carry their fair share of military spending, buttressed by repeated references to percentage of gross national product (GNP) devoted to defense and other explicit burdensharing indicators. In each case, the argument is made that the fair share borne by allies does not meet the standards even of simple objective arithmetic and that the likelihood that these shares will increase over time is nil.

---

[8] "The Effectiveness of NATO Strategy," DoD News Release, February, 1988, pp. 6 and 8. also see *Washington Post,* March 2, 1988, p. A18.

What the unilateralists miss in this calculation of interest is many of the other parts that their own arguments stress. Little is made of the fact that the general prosperity of the West has led to an overall rise in gross national product for every Western state. Shares of burden means shares of an increasing economic pie, which has led to the increasing prosperity of most if not all of the citizens of these states. Moreover, references to the "wimpy" Europeans who are not doing what they should in terms of contributing to the general competition between capitalist and socialist systems ignore a number of recent political developments. Despite articulate public protests and minority demonstrations, the NATO intermediate-range nuclear forces were deployed. European defense budgets have remained relatively stable. The NATO states have taken coordinated, if not common, action in terms of the Gulf war, and the assumption of equal risk sharing is the principle of continued cooperation of all European states around the Persian Gulf area.

A particular variant of the unilateralists' argument is heard on the Left as well as on the Right and involves U.S. flexibility to allocate its resources with the Soviet Union's to the general benefit of global stability. From the viewpoint of the Left, implementing the guarantee of extended nuclear deterrence to Western Europe stands in the way of efforts to develop an overall arms control strategy or arms limitation agreement. Without the burden of extended deterrence, U.S. forces could be smaller and could reach the levels promoted by proponents of minimum deterrence in the 1950s. Without the commitment to Western Europe, the United States would not be drawn into a promise of an escalatory nuclear spiral. Forward defense is the problem of deterrence in particular and of the Europeans in general. Without that, the United States and the Soviet Union could arrive at more stable and limited forces, which could contribute to lowered tension and a lessened risk of nuclear threat or use.

This interesting argument has been heard only occasionally in the forty years of NATO's existence. The assumption on which it is based is contradictory to the set of concerns that led to the formation of the alliance itself and the U.S. role in the postwar international arena. The principal point of these unilateralists is that the United States has a higher stake in nuclear stability and lowering the risk of nuclear war than it does in any other area of activity, including the stability and security of democratic regimes and open access to a preferred international economic order. This is close to the isolationism embodied by the America First movement in terms of U.S. limitation within its boundaries.

Again, the calculus is a very narrow one. The basis for the set of goals and objectives that animate American foreign policy is more limited than that embraced by any conceivable political leadership. In essence, this is another variation of the kind of argument that led to that well-known saying, "Better red than dead."

The Pragmatists

A second set of arguments concerning American interests comes from a group loosely called the *pragmatists*. The basis of their argument is that U.S. national interests have been well served by the relationships within NATO and that NATO has worked substantially well as a safeguard of American security in military terms and in providing for cooperative behavior in economic and political realms. The critical element, however, is the *but* that follows these statements. Here, the pragmatists divide into a number of different camps, yet with a single message, namely, that NATO may have embodied primary American interests in the past, but it will not likely do so in the future.

One set of reasons advanced for this change concerns what many in this group see as the economically determined basis for Atlantic cooperation. This group sees NATO as reflective of old economic trading patterns in which the United States was anxious to revive West European markets for its goods. The current situation these pragmatists see is one of direct conflict and competition between the United States and its major West European allies for markets in Third World countries. A number of voices in Congress and in the business community see a danger to U.S. interests: European allies are ungrateful in their efforts to compete economically with the United States. What makes this competition doubly unfair is that the European countries are unwilling to loosen their military dependence on the United States and to provide more for their own defense. They thereby weaken the United States and drain resources that otherwise would help increase U.S. productivity and promote long-term economic growth.

A particular variant of these arguments takes a different tack: that it is in the interest of the United States to have more resources available to devote to its area of greatest economic interest and potential, that is, the security of the Pacific rim. This interpretation, heard most strongly in the first years of the Reagan administration, is that the United States has evolved new, more attractive trading relationships in Asia that need the kind of security framework that has been so successful in Europe. Providing equal stability guarantees in both areas is beyond the resources of the United States. Advocates stress the need gradually to phase out conventional U.S. forces in Europe while devoting increased resources to maritime capabilities and some light ground forces in Asia. At a minimum, this would involve strengthened ties and guarantees to Japan, South Korea, the Asian countries, and the U.S. base point of the Philippines.

Another variant of this argument bases its analysis on the experience of the past, especially as recorded by David Calleo and Paul Kennedy.[9] The thrust is that the United States is now at the point of decline as a global power because its military spending (particularly spending for the defense of others) is outstripping its potential for economic control and for sustained economic growth. Calleo explores the parallels with British economic performance in the late nineteenth century; Kennedy charts "imperial declines" since 1500. Academicians and policymakers have joined the debate by challenging both the statistical basis and substantive evidence presented by the pragmatists. Many question the proposed absolute decline in U.S. power; others have asked if statistics or examples from a prenuclear, predemocratic era really are of major significance.

However, the analyst is struck by how shallow and how limited a range of U.S. interests the calculus involves. The principal economic arguments involve fairly limited indicators, specifically the percentage of gross national product devoted to defense and the particular short-range balance of trade measured in terms of direct exchanges of commodities. As expert analysis and testimony before congressional and parliamentary committees demonstrate, neither of these indicators has a single widely accepted definition. The burdensharing discussions show that percentage of defense effort is not summed up by simple share of GNP, even when controlled for relative level of productivity, relationship to working-age population, or expenditures for various other defense-related items. Moreover, these indicators do not capture the basic set of economic concerns about long-run prosperity and stability, for the United States and for those countries with which it shares democratic values, that still pervades U.S. interests. They hardly sum up the kind of economic underpinning that is needed to preserve a balance in Western Europe and to preserve the viability in the face of external threat or internal disruption. Third, economists in the mainstream would dispute whether or not competition is necessarily a zero-sum game, particularly when viewed in terms of long-run patterns of diffusion of technology and sharing through multi-national corporations and other economic arrangements.

---

[9] David Calleo, *Beyond American Hegemony: The Future of the Western Alliance* (New York: Basic Books, 1987). See also Paul Kennedy, *The Rise and Fall of Great Powers* (New York: Random House, 1988).

Last, Western economic growth is quite clearly not a zero-sum game. As Tables 4.1 to 4.4 well document, real growth and unemployment rates rise and fall together with only occasional lead-lag effects. Furthermore, the United States has increasingly drawn on European as well as American capital to fuel both general economic growth and the record military buildup under the Reagan administration. Independence at new levels is the result. Attempts to extract further "imposed" economic advantages could prove counterproductive at home as well as in bilateral relations with our European allies.

TABLE 4.1. *Real Economic Growth Rates for Seven Major Alliance Nations*

Year	France	Italy	UK	Canada	Japan	FRG	USA
1965	5.3	3.3	2.5	6.7	11.3	5.5	6.0
1966	5.2	6.0	1.6	7.0	10.6	2.7	6.1
1967	4.6	7.2	2.5	3.3	10.8	-0.1	2.7
1968	4.1	6.5	4.3	5.8	12.7	6.1	4.5
1969	7.1	6.1	1.7	5.1	12.3	7.3	3.0
1970	5.6	5.3	2.0	2.9	9.9	5.3	-0.4
1971	5.5	1.6	2.6	6.8	4.7	3.2	3.5
1972	5.8	3.2	2.1	6.1	9.0	4.1	5.7
1973	5.1	7.0	9.0	7.5	8.8	4.6	5.6
1974	3.4	4.1	-1.3	3.6	-1.2	0.3	-0.6
1975	0.0[1]	-3.6	-1.5	1.2	2.4	-1.6	-1.2
1976	5.2	5.9	5.0	5.8	5.3	5.6	5.4
1977	3.0	1.9	-0.9	2.0	5.3	2.8	5.5
1978	4.0	2.7	4.3	3.6	5.1	3.5	5.0
1979	3.3	4.9	2.2	3.2	5.4	4.0	2.8
1980	1.1	3.9	-2.8	1.1	4.8	1.9	-0.3
1981	0.2	0.0	-0.8	3.3	4.0	-0.2	2.5
1982	1.5	0.0	1.9	-4.5	3.3	-1.0	-2.1
1983		0.0	3.3	3.3	3.4	1.3	3.7
1984		0.0	1.7	4.7		2.6	6.8

[1] A value of 0.0 indicates real growth of less than plus or minus 0.05.
Source: Computed from International Monetary Fund, *International Financial Statistics*, various years.

Catherine McArdle Kelleher

TABLE 4.2. *Unemployment Rates of Seven Major Alliance Nations*

Year	USA	Japan	UK	FRG	France	Canada	Italy
1967	3.8	1.3[1]	2.2	2.1	6.1[2]	4.1	3.5[1]
1968	3.6	1.2[1]	2.2	1.5	7.1[2]	4.8	3.5[1]
1969	3.5	1.1[1]	2.1	0.7	2.8[2]	4.7	3.4[1]
1970	4.9	1.1	2.3	0.5	2.8[2]	5.9	3.2
1971	5.9	1.1	3.0	0.7	2.1	6.4	3.2
1972	5.6	1.4	3.4	1.0	2.3	6.4	3.6
1973	4.9	1.3	2.6	1.3	2.1	5.6	3.5
1974	5.4	1.4	2.9	1.5	2.7	5.4	3.1
1975	8.5	1.9	3.9	4.8	3.8	6.9	5.9
1976	7.7	2.0	5.4	4.7	4.2	7.1	6.7
1977	7.1	2.0	5.7	4.6	4.7	8.1	7.2
1978	5.9	2.2	6.1	3.5	5.1	8.3	7.1
1979	5.7	2.1	5.8	3.2	5.9	7.4	7.5
1980	7.2	2.0	7.0	3.4	6.3	7.5	7.6
1981	7.6	2.2	10.6	4.8	7.3	7.6	8.5
1982	9.7	2.4	11.0	6.9	8.0	11.0	9.1
1983	9.6	2.7	11.6	8.2	8.4	11.9	9.8
1984	7.5	2.7	11.6	8.2	10.0	11.3	10.3
1985	7.2	2.6	11.8	8.3	10.2	10.5	10.6

[1] Not seasonally adjusted.
[2] Ratio of unemployed to jobs vacant.
Source: Organization for Economic Cooperation and Development (OECD). *Economic Outlook*, Paris, various years.

TABLE 4.3. *American Net International Investment Position*

Year	TOTAL	With W. Europe	With Canada	With Japan	With Latin America	With Other Countries
1970	58,473	− 24,829	20,823	1,075	18,091	25,439
1971	45,511	− 35,843	23,221	− 7,814	19,996	29,529
1972	37,036	− 46,328	25,915	−11,648	21,854	29,162
1973	47,894	− 53,084	29,509	− 2,007	22,207	31,527
1974	58,731	− 48,030	35,466	2,045	29,104	18,222
1975	74,240	− 47,266	40,267	918	36,628	20,835
1976	83,578	− 47,819	46,241	− 2,116	52,005	10,775
1977	72,741	− 58,423	50,589	− 8,833	59,807	5,878
1978	76,115	− 71,559	56,566	−16,451	70,630	17,285
1979	94,457	− 67,770	60,704	1,371	64,719	15,645
1980	106,037	− 66,818	58,975	1,953	85,732	4,414
1981	140,704	− 52,243	66,272	− 1,840	100,236	2,485
1982	136,200	− 71,484	63,930	1,305	113,970	−1,936
1983	88,494	−111,615	64,990	− 1,675	97,442	4,249
1984	4,384	−150,522	56,511	−19,269	78,311	5,933
1985	−107,440	−198,480	52,926	−45,531	54,048	−5,966

1. All values in millions of current U.S. dollars.
Source: U.S. Dept. of Commerce, Bureau of Economic Analysis. *Survey of Current Business*. Parts were taken from Vol. 66, No. 6, June 1986, but much was also taken from unpublished historical tables obtained by mail from BEA.

TABLE 4.4. *American Net International Investment Position with Western Europe*[1]

Year	Net Position[2]	U.S. Assets in W. Europe	W. European Assets in U.S.
1970	- 24,829	42,191	67,020
1971	- 35,843	46,580	82,423
1972	- 46,328	51,829	98,157
1973	- 53,084	59,974	113,058
1974	- 48,030	70,020	118,050
1975	- 47,266	78,983	126,249
1976	- 47,819	90,243	138,062
1977	- 58,423	104,865	163,288
1978	- 71,559	131,782	203,341
1979	- 67,770	158,231	226,001
1980	- 66,818	186,786	253,604
1981	- 52,243	216,492	268,735
1982	- 71,484	251,055	322,539
1983	-111,615	258,219	369,834
1984	-150,522	272,148	422,670
1985	-198,480	316,552	515,032

[1] All values in millions of current U.S. dollars.
[2] Net position figure is the difference between columns 3 and 4.
Source: U.S. Department of Commerce, Bureau of Economic Analysis, *Survey of Current Business*, Vol. 66, No. 6, June 1986.

A second area of concern for pragmatic criticism of NATO as a framework for American interests is the consequences of nuclear parity. The argument of the pragmatists, as well as that of the unilateralists discussed earlier, proceeds from an assumption that in the past the United States enjoyed nuclear superiority or was able in some sense to afford "providing extended deterrence for European security." With the onset of strategic parity and thereby a greater mutual deterrence practiced by the Soviet Union and the United States, pragmatists thought that the United States could no longer provide this set of guarantees. Additionally, provision of adequate conventional defense by the United States or by the United States and its allies is currently not thought to be supportable economically. Conventional defenses are not an area, they argue, in which the United States has any particular natural advantage or possibility. Conventional defense is something the Europeans can and should provide for themselves. However, the United States should seek new means to maintain the strategic competition with the Soviet Union, whether in the area of defensive force development (SDI) or in terms of new technological breakthroughs in the offensive force area.

Close examination of this set of arguments raises many questions beyond the test of surface validity. The question of direct benefit to the United States of lowering the risk of nuclear war is not considered, nor is the relationship of that level of risk to the particular balance of forces in Europe made clear. Even more surprisingly, the easy assumption is made that the U.S. presence in Europe of some 320,000 conventional forces is secondary to the principal American deterrent of tactical nuclear weapons stationed in Europe and strategic offensive forces stationed in the United States. This argument, furthermore, is not consistent with NATO's doctrine of flexible response. It is also in conflict with the goal of strengthening conventional capabilities to correct asymmetrical East-West military balances.

Also ignored is the degree to which the U.S. presence in Europe, whatever its numerical level, suits a number of purposes. One is to establish a system of conventional and nuclear deterrence to deny the prospect of an easy conventional victory or the easy application of conventional military pressure against Western Europe. Another is to provide a level of reassurance not just to domestic populations, but especially in terms of the establishment of the intra-European political balance. For example, U.S. forces represent a specific balance weight to the military potential possessed by the Federal Republic of Germany. Lastly, the U.S. presence defines a U.S. commitment to the stability of the range of political systems that exist within the European continent and to the prospects of peaceful change within the European order. The numbers of specific deployments may change, but the basic facts of this commitment seem to require the continued presence of U.S. military forces for at least the foreseeable future. U.S. forces embody the stake the United States has in the evolution of the European political order, which extends the terms upon which the final settlement of World War II will be established.

Another concern of the pragmatists is what they regard as the unhealthy nature of the basic political relationship between the European allies and the United States. The reasons for this unhealthy turn are described variously. Some, particularly influenced by the INF demonstrations and discussions, portray the Europeans now as no longer interested in the true process of defense or even much in the basis for deterrence. They argue that the United States has remained true to particular political, military, and economic requirements of security, while the Europeans have substituted preferences for detente for serious security policies. This argument gives great emphasis to the concept of the "Eurowimp" and to the mobilized electorates that demand greater and greater welfare benefits under indulgent systems providing cradle-to-grave individual economic security.

A second variant puts the cause of the unhealthy situation in terms of American natural dominance. Here, as sometimes heard in the words of Henry Kissinger and even sometimes in the prescriptions of Jonathan Dean, the United States is purportedly getting in Europe's way.[10] It has by design, and perhaps also by inadvertence, led the Europeans to be too dependent on and too concerned with events in Washington and insufficiently concerned with coordinated European defense efforts. The prediction is that eventually the United States will begin to draw back from active involvement in European defense efforts. Western Europe will then pick up the challenge and go forward through the medium of the European Community or through some new European organization to mount its own coordinated defense. This defense could then be related to the United States through a series of new cooperative relationships and come to constitute the second pillar in the alliance.

This discussion later considers the possibility that such an alternative truly exists, particularly in the foreseeable future. In examining the pragmatic criticism on its own merits, however, again one sees a fairly narrow range of evidence that has been taken into account and an even more limited definition of what U.S. interests are. The heightened European consciousness of the possibilities for European cooperation is beyond question. To be taken into account, for example, are the increasing frequency of contacts among European defense ministers, the continuing coordinating efforts within the Eurogroup (the European caucus of NATO), intensified cooperation in the Western European Union (WEU), and the new salutary evidence of Franco-German and Franco-British defense cooperation.

This evidence of renewed discussion, planning of common brigades, and councils for consultation is a long way from the integration of a coordinated European defense structure. Moreover, U.S. interests, at least since the 1950s, have already been defined as fostering a cooperative framework, even if operationally the fostering has had somewhat of an edge. The question is how and to what extent the United States stands in the way of European efforts. The available evidence suggests that rarely does the United States get in the way of what was a serious effort at cooperation behavior. At least in some cases, U.S. behavior may act more as a catalyst to European activity, than as a barrier to it. Included here would be such cases as bounded competition of the sale of the century (the F-16 versus the Tornado); cases of direct European response to U.S. initiatives, as in repeated calls for a European out-of-area contribution; and questions of direct calls for coordinated European response, as in a number of the recent arms control initiatives.

---

[10] See Jonathan Dean, *Watershed in Europe: Dismantling the East-West Military Confrontation* (Cambridge, Mass.: Union of Concerned Scientists, 1987).

The Eurowimp argument seems similarly flawed. First, the proponents of this view ignore much of what has really happened in terms of alliance cooperation and in fact the implementation of alliance initiatives over the last ten years. Perhaps more importantly, they are deluded by an imperfect understanding of the nature of past cooperation and integration. Inspection of the available evidence shows decisively that the golden age of NATO never happened, and like all golden ages, it gained in luster as time passed and as sensitivity to present irritation and problems has continued. The management of the alliance, from both the American and the European points of view, always has involved questions of conflict as well as cooperation and of considerable irritation as well as harmony.

The Founding Fathers or True Believers

The last group of critics, the founding fathers or true believers, reflects a variety of American political perspectives united behind a common theme: disappointment with European reactions to American leadership within NATO and nostalgia for what they believe was NATO's golden age. For this group, American interests in NATO and in the guarantee of European security are self-evident and inevitable for all of the reasons advanced in the 1949–51 debates that were reviewed above. These reasons do not only depend on the particular intensity or probability of a Soviet threat; they are not dependent on the particular state or level of European economic health or even the relative trade balance. With the exception of extremist political groups, these interests are compatible with almost any coalition grouping and political arrangement within the European political spectrum.

What is critical, however, is the stable, assured role of the United States within the alliance, and the recognition by the allies of the burdens and the risks that the United States has assumed for the general good. This is where the greatest disappointments of the past decades purportedly lie. For this group, the burden of initiative and responsibility is largely the business of the United States and primarily subject to its definition. What has been lost, then, is the allied consensus on this issue and the understanding and acceptance of the U.S. lead on topics as diverse as the gas pipeline issue, the need for allied contributions to security tasks outside the NATO area, the development of economic relationships with Eastern Europe, or even political ties to Latin American opposition groups.

In essence, these critics see NATO not only as the umbrella framework for the priority problems of American foreign policy but also as the necessary subsuming framework for the NATO allies as well.

The primary focus of European allies supposedly is the regional balance; therefore, they should cooperate with American global initiatives as required or assume special regional burdens to offset American efforts required outside NATO. Implicitly, too, the cohesion of the alliance and the difficulties of coordinating policy within NATO place special demands for allied support and understanding. NATO therefore is to be both the primary vehicle of allied policy and the framework in which mutual irritation and disputes are muted for the advancement of the common good. Any deviation from NATO consensus, especially on issues defined in the domestic American political context as important to the United States, thus becomes a cause for anxiety about crisis, about the weakening of essential Atlantic ties, and about the future of the alliance.

Even this oversimplified précis of the founding fathers' argument suggests reasons to rebut this form and level of criticism. Much of the argument reflects the ahistorical nature of American political discourse. From its inception, the alliance has subsumed within it substantial areas of European-American disagreement over fundamental national policies and interests, including the debates over decolonization, Suez, nuclear sharing, nuclear independence, fiscal and monetary coordination, and the nature of relationships with Taiwan and the People's Republic of China, Vietnam, Cuba, and the Arab world, not to mention with the Soviet Union over the Nuclear Nonproliferation Treaty or, in contrast, the SALT II accord. The discussions have been fierce and lengthy and ended sometimes less through direct compromise than through external change and internal exhaustion.

However irritating this disagreement has been at any particular point, an objective definition of U.S. interests would seem to allow or even prescribe considerable room for diversity and debate. The values pursued over the long run are the critical questions, not the degree of loyalty to or alignment with the specific policy choices of particular American administrations or leading political personalities. NATO's strength is that of a free association, bound by particular common interests and by primary common values, which reaches decisions with difficulty but with rigor and stability. The double-track decision is an example of the risks and costs involved in common action, and also an example of a decision taken and implemented because majority governments decided to do so. The views of minorities were important and should be interpreted as cautionary indicators about the present parameters of consensus and toleration. However, they remain minority views, without electoral responsibility or overweening political significance in the immediate future.

Important to this diversity is also openness to change, clearly another factor compatible with basic American interests. Critical changes have occurred since NATO's formation, with specific implications for the sharing of burdens, the acceptance of risks, or even for the recalculation of particular military arrangements or political bargains. But, few of these obviate the basic definition of American interests or the need to manage change in common with the West European allies. A successor generation that has a different perception of risk sharing is, in and of itself, not grounds for anxiety. Rather, it is a challenge to be met with an explanation or perhaps a reexamination of the types of probable risks and the formulas for sharing consistent with base values. Managed in common, as risk has been throughout most of NATO's history, new perceptions are grounds for strength and renewal in light of a changing environment. Clearly, a dynamic interpretation of American interests can only welcome the flexibility and adaptability this allows, in contrast both to the rules of other alliance systems of the past and even some in the present.

THE FUTURE

If the United States does not completely go home and the American political system continues to support a broad NATO commitment, the question still remains as to whether alternative options are available for the organization of Atlantic security consistent with basic American interests. One option that has been around for some time, but remains a subject of renewed interest, particularly in the last year, is a revival of a European framework for defense. It would involve not Kennan's dumbbell or the European Defense Community concept of the 1950s, but rather something closer perhaps to President John F. Kennedy's "two-pillar concept," with a loose European organization linked to something similar on this side of the Atlantic. These two pillars would be sufficient for deterrence and would coalesce into a single, integrated organization in the event of war.

Here one stumbles into the same kinds of problems that were critical in the 1950s. What is the basic willingness of Britain and France to accord Germany a full role in such an organization, unbalanced by an equalizing American weight? What new problems of nuclear control would arise and assume ever-increasing importance as the British and French forces modernize toward the 1990s and toward a third, significantly different stage of nuclear weapons development? How would these forces be coordinated with the American guarantee? Would all these arrangements allow Germany and the smaller states direct roles in deciding whether or not nuclear weapons are used in their defense? Indeed, could they permit these states to develop nuclear weapons of their own, however unrealistic that now seems? What are the American interests to be preserved in an evolving political-military balance in Western Europe and between Western and Eastern Europe?

A second set of options, more consistent with the severe economic and demographic constraints Europe will increasingly face, emphasizes a drastic change in the kind of defense organization and level of effort European states would undertake. It might be a force structure "made in Europe" rather than in the United States. It might involve cadre divisions that could be filled out given sufficient warning or greater emphasis on the use of reserves along the lines of the Swiss model of the gun in the closet. NATO as an overarching organization would be of lesser importance, while bilateral (especially U.S.-German) ties would be crucial. However attractive, such concepts include a formidable set of political responsibilities and would require a willingness to go beyond some rather bad memories of the past.

A third alternative is one barely outlined in Egon Bahr's catchphrase, "mutual security through security partnership." Alluded to in the alternative strategy debates in Germany during 1983–84, this concept takes into account the special security responsibilities borne by the two halves of Europe (and especially the two Germanies) toward one another. Some versions also include a closely connected set of responsibilities toward all targets of Nazi aggression, particularly "the Soviet people." At issue is not only the rethinking of present doctrine and force employment guidelines but also the development of a "nonprovocative defense" in structure and operation. Remaining to be considered are the implications that this arrangement would have on the stationing of other forces on German territory (East as well as West) or on the future conduct of the European-American alliance. Moreover, what are the implications for a new system of conventional deterrence and for arms control guarantees?

These are but three alternatives; many others could be and have been considered. To most conceivable American leadership groups over the next decade, all of them will probably look less attractive than the basic NATO framework. This celebration of the status quo may be simply a tribute to our failure to imagine the full scope and impact of coming events. It certainly reflects the basic continuity of American interests and the set of beliefs and calculations that have always made the Atlantic tie the cornerstone of postwar foreign policy. Although dissatisfactions have grown, the probabilities for startling future achievements or new initiatives now seem very low. Along the crucial dimensions, the safest bet will almost certainly continue to seem sticking with policy stances that promise the fewest risks and preserve the greatest number of future options while assuring present benefits.

Still open, however, are major questions that turn on the degree of attention that will be given to European issues by future American administrations. How much strain will normalization and adaptation produce? Will the fundamental containment bargains struck in the 1950s be fully understood by the political leadership that will come to power in the United States during the 1980s and the 1990s?

POSTSCRIPT

Ten years after his first exposition of the containment doctrine, Kennan returned to the issue of NATO in the 1957 Reith lecture, "Strengthening NATO—To What End?"[11] Kennan recalled his notion of NATO as a "military shield" to stabilize the situation in Western Europe and reasure the European people. "Strengthening NATO," he argued, must be not a military end in itself, but the means to another end: "the piecemeal removal, by negotiation and compromise, of the major sources of the military danger, particularly, the abnormal situation now prevailing in Central and Eastern Europe, and the gradual achievement of a state of affairs in which the political competition could take its course without the constant threat of a general war." He concluded that the United States, as NATO itself, would be ill-advised to "put all our eggs in the military basket and neglect the positive things" that alliance members could do. The latter included cooperation on economic and technological issues and attention to domestic problems in each member country that undermine NATO's overall strength and utility.

Written over two decades ago, these words seem relevant to the world of the 1990s. Because radical departures from NATO as an instrument of U.S. policy seem unlikely, today's task is one of ensuring that NATO can continue to function and that U.S. interests are clearly and carefully defined. The greatest danger lies in attrition, fragmentation, and exploitation of internal weaknesses and divisions within countries and among allies. Here Kennan's caution against becoming wholly fixated on the military aspect of U.S. security interests is particularly pertinent. "Let us, then, while keeping our guard up and while never ceasing to explore the possibilities for progress by negotiation, not neglect those undertakings that are

---

[11] The following discussion substantially follows my argument in "Containment in Europe: The Critical Context" in Deibel and Gaddis, *Containment: Concept and Policy.*

necessary for the spiritual and economic advancement of Western society." In 1957 these undertakings included greater Western European integration, attention to the pound-dollar division, and establishment of common policies "in those areas where our concerns and responsibilities are common." Today the list would be somewhat different and far longer, but, as Kennan observed then, these things must not be "lost in the military shuffle." In fact, the future of American involvement and the success of American interests may depend on making them the subject of sustained and common Atlantic effort.

5

Is NATO Still in Europe's Interest?

By MICHAEL STUERMER

This chapter rests on the assumption that yes, NATO is still in Europe's interest, that it will continue to be so for a long time to come, and that it cannot be replaced but must be transformed from a U.S.-dominated protectorate into a more equitable relationship. The NATO of the future will be essential to world stability as much as to West European security, because the control of Europe's heartland, Germany, is still the most contested issue in world politics and, concomitantly, the control of Germany is the key to European domination.

Certainly, NATO would not have come into existence without the Soviet threat, perceived or real, in the last phase of World War II and the first phase of the postwar period. However, the role of NATO past and present cannot solely be described in terms of the dominant Soviet-American conflict; it is also, in a much wider context, a crucial element in the ongoing political and strategic contest between pax Americana and pax Sovietica—two mutually exclusive ideas of the order of the world or at least very large parts thereof. Raymond Aron was right in saying that the superpowers are enemy brothers "who can't make war and can't make peace." Whatever changes have occurred in the meantime, the basic relationship is still one of inescapable partnership and inescapable antagonism. Europe continues to be the bone of contention between the two sides as it provides the economic, psychological, and geostrategic element that would tip the balance in favor of one side or the other.

The Soviet threat was paramount at the beginning, and the Soviet Union's overwhelming weight on the Eurasian landmass will continue to be the dominant reason for NATO's existence as long as the bipolar structure of world politics persists. What this means for long-range risk assessment can be described in terms of continuity and change. Continuity is inherent in the direction of the geostrategic axes of Europe: the Turkish Straits, the central approaches across the Vistula, the Elbe, the Rhine, and the Baltic approaches. Only the northern route through the Norwegian Sea has been added during and after World War I. The ancient claim of the tsars expressed in the peace of Hubertusburg at the close of the Seven Years' War in 1763, to be the arbiters of Europe's destinies and to cast a veto on vital European matters, has not been lost on the way. After 1945 and the success of Western containment policies, it has been translated into a persistent policy of seeking a veto over West European defenses, distancing Europe from the U.S. protective role, and turning Western Europe into a high-technology farm. The domination of Poland as the empire's strategic glacis has been handed down as one of the *arcana imperii* from Catherine the Great to Lenin and Stalin and their successors, notwithstanding the rise and fall of Napoleon, the pax Britannica, the passing experience of the German Reich, and, finally, the emergence of the bipolar structure of global politics and nuclear parity.

Western Europe, especially Germany, had been the workshop of prerevolutionary Russia and its banker for a long time and is destined to continue that role in the age of high technology. This role will help the Soviet Union enter the twenty-first century as the other world power without having to give up, fundamentally, the unity of the sword, spiritual and secular.

No convincing evidence shows that the Soviet Union is a saturated power in the sense that it has ceased to aim for control of its strategic environment. The present period of reform and reconstruction is, alas, not aimed at the greatest happiness for the greatest number but at a leaner, more efficient political-military system for the next century. At best, the West perceives the chance of a strategic "pause" in Gorbachev's *perestroika*: a period of *"reculer pour mieux sauter."* The West could and should exploit this pause to win more influence and, perhaps, to establish interdependence in order to call into existence a more stable and calculable relationship with a power that will nevertheless remain, for a long time to come, the chief antagonist.

What has changed is the form and complexity of the threat, not the threat itself. Marxism, of course, has long ceased to have vitality and attraction, but it still provides a framework of ideology and legitimacy, superseded in the Soviet Union by the Great Patriotic War; in the East European satellite states, where the fascist specter no longer haunts Europe, Marxism is an attempt at national communism and modus vivendi with mostly passive populations resigned to their fates. Marxism notwithstanding, the Soviet Union is a variation on the theme of Russia and its heritage of paranoia and expansionism.

Is NATO slowly going out of fashion, a historical monument in search of political purpose? After four decades of the long nuclear peace of the postwar period, the North Atlantic Treaty Organization tends to become the victim of its own success. The beneficiaries on both sides of the Atlantic are tempted to take for granted the stability and equilibrium that NATO effected and that, without the NATO framework, would soon give way to instability and crisis. The argument is not that NATO is a work of art beyond time and space that cannot be improved and is better left alone. The argument is rather than it must be adapted to the transformations in the Atlantic system and the global arena; that it must be reconstructed so as to take account of the state of the West "beyond American hegemony," as David Calleo puts it; and that it must be transformed in order to accommodate a European situation that has outgrown most of its war and postwar traumas. As NATO cannot be replaced, it must surely be improved.

This chapter looks at the hidden agenda that was taken care of by the Western alliance. It then, in view of transatlantic unrest and uneasiness, suggests practical approaches that respond to the manifest need for reform without neglecting the unfinished business of the hidden agenda.

NATO'S TROUBLES

Precisely because NATO has delivered the goods for which it was created, many experts, not to speak of the general public, tend to forget the relationship of cause and effect. They claim the privilege of every new generation to look with ignorance and forgetfulness at the institutions of the past, their unspoken assumptions, and their achievements. But age and success are insufficient reasons to condemn NATO's institutions. Of course, the world of 1949 and the world of forty years later differ widely. Leaving aside the military aspects of the transatlantic relationship, U.S. hegemony has given way to inter-dependence and an uneasy and mostly unrecognized equilibrium. The virtual nuclear monopoly of the United States did not survive the late 1940s, and the last two decades have seen the United States accommodating Soviet nuclear parity while trying to preserve a technological edge over Soviet arsenals. The Strategic Defense Initiative (SDI) is an expression of three fundamental American beliefs: that the nation has a birthright to invulnerability; that "mutual assured destruction" is a grim hypothesis that is impossible to reconcile with the pursuit of happiness; and that political problems lend themselves to technical solutions. Client states in Europe and elsewhere have become complacent and uneasy partners, with the economic relationship changing thoroughly; in terms of security, the United States continues to be the lender of last resort. The Europeans resent their client status, yet at the same time they feel comfortable: whether they cannot change their status or whether they do not want to change remains an open question.

Today, the transatlantic relationship is in need not only of candid analysis but also of creative action. The following areas of concern can be identified:

1. Out-of-area conflicts (Central America, the Persian Gulf, Libya, Lebanon, Indochina, Afghanistan, to name but a few, to which emerging problems might be added such as those in South Africa) tend to underline existing geographic and philosophical differences and bring out conflicting views of national interest as opposed to alliance solidarity.

2. More equitable burdensharing is being demanded in the United States in an almost ritual way as the more important European partners, particularly the West Germans, tend to point at specific efforts that they make that defy quantitative comparison, including national conscription, financial aid for West Berlin, and the transformation of the country into a vast military base.

3. More important still seems to be political and philosophical differences rooted in the respective national cultures and experiences. Europeans are uneasy when faced with the oscillations of U.S. policy toward the Soviet Union; they dislike unpredictability whether it tends to veer in the direction of confrontation in hardware (SDI) and software ("evil empire") terms or in the direction of condominium without consultation (the Reykjavik trauma). Europeans, for external as much as internal reasons, tend to look at detente as a linear process; Americans suspect an inherent tendency to accommodate the Soviets at almost any price. Europeans resent the conspicuous tendency of the American political system, already observed by de Tocqueville, to worship the primacy of domestic politics, yet their own political processes, as de Tocqueville predicted for democracies in general, are subject to similar laws and tendencies equally ill received by the American side.

4. The nuclear class structure of NATO causes rifts and incompatibilities that are difficult and often impossible to bridge or reconcile through graduated participation in nuclear consultation, control, and sharing of the nuclear mystique. Concomitantly, the right of admission to the arms control club has become a fringe benefit of the possession of nuclear weapons, and their exclusion is thus resented to almost the same degree by the nuclear have-nots.

5. Imposing the assumption of equal security and risk sharing upon the unequal geography of the Atlantic system is difficult.

6. NATO countries are tempted to find some particular form of security—every man for himself and the devil take the hindmost— the United States through SDI, West Germany through *Ostpolitik*,

some countries through their conspicuous nonnuclear status, other countries through their nuclear posture.

7. The Europeans have become used to the fact that for the best part of forty years U.S. nuclear weapons gave them a margin of safety for their inadequate conventional defenses and helped them withstand Soviet blackmail while U.S. troops were in Europe in a triple role: hostages for U.S. commitment; support for European defenses; and forward defense of U.S. interests. Meanwhile, most of the nuclear armory has been immobilized through nuclear parity; the technological edge over the Soviet conventional buildup has been lost or given away. To strengthen conventional defenses would undermine the already shaky defense consensus in some European countries.

8. Most Europeans, and Canadians for that matter, have developed over the last forty years a kind of subvention mentality in security matters. They try to have the best of two worlds: as much nuclear security as the United States has and welfare systems much better than that of the United States. The rationale of European welfare systems is twofold: historical as well as political. European welfare systems have mostly been developed by conservative governments in the course of the nineteenth and twentieth centuries. Today, vis-à-vis the Marxist challenge, West European nations have to prove their superior way of life, including their superior welfare systems. At the same time, American budget restraints being what they are, American policymakers are not inclined to listen to European history lessons or accept geostrategic explanations for electoral accommodation.

9. Finally, a fundamental philosophical division makes itself felt between the American preoccupation with a technological experience and a history that has littered the European continent with the monuments of tragic failure and the futility of grand designs. The two world wars whose outcome the United States decided were thirty years of European civil war, and deep inside the collective European ethos, especially that of Germany, the traces make themselves felt.

Perhaps Raymond Aron summed up the complexities of the situation in a very European manner when he wrote, in 1983: "America is no longer able to guarantee peace. . . . The fact that the United States could not maintain its nuclear dominance while the Soviet Union disposes of forces that continue to increase, seems to be one reason for the growing moral disorientation in the Federal Republic of Germany."

NATO AND THE WAR OF THE GERMAN SUCCESSION

NATO is the centerpiece of a global economic system and of a global political framework that brought stability to central Europe, the part of the world that for many centuries had been the engine and the center of global conflict. In the nineteenth century, the balance of power, established at the close of the Napoleonic wars and presided over by Great Britain, prevented hegemony. It finally collapsed in 1914. After two world wars, bipolarity emerged, and NATO engaged American enlightened egotism in the long-term defense and stability of Western Europe. NATO's architects, British and American, did this not so much in order to close the book on European wars but rather to forestall Soviet control of the strategic heartland of Europe. Painfully and almost against their instincts, the Western victors of World War II had to learn the lesson that Stalin had never forgotten: he who controls Berlin holds the key to Germany, and he who controls Germany holds the key to the German succession and thus to the material wealth, the psychological energy, and the strategic geography of Europe and the adjacent seas. NATO was called into existence against the strongest of American foreign policy traditions: at the time of the French Revolution, Washington and Jefferson both warned their country against "entangling alliances."

Faced with a perceived threat of Soviet hegemony over the whole of Europe, however, the United States would have had to part with national self-respect, the traditional concept of manifest destiny, and the time-honored principle of world balance, or fill the vacuum in central Europe. No Vienna Congress was feasible in and after 1945, with Prussia destroyed beyond recognition, Austria reduced to a mere shadow of its imperial glory, France an uncertain victor, Britain thoroughly exhausted, and Stalin's Russia emerging from the trials and tribulations of war and revolution as the one and only power on the Eurasian landmass. Thus the role that Britain had played at Vienna—stabilizing the world balance through the European balance— fell on the United States of America—not by choice but by necessity.

NATO was created after the 1947 Truman Doctrine had pronounced the continuing antitotalitarian commitment of the United States and directed it against the Soviet Union, and after the Marshall Plan had changed the currency of global conflict from political-ideological to economic. The rationale was to stabilize Western Europe against Soviet pressure and to prevent the Red Army from filling the void that World War II and the breakdown of the victor's condominium had left. The United States was ready to invest power, prestige, and influence for the world balance without necessarily committing a large number of U.S. conventional troops to the task. Although the

Berlin blockade had finally brought U.S. military withdrawal to a halt, not until the shock of the Korean War did U.S. policy place a sizeable contingent of U.S. troops firmly in the heart of Europe and insist at the same time that the West European allies accept West German rearmament so as to make Western defenses credible and push them forward from the Rhine to the Elbe.

Since then, what changes have taken place in the overall correlation of forces? The "Sources of Soviet Conduct," to quote George F. Kennan's seminal *Foreign Affairs* article in 1947, have rarely been seen to have changed sufficiently to warrant a decisive abandonment of the Western posture, even though now may be the time for a thorough reappraisal. When NATO was about to reach age twenty, the Harmel Report stated that NATO's continuing defense effort should and must be coupled with a patient, firm attempt at reducing tension and creating a framework for detente. Whether nuclear weapons have really changed the nature of international politics since the time of Machiavelli or Hobbes remains a matter of faith. But two elements have changed:

1. Nuclear weapons have acted as a force in being, have prevented the conduct of conventional war where they are present, and thus have effected the long nuclear peace of the postwar period and integrated even the transition from U.S. monopoly to parity with the Soviet Union.
2. NATO has translated this ban into operative terms through its unwillingness, coupled with inactivity, to match Eastern conventional options numerically and its subsequent reliance on nuclear deterrence. Under the auspices of detente, a compromise between a conventional defense of Europe and U.S. extended nuclear deterrence was reached in 1967 in the form of the doctrine of "flexible response."

Without NATO, the pax Americana of the first postwar decade would have been but a fleeting moment. Through NATO and its economic and monetary corollaries, the initial U.S. commitment was translated into a structure that is as effective as it remains flexible.

NATO has come to operate as a framework of peace in the East-West context and as a structure of peaceful change on the Western part of the great European divide. It has brought into an equation the European need to have a friendly world power offsetting an unfriendly one and the U.S. concept of American long-term security and forward defense fastened to European soil, not in the traditional form of an understanding to intervene in an emergency but as a permanent expeditionary force.

Thus, for the Europeans, NATO serves as a conventional insurance policy coupled with a nuclear reinsurance policy. For the United

States, it keeps not only the Atlantic periphery in friendly hands, the West Europeans firmly on the American side, and the neutrals safely neutral. It also provides the groundwork for a stable and manageable economic and monetary environment for U.S. interests in Europe and beyond. Without this friendly periphery, the United States would still be the world's most powerful island but no longer its dominant force.

NATO'S HIDDEN AGENDA

"What will lie between the white snows of Russia and the white cliffs of Dover?" When Britain's wartime Prime Minister Winston S. Churchill posed this question a few days after Yalta, he thought of Poland ("I have no intention of being cheated over Poland, even if we go to war with Russia") and of Germany, of the French and Dutch coast opposite the British isles, the eastern Mediterranean, and the Baltic Sea. At Yalta, the answer was left in suspense. Roosevelt announced once again U.S. withdrawal from Europe within two years, as Congress and public opinion would not accept any other policy. Churchill's immediate reaction was to press for great power status for France. In May 1945 he warned Harry S. Truman of the iron curtain that the Soviets had lowered before the East European scenery and tried to postpone British and U.S. withdrawal from Saxony and Thuringia in the summer of 1945. Meanwhile, Stalin discovered a penchant for German unity, insisted on a bridgehead on the Rhine for the Red Army, and volunteered no fewer than 200,000 troops as a contribution to allied control of the Ruhr. Only after Truman firmly objected to this strategy during the final hours of the Potsdam conference did Stalin postpone, for the time being, his attempt to arrive at the Rhine in full war paint.

The signing of the North Atlantic Treaty in 1949 did not seal the answer to Churchill's question; it gave only a provisional reply: the continent divided, the Eastern part incorporated in the Soviet land empire, the Western part slowly forming the European side of the American sea alliance. Indeed, after condominium gave way to confrontation, NATO facilitated the long-term translocation of U.S. victory in Europe into the pax Americana of the postwar period. In 1951, Raymond Aron in *Les guerres en chaine* observed the unprecedented character of the situation:

> The present constellation is situated at the crossroads of three lines. The first one leads to the unity of the planet and the bipolar structures of international politics. The second one implies the extension of a secular religion whose metropolis is to be found in the middle of one of the superpowers. The third one points at the

development of weapons for mass-annihilation and total war, driven forward by
modern technologies and primeval passions; the terrorist and the nuclear bomb have
become the ultimate expression of violence unlimited.[1]

Forty years later, Aron's prophetic view is not outdated, but with the
benefit of hindsight some observations can be added concerning the
chemistry between U.S. superpower and European superimpotence
and the changes that have occurred since 1945:

1. Politics had indeed been globalized ever since the turn of the
   century. In 1918 the two dominant powers of the future had faced
   each other over Germany and posed the question of who would
   finally win control of Europe and thus inherit the earth. For a
   passing moment, Lenin's pax Sovietica stood against Wilson's pax
   Americana. World War I allowed the European system to be
   reconstructed and the Europeans to become, once again, the victims
   of the past, with Germany holding a precarious balance between
   East and West. But World War II resulted in a bipolar system, with
   the Roman Lines running, once again, through the heart of Europe.
2. Western Europe was defended against Stalin's power projection and
   Soviet expansionism. The price was the partition of Germany and
   of Europe between the Soviet system, controlling practically the
   whole of the Eurasian landmass, and the Atlantic sea alliance
   linking the United States to the Eastern shores of the Atlantic
   Ocean. The fundamental asymmetry was overcome through a
   combination of economic interdependence and the projection of
   nuclear and conventonal military power.
3. In conventional military terms alone, U.S. engagement in the
   conflict over Europe's future and entry into the war of the German
   succession would have been a hopeless proposition. Its nuclear edge
   over the conventional military machine of the Soviet Union
   permitted the United States to stabilize the situation and to call into
   being the Atlantic system. The war over Europe's future was
   suspended through the nuclear fact: nuclear deterrence and
   political reassurance entered into a prolonged phase of interdependence, as Michael Howard observed in 1980, when reassurance
   began to vanish. Stability had been the net result for Western
   Europe, with military containment of the Soviet Union linked to
   political containment of the German question.

Containment had begun in the Mediterranean and the neighboring
areas, and it was effected by the most conventional means available:
sailors and guns in the Turkish Straits, dollars and supplies to Greece,
and the Stars and Stripes finally replacing the Union Jack. In the

---

[1] Raymond Aron, *Les guerres en chaine* (Paris: Gallimard, 1951).

central European theater, however, containment began with the European Recovery Program, also known as the Marshall Plan, and went through its ultimate test when Stalin blockaded the access routes to Berlin and left only the three air corridors untouched. The question was put on the agenda whether "Germany as a whole"—the Potsdam formula—would be part of the pax Sovietica, or whether western Germany would be the keystone of the pax Americana. Implicit in this question was the future order of Western Europe and the world leadership of the United States. The airlift of 1948-49 not only displayed resolve and technological superiority on the part of the West but also reminded the Soviets of Western conventional striking power. Still, negotiations and access routes were unblocked only once the United States transferred B-29 bombers, potential carriers of nuclear weapons, to British airfields while demonstrating their ability to reach any place on earth without having to refuel on the ground.

The agenda of strategy and diplomacy in the decade before NATO was born comprised the European order after German hegemony and, inevitably, the balance between the superpowers. Meanwhile, the hidden agenda was derived from the 1945 vacuum in the center of the European system after the fall of the German Reich, the decline of the British Empire, the impotence of France, and, last but by no means least, the transition from wartime alliance to postwar antagonism between the Soviet Union and the United States. Only after NATO gave both a military framework to Western Europe and psychological reassurance to the Europeans was this hidden agenda slowly realized. In the light of past conflicts and potential future instability, it proved to be no less important than what happened in the central East-West strategic conflict.

1. The age-old nationalist conflicts of Europe, so prominent and explosive after World War I, were prevented from gaining currency, the trauma of Germany's neighbors being only the most conspicuous on the long list of accounts still awaiting settlement.
2. The war of the German succession inherent in the unsettled state of Europe between Victory in Europe (VE) day and the founding of NATO was kept in long-term suspense against Soviet and satellite pressure.
3. The Europeans were offered a system of double insurance: containment of the Soviet Union and containment of the perennial German question. What de Gaulle feared in 1945 was not only German revanche but even more a German-Soviet alliance, Rapallo or 1939-style, and most of all that the United States would, once again, leave Europe to the haunting specters of its past.
4. The democratic societies of Europe were stabilized by economic

well-being and political renaissance as well as through strategic stability. What troubled Germans most in the immediate postwar period was not want and hunger but the question of whether the U.S. commitment was there to stay and whether entering into any engagement with the West was worthwhile.

5. A sense of purpose and direction was injected into the devastated psychology of the Europeans. What de Gaulle said about France— *"il faut faire le travail d'un psychiatre"*—was true of the whole of Europe, and nowhere more so than in Germany: from Konrad Adenauer to Helmut Kohl, German leaders have been aware of the need for psychological support from Germany's neighbors and allies.

6. The Americans' sense of mission and self-respect, so sadly frustrated by the ill-fated League of Nations, was satisfied in a way that George F. Kennan alluded to when making the case for containment in 1947: "a certain gratitude to Providence . . . this implacable challenge . . . accepting the responsibilities of moral and political leadership that history plainly intended them to bear."

7. On the European side, the hidden agenda also comprised the mirror image of this policy, including the transformation of the initial unilateral, expeditionary type of U.S. involvement to long-term interdependence.

In the later part of the 1950s, the hidden agenda was complemented by designing a new role for Europe's great powers in decline. In the process of decolonization Britain and France were spared the agonies of carrying on regardless. Due to NATO's existence their survival and status no longer depended on control of outdated colonial empires. Rather, they developed nuclear forces of their own, their role being accentuated by the Suez crisis of 1956. The British used their nuclear posture to link North German defenses firmly to Britain's, and Britain's firmly to America's, while France opted for a more independent strategy of national sovereignty, combining a last-resort nuclear reinsurance policy under national control with a strategic situation that profited essentially from the presence of friendly troops in Germany and their protection through U.S. extended deterrence. NATO managed to integrate the British nuclear role and to accommodate even de Gaulle's bid for nuclear independence in and after 1966. Another part of NATO's hidden agenda in the 1960s was the transition from U.S. hegemony to Soviet–U.S. parity and, subsequently, detente. After almost twenty years of NATO, the Harmel Report attempted to implement a new political philosophy of firmness and openness that took into account the open-ended U.S. involvement in Vietnam, the blank check issued to Israel in the course of the Six-Day War, the nonproliferation policies of the two nuclear giants, the pressure of the Soviet Union on the West Germans in Berlin and elsewhere, and the growing uneasiness in the West about the reliance on nuclear weapons in the age of superpower equilibrium and, indeed, parity.

At the same time, the German bid for nuclear sharing was taken out of the impasse of the early 1960s over the creation of a multilateral nuclear force (MLF) for NATO and translated into permanent participation in NATO's Nuclear Planning Group. After 1965, the growing dynamism of West German *Ostpolitik* was kept within the framework of the Western alliance and made to strengthen rather than weaken its cohesion. Western nuclear security on the one hand and the European Community on the other hand provided the Western architecture for the Berlin Four-Power Agreement (1971) and for the subsequent German-German *Grundlagen-vertrag* (1972). Without the combination of firmness and openness, pronounced before, *Ostpolitik* could have been, in terms of Western cohesion and central European stability, an operation involving enormous political and psychological hazards. Instead *Ostpolitik* evolved within a framework that prevented it from going too fast and too far and thus destabilizing the global balance as well as the domestic setup, and from aiming too low and continuing the prevailing instability of the Berlin situation after the building of the wall.

In yet another part of NATO's hidden agenda, the arms control process, winning momentum after the Cuban missile crisis, was prevented from creating profound mistrust among the Western nations precisely because it could be and was indeed linked to their vital interests through NATO. By and large, Europeans left arms control to the U.S. negotiating teams because formal and informal channels of communication existed. Although the French and the British, on account of their nuclear potential, refused to be parties to the actual arms control negotiations, their respective interests were taken care of by the United States. Canadians and Europeans alike, as long as their security was not at stake, watched the process unsure whether to ask for more detente, less condominium, or both. Even the explosive material of nonproliferation was handled within its context: British and French nuclear status remained in its respective kind of semi-independence, while the specific nuclear dilemmas of West Germany, both military and civilian, were accommodated.

One problem, however, has steadily grown as a by-product of detente: out-of-area conflicts. In the early days, U.S. anticolonial enthusiasm had dictated the clauses limiting NATO obligations to the area north of the Tropic of Cancer so as not to be drawn into the declining colonial empires' bid for survival. The Korean and Vietnam wars never came close to being regarded as NATO business, but they had dramatic implications for the Atlantic relationship. Korea sealed the U.S. involvement in European defense. Vietnam put enormous strains on U.S.-allied relations, direct and indirect: directly through the thinning out of European defenses, on the one hand, and mass rallies in the streets and political uneasiness in the corridors of power on the other hand; indirectly through the erosion of the dollar and the decline of the Bretton Woods system, in fact, the self-destruction of U.S. economic leadership, and the preoccupaton of Washington with Pacific issues.

With detente gaining momentum and the Nixon-Brezhnev declaration (1972) on the rules of conduct and the prevention of nuclear war signed, an era of self-restraint and stability seemed to be born. But half a decade later, hope turned to illusion, and from Angola to Mozambique, from Ethiopia to Egypt, the Russians and their allies were seen violating the largely unwritten rules of the game. At the same time, the Europeans, especially the Germans, let it be known that they saw no alternative to the Harmel Report's basic philosophy. They seemed to believe that, if you could not have detente everywhere, you should preserve it somewhere: in Europe.

A policy of horizontal escalation, which the Americans wanted to apply, was feared by the Europeans. Most European governments were also eager to prove, for the domestic scene, that detente was infinite and that they were the guardians of its continuity, come what may. No West German government would have been able, without severe electoral punishment, to risk the special relationship with the German Democratic Republic that had been established, very much under Western guidance and pressure, in the early 1970s. When the Soviets invaded Afghanistan in 1979 and pressured the Poles into declaring marshal law in 1981, most European governments, instead of burning bridges, determined that the continuation of detente was all the more important. Thus the gas pipeline deal of the early 1980s was allowed to develop into a major test of will on both sides of the Atlantic. Out-of-area problems seemed to have a tendency to eat into the psychological and political foundation of the alliance.

A second set of out-of-area problems did not arise from divergent views of detente but from ideological differences and from divergent approaches to political problems. After Spain and Portugal—much to the surprise of some prominent Americans—had been prevented from turning Communist and were set on the path of democratic virtue, left wing parties in Europe hoped to repeat this success story elsewhere but failed dismally. Nicaragua continues to prove that the Iberian experience cannot easily be translated into Central American power games. In addition, the U.S. handling of the Nicaraguan morass did not create much confidence in inspired leadership.

A third kind of out-of-area problem presented itself in areas where the United States is called upon to play world sheriff, with most Europeans reserving for themselves the role of onlookers, commentators, and, perhaps, beneficiaries. The Persian Gulf has, since Khomeini returned to Iran and the second oil shock of 1979, provided a dangerous and continuing object lesson. Lebanon could also be cited here, and certainly Libya. South Africa may possibly be added in the foreseeable future, once land-based Soviet influence and sea-based U.S. influence face each other at the Cape. From crisis to crisis, any U.S. administration will find intervening on behalf of the West more difficult if no support or only a symbolic contribution is forthcoming from its allies. In 1987 this insight resulted in an enhanced West European effort in the Gulf, and developing the methodology and translating it, not necessarily within the existing NATO framework, into a framework of out-of-area crisis prevention and crisis management might be worth our while.

Otherwise, out-of-area problems and burdensharing—or rather its insufficiency—may develop into a psychological mortgage on the alliance. By definition, however, out-of-area problems are not NATO problems, even though they may be a grave concern for all of its members and contribute to ill feeling and dissatisfaction. They should, however, not be included in NATO's business but be kept outside and treated bilaterally and, if possible and necessary, multilaterally.

NATO IN DOUBT

Throughout the West, there is little criticism of NATO in general but much criticism of particular policies and strategies involving NATO. The 1950s witnessed passionate parliamentary and public opinion clashes. In France the left wing resented U.S. hegemony and German rehabilitation. For Britain's left, NATO was, above all, a nuclear alliance drawing the British isles into affairs and dangers not their own. Little Englanders, pacifists, and unilateralists joined forces, even if they did not march together, but when in power the Labour Party left largely unchanged the policies of its predecessors. In Germany, the parliamentary left saw the Western alliance predominantly as the framework for rearmament, and rearmament seemed to preclude national reunification; extraparliamentary forces displayed belief in pacifism and neutralism and resented Adenauer's grand design: sovereignty and equal rights for the Federal Republic in exchange for rearmament, readmittance to the Western club, and support for the West German national objective. The integration of all of the *Bundeswehr* forces and the renunciation of nuclear weapons—more specifically, their production and peacetime possession by Germany—helped not only to allay allied apprehensions but also to mute domestic opposition. In 1960, however, the Social Democrats in the *Bundestag* vowed continuity of German foreign policy, thus espousing Adenauer's policy and preparing their own entry into the corridors of power.

Other European nations share some of the mixed feelings in and around Germany. NATO was too American, too nuclear, and, for some, also too friendly to the defeated Germans. Although NATO was welcomed as a framework for reconciliation and as a last-resort insurance system of security, its moral and military price was resented. In Canada, the World War II tradition of conference diplomacy through the United Nations and subsequently through transatlantic channels, combined with a less explicit dislike of being just a minor cousin of the United States, led the country into its lasting European engagement. This engagement has been changed but not substantially challenged.

During one decade and a half of detente, NATO came under less attack than its leading power, the United States of America. In Germany, the United States was resented by part of the young generation because of moral disappointment. Elsewhere, that the United States was involved in the dirty war inherited from the French in Indochina sufficed. The nuclear issue was confined to the background, as the foreground seemed to be occupied very visibly, and also partly successfully, by nuclear arms control.

In 1966 de Gaulle demonstrated to Europeans of all political convictions that detente, entente, and cooperation might be possible and that this agenda would also help the Europeans get rid of too much American hegemony while preserving it as a fallback position. Others, largely right of center, argued that to reduce East-West relations to the technicalities of arms control did not address the real sources of conflict and rather obscured the nature of the Soviet system and the threat of its military power and ideological energy. In the heyday of detente, NATO was not so much criticized as taken for granted. After the Harmel Report, little time or effort was devoted to thinking about NATO's reappraisal and reform, and it was, explicitly or implicitly, accepted and acknowledged, right of center and left of center, as the framework that would help detente win momentum. Only a few voices were heard arguing that with more and more detente less of NATO and of the American umbrella would be needed.

All this changed rather rapidly and unexpectedly in the second half of the 1970s when the global climate of detente changed and finally collapsed. Within two or three years, growing East-West tension accentuated the out-of-area issue, especially in Africa and Indochina. The decline of the U.S. dollar brought back the problem of burdensharing, and allies clashed over a qualitative approach preferred by the Europeans and a quantitative one that was more in line with American thinking and American interests. Moreover, during the Carter years, the United States began to emphasize human rights in very broad terms in its approach to the Soviet Union and, after the Soviets had invaded Afghanistan, reacted very sharply, probably to the surprise of the Soviets and certainly not to the delight of the European left. As a result, for much of the European left, the United States became the rogue of international politics, while center-right thinking put the blame squarely on the Soviet Union. Domestic strife, accentuated through the first and second oil shocks, and international issues reinforced each other and brought NATO back into the focus of attention and into a more and more heated debate. Ever since the crisis of the early 1960s and adoption of the Harmel Report, detente has been the implicit condition for the stability of consensus on NATO. When detente fell on hard times and the grim old East-West conflict reappeared, undisguised by the paraphernalia of detente, the benign neglect of NATO ended. Strategy, burdensharing, out-of-area issues, leadership, and every other aspect came under scrutiny, often in very bitter terms.

The overriding issue, however, was once again nuclear security, the impotence of defense, and the predicament of peace resting on mutual assured destruction. In the United States, the nuclear freeze movement and some of the major churches had voiced a decided skepticism and even abhorrence of nuclear weapons. They emphasized the moral dilemmas and implicitly shifted the blame for America's involvement on the Europeans. A note of unilateralism was struck, and it allied itself with a new feeling of national identity and distance in the United States: *Eurosclerosis* and *europessimism* were the catchwords of the early 1980s, giving expression to the "Reagan revolution" and the strong dollar. Somehow, this America-first philosophy translated into the Strategic Defense Initiative, holding out the promise that once again America could and would be an island, alliances would not be entangling, and sovereignty and invulnerability could be regained.

In the light of this resurgence of what came to be called *unilateralism* on the American side, the new attempt at solving the nuclear dilemma of Europe and of sharing, once again, the European risk, came rather as a surprise. As it seemed to be at odds with fundamental and deep-rooted American feelings, some doubt was possible whether it would last. Nevertheless, after the failure of the neutron bomb (enhanced-radiation weapon) so militarily suitable to the specific threat to Europe, the alliance could not afford, or at least believed it could not, a second setback. Then came the issue of intermediate nuclear missile forces (INF), seemingly as a response to the Soviet buildup of a highly accurate new generation of INF missiles, code-named SS-20. However, reality was different. Independent of Soviet strategy and as an attempt to link, once again, the conventional defenses of Europe to the nuclear deterrence of the United States and thus to reinsure European security through the central systems of the United States and upgrade extended deterrence, INF missiles were sent to Europe and legitimized through NATO's double-track decision. Europe's risk—this was the rationale—should again be shared, almost on autopilot, by the United States. The deployment of the INF missiles encountered many antinuclear feelings in Germany and elsewhere. Therefore track one (deployment) was linked to track two (an arms control proposal to limit deployment in return for Soviet cuts in their SS-20 missiles).

The INF crisis, with the accompanying war of nerves and test of resolve, developed into the third major East-West crisis of the postwar period. It helped to give birth to Germany's Greens as a minor political force and a major factor of public opinion. It played a role in the erosion of Chancellor Schmidt's majority until its decline and fall in September 1982, and it accelerated the change that took place within the Social Democratic Party (SPD) after its fall from power. In France, the crisis gave rise to the French Communist Party's agonies, accompanied by the discredit of Marxism as a major political philosophy and the reemergence of the right as the decisive parliamentary force. In addition, French politicians left and right began to appreciate the importance of calculability and reliability on the part of Germany and began to engage France much more in matters of common defense, without ever being able to cross the threshold to full nuclear guarantees or to full reintegration in NATO. In England, the Labour Party went back to its old scruples and uneasiness concerning the U.K.'s ambiguous nuclear role. While British short-range nuclear weapons are stationed with the British Army on the Rhine and British nuclear subs are patrolling the adjacent sea areas, Britain itself is host to U.S. nuclear weapons, representing the special relationship. Thus, the British nuclear role came under attack in terms of both American bases and British missiles. After the electoral defeat of Labour in the summer of 1987, however, the defense consensus consolidated once again on more or less traditional grounds.

Again, not NATO itself came under attack so much as the alliance's nuclear posture and the U.S. arms control agenda—to the point that even President Reagan's sincerity was being questioned and accusations were voiced that the United States was considering fighting a nuclear war in Europe. In 1982, at the height of the missile crisis, the "Report of the Independent Commission on Disarmament and Security" (Palme Report), with the signatures of Soviet expert Juri J. Arbatov and former U.S. Secretary of State Cyrus Vance, summed up many of the misgivings of the European left. It concentrated on Europe's key geostrategic role and vulnerability, called for lowering of defense expenditures in general, accepted the peacekeeping role of nuclear weapons in principle, recognized some of the problems in lowering the nuclear threshold in particular, warned against the semiautomatic response inherent in the deployment of intermediate-range nuclear forces (INF) and short-range INF (SRINF), understood that the moment of truth in the nuclear age is not war but the crisis preceding war, insisted on maintaining political control in every phase of a military crisis, and finally came up with a proposal to establish a nuclear-free zone of 300 kilometers, including all of the German Democratic Republic, much of Czechoslovakia, a strip of Poland and, on the Western side, practically all of the Federal Republic of Germany. If accepted, it would have precluded the deployment side of the dual-track decision. The Palme Report proposed a notion of "common security" between East and West and expressed hope that a zone without battlefield nuclear weapons would help to build confidence and constitute a situation in which both sides "begin to organize their security together and not against each other." The report did not, however, address the problem of asymmetry on the European continent and between the two global superpowers, nor did it identify the role of arms control for the psychological penetration of Western societies or the fundamental conventional imbalance between the Vistula and the Atlantic. Thus, the report contained some seminal ideas, to emerge once again after the INF crisis, but it failed to impress or influence the ongoing INF negotiations, let alone prevent their breakdown. On the whole, the Palme Report was a left-of-center attempt to find a constuctive alternative to the NATO consensus that failed to set a new agenda or win majorities. The Soviet Union was no longer presented as a principal threat to NATO; a "security partnership" with Moscow was proposed instead. Nuclear weapons were reinterpreted from being the last resort of defense and deterrence in Western Europe to being the common enemy.

The role of Germany seems to be not only the focus of European geostrategic dynamism but also its workshop of ideas about the nuclear future of NATO and the East-West relationship. Most of the ideas and sentiments current elsewhere tended to find a more radical expression in Germany over the last 15 years. The Greens reject nuclear weapons and nuclear power altogether, and the NATO that they would readily accept would have to be very different indeed from today's NATO. Their threat assessment identifies the United States much more clearly than the Soviet Union, although they have a distinct dislike for the repressive and bureaucratic character of the Soviet system.

Althouth the French Socialist Party remains firmly within the French defense consensus—pronuclear and distanced from NATO's command structure—the SPD and its majority, with its long experience in and out of government and its strong international contacts East and West, thinks predominantly in terms of East-West stability, confidence building, and nonaggressive defense, and the postnuclear and post-NATO European security order is being envisaged in a very long-term framework indeed. Most of this is being summarized—somewhat misleadingly—under the name of the second phase of *Ostpolitik*. This second phase is seen as including the eventual replacement of nuclear deterrence by a defensive conventional force posture, the creation of nuclear-free zones in Europe as a step toward denuclearization, strengthening of the European voice in the alliance, and negotiating a security partnership with the Soviet Union and its Warsaw Pact allies.

In sum, the first phase of the INF crisis, having sent ripples through the accepted wisdom about detente, weakened much of the defense consensus in Germany and elsewhere and renewed attention to the nuclear threat and the price of deterrence. The second phase (1979–84) of the INF crisis contributed to the disintegration of consensus and major power shifts in some West European countries, while resulting, after a breakdown of the Geneva INF negotiations, in Western deployment of INF missiles in Western Europe and Eastern counterdeployment of SRINF in Eastern Europe. The arms control process seemed to be at an impasse.

The third phase of the INF crisis (1985–87) brought the double-zero agreement, took out key elements of NATO's deterrent posture, and gave much of the initiative back to the Soviets, who had made sure in advance that, whatever *zero* means mathematically, it would not leave them bereft of important nuclear options and still allow them to bring heavy pressure to bear on the key country of Western Europe, West Germany.

Thus, after INF, the domestic scene in most West European countries is dominated by the following questions, and some of them have as much destructive potential as the agenda of phases one and two had in their time:

- how to proceed with arms control, how to set the agenda, and how to define priorities;
- how to substitute for the nuclear options negotiated away, without undercutting the INF agreement; and

- how to avoid the singularization of any one country—this is traditionally a particular German concern—and how to give new credibility to European-American coupling.

Although America is no longer able to guarantee peace, the nuclear architecture of European security and, in its center, the postwar settlement of the German question will begin to move; they may move together but not necessarily in harmony. Thus, the two key issues of European security are being set in motion. With a much weakened defense consensus in North America and within Western Europe how alliance stability can be reestablished as the essential precondition, identified by the Harmel Report 20 years ago, of East-West stability is hard to see, unless many of the European left wing party wishes are accommodated. To what extent this accommodation would result in a new phase of detente, a gradual falling apart of NATO, or both depends to a large extent on NATO's ability to

- set the future arms control agenda;
- establish a more equitable transatlantic relationship; and
- maintain nuclear deterrence while convincing the general public that this is the condition of peace.

TOWARD THE FUTURE

NATO is an alliance that defies generalizations. It is composed of countries that are all different. They are part of NATO precisely because they insist on preserving their different ways of life and political philosophies. The standard NATO member does not exist, and thus the standard approach to NATO problems does not exist. The allies differ in almost every conceivable dimension, from nuclear haves to nuclear have-nots and want-nots, from rich to poor, from highly industralized to predominantly rural, from those close to the Warsaw Pact countries to those thousands of miles away, from being efficient to being inefficient, from being militarily integrated to being fully sovereign. They also differ dramatically in the way they conceive of their own natural identities and destinies. These differences will not change, and nothing is more futile than to wish they would.

After amost 40 years, the process of redirection and adaptation expressed in the Harmel Report should and must go on. The Harmel Report was adopted as the alliance approached its twentieth anniversary, and after another 20 years within a fast-changing political and strategic environment, NATO's purpose, structure, and identity must again be redefined. The following points might prove to be useful in the process:

1. Prudence may still be the better part of valor—and optimism—and containment of the Soviet Union must still prevail. However, after cold war, containment, and the era of detente, a long period of conflict management and perhaps conflict prevention may be possible, especially as the Soviet Union seems to be in need of a strategic pause.

2. NATO will have to formulate its role in the future less in terms of an Atlantic structure solely for stability and the prevention of both conventional and nuclear war. Therefore, nonmilitary sides of NATO need to be developed and expanded, publicized and talked about, and NATO as such must also play a visible role in arms control.

3. Arms control between the superpowers will continue to be the continuation of strategy by other means. Much as the containment role of NATO in the past needed substantial public support, NATO's arms control profile of the future will help the general public not only to better understand NATO's role but also to accept the paradoxes and contradictions of arms control. Emerging technologies should at an early stage be assessed according to their impact on strategy, arms control, and alliance cohesion. The same is true of activities that involve both military and civilian uses of outer space.

4. The European pillar needs a robust and simple architecture and agenda. It cannot be constructed without a measure of U.S. enlightened self-interest, and it cannot work without leadership from Britain, France, and Germany in their respective fields of strength and expertise. The ultimate nuclear responsibility cannot be divided, but a vast variety of business can be handed over to the European pillar, including arms procurement, wartime host nation support, solid consultation on arms control and threat assessment, and division of labor concerning out-of-area problems.

5. Out-of-area problems cannot and should not be treated on a standard basis because
   • they tend to drive NATO allies apart;
   • they are mostly none of NATO's formal business;
   • allied nations should be called upon to make contributions that relate to specific interests and capabilities; and
   • indirect burdensharing may be the answer in many cases. German vessels could replace U.S. vessels in the Norway Sea instead of steaming to the Gulf and creating endless domestic trouble and constitutional debate. Specific national restrictions and inhibitions must be respected.

6. The quantitative approach to NATO is valid but insufficient for a comparative analysis of national effort. Probably no system can be devised that combines quantitative criteria to everybody's

satisfaction. We must accept the fact that NATO nations are different and understand from their culture and history why this is so and why this is difficult to change. Our respective tax systems have long established that obligations increase with strength; why not translate this healthy principle into NATO philosophy?

7. As member states differ greatly, we should agree to and indeed support the concept that within the alliance special relationships can be formed (for example, nuclear between France and Great Britain, conventional and otherwise between France and West Germany). Such relationships contribute to the overall potential and performance of the alliance.

8. Especially with respect to strategic planning, as long as the first shot has not been fired by the other side, NATO is about deterrence and not about war fighting. The man in the street has a feeling that peace is held in balance through mutual assured destruction, but his understanding and common sense are taxed if he has to cope with war-fighting scenarios, most of them apocalyptic, patently absurd, or both. That NATO is not a war-fighting alliance but a complex system for the maintenance of stability and the conduct of conflict management must be emphasized time and again.

9. The more intelligent and flexible the Soviet leader's approach to the East-West conflict becomes, the more necessary is the development of a structure of consultation and concentration for the broad range of East-West issues, most of them not directly within NATO jurisdiction but mostly invariably of key importance for alliance cohesion. Trade in general and technology transfer in particular should not be negotiated without reference to long-term alliance objectives concerning arms control. Berlin questions and *Deutschlandpolitik* should be part of a continuous effort at consultation and concentration that relates them to broader alliance policy toward the East.

10. Last but by no means least, different national experiences, traumas, and visions have their expressions within NATO, and they have to be taken care of. The military-bureaucratic elements in NATO may have to be supplemented, more than in the past, by parliamentary concentration and deliberation. NATO should develop a think tank of its own with a not too small educational role. All those divergent views of history and destiny, of Europe and the world at large, can probably be accommodated through NATO, and through NATO alone, if the alliance keeps changing and if indeed its leaders understand, and make it understood, that NATO has graduated from an American containment system to the centerpiece of a global economic system and a framework for stability in East-West relations.

III

The Contemporary Setting

6

The New Soviet Foreign Policy Approach: Challenges to and Opportunities for the West

By DIMITRI K. SIMES

Intriguing, potentially very important changes are taking shape in the conduct of Soviet foreign policy. After Mikhail S. Gorbachev's first three years in power, clearly the new team in the Kremlin is eager to modify not only the style but also the substance of Soviet international behavior. Changes in the Soviet performance in the world arena are bound to have an impact on the West. They bring, simultaneously, both new opportunities for reducing international tensions on terms beneficial to the interests and values of industrial democracies and new challenges in dealing with a more sophisticated, attractive, dynamic, but not necessarily less ambitious and assertive superpower.

A great deal depends on whether Western nations can be open-minded and at the same time realistic about the nature of changes in Soviet foreign policy. Even more is contingent upon making prudent judgments concerning the effects of Moscow's new approach on the security and prosperity of North Atlantic Treaty Organization (NATO) nations. The West should be aware of two dangerous temptations when assessing the Gorbachev-inspired evolution in Moscow's global activities. The first temptation is to dismiss all changes short of an unqualified abandonment of traditional Soviet objectives as mere cosmetics. The second is to ignore the distinction between the kinds of changes that make Soviet foreign policy more effective, but do little for the West, and those that correspond with key Western security and economic interests.

The West is not and cannot be a neutral observer vis-à-vis the Soviet superpower. Common sense suggests that before hailing the Kremlin's new domestic and international accomplishments the United States and its allies should engage in a probing examination of the likely consequences of such changes for NATO: its relative power, cohesion, prosperity, and values. Well-intentioned Soviet actions may sometimes complicate Western dilemmas, and, conversely, on other occasions threatening moves can prove to be a blessing in disguise.

Soviet analysts would do well to remember that excessive certainty over the direction and pace of unpredictable developments is a vice. Events may not be moving as quickly or even in the direction many perceive. Speaking at the February 1988 Communist Party Central Committee Plenum, Mikhail Gorbachev stressed that as far as Soviet foreign policy is concerned, "both a scholarly development of new thinking problems and their ideological justification still remain in the initial stage."[1]

Few statesmen enjoy making difficult and domestically controversial choices unless the alternatives are even worse. Accordingly, the magnitudes of Soviet foreign policy transformation are bound to be influenced by the Kremlin's attempt, through trial and error, to discover how much change is necessary to achieve desirable results. In this context, NATO's statements and deeds will become factors in Moscow's foreign policy review.

CHANGES IN SOVIET FOREIGN POLICY CONDUCT

A lot has changed in the Soviet approach to foreign policy since Gorbachev took over in March 1985. The policy formulation process has been reformed. Key personalities in party and government agencies have been replaced. The Soviets now practice diplomacy with new vigor, purpose, and flexibility and an unparalleled penchant for public relations.

Substantive changes have occurred in all areas of Soviet international activity as well: relations with the West, involvement in the Third World (including attitudes toward regional disputes), and control over Eastern Europe.

Under Gorbachev, Moscow has made a number of concessions to the West. Some of them, like the commitment to withdraw Soviet forces from Afghanistan, are of major importance both substantively and symbolically. Moreover, the Soviets have not hardened their position on any of the serious East-West issues. By the general secretary's own admission, "new thinking" is only beginning to be translated into practical foreign policy. Hence, many in the West believe that the best is yet to come.

Recently, the list of Moscow's international initiatives has been growing rapidly. The Soviet leadership, in late 1987, signed a treaty with the United States eliminating two classes of nuclear weapons.

---

[1] *Pravda*, February 19, 1988.

The agreement was made possible when the Soviet Union agreed to dismantle approximately three times as many missile launchers as the United States and accepted for the first time in history intrusive on-site inspection procedures. Now the Kremlin, after much hesitation, has abandoned its unqualified opposition to the Strategic Defense Initiative in order to clear the road for a START agreement cutting strategic nuclear arms by 50 percent. This new Soviet position allows space-based antimissile systems to be developed and tested as long as they do not contradict the 1972 Anti-Ballistic Missile Treaty. Additionally, Soviet negotiators have signed on to the U.S. notion that some nuclear weapons are more destabilizing than others (though they do not agree on which ones), and accordingly they accept the absence of complete freedom to mix types.

Although the Warsaw Pact and NATO differ in their approaches to conventional arms cuts in Europe, Moscow for the first time has subscribed to the idea of asymmetrical reductions. Gorbachev has also fascinated the West by espousing a military doctrine of "reasonable sufficiency." As explained by Soviet spokespersons, this doctrine will lead to a more defense-oriented force posture, a less threatening mode of military maneuvers, and an effort to negotiate deep cuts in the two alliances' military machines. These cuts would aim for the lowest possible level that would be incompatible with aggressive designs. What is new about this doctrine is not the concept of sufficiency, which was a part of public U.S. defense policy during the early 1970s. What is new is that the Soviets for the first time have said that they accept it.

Arms control is not the only area where Gorbachev and his colleagues have moved to accommodate Western concerns. The Soviets have taken a more forthcoming attitude toward human rights. In the past, Leonid I. Brezhnev and his Minister of Foreign Affairs Andrei A. Gromyko stubbornly refused to discuss allegations of Soviet repression with Western leaders. Their standard response was that foreigners are not supposed to interfere in the USSR's internal affairs. Conversely, Gorbachev and his foreign minister, Eduard A. Schevardnadze, are frequently the first to raise human rights problems with their Western counterparts.

The Kremlin has also begun shifting its attitude concerning regional disputes. The Soviet decision to withdraw troops from Afghanistan was probably less motivated by "new thinking" than by the painful realization that the war was unwinnable. With escalation far too costly and provocative, Moscow had to look for an exit from what the general secretary himself described as a "bleeding wound" during the Twenty-Seventh Party Congress in February 1985.[2] Gorbachev's predecessors might also have seen the need to find a way out of the Afghan mess, but whether they would have found the courage to face the moment of truth and the ingenuity to portray it as something other than a humiliating defeat is unknowable.

Even if, from the Soviet standpoint, Afghanistan is in a category by itself, Gorbachev put his handling of the war in the context of a general call relying on "national reconciliation" as a method for settling regional disputes. Addressing the Twenty-Seventh Communist Party Congress, the general secretary not once mentioned "national liberation movements." He and other Soviet officials have made no secret of their disillusionment with Third World radical regimes, which more often than not have turned into strife-torn economic basket cases instead of serving as revolutionary bridgeheads. Although their usefulness to the Soviet cause has been limited, their desperate requests for aid just to stay afloat have not.

Of particular significance is the growing Soviet recognition that Moscow's Third World adventures played a role in destroying detente during the 1970s. Top Soviet international experts have begun to acknowledge that the Soviet Union took too cavalier an attitude toward Western warnings that the Kremlin was undermining detente through its persistent exploitation of regional instabilities.

The simple lack of opportunities, coupled with a sense of overextension dating back to the end of the Brezhnev era, may have had at least as much to do with relative Moscow moderation as Gorbachev's "new thinking." Whatever the reasons, the Soviet Union lately has shunned new large-scale investments in Third World revolutionary struggles, even while continuing to seek ways of harming Western interests in those regions.

The Soviet approach to its own sphere of influence in Eastern Europe is also evolving. Under Gorbachev, the Soviet Union has gone from attempting to block reforms to actively promoting them. More significant than the sharp reversal in Moscow's guidance to satellite states is that Gorbachev increasingly appears to be signaling East European nations that blindly following Soviet guidance is no longer required.

Only two years ago, addressing the June 1986 Polish Party Congress, Gorbachev, despite his appeals for change, in effect endorsed the Brezhnev Doctrine. As the general secretary put it, "socialism now manifests itself as an international reality, as an alliance of states closely linked by political, economic, cultural and defense interests. To threaten the socialist system, to try to undermine

---

[2] *Pravda*, February 26, 1985.

it from the outside and wrench a country away from the socialist community means to encroach not only on the will of the people, but also on the entire postwar arrangement, and in the final analysis on peace."[3]

A very different approach to East European rights, however, was articulated by the March 1988 Soviet-Yugoslav Declaration personally signed by Gorbachev. According to the document, "the sides attach particular significance to the unfailing observation of the U.N. Charter's universally binding principles, the Helsinki Final Act and other key international legal documents, which ban aggression, violation of borders, conquest of foreign territories, any forms of force and coercion, and interference in internal affairs of other states through whatever pretext."[4] Throughout Eastern Europe, this statement was widely portrayed as a Soviet commitment to allow the satellites much greater latitude, if not complete independence, in determining their own destiny. Strictly interpreted, the language of the Soviet-Yugoslav Declaration is definitely incompatible with crushing a Prague Spring or suppressing an uprising in Hungary.

THE CHALLENGE IN DISGUISE?

Some in the West, of course, would not be impressed by this list of Gorbachev-inspired changes in Soviet foreign policy behavior. For this constantly shrinking community of skeptics, Moscow's new thinking is a mixture of marginal tactically motivated adjustments, delivered in the context of a shrewd public relations charade. Even if the new Kremlin's message is as good as it sounds, however, the West has serious reasons for concern. If nothing else, the Soviet leader's bold changes both at home and abroad risk shattering the traditional concepts and structures upon which Western security has been based for four decades. What will replace those concepts and structures and what Gorbachev's brave new world will yield for the West remain disconcertingly unclear.

Three interconnected groups of problems could transform exciting and appealing Soviet developments into a challenge in disguise for the West. First, Gorbachev makes no secret that one of the main rationales for *perestroika* is to ensure and to enhance the Soviet status and role in global politics and economics. Even giving the general secretary's intentions every benefit of the doubt, the strengthening of the Soviet superpower cannot but impose constraints upon the United States and

---

[3] *Pravda*, July 1, 1986.
[4] *Izvestia*, March 19, 1988.

its allies. Second, changes in Soviet international conduct may go just far enough to make it more efficient but not far enough from the Western point of view to make a difference where it really counts.

Finally, Gorbachev is skillfully and purposefully eliminating the image of a Soviet threat that has been crucial in keeping the NATO alliance together. Finding a new, positive foundation for Western unity may prove to be an extraordinary task. Yet the absence of such unity may cost industrial democracies dearly, not just vis-à-vis the Soviet Union but also more generally in a world environment filled with rivalries, jealousies, poverty, and fanaticism.

Gorbachev regularly tells the West that *"perestroika* threatens no one." According to the general secretary, "transformations in a country such as the Soviet Union require huge efforts. This is an extremely complex undertaking. Therefore, it is natural that we are interested in reliable, peaceful external conditions."[5] The Soviet leader is probably sincere to the extent that the motives for the reformist crusade have more to do with Soviet internal requirements than with any immediate aggressive designs. Also, in the short run, the preoccupation with domestic economic change may discourage both defense spending increases and expensive international adventures. It may even persuade the Politburo to be more accommodating toward the West in the interest of acquiring much needed credits and technology.

From a long-term perspective, however, a stronger economy may allow Gorbachev and/or his successors to improve Soviet military capabilities. A direct connection between Soviet economic growth and defense appropriations has been traditional. According to most Western estimates, growth in the Soviet gross national product (GNP) fell from about 4 percent between 1969 and 1975 to roughly 2 percent between 1974 and 1985. This decline had a major impact on Soviet weapons procurement, which began to level off in most categories. Gorbachev's first three years in office have failed to bring positive changes for the Soviet economy. As the official summary of the 1987 economic performance concludes, in a rather understated fashion, "during the past year there were no fundamental improvements in the areas of machine building and light industries, especially as far as the quality of goods is concerned."[6] If the Soviets manage by the early 1990s, as Gorbachev promises, to achieve a GNP growth rate of approximately 4 percent, and to narrow their expanding technological gap with the West, Moscow could accelerate the arms buildup from a

---

[5] *Pravda,* March 12, 1988.
[6] *Izvestia,* January 24, 1988.

stronger economic and technological base. The military implications of Gorbachev's intent to increase industrial output in the electronics sector tenfold by the year 2000 do not require elaboration.[7]

Most Western specialists doubt that Gorbachev can make the Soviet economy work successfully. But the real issue is not whether the Soviet Union will approach Japanese or American levels of productivity. The issue is whether or not reform can reverse, at least temporarily, Soviet economic decline sufficiently to provide a base for future expansion of military efforts.

Predictions are risky. Soviet reform is only in a preliminary stage and Soviet officials are the first to admit that more time, effort, and change are needed before it begins to bear fruit. The economic accomplishments of South Korea, Taiwan, and Singapore demonstrate that market mechanisms may coexist with authoritarian political structures. Moreover, Russians have their own peculiar work habits and managerial techniques. To evaluate their chances for economic progress on the basis of Western norms and criteria may be misleading. If the Soviets lived by Western standards, their whole system of government would have collapsed long ago. Instead, the Soviets have proved capable of developing enough resources to turn the Soviet Union into a genuine global military power.

Gorbachev's new, more moderate foreign policy course does not guarantee that this power will not be used against Western interests. We have no assurances that the general secretary will not be ousted from office or survive there at the price of becoming "brezhnevized." He certainly would not be the first Russian leader (others being Emperors Alexander I and Alexander II) who, after brave experimentation with structural changes, began to repudiate them in the fear that reform policies were generating too many unintended challenges to a government whose preservation was the original rationale for pursuing them. Even Leonid I. Brezhnev was initially not adverse to allowing the then-chairman of the Council of Ministers, Aleksey N. Kosygin, to try economic reforms, until Brezhnev realized that the reforms were detrimental to the power and privileges of the party elite.

Gorbachev's changes in Soviet international conduct are only beginning to acquire shape. They have been neither seriously tested nor are they irreversible. Contradictory signs abound. Even Gorbachev himself probably remains ambiguous about many key issues on the Soviet foreign policy agenda. Until now, with the sole exception of Afghanistan, the general secretary and his colleagues have not made a

---

[7] *Pravda*, April 9, 1988.

single major foreign policy decision that would dramatically address the root causes of East-West conflict.

To start with, Soviet military policy until now has changed more in terms of rhetoric than in practice. Gorbachev categorically denies that the Soviet Union seeks military superiority. He and other Soviet spokespersons call for the elimination of nuclear weapons and articulate a Soviet military doctrine of "reasonable sufficiency." However, such talk is not entirely new. In a January 18, 1977, speech in Tula, Leonid Brezhnev took the position that a nuclear war was inherently unwinnable and rejected the very notion of strategic superiority.[8]

More was involved in Brezhnev's speech than just reassurances for foreign consumption. Top Soviet military leaders began calling for a reassessment of the Soviet Union's strategy, including the political and military utility of nuclear weapons. Marshal Nikolai V. Ogarkov, then Soviet general staff chief, became particularly outspoken, deemphasizing nuclear arsenals whose ever-growing overkill capabilities ironically reduced their value in war. "One does not have to be a military specialist to understand: further accumulation of these weapons becomes simply senseless," Ogarkov wrote in his 1985 alarmist book about the urgent need to improve Soviet defense capabilities.[9]

Thus, the new Soviet attitude toward nuclear weapons predates Gorbachev, and it has been shared by civilians and the military alike. What Gorbachev has done is, first, appreciated the logical implications stemming from this attitude and applied them to Soviet arms control proposals, and, second, displayed an enviable mastery in exploiting this new attitude for public relations purposes.

Truly unprecedented are appeals by Gorbachev's academic advisors for "an optimization in the proportions of defense and socioeconomic development appropriations," in other words, cutting the military budget.[10] No less unusual are demands by other influential experts, such as Director Vitaly V. Zhurkin of the newly created European Institute, in the top party journal, for "a reassessment of quantities of these or those kinds of armaments (tanks among them) and the character of military maneuvers."[11] Such statements cannot be easily dismissed. Neither can they be taken as evidence that Moscow has already made decisions about far-reaching defense reforms.

In a manner of speaking, "reasonable sufficiency" in defense is like

[8] *Pravda,* January 19, 1977.

[9] N.V. Ogarkov, *Istoriya Uchit Bditelnosti* (Moscow: Voennoie Izdatelstvo, 1985), p. 88.

[10] Interview with academician Ye. M. Primakov in *Sovetskaya Kultura,* November 7, 1987.

[11] V. Zhurkin, S. Karaganov, and A. Kortunov, "Vyzovi Bezopasnosti—Stariye and Noviye," *Kommunist* 1 (1988): 46.

glasnost. Once the general secretary turned them into official slogans, nobody dared to challenge them openly. But what they supposedly mean lies strictly in the eyes of the beholder. The military hierarchy does not seem to object to Gorbachev's denuclearization schemes, but suggestions that the Soviet armed forces should be reduced or deprived of the ability to conduct offensive operations get a highly negative response. In an apparent rebuff to Zhurkin and his coauthors, General of the Army Ivan Tretyak, commander-in-chief of the Soviet air defense forces and a deputy minister of defense, declared that "defense of the country should be absolute." Reflecting long-standing Soviet military thinking, the general stated point-blank that a defense-oriented strategy is inadequate to "assure the final destruction of the enemy." He warned against any major spending or personnel reductions, which in his view would cripple Soviet defense capabilities and morale.[12] Public statements by other senior military commanders, including Gorbachev's hand-picked minister of defense, General of the Army Dmitriy T. Yazov, indicate that the views expressed by Tretyak are representative of the defense establishment.

In disputes with the military, the task of civilian advisors is complicated by the continued lack of an interagency forum where officials outside the Ministry of Defense can have a large say in determining the Soviet posture. The Defense Council, chaired by Gorbachev and considered the Politburo's national security commission, is empowered to give orders to the military on all issues, but it does not have a professional staff and has to rely on information supplied by the appropriate agencies. Because the Ministry of Defense, specifically the General Staff, is the only institution possessing full information about Soviet defense capabilities, civilians willing to challenge them at the Defense Council and other forums are at a disadvantage.

Gorbachev's forceful personality, however, may prove to be a new determining factor in the civilian-military dispute. Since the death of former Minister of Defense Dmitriy F. Ustinov in 1984, the military, unlike the KGB and the Ministry of Foreign Affairs, does not have full representation on the Politburo. General Yazov is only a candidate member, as was his predecessor Marshal Sergei L. Sokolov. But will Gorbachev be prepared to risk the wrath of the defense hierarchy by decreeing radical changes in Soviet military doctrine and posture? Is he even inclined to go in this direction? Nothing the general secretary has said or done provides a definite answer.

---

[12] Interview with General of the Army Ivan M. Tretyak, *Moskovskiye Novosti*, February 21, 1987.

Beyond the issue of nuclear reductions, Gorbachev's arms control initiatives are vague. Moscow currently advocates asymmetrical cuts in conventional forces in Europe, but the Soviets continue to insist that NATO and the Warsaw Pact already have an overall balance, with each side enjoying superiority in some categories of military power. Neither official Kremlin pronouncements nor private hints from Soviet officials and analysts give the impression that the Soviet Union is ready for dramatic shifts in the size and the composition of its forces in Europe.

Similarly, Soviet Third World policy combines new diplomatic flexibility and a predisposition against both overcommitment toward and provocation of the West. It retains the tendency, Moscow's denials notwithstanding, to view most regional issues through the East-West prism and is prepared to support extremist regimes and factions as long as they fit into the Kremlin's foreign policy objectives. In every Third World conflict involving the United States, Moscow cannot resist the temptation to adopt an anti-American stand. U.S. military retaliation against Iran was described as "banditry" by the Soviet media.[13] The Reagan administration's efforts to get rid of General Manuel Antonio Noriega have been typically portrayed by Soviet publications as an imperialist attempt to take a small country "by the throat."[14] On North-South economic issues, the Soviet Union is unquestionably on the side of developing nations. Moscow calls for the cancellaton of Third World debts, and Gorbachev periodically refers to a "new world economic order" that would redistribute global wealth at the expense of the industrial democracies.[15]

The new Soviet Third World policy has three major dimensions. First, Moscow is explicitly unenthusiastic about endlessly subsidizing its clients' failures and corruption. Soviet junior allies such as Nicaragua, Angola, and even Vietnam are actively encouraged to reduce their economic dependence on the Soviet Union and to look for assistance elsewhere, including the United States. Second, the Gorbachev leadership is much less preoccupied with the ideological purity of Soviet Third World associates than were its predecessors. Whether Third World models of development satisfy some abstract philosophical standards is considered much less important than their ability to become politically and economically self-sufficient.

Finally, the Soviets are taking greater precautions in adopting additional clients, especially among those groups still struggling for power in poor and strategically unimportant postcolonial nations.

---

[13] *Pravda*, April 20, 1988.
[14] *Pravda*, March 11, 1988.
[15] *Pravda*, February 19, 1988.

As influential Director Yevgeniy Primakov of the Institute of World Economy and International Relations stated, "To exclude the export of revolution is the imperative of the nuclear age."[16] In this spirit, the Soviet Union is prepared to expand its diplomatic communications at least on an informal level to such "outcast" states as South Africa and Israel. Gorbachev's diplomacy operates on the assumption that talking to everyone is beneficial, openly when possible and clandestinely when necessary (as in Pretoria's case).

Nevertheless, Soviet Third World moderation should not be exaggerated. The volume of Soviet arms supplies to its radical clients has not been reduced. While building diplomatic bridges to the Israelis and the South Africans, Moscow has also been busy consolidating its influence over the PLO and opening official representation in the Soviet Union to the African National Congress.

In his Third World policy, Gorbachev is not entirely a free agent. Neither Cuba, Syria, nor Vietnam, for example, would win a popularity contest within the Soviet foreign policy establishment. Their constant demands for aid and stubborn pursuit of their own agendas generate considerable resentment in Moscow. Still, Moscow appreciates that these happen to be the most reliable and successful allies the Soviet Union has in the Third World. Distancing the Soviet Union from them, to say nothing about realignment, by all appearances has few, if any, advocates among Soviet decision makers.

Because the Soviet Union is a superpower almost exclusively in military terms, and Gorbachev seems determined to protect and to enhance Soviet global status, Moscow regularly finds itself tempted, indeed pressured, to act as a counterbalance to the United States. The nature of the Kremlin's Third World allies, coupled with the Soviets' own competitive instinct vis-à-vis the United States, virtually assures that, unless Gorbachev and his colleagues go much further in redefining the Soviet Union's international interests, vigorous East-West competition in the Third World will continue, even if in a somewhat more subdued form.

Last, but certainly not least, Soviet policy toward Eastern Europe has not yet been subjected to the tough but inevitable tests that alone can determine how much of a departure Gorbachev's thinking on international affairs really is. What form these tests will take and where will they occur is impossible to know. Most East European economies are in deep trouble, most local Communist leaderships enjoy little popular legitimacy, political successions are about to

---

[16] *Pravda*, July 10, 1987.

happen in most nations of the region, and fresh winds from Moscow are encouraging populations from East Berlin to Sophia to oppose old oligarchies. In the course of the next several years, the Kremlin will certainly be confronted with powerful centrifugal forces gathering momentum inside its orbit.

The Soviets are not known for devising contigency plans to respond to hypothetical situations. Chances are that Gorbachev himself cannot predict at this point how he and his colleagues would act if given a choice between the disintegration of the Soviet empire and a brutal display of force that would shatter Moscow's new, more benign international image. As long as the Kremlin persists in dominating Eastern Europe, reaching a genuine East-West equilibrium in conventional military forces remains an unattainable goal. The Soviets cannot settle for military parity if their armies in Europe are to be sufficient to fight simultaneously against NATO and rebellious East Europeans. Thus, meaningful conventional reductions in Europe may have to wait for geopolitical changes on the continent. Despite all his talk about the "common European home," Gorbachev has still given no indication that his new thinking contemplates the elimination of the Soviet sphere of control as established by Stalin's troops forty years ago.

WESTERN CHOICES: DEALING WITH GORBACHEV

Overall, in evaluating the practical implications of Gorbachev's new thinking for Western interests, the issue is more complicated than simply deciding whether the glass is half full or half empty. A dynamic process of the evolution of international strategy has been set in motion by Moscow. Even if this process cannot be reversed, multiple outcomes are entirely possible. No particular cynicism is required to imagine that one of the strategies may amount to the pursuit of the old imperial course, but with more skill and calculation and without unnecessary and counterproductive provocation.

Meanwhile, the Soviets are well aware that their new diplomacy is a potent political tool for outmaneuvering Western opposition to the Kremlin's actions. According to Primakov, "flexible and dynamic, constantly evolving and becoming more precise, Soviet proposals deprive the militarist forces of breathing space, and keep those who felt much more comfortable without such flexibility and dynamism on our side, in the state of constant alert."[17]

Gorbachev is the first to understand that the new Soviet image undermines the very foundations upon which Western security policies

---

[17] *Pravda*, February 19, 1988.

have been based since the inception of the alliance. He argues that his successful elimination of the image of the Soviet Union as an enemy "destroys what used to reliably serve the reactionaries for decades."[18] The general secretary has a point. Populist democracies find dealing with the subtleties and nuances of international relations difficult. To develop a Western consensus on how to deal with the Soviet Union as a respectable, long-term adversary rather than an ugly and irrational one is perhaps the greatest challenge NATO faces at the moment.

The threat is not in *perestroika* per se. Rather it is in Western difficulty in mastering new rules of international politics brought about by Soviet changes. As Pericles told his fellow Athenians almost twenty-five centuries ago, "What I fear is not the enemy's strategy, but our own mistakes."[19] Unfortunately, the West does not have the luxury of waiting until we have greater certainty regarding the direction and fate of Gorbachev's reforms. The impatient general secretary would then exploit NATO procrastination to impose his own diplomatic agenda and to undermine cohesion of the alliance.

Whether Gorbachev's changes in Soviet foreign and domestic policies prove to be an opportunity or a menace to the West depends a great deal upon our own ability to maintain conceptual clarity and to develop fresh policies corresponding to the evolving international environment.

---

[18] *Pravda*, February 19, 1988.
[19] Thucydides, *History of the Peloponnesian War* (Penguin Books, 1986), p. 122.

7

Public Opinion and the Alliance: European and American Perspectives on NATO and European Security

By STEPHEN F. SZABO*

THE PUBLIC DIMENSION OF DEFENSE

The public dimension of defense in a democratic alliance reemerged unexpectedly and dramatically in the 1980s. The widespread debate over the double track decision on the intermediate-range nuclear force (INF) missiles mobilized large numbers of demonstrators and forced security issues to the attention of European publics. The nuclear freeze movement and the Reagan administration's Strategic Defense Initiative (SDI) also reopened an extensive public consideration of the fundamentals of nuclear deterrence in both Europe and the United States. The Reykjavik summit and the swift movement to an agreement to eliminate all INF and short-range nuclear (SRINF) missiles kept alive the public dimension of what promises to be the first significant reassessment of NATO strategy since the movement away from massive retaliation to flexible response in the 1960s.

In addition to these strategic questions, the emergence of a new Soviet leadership that is dynamic and sophisticated in its public approach to the West creates a new public diplomacy challenge for the alliance. By the middle of 1987, polls began to show that General Secretary Gorbachev was viewed as more sympathetic toward and interested in arms control than President Reagan by the public in a number of key European states.

* The views expressed in this chapter are solely those of the author and do not necessarily represent those of the U.S. government. The author wishes to thank Dr. Alvin Richman of the Office of Opinion Research, Bureau of Public Affairs, U.S. Department of State, for his generous assistance in providing a portion of the data for this chapter.

The *social dimension of strategy*,[1] the social cohesion and will that is necessary to sustain defense policy, is likely to remain a crucial element in the evolution of the alliance for the rest of this century. The increasing role of the media, the democratization of higher education, and the emergence of a postwar generation to power are only a few of the elements that ensure the heightened attention of the Western public to security issues in the years to come. Events and images in Western Europe and the United States have become as closely linked as their financial markets, creating a political stock market with dramatically reduced reaction times.

This chapter examines public images of the Atlantic alliance and of security in Europe and the United States in hopes of providing a portrait of where consensus and disagreement exist among Western publics and which factors appear to be important in shaping perceptions. It identifies where American views differ and agree with those in Europe on the Soviet threat and how to deal with it, security interests and the role of NATO, the U.S. troop presence and burdensharing, alliance strategy, and the role of nuclear deterrence in that strategy.

To what extent is American opinion different from European opinion on these concerns? Is there a "European opinion," or are the differences in Europe greater than the similarities? How do leadership opinions compare with those of the public? How does party opinion affect public opinion? Does a substantial gap divide the generations on attitudes toward security and the alliance? What do trends in public opinion imply about the future of the alliance? These questions are addressed in this brief analysis.

In order to be concise and readable, percentages and data are held to a minimum in the text, and tables are provided for those who would like more detail. What follows is a synthesis and an interpretation, forests, or at least patches, rather than trees.

Finally, something needs to be said about the limitations of public opinion surveys in the areas of foreign and defense policies. Levels of public interest, knowledge, and involvement in foreign policy are far lower than they are on issues closer to home. Questions on social security, inflation, unemployment, and crime attract a great deal more interest and intensity than do those dealing with alliances, security, and diplomacy. As a result, public attitudes are more likely to be volatile and subject to elite direction in the latter than in the former.

Yet systematic surveys still provide a better picture of what people think than do the more impressionist techniques of journalism and

---

[1] The term is Michael Howard's. See his essay, "The Forgotten Dimension of Strategy," *Foreign Affairs* 57 (Summer 1979): 975–86.

reports of well-informed observers on what country X thinks based on informal samples of opinion. The distinction between attitudes and beliefs needs also to be kept in mind. Opinions on specific issues may fluctuate a great deal while deeper beliefs about the structure of international politics, national interests, and national stereotypes remain more stable. Polling data looked at over a long period of time can offer a glimpse into trends in images and beliefs and at the impact of key political and social factors in shaping those images and beliefs.

Public opinion should not be the decisive factor in the shaping of foreign and defense policy, but in democracies it is an important consideration for policymakers. It is no longer articulated largely through groups of interest articulators (interest groups, political parties, the media), but is now expressed directly to policymakers through polls. In the U.S. government, the National Security Council and the State Department have offices that deal primarily with the summarization and interpretation of surveys.[2] Therefore, they should have the best available image of the pictures in people's heads about the world.

IMAGES OF THREAT AND OF THE SOVIET UNION

The cycle of public moods in the United States and Western Europe on the nature of the Soviet threat has resynchronized after a major disjuncture in the early 1980s. The Reykjavik summit, the INF agreement, and the new period of Soviet-American rapprochement have resulted in a new Western consensus on the need for dialogue and agreements with the Soviets.

In the early 1980s, the public mood in Western Europe and the United States diverged in important ways. The Soviet invasion of Afghanistan came at time of a new assertiveness in the American public mood. American opinion has tended to alternate between phases in which concerns for peace were dominant to those in which concerns for strength took priority.[3] During the Vietnam period, peace concerns dominated the public but by the late 1970s the mood had begun to swing back to a preoccupation with strength. Support for increases in defense spending were on the rise prior to the Iran and Afghanistan events that reinforced this new mood.

---

[2]See Ronald Hinckley, "Public Attitudes toward Key Foreign Policy Events." Paper delivered at the 1987 Annual Meeting of the American Political Science Association, Chicago, Illinois, September 3-6, 1987, pp. 3-4.

[3]See William Schneider, "Conservatism, not Interventionism: Trends in Foreign Policy Opinion, 1972-1982," in Kenneth A. Oye et al., eds., *Eagle Defiant: United States Foreign Policy in the 1980s* (Boston: Little, Brown, 1983), pp. 33-64.

The European mood, in contrast, remained primarily concerned with peace. The Soviet action in Afghanistan was seen as largely defensive and limited in its objectives, not as a prelude to a larger move toward the Persian Gulf nor as sufficient reason for risking the concrete benefits of detente in Europe. The Soviet image suffered a setback in 1980 but recovered to pre-Afghanistan levels within a year after the invasion. Support for defense spendng remained relatively stable during this period with the exception of a minor boomlet of support for more defense in the United Kingdom.

The war scare in Europe of the early 1980s that was produced by the deterioration of Soviet-American relations after the Soviet invasion of Afghanistan and the large demonstrations opposing the NATO two-track INF decision arose out of a fear that war could result from superpower conflict rather than exclusively from a Soviet threat. The fear was of August 1914, of a war brought on by the dynamics of great power rivalries and alliance entanglements, rather than of 1939, of war caused by appeasement of a reckless and expansionist totalitarian power.

Surveys throughout the early to mid-1980s found a consistent view, especially in Britain and the Federal Republic of Germany, that *both* superpowers were threats to peace. This view persisted after the Reykjavik summit and the double-zero option on medium- and shorter-range nuclear forces in Europe. As Table 7.1 indicates, by the mid-1980s confidence in the American ability to deal with world problems had fallen to new lows in Britain and the Federal Republic. A number of surveys found that Mikhail Gorbachev rather than Ronald Reagan got more of the credit for the INF agreement.

A substantial delinking had occurred between European views of Soviet and American societies on the one hand and the behavior of these nations as international actors on the other. Both came to be viewed as behaving in equivalent or similar ways as great powers, intervening in the affairs of smaller states, disregarding the views of allies, pursuing military superiority at the expense of the other, and aggressively thrusting their ideological conceptions upon a generally unreceptive world.

These trends were most pronounced in Britain and West Germany and least noticeable in France and in southern Europe. They were symptoms of a clash between European views of the Soviet threat and those of the Reagan administration and substantial portions of the American public.

Europeans have alternated in their concerns about the U.S.–Soviet relationship between a fear of collision and a fear of collusion, between the specters of Sarajevo and Yalta. During periods of superpower confrontation, West Europeans have worried about being

TABLE 7.1. *Trends in West European Confidence in the Ability of the United States to Deal Responsibly with World Problems (Differential between Percentages Responding Favorably and Unfavorably)*[1]

Question: *In general how much confidence do you have in the ability of United States/Soviet Union to deal responsibly with world problems—a great deal, a fair amount, not very much, or none at all?*

Survey Date		Great Britain	France	West Germany	Italy
May/June	'60	-16	4	35	17
June/July	'61	21	11	68	35
June	'62	- 1	-10	50	33
February	'63	18	-16	66	46
May/June	'65	35	- 1	40	49
December	'68	2	- 4	- 5	24
Sept/Nov	'69	34	30	65	41
June	'70	-14	-13	0	—
July	'71	26	28	51	—
January	'72	32	-18	- 3	28
Mar/April	'72	50	14	53	48
June	'72	20	-22	4	14
April/May	'73	—	3	—	46
Oct/Nov	'74	41	1	34	—
May/June	'75	9	-22	- 3	—
March	'81	13	17	19	45
October	'81	- 2	5	1	26
December	'81	- 9	—	-14	—
January	'82	—	—	-13	—
April	'82	- 2	3	19	28
July	'82	14	3	-12	24
December	'82	14	11	6	45
April	'83	-13	—	-18	13
June	'83	- 4	—	-17	4
July/Aug	'83	0	—	-24	27

[1] In the interest of brevity, the full data for these long-term comparisons are not presented in the table, only the net lead or predominance of favorable over unfavorable opinion. Minus signs indicate that unfavorable opinion (low confidence) predominates.
Source: U.S. Information Agency, *Research Report,* December 1983.

dragged into a war by alliance commitment, but in eras of detente the concern has been of a deal being made over their heads without regard for their interests. The Yalta complex was evident in the reaction of Helmut Schmidt to the Carter administration's handling of SALT II and his concern that the United States was ignoring European interests in its desire to achieve strategic stability. The early Reagan years led to the other fear, that of being drawn into a conflict by an overly confrontational American approach. Following the Reykjavik summit and the signing of the INF agreement, some governing elites began to talk of a Munich agreement or Yalta II at their expense. Public opinion, however, did not share this concern.

The waning of the Soviet threat in Western Europe has an internal as well as an external dimension. Images of the Soviet threat may change as much for internal domestic political reasons as they do in reaction to Soviet behavior.[4] The Soviet Union has been viewed as both an internal and external threat in postwar Western Europe. The internal threat was one of subversion and the use of local Communist parties as fifth columns. This dimension preoccupied Europeans in the late 1940s and early 1950s, and the Marshall Plan and early containment policy were directed to this concern.

The internal threat is no longer a real one for European publics. The decline of the Soviet model among West European publics and of Communist parties throughout Western Europe (with Italy the notable exception) has removed the ideological concern. The East is now an antimodel to all but a few isolated groups. This trend can be associated in part with the rise of Socialist or Social Democratic parties in southern Europe, which spawned Eurocommunism and the corresponding decline in Communist influence in France, Spain, Greece, and to a lesser extent, Italy. The "Gulag effect" in France is the most dramatic example of this trend. Here intellectual and political trends resulted in a discrediting of the Soviet Union and a marginalization of the French Communist Party. Growing concern among French elites over a perceived drift toward pacifism and neutralism in West Germany was also an important factor pushing this reassessment. The critique by the Italian Communist party of the Soviet Union following the invasion of Czechoslovakia, combined with the Christian Democrat–Socialist coalition of the 1980s in Rome, served to limit the ideological appeal of the Soviets in Italy. The displacement of the Communists by the Socialists had a similar effect in Spain.

Europeans now view the Soviets more as a traditional great power and less as a revolutionary and ideological one. Although distrusted in the international arena, the Soviets are believed to have a stake in stability, at least in Europe, and to be preoccupied with internal economic problems and unreliable allies. The potential for intimidation that that military power represents remains a concern, but only for minorities.

European images of the Soviets are not clearly linked to their images of the United States, and "views held about either one (superpower) do

---

[4] North Atlantic Assembly, Civilian Affairs Committee, "General Report on the Atlantic Alliance and Public Opinion" (Brussels: North Atlantic Assembly, September 1987), p. 4. See also Edwinea Moreton, "Images of the Soviet Union: A More Typical Adversary" in Gregory Flynn, et al., eds., *Public Images of Western Security* (Paris: The Atlantic Institute, 1985) pp. 22–24.

not seem to affect the views held on the other."[5] Similarly, a lack of confidence in the foreign policy of one does not translate into confidence in the policy of the other. Both the United States and the Soviet Union seem to benefit in European opinion, however, when tensions between the two are low.

The delinking of European images of Soviet society from Soviet foreign policy also means that criticism of the Soviet human rights record has had little impact on the Soviet foreign policy image. Then again, the favorable overall American political and social image has not translated into broader support for U.S. policies.

When European publics are asked how they see the major threats to international security, they tend to list the Soviet military buildup, the U.S. military buildup, and superpower activities in the Third World. With the exception of France, the extension of Soviet influence is not viewed as a major source of tension. In Greece, Turkey is viewed as a more immediate threat than the Soviets, and in Turkey both Greece and Bulgaria are viewed as more immediate problems. In the Netherlands in the mid-1980s, nuclear weapons were viewed as a greater threat than the military threat of the Soviet Union.[6]

This relaxed perception of threat is reinforced by a relatively sanguine assessment of the military balance. The Reagan years saw a reversal in the trend viewing the Soviets as increasingly more powerful and resulted in a growing view that the superpower military relationship was one of parity. Most Europeans preferred parity and believed that the superiority of one superpower would only lead to a new arms race and that peace was best ensured by the equilibrium of a rough balance. The public in most West European states believes that both the United States and the Soviet Union are striving for military superiority and thus increasing international tensions.

The European conception of security is embodied in the Harmel Report's formula for NATO's strategy of defense and detente. The strong reaction against what was viewed as the confrontational approach of the Reagan administration toward the Soviets and the "evil empire" rhetoric of the first few years of the new administration resulted in a sharp decline in confidence in U.S. foreign policy leadership because the administration was viewed as stressing the defense side and ignoring the detente aspect.

The Soviet image, despite detente, remained negative in most of Western Europe. Europeans continued to view the Soviets as a power that could not be trusted, and one that continued to seek military superiority

---

[5] NAA, "The Alliance and Public Opinion," p. 4.

[6] North Atlantic Assembly, Civilian Affairs Committee, "Interim Report of the Sub-Committee on Public Information on Defense and Security: the Netherlands, Turkey and Canada," September 1987, pp. 8, 26.

and domination of smaller states. They have little trust in Soviet goodwill and a consensus that verification of any arms control agreement with them is vital. Yet the publics in most European countries believe that the Soviets can and must be dealt with and that they are motivated by self-interest in reaching agreeements with the West. As the West German historian Hans Peter Schwarz has noted concerning German opinion, "Despite a majority's basic mistrust of the Soviet Union, there is still a marked desire for fairly harmonic relations with the East."[7]

Trends in the American image of the Soviet threat have been more volatile. The increased perception of the Soviets as a threat began before the Soviet invasion of Afghanistan. Support for higher levels of defense spending grew from 1978 through 1982 and frustration with European "wimpishness" was prevalent in the press and the Congress. However, the U.S.–Soviet summits and the INF agreement, combined with a growing preoccupation with the problems of the domestic economy, have promoted a shift in attitudes. By 1986 the American mood was closer to that prevailing in Europe than it had been for a decade.

Americans continued to view the Soviet Union as "unfriendly" toward the United States, but 49 percent in a mid-1984 poll who viewed the Soviets as "an enemy" dropped to 32 percent by May 1987. Forty-four percent in 1987 continued to regard the Soviets as "unfriendly," a proportion that held steady over this three-year period. Although a majority continued to believe that the Soviets sought global domination, the proportion thinking that the Russians would risk a war to get it dropped by more than 50 percent between 1980 and 1986.[8]

The series of surveys conducted by the Chicago Council on Foreign Relations also found that, although the Soviets have consistently ranked at or near the bottom of thermometer ratings of feelings toward a country, substantial support has existed since 1978 at least for arms control agreements with the Soviets, with 80 percent of the public and 95 percent of elites favoring negotiating such agreements. Majorities supported as well the resumption of cultural exchanges, increases in grain sales, and the exchange of scientists. Only a small minority opposed limiting sales of advanced computers or favored the sharing of antimissile defense information.[9]

---

[7] Hans Peter Schwarz, "The West Germans, Western Democracy and Western Ties in the Light of Public Opinion Research" in James Cooney, et al., eds., *The Federal Republic of Germany and the United States* (Boulder, Colo.: Westview, 1984), p. 68.

[8] Roper national sample conducted in May 1987.

[9] John E. Reilly, ed., *American Public Opinion and U.S. Foreign Policy 1987* (Chicago: Chicago Council on Foreign Relations, 1986), pp. 14–15.

Similarly, the preference for a dual-track approach toward the Soviet Union increased during the 1980s while support for a confrontational approach was reduced from one-third in February 1980 to about one-fifth of the public by May 1987.[10] Comparisons with Gallup polls in Europe reveal that the proportion of Europeans holding a confrontationalist view is about 10 percent less and the proportion of accommodationists is about 10 percent greater. The defensive or status quo interpretation of Soviet behavior is apparently somewhat more prevalent in Europe, but the gaps with American opinion are not substantial.

The ideological component of the American perception of threat did not increase during the Reagan years. The Chicago Council study concluded that a Communist takeover by peaceful means was viewed as somewhat of a threat, but with the exception of the hypothetical case of Mexico, only minorities believed that this would be a "great threat."[11] Elite opinion on this question was actually more concerned than general public opinion.

Support for increased defense spending has also tapered off substantially so that by 1986 consensus in Europe and the United States was that defense spending should remain at current levels. Dissatisfaction in the United States continued, however, with the magnitude of European defense spending, given the higher overall proportion and amount of American spending. On this issue of defense spending levels, European opinion has been stable over the past decade, while American opinion has fluctuated widely.

Several factors seem to be behind this muting of the American perception of threat. The large increases in defense spending under the Reagan administration led in the United States, as it did in Europe, to a shifting assessment of the military balance.[12] The trend is similar to that which developed in Western Europe, namely a slight increase from 1982 to 1986 in the perception of American strength, a

---

[10] A May 1987 Roper survey found 57 percent agreeing to a dual-track approach toward the Soviet Union, combining strength with good relations. This was up from 44 percent in February 1980.

[11] Reilly, *American Public Opinion*, p. 20.

[12] The Chicago Council on Foreign Relations surveys found that the proportion of Americans who believed the United States was militarily stronger than the Soviet Union decreased from 33 percent in 1979 to 21 percent in 1982 but then increased to 28 percent in 1986. Those who thought the Soviets were more powerful fell from 32 percent in 1979 to 29 percent in 1982 and then further to 17 percent in 1986. During this period, those who believed that both sides were about equal climbed from 26 percent in 1979 to 42 percent in 1982 and up to 48 percent in 1986. The leaders sample found less of a shift in assessments of the balance and a greater tendency to view parity as the condition of the balance (62 percent in 1982 and 59 percent in 1986) and far fewer seeing the Soviets ahead (15 percent in 1982 and 11 percent in 1986). As with the general public, leaders also saw an increase in U.S. power as the proportion of leaders who believed the United States to be ahead climbed from 20 percent in 1982 up to 28 percent in 1986. Ibid., p. 14.

corresponding decrease in the number believing the Soviets to be more powerful, and close to a doubling in the number seeing parity as the condition of the superpower balance.

Although Americans remain more likely to see the United States as more powerful and more Europeans take the view that the Soviets have an edge, publics on both sides agree that parity is the condition of the balance. Leaders and the better educated on both sides of the Atlantic were even more inclined than the public to see parity as the condition. As the Chicago Council's study concludes, this shift in the perceived balance "represented a triumph for the Reagan administration's arms buildup. But this success may have undermined support for a continuation of that buildup. And the changed perceptions probably also contributed to some increase in the already strong public support for cooperative relationships with the Soviet Union."[13]

Growing concern over economic issues and the federal budget deficit, a shift back to some increased support for domestic programs, and dissatisfaction with the problems of waste in the Department of Defense have also played a role. A Roper survey conducted in December 1986 found that majorities thought that the United States was spending too little on education, fighting crime, improving the health system, dealing with drug addiction and improving the environment, but only 15 percent thought that too little was being spent on the military, armaments, and defense.

Thus by the end of the 1980s, Americans had replaced their concerns about strength with a preoccupation with peace and internal economic problems. Opinion surveys early in the 1988 presidential campaign provided evidence that the public was worried more about loss of control over the nation's future and less with the military threat posed by the Soviet Union.[14]

THE GORBACHEV FACTOR

Mikhail Gorbachev is the most popular Soviet leader in the postwar history of polling in the West. He is the first to outpoll an American leader in West European opinion in popularity and in dedication to peace.[15] The major thrust of Gorbachev's public diplomacy toward the

[13] Ibid., p. 15.

[14] For a summary of these opinion and political trends, see Ronald Brownstein, "Losing Its Grip?," *National Journal*, February 6, 1988, pp. 308-13.

[15] Khrushchev's popularity reached a high of 33 percent (having a very good or good opinion) in Britain and Italy, 30 percent in France, and 5 percent in the FRG in 1960 during another period of U.S.-Soviet summitry and detente, the spirit of Camp David. See Richard L. Merritt and Donald J. Puchala, *Western European Perspectives on International Affairs: Public Opinion Studies and Evaluations* (New York: Praeger, 1968), p. 278. At least among the West German public, Gorbachev outpolled Mitterrand and Thatcher as well as Reagan. See "Ganz besonders zweispaeltige Gefuehle," *Der Spiegel* 39 (1987): 21.

West has been an emphasis on his dedication to peace and international stability. His stress on "new thinking" and the interdependence of security plays on the strengths of the Soviet image, and his campaign for *glasnost* helps mute the negatives associated with Soviet society.[16]

By late 1987, some evidence that his personal image was translating into a better Soviet image began to appear in survey data. For the first time in thirty years, in September 1987 more Britons and West Germans had a favorable image than an unfavorable image of the Soviet Union.

The changes were most dramatic in those countries where the Soviets have been most critically regarded in the postwar period. In West Germany, a country whose public has had the most consistently negative image of the Soviet Union in the postwar period, the swing in Soviet image has been remarkable. Starting from only 8 percent with a favorable image of the Soviet Union in October 1981, by September 1987 a majority (54 percent) held a positive view. During that period the proportion holding an unfavorable image fell from 77 percent to 34 percent. By October 1987, 59 percent of West Germans had confidence in the peace and disarmament policies of the Soviet Union, compared to 52 percent with confidence in the policies of the United States.[17]

Similarly in Britain, the other of the major European nations with a consistently negative image of the Soviet Union, the Soviet image swung into the positive, beginning in 1985. However, both France and Italy remained more resistant to Gorbachev's magic, perhaps because they have been less critical of the Soviets over the postwar period and had a lower euphoria potential. Conservatives and older people tended to remain more skeptical of Gorbachev and the Soviets.[18]

Gorbachev had a similar reception among the American public. Just prior to the Washington summit, the Soviet leader had created a favorable impression among 59 percent of the public compared to 35 percent with an unfavorable impression. Unlike European opinion, however, President Reagan remained viewed as more sincere in his desire for an arms control agreement.

Certainly the trend toward treating both the United States and the Soviet Union as equivalent in their foreign policy behavior has not found much resonance with the American public, and this divergence

---

[16] On Gorbachev's approach to Europe, see NAA, *The Alliance and Public Opinion*, p. 4; Stanley Hoffmann, "Coming down from the Summit," *New York Review of Books*, January 21, 1988, pp. 21-25; and Robbin F. Laird, ed., *Soviet Foreign Policy* (New York: The Academy of Political Science, 1987), pp. 93-118, 235-53.

[17] USIA data for September 1987. October data reported in *Der Speigel*, November 2, 1987, p. 44.

[18] For data on this tendency in West Germany, see *Der Speigel*, November 2, 1987, p. 44.

could be a source of growing resentment in the United States, especially if it continues into the next administration.

These turnarounds have led to concern among a number of Western leaders that the Soviet leader has "become too popular for Western comfort."[19] However, little evidence suggests that Western publics have been swept up by "Gorbymania" or that they have changed their fundamental view of the Soviet Union, at least not yet. In both Europe and the United States, large portions of the public continue to have a very negative view of Soviet society but believe the new leader is trying to improve relations with the West and to open up his own society.

Both Gorbachev's and the Soviet Union's images remain soft as Western publics were hopeful but cautious in their assessments.[20] Much of the improvement in the overall Soviet image was linked to the personal popularity of the new Soviet leader and was therefore more fragile than the American image, which remained sound despite the unpopularity of its leader in Western Europe.

Based on the best evidence available in the survey data, *glasnost, perestroika*, and new thinking are not about to dissolve NATO. The public is open to a changed relationship and desires reduced tensions, but its expectations remain far from millennial. Proof of this can also be found in public attitudes regarding the alliance.

SECURITY INTERESTS AND THE ALLIANCE

A clear consensus exists among Europeans and Americans over the importance of the alliance to the security of their nations. In spite of all the antimissile demonstrations, the poll results showing drops in confidence in U.S. leadership, and trends toward viewing both superpowers as threats to peace, surveys surprisingly indicate that the sense of the commonality of security interests of Europeans with the United States has increased during the 1980s. The Federal Republic of Germany was the only, if important, exception to this trend.[21] There the 1980s witnessed a decline in the view that German interests were compatible with those of the United States, but the number who

---

[19] "The Gorbachev Effect," *The Economist* (February 17–March 4, 1988): 38. The article quotes Prime Minister Thatcher as saying, "The Russian bear was easier to deal with when it looked more like a bear than it does now."

[20] For example of the 54 percent of West Germans with a favorable image of the USSR in September 1987, only 4 percent had a "very favorable" image compared to 50 percent with a "somewhat favorable" view. The same tendency was apparent in the other European and American polls.

[21] In the 1950s and early 1960s, from 56 percent to 81 percent of West Germans believed that German interests were in agreement with those of the United States. By 1982 this proportion had dropped to 35 percent in comparison to 53 percent who regarded the interests of the two countries as different. USIA, *Research Memorandum*, September 19, 1984.

believed that the basic interests of their country were in agreement with those of the Soviet Union remained small.

Support for NATO membership and belief in the essentiality of NATO for European security were higher in the 1980s than in the golden years of the 1950s and early 1960s. In the mid-1950s, NATO was less preferred as a security alternative than a general security system that included both the United States and the Soviet Union, and one-fifth of West Germans, French, and Italians preferred neutrality in the East-West struggle to an alliance with the United States. Neutrality was viewed then as a way of avoiding polarization through a European security system.[22] Table 7.2 provides a national profile on NATO essentiality in September 1987.

TABLE 7.2. *European Views of the Necessity of NATO, 1987*

Question: *Some people say that NATO (the "Atlantic Alliance" in France) is still necessary to our country's security. Others say it is no longer necessary. Which view is closer to your own?*

Country:	Denmark	Norway	France	FRG	Great Britain	Italy
Sample Size:	(845)	(1009)	(961)	(1022)	(970)	(1061)
NATO still necessary	61%	71%	49%	70%	72%	65%
NATO no longer necessary	22	14	19	15	16	23
Don't know	16	15	32	15	12	12
Total	99%	100%	100%	100%	99%	100%

Source: U.S. Information Agency, Office of Research, *Research Memorandum*, February 10, 1988; surveys conducted in September 1987.

By the 1980s, alternatives to NATO lacked any real public resonance and centered around West European defense cooperation rather than a pan-European system of security. In the 1950s about a third of Britons and West Germans preferred a security system that included the Soviet Union; by the 1980s less than 5 percent chose greater accommodation to Soviet interests as an alternative to NATO. NATO remained the most popular choice of majorities and pluralities, and the only major competing alternative, some version of a stronger European pillar of NATO or of a version of an independent European defense system, received the support of not more than a third of the public.

---

[22] U.S. Information Agency, *Research Report* No.23, January 19, 1956, and No.53, February 1958.

TABLE 7.3. *Necessity of U.S. Military Presence (September 1987)*

Question: *"Now, I am going to read to you several statements about defense issues concerning (survey country). Please use this card (HAND CARD) to tell me how much you agree or disagree with each statement—do you agree strongly, agree somewhat, disagree somewhat, or disagree strongly."*
"The United States military presence in Europe is necessary in order to deter an attack on (survey country)."

Country:	Denmark	Norway[1]	France	FRG	Great Britain	Italy
Sample Size:	845	1009	961	1022	970	1061
Agree strongly	29%	39%	18%	29%	23%	17%
Agree somewhat	30	29	37	41	35	33
Disagree somewhat	16	11	15	16	21	33
Disagree strongly	17	10	13	8	16	21
Don't know	8	11	17	7	6	6
Total:	100%	100%	100%	101%	101%	101%

[1] In Norway, the phrase "in order to deter an attack on West Europe" was used in lieu of "an attack on Norway."
Source: U.S. Information Agency, Office of Research, *Research Memorandum*, February 10, 1988. Based on surveys conducted in September 1987.

Europeans, as Table 7.3 illustrates, continue to believe that the U.S. military presence is necessary to deterrence. Support for the presence of U.S. troops was substantially higher in the 1980s than it was in the 1950s, at least in Britain, Italy, and West Germany. In the mid-1950s, about one-quarter of the publics in these three countries believed that the presence of U.S. troops increased the chances of war, and qualified support existed for the withdrawal of U.S. and British forces in return for a Soviet withdrawal from Eastern Europe.

By the 1980s, only small minorities wished to see U.S. troops leave. The troops have become a symbol of the American defense commitment and are seen as an effective deterrent to the Soviets as well. In the country with the vast majority of American troops, the Federal Republic of Germany, 81 percent in a 1984 poll believed that the presence of U.S. troops deterred a Soviet attack, and only 16 percent believed they increased the possibility of such an attack. Two-thirds of West Germans in this survey also wanted the current level of deployments to be maintained, and 4 percent desired an increase in the levels. Only 17 percent wished to see a reduction and 7 percent their total withdrawal.[23]

---

[23] Security Survey conducted by EMNID in the Federal Republic of Germany, September 1984. See also USIA *Research Report* No.53, February 1958, and *Research Report*, December 20, 1979.

In southern Europe, however, erosion of popular acceptance of the American troop presence and American bases is apparent. In Italy, a fall 1987 poll found that the public was almost evenly divided on the American presence. A majority (53 percent) believed that the U.S. bases were "not a good thing," while 43 percent had favorable attitudes on the American presence. A majority of those opposing the bases believed the American presence increased the danger of an attack on Italy. The general consensus among the ruling parties in support of the bases, however, had limited the impact of these attitudes.[24]

In Spain, where a strong majority favors the removal of the American military presence, attitudes have been shaped by a number of factors. Spain has had a long tradition of neutralism and fought its last foreign war in 1898 against the Americans. In addition, the U.S. bases are viewed as a legacy of the Franco era and as a symbol of Spanish dependence. NATO is generally seen as a body dominated by the United States, and even those who argued in favor of remaining within the alliance do so on the grounds that leaving NATO would increase Spanish dependence on the United States, but staying in would allow the alliance to develop as a more European institution.[25] Similar sorts of concerns are present in Greece as well but not in Turkey.

Although the 1980s witnessed a decline in confidence in both the U.S. defense commitment and the ability of NATO to deter a war or to defend Europe in case war breaks out, the majority of European publics (in contrast to Charles de Gaulle's assertion that the Americans would not and should not sacrifice New York for Hamburg) remains confident that the United States would come to their defense if their security was threatened by the Soviet Union. Trust in the defense commitment of other European states remained lower than trust in the American guarantee.

Confidence in the ability of NATO to deter and defend remained relatively stable except in the Federal Republic, where it slipped in the 1980s. The publics in most NATO European states were evenly divided between those who had confidence in the alliance and those who did not. Within this uncertain public context Europe enters a post-INF era in which the American commitment becomes even more important.

Americans have been consistently willing in the postwar period to see the United States take an active role in world affairs and go against a century-and-a-half-old tradition of limited involvement in world affairs. A series of polls conducted since 1948 have found that from

[24] USIA, *Research Memorandum*, December 29, 1987, pp. 3-4.
[25] For a survey of Spanish attitudes during the 1986 referendum on NATO, see the NAA's *General Report on NATO's Public Relations Problems*, November 1986, pp. 3-9.

two-thirds to three-quarters of the public wish the United States to play an active international role and oppose going it alone. Similar proportions feel that the United States should take into account the views of its major allies in deciding on its foreign policies. The segment of the public that would like to see a diminished U.S. international role is a third or less. Pure isolationists are less than a fifth of the public and the trend over the past decade has been toward more internationalism.[26]

The American public's commitment to NATO and the defense of Europe, which has been consistent throughout the postwar period, reached its apex in the 1980s. A number of surveys taken in 1986 and 1987 found that Americans believe that Western Europe is an area of vital interest to the United States and that it is the one region where a majority of the American public would commit U.S. troops in case of a Soviet invasion. Support for the U.S. commitment has remained stable at high levels, with 70 percent of the public and 85 percent of the leaders in the Chicago Council's 1986 sample supported keeping the commitment at present levels or expanding it (only 8 percent favored an expansion). Eleven percent would decrease the commitment, and another 5 percent would withdraw entirely from NATO.[27]

More Americans would favor coming to the defense of major European allies if they were attacked by the Soviet Union than would support the defense of any other global region. From 55 up to 76 percent of Americans would use American troops in response to a Soviet invasion of Europe, with only from 16 percent up to a third opposing such a response. This support for European defense is a major increase compared to the Vietnam period. In 1974 and 1975, 48 percent would have responded with military force in Europe

---

[26] Reilly, *American Public Opinion*, p. 11; and William Schneider, "Conservatism, Not Interventionism: Trends in Foreign Policy Opinion, 1972–1982," in Kenneth A. Oye et al., eds., *Eagle Defiant*, pp. 50–51. Roper poll conducted in July 1987. However, a Gallup poll commissioned by the European Community and conducted in November and early December 1987 found that 44 percent would like to see the United States stop getting involved in world affairs compared to 49 percent who would like to see it play a leading role. Yet these figures represent a decline in the "isolationists" from the 55 percent who held their view in 1973. A separate sample of opinion leaders also revealed much stronger support for an internationalist position with 83 percent wishing the United States to play a leading world role compared to only 9 percent who would like the country to stop getting involved. The Gallup Organization, *Attitudes toward U.S.–European Relations: A Report on American Public Opinion about Western Europe* (Princeton, N.J.: The Gallup Organization, January 1988), p. 56 (hereafter referred to as the EEC poll).

[27] Reilly, *American Public Opinion*, p. 21.

compared to 34 percent who would not.[28] Less than a fifth would withdraw American troops today. The public also gives a clear priority to U.S. interests in Europe over those "out of area."[29]

Leaders and the better educated are more favorable to the American commitment than the less educated and less influential segments of the public. Regional breakdowns of the Chicago Council data revealed no major differences between the Sunbelt and the East Coast over Europe and NATO. Nonwhites were less favorable to the U.S.–European relationship than were whites, but a 1987 Gallup poll found that 68 percent of the people in their sample traced their ethnic roots to Western Europe and that a similar proportion felt close to Europe because of common cultural ties and religious roots.[30]

Thus in spite of numerous articles and commentaries in the press and critical voices on Capitol Hill, neither the general public, the attentive public, nor elites seem to be ready to make a substantial change in the U.S. commitment to Western Europe.

However, sentiments are widespread among both public and elites that the United States is carrying a disproportionate share of the alliance defense burden. About half of the public and two-thirds of opinion leaders at the end of 1987 felt that the West European contribution to world defense was too small. About one-quarter of the public and one-third of leaders felt the United States was contributing too much, with most feeling the U.S. contribution to European defense was just about right.[31]

The political and intellectual debate over the "solvency" of American foreign policy found in David Calleo's *Beyond American Hegemony*

[28] See Ibid. and a report of a Potomac Associates poll in "Japan and America," *The Economist* (January 9, 1988): 18.

[29] A September 1986 survey, for example, found that 59 percent believed that the United States should not cut back its commitment to Europe's defense in response to a lack of allied support for United States raids against Libya because the issue was not big enough to affect our relationship with our European allies (National Strategy Information Center survey, November 1986). Survey conducted by G. Lawrence Co., September 1986. The EEC poll conducted in late 1987 found that, while 75 percent of the public and 66 percent of the opinion leaders in their sample believed the United States did not get engouh support from its European allies in the attempt to stop terrorism, this did not translate into a "feeling of repudiation of the countries in Western Europe," Gallup, EEC Poll, p. 16. The same poll found that 70 percent of the general and elite publics believed that U.S. troops were necessary in Europe while only a quarter felt they were not. See also Schneider, "Conservatism, Not Interventionism," p. 51; Reilly, *American Public Opinion*, pp. 16–22; Roper August 1986 survey.

[30] Gallup, "EEC Poll," p. 63.

[31] Gallup survey conducted for the European Economic Community. See Delegation of the European Communities, *American Attitudes toward U.S.-European Relations* (Washington, D.C.: Office of Press and Public Affairs, 1988), p. 14.

(Basic Books: 1987) and Paul Kennedy's *The Rise and Fall of the Great Powers* (Random House, 1988) and the attention they bring to the economic aspects of foreign policy commitments are finding resonance among the public and elites.[32] The growing public and elite concern over national economic decline is beginning to translate into an expectation that the Europeans must take on a greater burden of the alliance. According to some evidence, Americans are also beginning to realize this change means devolution of control and a diminished U.S. leadership role in the alliance.[33]

In summary, NATO remains viewed as still necessary on both sides of the Atlantic in spite of the muting of the Soviet threat. Attitudes toward the alliance seem to be independent of concern about the Soviets and to be based on a sense that NATO serves as an insurance policy against an unlikely but not insignificant threat. An attitude of "if it works don't fix it" persists, rooted on an attachment to a status quo that has preserved peace for over forty years.[34]

For many Europeans, the European dimension of NATO is at least as important as the Atlantic one. In Spain, NATO membership was seen as a necessary prerequisite for entry into a European Economic Community. In Greece, the alliance is seen as primarily containing Turkey rather than the Soviet Union. Discussion of the European pillar of NATO, which revived in the 1980s, is further evidence of the importance of this European aspect.

However, sentiment for replacing NATO as currently structured with an independent European defense alliance remains limited to less than a fifth of most European publics.[35] European public support for the alliance persists despite widespread doubts about the wisdom of American policies. Although both NATO and the American connection remain viewed as essential to European security, conceptions of NATO seem, at least in Europe and perhaps in the United States as well, to be slowly shifting in the direction of a Europeanization of the alliance.

---

[32] See Brownstein, "Losing Its Grip," for a fuller discussion of this debate and its impact on the 1988 presidential campaign.

[33] See Gallup, "EEC Poll", pp. 17–19, which finds substantial American public support for European unification and a recognition among elites that this would give Europe a stronger voice in world affairs. Elites were evenly divided over whether this would make Europe a stronger competitor of the United States in world markets.

[34] An example of this type of support can be seen in the Netherlands, where NATO is viewed separately from nuclear weapons and the United States. As one NAA report put it, "NATO seems to be like national defense, part of the stable scenery to which the Dutch public is used." NAA, "The Netherlands, Turkey and Canada," p. 13.

[35] USIA, *Research Memorandum*, February 10, 1988, p. 10.

NUCLEAR WEAPONS AND NATO STRATEGY

The reemergence of antinuclear movements in the 1980s after a two-decade dormancy and the renewed debate within NATO of the role of nuclear deterrence in Western strategy following Reykjavik, the INF agreement, and SDI have opened a serious reassessment of the future NATO strategy. Many Western leaders, including Chancellor Kohl, have called for a new comprehensive concept or grand strategy in the wake of the INF agreement.[36] The degree of public acceptance of nuclear deterrence and for alternatives to it will be a key factor in this strategic reassessment.

Although the majority of Western security elites continue to believe that nuclear deterrence will be unavoidable for the foreseeable future, the prospect of a major gap between elites and publics and between publics of various nations of the alliance is one that holds the danger of fragmentation, an opportunity that the new Soviet leadership appears ready and able to exploit. This section briefly examines the extent of antinuclear sentiment in Western Europe and the United States and assesses the degree of public support for alternatives to NATO's flexible response doctrine.

European Opinion

With all the attention given to the antinuclear movements of the 1980s, we should not forget that European and American publics have been uncomfortable with nuclear deterrence since its inception. A profile of European public views in the 1950s and early 1960s, a period of clear American dominance in the nuclear balance, finds little support for the use of nuclear weapons, even in response to a conventional attack that threatened to overrun Europe. A U.S. Information Agency study written in 1955 described "a widespread revulsion against the use of atomic weapons so strong that it is overcome only in the contingency of prior use of atomic bombs against Western Europe."[37]

Opinion at this time believed that a nuclear war would not be limited to the battlefield but would include cities, and few thought they would survive it. Nuclear angst was tempered by confidence that the United States would use nuclear weapons only in an emergency and would not act rashly.

---

[36] Helmut Kohl, "For a Comprehensive Defense Strategy." Speech at the Wehrkunde Conference, Munich, February 6, 1988, *Statements and Speeches* Vol. 11, No. 5 (New York: German Information Center, February 10, 1988).

[37] Office of Research, U.S. Information Agency, *Report*, June 11, 1955, p. 31. For attitudes on use of nuclear weapons in the mid-1950s, see Richard Merritt and Donald Puchala, eds., *Western European Perspectives on International Affairs* (New York: Praeger, 1968), p. 381.

By the 1980s this aversion to the use of nuclear weapons, which was always below the surface, was activated by the antinuclear movements and the rhetoric of the early Reagan years. A new dimension was the Three Mile Island (Harrisburg) and Chernobyl effect, the fear over the dangers of civilian nuclear power. Much of the antinuclear movement in Europe began with concern over civilian uses of nuclear power and then spread to the missile issue.

As Table 7.4 indicates, the tenets of flexible response, which relies on first use of nuclear weapons if conventional defenses begin to give way under attack, have very little public support. Trend data also indicate that nuclear anxieties probably peaked late in 1981 or early 1982 and then turned down, except in the Federal Republic, where they remained high.

A few key conclusions can be drawn from the broad sweep of thirty years of polling on this complex of issues. First, nuclear anxieties are not a phenomenon unique to the 1980s and, with the exception of West Germany, survey data do not show that they are any more intense than they were in the 1950s.

Second, publics in the nuclear states are not in favor of unilateral nuclear disarmament and tend to believe that nuclear weapons "are better if they are yours."[38] The nuclear allergy seems to be more acute in the nonnuclear states and to be associated with the presence of foreign controlled nuclear systems and a decline in confidence in the American leadership that controls Europe's fate. Germany and Italy show a concern with French and British nuclear systems and a willingness to include them in negotiations with the Soviets, suggesting a possible fissure within the alliance. In the two European nuclear states, Britain and France, the national deterrents are closely linked to the concept of sovereignty and nationalism. Yet even in most of the nonnuclear states majorities still support nuclear use under some conditions.

---

[38] Marplan poll reported in *The Economist*, February 21, 1987, p. 52.

TABLE 7.4. *West European Opinion on NATO's Use of Nuclear Weapons in the 1980s*

"There are different opinions about the use of nuclear weapons in Europe by NATO. Which one of the following is closest to your own?

A. NATO should not use nuclear weapons of any kind under any circumstances.
B. NATO should use nuclear weapons only if the Soviet Union uses them first in attacking Western Europe.
C. NATO should use nuclear weapons to defend itself if a Soviet attack by conventional forces threatened to overwhelm NATO forces."

	Britain		Germany		Italy		Belgium			Netherlands			Denmark	Norway
	7/82	5/84	7/82	5/84	7/82	5/84	10/81	7/82	3/84	10/81	7/82	5/84	5/84	5/84
A. Not under any circumstances	30%	24%	38%	44%	38%	41%	47%	51%	35%	50%	37%	36%	43%	30%
B. Only if Soviets use them first	45%	51%	33%	42%	40%	44%	26%	28%	34%	31%	32%	30%	35%	48%
C. Against an overwhelming conventional attack	19%	18%	16%	11%	14%	9%	16%	14%	14%	11%	16%	16%	7%	11%
D. Don't know	6%	7%	13%	2%	8%	5%	10%	7%	17%	8%	15%	17%	15%	10%

Source: U.S. Information Agency, Office of Research, *Research Memorandum*, September 19, 1984.

TABLE 7.5. *European Attitudes on Nuclear Deterrence (September 1987)*

"Some people say that nuclear weapons are necessary to deter an attack against our country. Others say that we should rely only on conventional—that is, nonuclear—weapons for such deterrence. Which view is closer to your own?"

	France	FRG	Italy	Great Britain
Nuclear weapons are necessary to deter an attack	47%	24%	22%	59%
Should rely only on conventional weapons for deterrence	29%	50%	64%	36%
Don't know	23%	25%	14%	5%
Total	99%	99%	100%	100%

Source: U.S. Information Agency, Office of Research, *Research Memorandum*, November 18, 1987.

Although support for nuclear use remains understandably low, support for nuclear deterrence is somewhat higher, and willingness to enhance conventional deterrence is mixed at best. A series of surveys in the mid-1980s found that the French clearly continued to support nuclear over conventional deterrence, and the Germans had become the most concerned of the major states over the role of nuclear weapons.[39] Table 7.5 presents the results of a 1987 sampling of opinion in four major countries.

The concern over nuclear deterrence and nuclear weapons is not so intense that publics are willing to support conventional modernization in order to raise the nuclear threshold. Even in West Germany, only one-third in a 1984 survey believed that the conventional deterrent should be strengthened to raise the nuclear threshold. Support for increased defense spending, as noted above, is not present in any European country. Perceptions of threat and the balance being what they are, an elite consensus would be needed to push through major increases in spending for conventional defense, a consensus that is not on the horizon.

[39] The July 1986 security survey conducted in Britain and France found that 40 percent of French respondents agreed with the statement that nuclear weapons were necessary to deter a Soviet attack, and 27 percent believed that only conventional weapons were necessary; in Britain the proportions were 45 percent nuclear, 46 percent conventional. A 1984 survey found that in the Federal Republic 43 percent believed strengthening conventional forces was the preferable way to deter a Soviet attack, while only 20 percent supported the modernization of NATO nuclear forces.

Opinion in the United States

Americans, like Europeans, are skeptical about nuclear deterrence, especially the doctrine of mutually assured destruction. During the early 1980s as Europeans were demonstrating against INF, polls found over 70 percent of Americans favoring a freeze in nuclear arsenals.[40]

These latent concerns are also evident in the stronger support of Americans for the Strategic Defense Initiative than is found in European opinion. In polls taken in November and December 1986, when asked which was the better way to avoid nuclear war, 68 percent chose a strong antimissile defense and only 29 percent favored having enough nuclear weapons to be able to inflict unacceptable damage in retaliation for an attack. These surveys also indicated that Americans preferred a good strategic defense (69 percent) over the complete elimination of nuclear weapons (30 percent). However, when given the option of a combination of SDI plus some reduction in nuclear weapons, a majority of 58 percent preferred it to the other two options.[41]

Americans share the European aversion to the use of nuclear weapons in response to a conventional attack; they reject first use in such a case by a 73 to 19 margin in a late 1985 poll. They are more likely, however, to support nuclear use in retaliation for a Soviet nuclear attack against Western Europe (the margin was 58 to 32 in favor).

The public in the United States is even more optimistic than those in Europe concerning the assessment of the state of the conventional balance. A majority (59 percent) believed that if all nuclear weapons were eliminated, the United States would have conventional superiority, and 38 percent believed that the Soviets were conventionally superior. Only a quarter to a third of Europeans believed the United States and NATO to be ahead in conventional forces.[42] When asked further what U.S. arms policy should be if the Soviets were conventionally superior, a majority answered that a reduction but not elimination of nuclear arsenals would be the best policy. When faced with the question of what the United States should do if faced with Soviet conventional superiority if all nuclear weapons were eliminated, 37 percent stated they would be willing to increase taxes and reduce

[40] David Capitanchik and Richard Eichenberg, *Defense and Public Opinion* (London: Routledge and Kegan Paul, 1983), p. 76.

[41] Ronald H. Hinckley, "Domestic Public Opinion and U.S. National Security Issues" (Washington, D.C.: National Strategy Information Center, December 16, 1986), pp. 40, 44.

[42] USIA, *Research Memorandum*, November 18, 1987, p. 3.

166   *Stephen F. Szabo*

domestic programs to pay for conventional improvements, 38 percent would accept conventional inferiority, and 24 percent would opt to keep some nuclear weapons.[43]

THE PUBLIC AND THE INF TREATY

Overwhelming majorities in both the United States and Western Europe support the INF agreement signed in Washington in December of 1987. In Europe a series of surveys prior to the Washington summit found that between 66 percent in France and up to 93 percent in Italy favored the INF agreement.[44] These proportions increased after the summit, with from 78 percent in France up to 97 percent in West Germany favoring the treaty. Table 7.6 provides an overview of the national responses.

TABLE 7.6. *Support for INF Zero-Option Treaty*

Question: *"In particular, the United States and the Soviet Union are discussing an agreement which would eliminate all American and Soviet intermediate range nuclear missiles (such as the Pershing II, the Cruise, and the SS-20 missiles) from Europe. Do you strongly favor, somewhat favor, somewhat oppose, or strongly oppose an agreement which would eliminate all American and Soviet intermediate range nuclear missiles from Europe?"*

	Denmark	Finland	Norway	Sweden	France	FRG	Great Britain	Italy
Sample Size:	845	1057	1009	920	961	1022	970	1061
Strongly favor	71%	83%	69%	87%	39%	52%	58%	75%
Somewhat favor	21	9	17	7	27	23	21	18
Somewhat oppose	2	1	3	1	7	7	9	2
Strongly oppose	1	1	3	1	5	3	3	1
Don't know	5	5	8	4	23	15	10	3
Total	100%	99%	100%	100%	101%	100%	101%	99%

Source: Based on polls conducted for the U.S. Information Agency in 1987.

[43] Hinckley, "Domestic Public Opinion," p. 62.

[44] The U.S. Information Agency commissioned a series of polls in September 1987 and immediately after the Washington summit in mid December 1987. The results of these are the basis for the following discussion of European reaction to the INF treaty and can be found in Office of Research, U.S. Information Agency, *Research Memoranda*, dated November 17, 1987; November 18, 1987; and December 21, 1987.

American opinion was no less robust in its support for the treaty, with 79 percent of the public in favor in a January 1988 survey.[45] American public interest in and knowledge about the agreement was considerably lower than in Europe. Approval for the treaty also increased substantially after the Washington summit in December 1987, reflecting the impact of President Reagan's identification with it, especially among Republicans.

Europeans tended to believe the agreement would reduce U.S.-Soviet tensions. This motivation is consistent with the view among large numbers of Europeans that arms control serves more a political than a military purpose as an important symbol of detente and reduced tensions. The polls also found little concern that the treaty was motivated by an American desire to decouple from the defense of Europe. Post-summit polls indicated that confidence in the American defense commitment was heightened by the INF agreement.

American policy was seen as driven more by a desire for a reduction of tensions and by domestic political considerations, especially Ronald Reagan's desire to leave office as a peacemaker. Soviet interest in the treaty was viewed as the result of a desire to shift more resources from the military to the civilian sector. Few Europeans in these surveys were concerned that the Soviets wanted an agreement to intimidate Western Europe with their conventional military superiority.

Although pluralities believed that the Soviets would have a conventional edge after the agreement, not more than a third believed that Western Europe would be more vulnerable to Soviet or Warsaw Pact conventional forces, and fewer than 30 percent believed that Soviet troops were in Eastern Europe for purposes of domination or intimidation of Western Europe.

Neither in Europe nor in the United States was support for the INF treaty accompanied by a large degree of trust in the Soviet Union. In the four European publics sampled, majorities believed that the Soviets would comply with the agreement, but in the United States mistrust was much higher, with only 23 percent believing the Soviets would comply and 61 percent believing they would cheat. Majorities in Europe, however, also believed that NATO should not continue to remove its INF systems if it found that the Soviets were cheating on the treaty.

Unsurprisingly, Europeans were more skeptical of U.S. intentions than were Americans. Roughly one-third of the Europeans did not

---

[45] The European data are based on USIA surveys conducted in September 1987 in Britain, France, the Federal Republic, and Italy. The U.S. data are reported in *The Washington Post*, Janaury 31, 1988, p. A4.

believe the Americans would comply, and about a quarter of the latter held this view. Finally, the Americans overwhelmingly believed (by a 66 to 20 percent margin) that Reagan was more interested in arms control, and the Europeans were more evenly divided. In both West Germany and Britain, pluralities believed the Soviet Union was making greater efforts in arms control than the United States.

Initial reaction to the INF agreement indicated a broad transatlantic consensus of support but also some important divisions between governing elites, many of whom have decoupling and denuclearization concerns, and publics who do not share these anxieties. In addition, the gap between nuclear and nonnuclear Europe is apparent in responses to questions on the future role of nuclear weapons in Western strategy.

Overall on the nuclear question, the Western publics appear to be divided but tend to support the idea of nuclear deterrence if not nuclear defense. Their concerns are eased by an ongoing East-West dialogue and are revived during periods of confrontation. A reduction of what may be viewed as war-fighting nuclear weapons would be favored, as would the retention and modernization of longer range deterrent systems. Public concerns are not so intense that majorities are willing to spend more on conventional defense as an alternative to nuclear deterrence. The American deterrent continues to be viewed as essential by most Europeans to their security. Although public support for the nuclear element has eroded, it is inaccurate to refer to its demise, and the political benefits of antinuclearism have clear limits.

IMPLICATIONS FOR NATO IN THE 1990s

This brief look at the public's views of the alliance as it enters the 1990s offers a portrait of a relationship whose fundamentals remain sound and resilient after almost four decades. The public has emerged from seven years of debate, protest, and shifts in strategic thinking with a renewed appreciation for the importance of the alliance.

On both sides of the Atlantic, solid majorities continue to see U.S. and West European interests as compatible. Public support for the alliance is probably higher than it has ever been, and neutralism remains confined to a minority. Support for the U.S. defense commitment and the deployment of U.S. troops remains high as well.

The gap that opened up between Americans and Europeans in the first half of the decade on how to deal with the Soviets had substantially narrowed by 1987. Although perception of the Soviets as a threat has receded, it has not disappeared and no one wishes to cancel the insurance policy. The Gorbachev phenomenon remains (at least at the start of 1988) largely a personal one that has not led to a public euphoria about the Soviet Union or its policies.

The fundamentals of the relationship remain sound, but portents of change and possibly fissure are also discernible. Several elements of public and elite opinion show signs of erosion. Manifestations of change can be seen in the decline of European confidence in U.S. leadership and policy as well as in some erosion in public confidence in the U.S. defense commitment to Europe. The growing tendency to view both superpowers as threats to peace and as similar in their foreign policy behavior appears to be new.

What makes these trends more significant is that the better educated portions of European opinion appear to be the most likely to hold critical views of the United States and of NATO strategy. In the first two decades of NATO, the better educated and higher socioeconomic groups were the most proalliance and supportive of close ties to the United States.

Similar trends can be seen regarding party opinion. Party affiliation seems to be the most important factor in explaining public attitudes on foreign and security policy in Europe. This trend is due to the relatively low interest in foreign affairs of the general public and a consequential tendency to follow the cues of elites in this policy area.

With the notable exception of France, left and right are further apart in their views of the American connection and of strategy, especially concerning the role of nuclear weapons in that strategy, than they have been since the 1950s. This divergence has resulted in the shattering or straining of the security consensus in Britain, the Low Countries, parts of Scandinavia, and West Germany.

Although these strains are real, we should remember that Socialist or Social Democratic parties tend to be more radical in opposition and moderate their positions once in government. The Socialist parties in power, largely in the south, would probably have more antinuclear positions if they were in opposition.[46] Clearly the antinuclear strains go deeper within the northern European left. If a new consensus does not emerge, the fragmentation of public opinion on fundamentals could follow.

The impact of these trends is less perceptible in elections. Given the relatively low priority the Western voter gives to foreign and defense issues at the polls, elections continue to be decided largely on economic and social issues. Britain is perhaps the major exception; the elections of 1983 and 1987 were influenced by the perception that Labour was not credible on security policy. This lack of credibility on foreign and defense policies prevented Labour from convincing the

---

[46] See Subcommittee on Europe and the Middle East, Committee on Foreign Affairs, U.S. House of Representatives, "Challenges to NATO's Consensus: West European Attitudes and U.S. Policy," *Report* (Washington, D.C.: Government Printing Office, May 1987), p. 25.

electorate of its ability to govern and to defend British national interests.[47]

However, in the elections held in those same years in the Federal Republic, studies of voting found little evidence that foreign and defense issues played a significant role.[48] In France the overarching consensus on defense among the major parties limits the electoral potential of these issues.[49] In the Netherlands, the Lubbers government was reelected in 1987 in spite of the unpopularity of its position on the INF deployment, and in Belgium the internal linguistic division and economic issues continue to overshadow defense concerns.

In Italy, the parties on the left supported NATO membership as a means of enhancing their nationalist credentials, and the nature of coalition governments tends to diffuse security policy as an electoral issue. Similarly, in Spain the left has come to support a Spanish role in NATO as a means of Europeanizing the country as well, playing on nationalist sentiments.

The tendencies in American opinion have moved in the opposite direction from those in Europe, with the best-educated portions of the public being the most supportive of the alliance and the U.S. commitment to Europe. The major question regarding American opinion concerns its intensity, and signs suggest that this has declined among younger American elites. While some generational differences appear in Europe, especially in Italy and West Germany, there are no signs of any generational or partisan break in the United States on issues relating to Europe and the alliance.

On both sides of the Atlantic, generational change is bringing a less emotional, perhaps more realistic, skeptical, and limited assessment of the relationship. The Europeanism of the Monnets and Adenauers has been replaced by a more businesslike attitude, and no generation of "Wise Men" in the United States is committed to shaping an Atlantic community. This skeptical approach is most pronounced in those countries where the idealization of a new beginning and of the American connection was greatest, especially in West Germany, and in France the image of the alliance and of the United States has improved from traditionally lower levels.

Another important fissure seems to be developing between the public and governing security elites in Europe. The negative elite reaction among conservatives in Britain and West Germany and among Socialists and conservatives in France to Reykjavik and double

---

[47] See NAA, "The Alliance and Public Opinion," pp. 16–19.
[48] See for example, Forschungsgruppe Wahlen Mannheim, *Bundestagswahl 1987* (Mannheim, mimeograph, January 28, 1987), as well as their study, *Bundestagswahl 1983*.
[49] NAA, "The Alliance and Public Opinion," p. 22.

zero and the fears of denuclearization that were raised find little resonance among the public. Public support for arms control and any reductions in nuclear forces is widespread, and this gap opens up possibilities for Soviet public diplomacy to increase the distance between elites and public. Similar possibilities also exist to exploit differences between nuclear and nonnuclear Europe. Comments made by Foreign Minister Schevardnadze in raising the third zero option for shorter-range nuclear weapons during his visit to Bonn in January 1988 are an example of an attempt to exploit these gaps.

The disquiet over the future of Western strategy is another area of possible change. Both American and European opinion remain uneasy over reliance on nuclear weapons and especially with first use and foreign control of nuclear systems. Yet the public shows little recognition of a conventional defense problem and little willingness to pay more to enhance conventional defense. This extends to attitudes toward NATO itself; although support for the alliance is broad, willingness to spend more for defense to strengthen it is weak.

The alliance should consider writing a new Harmel Report in order to reach a consensus on where NATO should go in terms of its strategy and arms control policies. A new consensus is needed not only to explain the alliance posture to Western publics but also in order to limit the Soviet ability to play upon divisions within the alliance.

Public diplomacy will be a high priority in post-INF Europe. Public opinion will be monitored, and attempts will be made to manipulate it. It will be one of a number of factors that will shape the future of the alliance. A number of guidelines may be worth considering in shaping a public diplomacy strategy for the alliance.

First, the tendency toward more European political and defense cooperation that emerged from the 1980s, although largely an elite trend, will find public support as long as it is viewed as an adjustment of the alliance and not a substitute for it. Little public demand exists for a major and rapid restructuring of the alliance, but a gradual devolution or enhanced Europeanization of NATO will find a generally positive response among American publics and elites. The irritations of dependency lie behind much of the erosion that can be seen in European attitudes toward the United States and the alliance.

As a consequence of the enhancement of the European pillar, European governments will have to coordinate their public postures and argue for NATO programs. More of the explaining and arguing should be taken on by the European allies. A high priority should be given to educating the public on the state of the conventional balance in Europe, with one possibility being a NATO European effort to publish an official survey on the military balance. Conferences with journalists and defense specialists should be organized to discuss issues related to the conventional balance and arms control.

NATO's public opinion research capabilities and public information efforts should be expanded and greater national coordination of information efforts encouraged. An annual security survey should be commissioned by the North Atlantic Assembly in order to monitor public opinion on key alliance questions, with the aim of identifying areas for future educational emphasis. Special efforts must continue to involve younger elites and attentive publics in NATO programs and conferences. A NATO Washington office similar to that of the European Community would be a valuable means of providing speakers and information for the American public and generally giving the alliance a higher profile in the United States.

These and other initiatives should be part of a renewed recognition of the importance of public opinion to the future of alliance cohesion and evolution.

IV

Challenges and Opportunities

8

Defense Burdensharing: European and Canadian Contributions to NATO's Defenses

By DAVID GREENWOOD

In the 1990s, for 15 of NATO's 16 nations—the West European members of the alliance and Canada—the security agenda will be dominated by two issues: how to deal with their superpower adversary and how to deal with their superpower ally.

The first is a contentious matter even now, as in both popular and professional evaluations the perception of Mikhail Gorbachev's Soviet Union accords less and less with the stereotype of the implacable opponent. As time goes by, the second is becoming more and more problematical too, because of increased American questioning of the scale and priority—and, in some quarters, even the principle—of the U.S. commitment to its Atlantic affiliation.

This American disenchantment reflects the facts that the allies have been seriously at odds over a variety of policy matters in the 1980s: the conduct of trade relations with the Eastern bloc (e.g., the gas pipeline affair); the management of the bilateral arms control process (e.g., the surprises of the Reykjavik summit in 1986); how best to handle security problems arising outside the NATO area (from southwest Asia to Central America); and how best to tackle terrorism (in Libya and Lebanon, for example). The allies have even had sharp differences over fundamental alliance concerns: the merits of President Reagan's Strategic Defense Initiative, especially its implications for extended deterrence, and the wisdom of promulgating a new maritime strategy and prescribing revisions to tactical doctrine for the defense of northwest Europe. In fact, dissonance and dissent have almost become the norm in translantic dealings. Small wonder, then, that American sentiment ranges from exasperation to indignation, especially among those who take the uncomplicated view that, in return for the considerable and crucial contribution the United States makes to its allies' security, those allies owe Washington an obligation of across-the-board support if not uncritical compliance.

Yet discord about policy is not the heart of the matter. What most infuriates Congress, the media, and the public at large in the United States is not ambiguous or qualified approval of American behavior, the frequent absence of such endorsement, or even the occasional condemnation of American action. Rather, the irritation arises from the fact that the dissident voices come from partners who, although seemingly pleased to accept the U.S. protection and patronage, politely decline to pay what Americans regard as an appropriate proportion of the costs of the common defense.

In short, the focal tension in intra-alliance affairs is the perennial burdensharing question and specifically the widespread perception in the United States that West Europeans and Canadians quite simply do not contribute enough to NATO. Nor is this just a judgment on the present-day condition. Clearly, if the tension persists—and, more important, if it grows as the United States grapples with burgeoning trade, payments, and budgetary problems—this augurs ill for the alliance's prospects in the 1990s. What NATO's members must do in the forthcoming decade is concentrate attention and energy on managing relations with the East, not arguing among themselves.

Plain yearning for an end to family squabbles counts for nothing, though, and supposing that burdensharing disputes will quietly subside is idle thinking. What, then, can the alliance do? The answer is threefold: first, look critically at the bases of existing judgments on "fair shares" and recognize the dubious reasoning that underlies so many of them; second, consider alternative measures of members' contributions to the joint defense—especially measures based not on the value of resource inputs to military effort narrowly defined but on the real output produced by different states' all-around security provision—and ascribe greater weight to these, if crude cross-national comparisons must be made; and third, acknowledge the existence of more efficient means of transforming inputs into outputs than those which NATO now uses and that exploiting these—to get a more effective defense for our taxpayers' money—is a more constructive aspiration for the 1990s than pursuit of an elusive equity.

BURDENSHARING CONCEPTS AND CRITERIA

To take up the first of these themes, how sound are the measures that underlie most burdensharing judgments, especially comparisons of the alliance contributions of the United States on the one hand and its allies (non-U.S. NATO) on the other?

The main characteristic of these measures is that they rest on the presumption that equality of sacrifice is important in any joint security arrangement. This reflects a view of alliance defense as an international collective good, from which individual nations benefit as individual citizens do from collective (or public) provision in a single country. Just as citizens pay taxes, which are burdensome, so states pay dues for their defense by committing resources to military purposes on their own account, and that payment, likewise, is a burden (in the sense that the resource commitment means that other worthwhile things must be forgone).

The parallel with domestic public finance explains the basic assumption made about equity in alliance burdensharing. What is appropriate here is what is appropriate where personal direct taxation is concerned: dependence on ability to pay. On this criterion, sacrifice in proportion to wealth and income seems intuitively fair. In fact, it is not. At least no advanced economy in the West has adopted the (equi-) *proportional* model for its domestic tax regime. The arrangements favored are, instead, *progressive*. Successively larger slices of the individual's incremental (marginal) income are claimed for the revenue. The average tax take thus rises progressively with increasing ability to pay. The better-off pay not just absolutely more than the less well-to-do (as under an "equal proportions" system) but proportionately more—progressively—in line with their capacity to contribute.

Applying this reasoning in the alliance burdensharing context, the simplest and most frequently cited indicator of defense burden—the percentage of each nation's gross domestic product (GDP) allotted to defense (D)—is an inadequate, if not perverse, measure of sacrifice. Certainly the proposition that a high D/GDP proportion denotes an inordinately onerous burden (and vice versa) is erroneous. So, too, is the contention that "fairness" requires an exact equalization of D/GDP proportions.

Within NATO, though, much burdensharing disputation has been carried on in just these terms. In particular, American spokespersons—in the administration and in Congress—have regularly used data on D/GDP proportions as a rod with which to beat their West European and Canadian partners. The point of departure is numbers such as those in Table 8.1. The argument is, typically, that such figures "speak for themselves." The U.S. allies are manifestly "not pulling their weight!" For reasons apparent from the table, Greece and the United Kingdom may be spared sharp castigation. Conversely, Canada, Denmark, Italy, and Spain are often singled out for special condemnation.

TABLE 8.1 *Burdensharing: Measurement of Sacrifice (A) 1985*

Country	D/GDP Proportion (in percent)
Belgium	3.0
Canada	2.2
Denmark	2.2
France	4.1
Germany	3.2
Greece	7.1
Italy	2.7
Luxembourg	1.1
Netherlands	3.1
Norway	3.3
Portugal	3.1
Spain	2.7
Turkey	4.5
United Kingdom	5.3
Non-U.S. NATO average	3.5
United States	6.7
NATO average	5.4

Source: Congress of the United States, Congressional Budget Office, *Alliance Burdensharing: A Review of the Data*, Staff Working Paper, June 1987.

The underlying assumption in such argument—sometimes explicitly stated, sometimes not—is that equal, or more nearly equal, proportions would be "fair," and the typical conclusion is that what is required, therefore, is the raising of allies' D/GDP ratios to the U.S. level. In fact the figures bear false witness and offer no basis for inferring which countries are or are not "pulling their weight." The assumption is mistaken, and the conclusion is absurd. Certainly in domestic public finance no one would say that, in the name of equity, the proportion of income taken in taxes from every worker should be equated with that levied on the wealthiest in the land.

Still, the argument *is* voiced, often by people who should know better. For instance, in June 1987 then Assistant Secretary of Defense Richard Perle told the North Atlantic Assembly's Military Committee that D/GDP proportions must be *the* benchmark for burdensharing calculations: "Everything else," he added, "is special pleading." The slick throwaway line was, of course, particularly pernicious nonsense. A moment's reflection shows that it is a total misrepresentation. In fact, what exclusive attention to D/GDP proportions does is to load the equity argument in favor of the United States.

The Pentagon official's assertion is also curious because until very recently the Department of Defense did not so scathingly dismiss the progressive approach to assessment of international "taxable capacity."

Indeed, in *Allied Contributions to the Common Defense*, its annual submission to Congress, it regularly presented a so-called prosperity index for each NATO member (and Japan); and this measure was commended in the 1981 report as "the most comprehensive and the most equitable indicator of ability to contribute" (p. 13), precisely because of its approximation to "a graduated income tax on nations" (p. 15).

The prosperity index (*PI*) represented, in the words of the 1986 report, a means of "taking economic development and standard of living into account in assessing fair shares of the defense burden" based on the premise that "the collective interest of the Free World is best served if the relatively more prosperous nations . . . carry a proportionately larger share of the collective military burden, thereby allowing relatively less prosperous nations to concentrate their limited resources . . . on basic domestic problems" (p. 23).

The prosperity index was calculated by (1) multiplying (i.e., weighting) each nation's share of the aggregate GDP of NATO members plus Japan by that country's per capita GDP (a reasonable gauge of relative prosperity); and (2) "normalizing" the resulting products so that they totalled 100 percent. The resulting value for each nation signifies the country's share of the overall "taxable capacity" of the collectivity (that being, in these computations, the United States, non-U.S. NATO, and Japan). These values are not without interest in their own right. They highlight the huge disparities in economic strength among the NATO nations, notably the towering stature of the United States. For burdensharing assessments, however, what is significant is that an individual country's share of "taxable capacity" can be compared with that particular nation's share of the total defense expenditure of the group, the ratio between the two proportions providing a direct and graphic indication as to whether a country is oversubscribing or undersubscribing militarily.

The idea sounds complicated but is simplicity itself, however, as examination of data from two recent Pentagon reports on allied contributions will make clear.

The numbers are in Table 8.2. They come from the 1983 and 1986 submissions to Congress. In this tabulation column 1 of each "year panel" records national shares of the aggregate military spending of NATO members plus Japan. National shares of the overall "taxable capacity" of these countries—as given by the prosperity index computation—are recorded in column 2 for 1983 and 1986. The ratio between the proportions—set out in column 3 of each panel—is a pure "measure of merit" for each country or group of countries. The closer the ratio is to 1.0 (unity), the nearer the country is to the norm that represents equality of sacrifice assessed in a progressive fashion.

TABLE 8.2. *Burdensharing: Management of Sacrifice (B)*

Country	1983 Report			1986 Report		
	(1) Defense Spending Share (percent)	(2) Prosperity Index (percent)	(3) Col. (1) divided by Col. (2)	(1) Defense Spending Share (percent)	(2) Prosperity Index (percent)	(3) Col. (1) divided by Col. (2)
Belgium	1.22	1.30	0.94	0.71	0.64	1.11
Canada	2.03	4.39	0.46	2.20	4.82	0.46
Denmark	0.52	0.88	0.59	0.37	0.64	0.57
France	8.56	8.14	1.05	5.89	4.78	1.23
W. Germany	8.31	10.26	0.81	5.87	6.74	0.87
Greece	0.93	0.19	4.90	0.70	0.12	5.68
Italy	3.12	2.91	1.07	2.73	2.34	1.17
Luxembourg	0.02	0.05	0.32	0.01	0.03	0.36
Netherlands	1.63	1.88	0.87	1.16	1.15	1.01
Norway	0.59	1.08	0.55	0.45	0.79	0.57
Portugal	0.30	0.07	4.06	0.18	0.04	4.56
Spain				1.36	0.74	1.84
Turkey	1.08	0.10	11.02	0.64	0.06	11.42
UK	9.50	5.98	1.59	6.82	3.50	1.95
US	58.39	48.98	1.19	67.49	61.19	1.10
Japan	3.80	13.79	0.28	3.41	12.42	0.27
Non-U.S. NATO	37.81	37.23	1.02	29.10	26.39	1.10
Non-U.S. NATO and Japan	41.61	51.02	0.82	32.51	38.81	0.84
NATO total	96.20	86.21	1.12	96.59	87.58	1.10
Total (NATO and Japan)	100.00	100.00	1.00	100.00	100.00	1.00

Source: Compiled from data in *Report on Allied Contributions to The Common Defense* (DoD, March 1983 and March 1986).

The perspective on burdensharing provided by this presentation is very different from that gained by inspecting the D/GDP proportions of Table 8.1. Consider the summary figures at the foot of the table, for example. In each year panel the non-U.S. NATO ratio is greater than unity, that is, above the norm, most clearly so in 1986. That is to say, in the mid-1980s the United States' Atlantic alliance partners taken together were shouldering at least their "fair share" of the common defense burden on this more legitimate reckoning.[1]

Consider, too, the values for individual countries. The defense efforts of the alliance's least economically advanced members—Greece, Portugal, Turkey, Spain—are here seen clearly for what they are: disproportionately burdensome exertions for these still-developing societies of the southern tier. That of the United Kingdom is seen for what *it* is: a commitment of resources to defense that would not disgrace an economy twice as strong. Italy, France, Belgium, and the Netherlands are not shamed by their showing. Discounting tiny Luxembourg—and Iceland, which is omitted from all these calcualtions because it fields no armed forces—leaves only four apparently freeloading NATO members (Canada, Norway, Demark, and the Federal Republic); and each of those, as later argument will show, has an explanation for modest financial sacrifice that—*pace* Mr. Perle—cannot be dismissed as special pleading.

This analysis has a curious footnote. The latest figures in Table 8.2 are those from the 1986 report on allied contributions because, despite having lauded defense-spending prosperity index share ratios as the soundest basis for burdensharing assessment until 1986, the Department of Defense (DoD) presented no such calculations in its 1987 submission to Congress. DoD neither explained this lapse or change of practice, nor invited attention to it. One wonders whether the sums, duly done, revealed the United States itself to be falling below the norm of military effort commensurate with economic stature.

---

[1] I say "at least" and not "more than" advisedly. Following the practice in the *Allied Contributions* documents, the data in Table 8.2 lump NATO members and Japan together. Thus in 1986 non-U.S. NATO countries bore "more than" their fair share of the *NATO and Japan* defense burden, that being the meaning of the ratio of 1.10 in column 3. However, because the U.S. column 3 ratio for the year is 1.10 also, for the *inter-alliance* comparison that is of interest "at least" is the most that can be claimed. Note also that, as in all previous *Allied Contributions* volumes, the calculations in the 1983 and 1986 reports were based on data about defense budgets, GDP, and the like of two years earlier. Thus the 1986 report panel of Table 8.2 actually portrays the position in 1984, hence my formulation "in the mid-1980s."

In any case, the Major Findings section of the 1987 report (pp. 10-11) contains the clear overall judgment that "the non U.S.-NATO allies as a group are shouldering roughly their fair share of the NATO and Japan defense burden." Moreover, it concedes that virtually all the other ratios computed by the DoD concerning specific resource contributions in relation to ability to contribute show that these same partners' ratios "are in the vicinity of, or exceed, 1.0" (i.e., the norm of equal sacrifice).[2]

These are the conclusions of the most comprehensive, thorough, and technically proficient analysis of burdensharing regularly conducted in the West. The results (and methods) of the Pentagon's exercise have, moreover, been scrutinized by the independent Congressional Budget Office, which said of the 1987 report just cited that it "draws reasonable and fair conclusions" (Staff Working Paper, June 1987, p. 1). Why then the persistent misperception, especially but not exclusively among Americans, that the United States does too much for NATO while Western Europe and Canada contribute too little? Why is the myth of inequitable sacrifice so robust?

Of the two reasons, one is a product of the last decade, and the other is much more fundamental. Fortunately, NATO can do something about them both.

Opportunities for misinformation about who bears how much of the defense burden have multiplied in recent years because the alliance has itself encouraged attention not to equality of *overall* sacrifice—which is what all the discussion here thus far has been about—but to equality of *incremental* sacrifice. That was the effect of the NATO members' decision in 1977-78 to aim for three percent real increases in defense spending annually, that is, equiproportionate increments of endeavor, regardless of individual nations' economic or other circumstances. At the time the initiative made some sense. It signaled solidarity and resolution to the adversary, not unimportant in the later 1970s. Also, it gave defense ministers useful ammunition—an alliance "obligation"—for their permanent struggle with parsimonious treasury ministries. It was, however, a dangerous hostage to fortune that gave nations a new yardstick with which to beat each other, which is exactly what they have done for the last ten years.

Yet the pledge has no foundation in equity, and fulfillment or nonfulfillment has nothing to do with burdensharing proper. In

---

[2] The single exception—the message of Table 8.1 restated—is son of shares of aggregate (NATO and Japan) defense spending on the one hand and shares of aggregated GDPs (unweighted) on the other. On this indicator the non-U.S. NATO countries score just 0.74, but then—as the report points out—"the non-U.S. NATO per capita GDP average is less than half the U.S. figure."

terms of the domestic finance analogy of earlier pages, no government or legislature would think itself fair to demand of every taxpayer a set percentage more each year regardless of whether his or her income had risen, fallen, or remained the same, and regardless of his or her domestic circumstances. But NATO did the equivalent of that in 1977–78 and, admittedly with decreasing emphasis, the 3 percent target has been featured in the resource guidance accepted by member nations ever since.

TABLE 8.3 *Burdensharing: Measurement of Incremental Sacrifice; Real Increase in Defense Spending (Percentage change from previous year)*

	1979	1980	1981	1982	1983	1984	1985	Annual Average 1975–85	Forecast 1986
Belgium	2.2	1.9	0.9	-0.1	-0.4	-1.3	-1.7	0.2	2.0
Canada	-0.9	5.1	3.1	4.5	8.0	7.2	2.4	4.2	3.7
Denmark	0.2	0.7	0.6	-0.3	0.8	-1.1	0.9	0.3	2.8
France	2.5	3.7	3.9	1.3	1.8	-0.2	-0.2	1.8	0.7
Germany	1.8	2.3	3.2	-0.7	0.8	-0.4	0.3	1.0	0.1
Greece	-2.9	-9.4	22.8	-1.1	-7.9	17.1	0.7	2.1	-5.2
Italy	2.6	4.9	-0.5	3.1	2.5	2.8	3.0	2.6	1.8
Luxembourg	3.5	16.3	4.3	0.2	3.4	0.5	-1.5	3.7	9.5
Netherlands	4.2	-2.1	4.2	2.2	0.5	3.2	0.2	1.7	3.4
Norway	1.9	1.8	2.7	4.1	4.0	-4.6	15.2	3.4	-4.9
Portugal	2.9	6.0	1.2	0.6	-3.1	-4.6	-0.3	0.3	5.2
Spain	n.a.	n.a.	1.8	3.5	2.1	2.6	2.5	2.5	3.0
Turkey	2.6	2.0	1.8	4.6	-4.4	-1.3	8.5	1.9	13.0
United Kingdom	3.0	2.8	1.4	6.0	0.4	4.0	-0.2	2.5	0.2
United States	3.4	4.9	4.6	7.0	7.9	4.7	7.8	5.7	6.5
Non-U.S. NATO Average	2.2	2.6	2.8	2.5	1.3	2.0	1.0	2.0	0.9
Total NATO	3.1	4.0	4.0	5.5	5.8	3.9	5.8	4.6	5.0

Source: Congress of the United States, Congressional Budget Office, *Alliance Burdensharing: A Review of the Data*, Staff Working Paper, June 1987.

Predictably, few allies have consistently met the target, as the figures in Table 8.3 make clear. The United States has done so, real growth in military spending having been a high priority for both the Carter administration in its later years and the Reagan administration until its final years. So have Canada and Norway, two of the alliance's four "freeloaders," according to overall burdensharing criteria. The West Europeans generally have not, as their American critics have repeatedly pointed out. What was conceived as a unifying gesture—the shared commitment to spend more—has thus become divisive. Lacking as it did a basis in equity, that was bound to happen.

What of the second and more fundamental reason for persistent misinformation and misunderstanding about NATO contributions and the associated economic sacrifice? In alliance affairs as in other contexts, perpetrating and perpetuating myth and misperception suits some people, those whose convictions are chronically refractory to objective evidence. What makes things easy for such people (and institutions) is the fact that they can select the statistics that support their prejudices—unweighted D/GDP proportions like those in Table 8.1, the low or negative percentages of Table 8.3—and write their own rules for the "numbers game as to the relative contribution of each ally" (Senator Sam Nunn's expression). In this sport, of course, self-justification is the cardinal rule and team spirit is unheard of.

Putting an end to this game will not be easy. The prime requirements are to improve the supply, and strengthen the standing, of "objective evidence" and to enunciate some standard rules relating to its use. Ideally, the NATO bureaucracy in Brussels should undertake, as an alliance exercise, the audit of national contributions to the joint defense. The work done by the DoD for Congress is a model (provided "the most comprehensive and . . . most equitable indicator of ability to contribute" is reinstated). At the same time, the North Atlantic Council should frame guidelines for interpretation of the data so collected. The gain would be dual. Outlawing blatantly self-serving arguments would bring to an end NATO's long-running orgy of mutual recrimination. Legitimizing truly comprehensive and equitable burdensharing tests would give much-needed authority to any necessary censure of reprobate or delinquent allies.

ALTERNATIVE MEASURES

An alliance-wide consensus on the calculation and interpretation of financial burdensharing measures would not, however, eliminate all controversy concerning the evaluation of different countries' contributions and the meaning of comparisons among them. Scope for argument would remain on several matters.

The Norwegians and Danes might contend, with some justification, that because of their total defense approaches to security provision their military budgets understate the true scale of their national commitment of resources to defense. The West Germans might make a similar claim because they have borne much expense in providing facilities for other countries' stationed forces (over $20 billion worth of land and buildings, for instance). The Canadians, for their part, could point out that, because of their country's size and population distribution, they must devote to certain civil public programs larger shares of their GDP than most of their allies are required to do.

Exclusive reliance on nations' defense expenditures as the means of gauging their NATO contribution also has a general and fundamental drawback: budgeted funds may or may not be used efficiently. Thus a nation might increase its outlays in one year quite spectacularly, without any augmentation in its real contribution to the alliance in terms of manpower and fighting formations fielded or equipment improved and modernized.

All these arguments lead in the same direction. NATO contributions cannot be looked at wholly in terms of countries' resource inputs, equity should not be construed solely in terms of equality of sacrifice. There is an obvious case for recognizing the relevance—the superiority even—of alternative judgments based on the security *outputs* and on equity construed as equality of *effort* in relation to circumstances.

In fact such considerations are already featured in the burdensharing discourse, and not just in the guise of special pleading. Two examples must suffice. First, when Senator Nunn sought, in 1984, to make the maintenance of United States' troop levels in Europe conditional on extra West European effort, he chose to define the "conditions" principally not as some absolute or proportional increment in money spent (inputs) but as fulfillment of certain specific enhancements of combat effectiveness (outputs). This prescription was shrewd and sensible, and it worked. Second, in its now long-running campaign to counter the stubborn American perception of feckless allies who do not pull their own weight, the Eurogroup—comprising all NATO's West European members except France (and Iceland)—has consistently emphasized not how much Europeans spend but how much they contribute to the alliance's order of battle. Its publications stress, among other things, that of the allied forces stationed in Europe in peacetime—upon whom would fall the task of providing the initial resistance to any sudden attack—the Europeans provide 90 percent of the manpower, 95 percent of the artillery, 85 percent of the tanks, and 80 percent of the combat aircraft.

Should outputs enter the reckoning even more? Surely they should, if only because of the very diversity that characterizes the Atlantic fraternity. What is so easily lost sight of when the focus is on the minutiae of financial burdensharing is that *all* NATO members make an important contribution to the alliance, that each member's contribution is a distinctive contribution, and that each is in its own way an indispensable contribution. Examination of outputs reveals this in a way that preoccupation with inputs cannot do.

That national contributions vary as they do in nature, scope, and scale is hardly surprising. After all, each is the product of a unique interplay of economic, environmental, geographical, historical, political, social, strategic, and psychological determinants. Even the three countries of apparently comparable stature and circumstances—France, the Federal Republic, and the United Kingdom—have major triangular asymmetries: France and the Federal Republic have conscript forces, the United Kingdom does not; France and the United Kingdom possess significant nuclear capabilities (strategic and tactical) and maintain forces for out-of-area contingencies, the Federal Republic does not; the troops of the Federal Republic and the United Kingdom take their places in the layer cake of corps dispositions along the inner German border, those of France do not. That is the position with respect to three medium powers that are more alike than most. When comparison extends to embrace the other allies, the diversity is considerably more complex.

Because allies' contributions are so disparate, evaluating them according to a simple common denominator is certain to be misleading. On top of that, almost all of them incorporate nonquantifiable elements. These can be enumerated and described, but they defy measurement and frustrate the facile comparison.

The message here is a general one, but directed particularly at the American critics of West European and Canadian contributions: judge allies not only by how much they pay but also by what they do (the Nunn technique), and, from time to time, look behind and beyond the customary burdensharing indicators and note the substance of what partners subscribe to the alliance's defenses (the Eurogroup approach).

So far as individual force subscriptions are concerned, what the West Europeans and Canadians do—the "substance"—is well summarized in numerous reputable publications. The International Institute for Strategic Studies' annual compilation, *The Military Balance*, is one. The Mönch Publishing Group's impressive *World Defense Almanac* is another. What inspection of such detailed information conveys most strikingly is that the image of the inveterate freeloader that several countries have acquired is invariably a mistaken impression.

Take the case of Canada. Despite the constraints on their resources—the country has half the population but forty times the territory of the United Kingdom, for example—the Canadians will enter the 1990s committed to three-ocean maritime deployments (including the provision of an all-important presence in the high Arctic), comprehensive surveillance and protection of their crucial national airspace (including a new North Warning System and upgraded facilities for AWACS planes and interceptors), plus a consolidated and enhanced contribution of both in-place formations and reinforcements to NATO's order of battle in the Allied Command Europe (ACE) area. In addition—and this is something that even the force structure facts do not reveal—Canada generously provides test and training facilities for others, including the United States, the United Kingdom, and the Federal Republic. These are all valuable "outputs," some of them uniquely so. The alliance would be ill-advised to underestimate their worth.

Like Canada, NATO's Scandinavian members have also attracted the freeloader tag, not without justification according to the testimony of Table 8.2. Regarding Norway, though, one must acknowledge that the demands of small population and extensive territory arise as in the Canadian case. One must also respect the Norwegians' long-standing insistence that, sharing as they do a common border with the Soviet Union (and near one of the superpower's biggest concentrations of naval and military facilities at that), prudence dictates that security policy should combine deterrence with reassurance that Norway itself poses no threat to its eastern neighbor. Against that background and taking account of the country's philosophy of total defenses already mentioned, Norway's military outputs are not to be disparaged.

As for Denmark, no country has been chastised more often for unwillingness to pay its way. Critics should pause, however, to reflect on the circumstances in which the Danes joined NATO in the first place. The Danish government of the day was coaxed into membership by use of the argument that Denmark's strategic location, commanding the Baltic approaches and forming the northern flank of NATO's central front, was a priceless asset. Without it, the argument ran, defense of the North Atlantic and the security of northwest Europe could not be assured. Thus, however much or little Denmark may have paid for its defenses since 1949, in a real sense the alliance as a whole has been the beneficiary. However adequate or inadequate the Danish military effort may be judged, if the country were to defect to nonalignment, NATO would unquestionably be the loser.

A territorial contribution must also be counted as part of the Federal Republic's dues to NATO. This contribution is not just the battlefield, though it is certainly that. It is also the airspace and land for half-a-dozen nations' training and exercises, plus all the "maneuver damage" and "environmental pollution" associated with them. The extent of this imposition is not widely appreciated. The Germans accommodate 5,000 military exercises a year and 600,000 military aircraft sorties (many at low level), in an area the size of Oregon. Subsidies to Berlin and practical host nation support for allies' stationed troops and reinforcements are other German outputs that must be added to the country's provision of the active and reserve forces that are NATO's backbone on the central front. Taking a broad view of contributions to security, the military help that Bonn gives to

Portugal, Greece, and Turkey should be included in the reckoning too.

West Germans themselves would add that, in addition to this aid burden, they bear a disproportionate share of the burden of risk associated with the NATO–Warsaw Pact confrontation in Europe, and a singular risk of nuclear devastation if deterrence were to fail. This is a more contentious proposition. On the one hand, the facts of geography make the Federal Republic the first line of alliance defense in the event of war on the European continent, with all that this implies. On the other hand, which NATO member is making the greatest sacrifice in terms of additional vulnerability assumed because of alliance membership cannot be objectively determined; countries like the United Kingdom and the United States—especially the United States—have obviously taken on nuclear risks they would not necessarily face without NATO.

The essential point is that each alternative perspective—output and input, effort and sacrifice—is illuminating. The thesis here is not that the one should somehow supersede the other. It is that for a fully rounded picture and a true and fair representation of the burden borne or contribution made by each ally, the one must be used to complement the other.

Certain conclusions arise naturally from the foregoing analysis. Intra-alliance relations in the 1990s would greatly improve if a way could be found to stop the persistent infighting about the comparative sacrifice involved in defense provision and especially the strident transatlantic rhetoric that goes with it. To this end, NATO itself should marshal objective evidence on nations' spending and ability to spend (using comprehensive and equitable indicators) and should monitor allies' performance according to these measures. At the same time who pays what (and how much it hurts) should not be the be-all and end-all in comparative evaluation of security provision. Who contributes what in real terms (and how much it matters to the alliance) ought to have a place in such assessment too.

Needless to say, none of this would put an end to debate and dispute about burdensharing and equity in alliance arrangements, but less scope would be available for spurious and self-serving argument. The allies might also recognize that NATO has strength in diversity and that each member's subscription has a singular and special value.

BEYOND BURDENSHARING

The way might then be clear for both North Americans and Europeans to tackle the big intra-alliance challenge of the next decade: to work out who can best contribute what to the security of the Atlantic community and to plan the evolution of national force subscriptions on the basis of a rational division of labor (between Europe and North America and among the European states themselves).

That this is the big future challenge ought to be self-evident. NATO has a solid consensus on the need to maintain, modernize, and, if possible, strengthen the alliance's nonnuclear capabilities, pending progress in conventional arms control. The allies have broad agreement on the desirability of reducing dependence on nuclear weapons, without rendering the fabric of deterrence threadbare by premature denuclearization. However, NATO members are not planning big increases in their allocations of resources to defense. A few (Canada for example) have long-term programs based on modest real growth. Most will be content to hold their expenditures, expressed at constant prices, to around the present level (taking one year with another). Some (e.g., the United Kingdom) are projecting what amount to reductions in their defense budgets after inflation. In these circumstances, the only way nations can get the conventional force improvements that they want (together with such essential nuclear modernization as they may eventually decide upon) is by making more efficient use of the resources they devote to military purposes.

Economies produced by "good housekeeping"—diligent searching for better value for money throughout defense organizations—can help in this regard. But economies can only alleviate the problem; they cannot solve it. Measures to manage weapons research, development, and production more effectively have a part to play, too. Much effort is going into the promotion of cooperation bilaterally and multilaterally in both the transatlantic and intra-European contexts. Here also, however, the budgetary savings that can be expected have limits, not least because the rising real cost of military equipment erodes the efficiency benefits yielded by collaboration.

The alliance must look to the distribution of tasks among its members and to remedying the fundamental inefficiency that exists because each member seeks to maintain a broad spectrum of national military capabilities. In short, NATO must contemplate some measure of role specialization, an intra-alliance division of labor, in the performance of roles and missions based on the comparative advantage(s) of different countries in different forms of defense provision.

In recent years, reputable analysts on both sides of the Atlantic have examined options and prospects for such specialization: Steven Canby in the United States and Peter Volten in the Netherlands spring to mind. Particular opportunities for worthwhile marginal change have been identified. The considerable benefits that might be achieved by a series of such force-structure adjustments—each based on nations concentrating on what they do best—have also been demonstrated. The practicalities have not been ignored: how the required "adjustments" might be arranged, by transforming NATO's present joint-programming procedures into a genuine collective planning process, has received attention, too.

This chapter is not the place for a detailed account of division of labor possibilities, but a brief review of selected options is in order.

In the maritime domain, for instance, the U.S. Navy and the Royal Navy—perhaps with Canadian help—ought to be able to provide an ASW capability in the eastern Atlantic sufficient to allow the smaller European navies to concentrate on shallow-water and sheltered-water missions. If efficiency is the goal, the commitment of resources by Belgium, the Netherlands, West Germany, and Denmark to small, disproportionately costly numbers of oceangoing escorts and long-range maritime patrol aircraft is manifestly ill-advised. What these countries should do and can do well—and what only they can do—is provide short-range maritime surveillance and presence in the eastern Channel, the southern North Sea, and the Baltic, plus a good mine-warfare capability and—in the case of the Danes and the Germans—many missile-armed, fast attack craft, which are the most effective surface units in the confined waters of the Baltic and its approaches.

So far as tactical air capabilities are concerned, a similar argument holds. Many European countries, in striving to sustain all-purpose air arms, are fighting a losing battle. Yet several hundred combat aircraft in the U.S. inventory (navy, air force, and air national guard) do not have a NATO wartime commitment. Clearly, a big payoff might result from greater use of the American assets, given appropriate investment in reception and protection facilities at British and continental airfields, and some rundown of West European air forces, which over time would release resources for, say, additional ground troops.

A further source of extra manpower for land warfare would be the more effective mobilization and employment of West European nations' reservists. Almost all continental countries have an untapped potential for taking up recently released conscripts and embodying them in strong field force formations. Among other things, that would allow some of the best regular troops, now required to fulfill covering-force tasks as part of the cordon defense of the central front, to be reconstituted as the mobile operational reserve for counterpenetration, counterattack, and the telling counterstroke, which are what NATO so badly needs to strengthen its conventional defenses.

One could add to these illustrations of opportunities for worthwhile marginal change; obviously, if a number of such options could be pursued simultaneously, substantial benefits in the more efficient use of resources might accrue.

Equally obviously, this is the way the alliance should go, because it offers governments a possible escape—perhaps the only escape—from the dilemma of rising defense demands and static or shrinking budgets. Presumably that is why role specialization is coming back onto NATO's political agenda.

CONCLUSION

We have thus the prospect of a new and more productive emphasis in alliance deliberations: not on who pays what, not even on who contributes what, but on who can *best* contribute what. This new emphasis is to be wholly welcomed. Among other things, it would set new terms for the debate on comparative evaluation of national force contributions, including the assessment of the U.S. defense effort vis-à-vis those of its West European and Canadian allies. Discussion would be not about how to share the burden more equitably, but about how to divide the labor most efficiently.

9

Measuring U.S. Contributions to NATO Defense

By LAWRENCE KORB

In a recent essay, Zbigniew Brzezinski, President Carter's national security advisor, argued that "374 million (West) Europeans with an aggregate economy of $3.5 trillion—faced with an opponent with 275 million people and a GNP of only $1.9 trillion—should not need to depend as they do on 241 million Americans with a $4.3 trillion economy."[1] The clear implication of Brzezinski's argument is that the United States is carrying too great a burden in NATO, yet nowhere does Brzezinski say what that burden costs.

An accurate estimate of the annual U.S. contribution to North Atlantic Treaty Organization (NATO) defenses is difficult to present. The yearly figure varies significantly, depending upon how one defines "U.S. contributions." For example, should such an estimate include only those U.S. troops actually deployed in Europe, or should it include also the U.S.-based forces that are designated for NATO's defense? How does one account for arguments that the U.S. contribution to NATO cannot be separated from our own security interests? An extreme example of this claim would be that the U.S. contribution to NATO is the entire $300 billion U.S. defense budget because "North America is part of NATO's line of defense." The extreme low estimate would be the $2 billion "incremental operating costs incurred by stationing forces in Europe rather than in the United States."[2]

---

[1] Zbigniew Brzezinski, "Reagan's INF Treaty Moves Us Toward a New Europe," *Washington Post,* September 27, 1987, pp. D-1-2.

[2] David C. Morrison, "Sharing NATO's Burden," *National Journal,* May 1987, p. 1398; and Alice C. Maroni and John J. Ulrich, "The U.S. Commitment to Europe's Defense, A Review of Cost Issues and Estimates," Congressional Research Service, November 1985, pp. 10-11.

Unfortunately, as Brzezinski's article demonstrates, these discussions are not merely semantic. Political leaders on both sides of the aisle and on both sides of the Atlantic use a wide range of estimates to buttress arguments for or against the U.S. role in NATO. Moreover, in light of the debate about the conventional balance in Europe that is certain to follow the ratification of the INF treaty, these arguments are likely to become more intense.

Estimates of the U.S. contribution to NATO can be expressed either absolutely or relatively. On an absolute basis, one can measure the dollar value of the U.S. contribution to NATO; on a relative basis, that contribution can be evaluated against some standard that measures a nation's ability to allocate funds to defense. Absolute costs can be measured in four ways: direct, indirect, proportional, and as a percentage of the defense budget. Relative costs are usually measured against a nation's gross national product (GNP).

The direct costs of the U.S. contribution to NATO may include only the incremental cost of stationing U.S. troops in Europe; it could also combine that cost with the total cost of maintaining these European-deployed U.S. forces in the active force structure. The direct U.S. contribution can also be viewed as the total cost of European-based troops plus the U.S.-based troops that would be sent to Europe early in a conflict. Troops that would be sent to Europe later in a prolonged conflict can also be included in direct costs.

The "Defense Planning Questionnaire" (DPQ), which all military members of NATO submit annually, provides one estimate of the U.S. direct and indirect contributions. The direct costs are defined as those of the European-based troops plus pledged reinforcements. The DPQ includes, in addition to the direct costs of the combat forces, an allocated share of the costs of new equipment, a proportionate share of U.S.-based training and logistical support, research, development, test and evaluation, and Department of Defense (DoD) administration.[3]

The proportional method for examining the U.S. contribution divides the defense budget into four separate force categories: forces rapidly available to NATO, multipurpose forces, forces for other contingencies, and unallocated costs. The U.S. NATO contribution may be calculated by costing out the first two categories. The defense budget can also be divided on a regional basis, with the U.S. NATO commitment being defined as its "European commitment." U.S. contributions to NATO on an absolute basis can be analyzed by employing each of these methodologies.

Accordingly, the total cost of the U.S. contribution to NATO defenses in FY 1988 can be viewed as ranging from about $60 billion to

---

[3] Maroni and Ulrich, pp. 10–11.

approximately $195 billion.[4] The $60 billion estimate includes only the cost of U.S. troops based in Europe; it rises to about $100 billion when one includes the U.S.-based troops that would be sent to Europe within 15 days of mobilization.[5] If one also includes the U.S. force that would be sent to Europe 15 days after the actual outbreak of a conflict, the figure goes up to $140 billion. If the cost of U.S. forces is based on the listing in the DPQ (troops in Europe, plus early and late reinforcements based in the United States and their indirect costs), the estimate for annual U.S. contributions would be $158 billion.[6] Finally, if one includes all the troops (not just those included in the formal DPQ estimate) that could be sent to Europe during a prolonged conflict, the contribution goes up to $195 billion. These costs are summarized in Table 9.1.

TABLE 9.1 *Cost of U.S. Contribution to NATO in FY 1988*

Definition of U.S. Contribution	Cost
Incremental cost of U.S. troops based in Europe	$60 billion
Cost of U.S. troops based in the United States that would be sent to Europe within 15 days of mobilization	$100 billion
Cost of U.S. troops based in Europe plus early reinforcements and U.S. forces that would be sent to Europe 15 days after the beginning of the conflict	$140 billion
DPQ	$158 billion
All planned troops including troops not formally mentioned in the DPQ	$195 billion

A fourth means of examining the absolute contributions of the United States to NATO defenses is to assess the contribution as a percentage of the total U.S. defense budget. Most analysts agree the United States spends between 40 percent and 60 percent of its total annual defense budget on NATO defense, depending upon the assumptions used about the length of a European conflict. This range has remained constant during this decade. Based on the DPQ estimate, in 1980 52 percent of the total annual defense budget went to NATO,

---

[4] The DoD stopped submitting unclassified cost estimates of the U.S. commitment to NATO several years ago because it felt that the public was misusing them. David C. Morrison, "Sharing NATO's Burden," p. 1398. This chapter has taken then DoD's unclassified earlier figures as quoted in Maroni and Ulrich, "U.S. Commitment," pp. 1-11, and has put them in FY 1988 dollars.

[5] DoD, June 1984 for FY 1985, as quoted in Maroni and Ulrich, "U.S. Commitment," pp. 10-11.

[6] DoD, $115 estimate for 1982, $113 estimate for FY 1983, as quoted in ibid.

in both 1981 and 1982, 54 percent, and in 1983 52 percent.[7] My DPQ estimate for FY 1988 would be about 52 percent.

A discussion of the cost to the United States incurred by the maintenance of troops in Europe rather than in the United States is pertinent to any analysis of the cost of the absolute U.S. contribution to European defense. In May 1987 the Congressional Budget Office estimated that if 100,000 U.S. troops were withdrawn from Europe and demobilized, $4.6 billion in savings would result. However, if forces were withdrawn from Europe but remained on active duty in the United States, the United States would spend $5 billion (per 100,000 troops) building new facilities for them in addition to a $1 billion expenditure for their actual relocation. Although DoD has an excess of base facilities in the United States, not many of these are suitable for the 100,000 combat and combat-support troops that could be redeployed to Europe. For example, an army division could not be relocated from Europe to one of the excess shipyards in the United States.

If a conflict in Europe required a return of all the U.S. forces, the cost of training and preparations for redeployment would reach $12 billion. As Deputy Assistant Secretary of Defense for European and NATO Policy John J. Maresca asserts, "The idea that there would be economies is false. . . . There's no question that (withdrawals) would not save you money."[8] Table 9.2 summarizes the savings and costs of a few options for withdrawing troops from Europe.

Table 9.2 *Savings and Costs of Withdrawing U.S. Troops from Europe*

Option	Savings	One-time costs
Withdrawal and demobilization of 100,000 from Europe	$4.6 billion annually	$670 million
Withdrawal of 100,000 but remaining on active duty[a]	$540 million annually	$5 billion (bases) $1 billion (relocation)
Equipped and trained for possible redeployment to Europe in a crisis		$12 billion

[a]no prepositioning

---

[7] Ibid., p. 1.
[8] Morrison, "Sharing NATO's Burden," p. 1378.

Although some people focus on absolute measure of U.S. contributions to NATO, many others concentrate on relative measures. One frequently used relative measure is defense spending per capita. Table 9.3 lists the per capita defense expenditures of the NATO nations. By this index, the United States ranks far above its major allies, spending almost $1,100 per American citizen on defense. As is indicated in Table 9.3, this is more than double that of any other NATO nation and about four times greater than the average contribution for the rest of NATO. Moreover, no non-U.S. NATO nation spends more than $450 per capita on defense, and two nations, Portugal and Turkey, actually spend less than $100 per capita on defense.

A similar picture emerges if one compares the percent of GNP that each member of the alliance spends on defense. Currently the United States spends in excess of 6 percent of its GNP on defense, the rest of the alliance allocates only about 3 percent to defense, and no other nation allocates even 5 percent.

TABLE 9.3 *Per Capita Defense Spending in FY 1985 Dollars*

Country	Amount
Turkey	47
Portugal	64
Luxembourg	104
Spain	124
Italy	170
Greece	234
Belgium	242
Denmark	246
Netherlands	268
Canada	298
Germany	327
France	377
United Kingdom	420
Norway	433
United States	1,079
Non-U.S. NATO	255
Total NATO	564

TWO DECADES OF CONTROVERSY

Absolute and relative indications appear to suggest that the United States is spending a disproportionate share of its national wealth on alliance defense. Over the past 20 years, focusing on these indications has led many public officials in the United States to call for a more equitable sharing of the burden.

The 1967 offset payment conflict between the United States and the Federal Republic of Germany shows this cycle clearly. In 1967 West Germany felt that its economy was not strong enough to continue making offset payments to the United States. At the same time the United States was concerned about its large balance of payments deficit, coupled with huge defense expenditures for Vietnam.[9] Great Britain too was concerned about its own deficit. In 1967 and 1968 both the United States and Great Britain withdrew troops from Europe (Britain withdrew 6,000; the United States withdrew 35,000) as part of their agreement with West Germany. The withdrawal reportedly saved the United States about $100 million a year.[10] A further withdrawal of about 20,000 between 1967 and 1969 saved the United States another $75 million annually.[11]

In 1970 the United States announced its "total force" plan, whereby the troop reductions that had taken place in the late 1960s would become permanent. At this time the idea of "dual basing" was emphasized to reassure West Germany that the United States was not in the process of lessening its support to the NATO alliance. *Dual basing*, developed as part of the flexible-response strategy, meant that troops in the United States were designated in the DPQ to be deployed rapidly to Europe in the event of a conflict.

During the early 1970s, the conflict over the stationing of U.S. forces abroad continued. Former Senator Mike Mansfield repeatedly pushed for the withdrawal of U.S. troops. In 1973, the U.S. Congress passed the Jackson-Nunn Amendment stating that a number of U.S. troops would be withdrawn if the American balance-of-payment deficit was not covered by the allies.

In 1974, West Germany agreed to its eighth and final offset payment agreement, which the United States had sought in part to help deal with continuing balance-of-payments deficits. An element distinguishing this agreement from those before it was a provision for German purchase of civilian rather than purely military goods. The next year Germany also promised to contribute more to the NATO defense improvement program instead of being party to a new offset agreement.[12]

---

[9] Daniel J. Nelson, *A History of U.S. Military Forces in Germany* (Boulder, Colo.: Westview Press, 1987), p. 78.

[10] Morrison, "Sharing NATO's Burden," p. 1394.

[11] Nelson, *A History*, p. 96. These estimated savings do not take into account any potential redeployment costs.

[12] Ibid., pp. 135–138.

The West German acceptance of greater responsibility encouraged the United States to increase its combat strength in Europe in 1976. The Nunn-Bartlett initiatives promoted the idea of a strengthened U.S. commitment to European-based conventional forces. Two combat brigades were returned to Europe as part of a new strategy to move American troops closer to the East European border.

In 1980, the cycle of U.S. demands, then threats, followed by concessions on the part of West Germany began again. The Stoessel Demarche (named for U.S. Ambassador to West Germany Walter Stoessel) began with the United States outlining its plan for storage of additional U.S. weapons in West Germany and for the relocation of U.S. troops closer to the border with Eastern Europe. The United States insisted that West Germany help with payment for these strategic changes. The West German response was negative. In view of their efforts to reduce their own budget deficit, the Germans saw the request for contributions to a new project as unreasonable. West Germany did in April 1982 accede to the U.S. position on a Wartime Host Support Treaty, under which the West Germans would provide support to U.S. forces in the areas of transportation, supply, airfield repair, logistics, and security of U.S. army facilities in addition to those German troops who would already be on active duty. The investment costs of the treaty were approximately $570 million. These costs in addition to all operating expenses were to be shared equitably by the United States and the Federal Republic.[13]

At the same time, Senator Ted Stevens attempted to revive efforts to cut U.S. forces in Europe. Senator Stevens sought a reduction of approximately 20,000 in the number of troops the Reagan administration intended to station in Western Europe in FY 1983. In October 1982 the measure was approved by the Senate Subcommittee on Defense Appropriations, which Senator Stevens then chaired. As passed by the Congress in December, however, the measure was modified to limit U.S. troops on shore in Europe to the September 1982 level of 315,600.[14]

In 1984 Senator Nunn proposed, in the form of an amendment to the FY 1985 defense authorization bill, that the United States withdraw 90,000 troops from Europe unless the Europeans made specific improvements in their defense posture. His amendment was not successful. Senator Nunn nonetheless continued to press for more allied defense efforts, as well as U.S. improvements in conventional

---

[13] Ibid., pp. 186–187.
[14] Stanley R. Sloan, "Defense Burdensharing: U.S. Relations with NATO Allies and Japan," *Congressional Research Service Report for Congress*, June 24, 1988, p. 16.

forces. The chairman of the Senate Armed Services Committee argued
"that the future of the U.S. troop withdrawal issue in NATO depends
on the perception that we are all equally committed to a credible
conventional defense in accordance with NATO's declared strategy.
That was the measuring stick when I introduced my amendment in
1984 and it remains the measuring stick today."[15]

Although no congressional initiative has so far succeeded in forcing
a withdrawal of troops from Europe, the Congress in recent years has
kept a ceiling on U.S. troops deployed there, most recently set at just
over 326,000. The DoD asserts that the current limit on troop strength
in Europe is an artificial subceiling within the overall ceiling on
service and strengths. Defense officials argue that this subceiling
distorts the process of allocating available manpower to meet the
threat and confuses the general debate about how much is enough for
defense.

No "correct" number for U.S. troop strength in Europe can be
determined. There is no exact level below which Europe is hopelessly
vulnerable, nor is there a level above which it is completely secure. As
Table 9.4 indicates, over the past thirty years the level of U.S. troops in
Europe has ranged from a high of 427,000 to a low of 291,000.

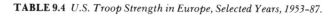

TABLE 9.4 *U.S. Troop Strength in Europe, Selected Years, 1953–87.*

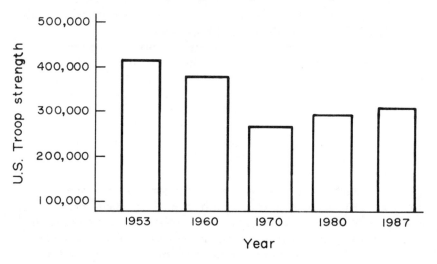

---

[15] Senator Sam Nunn, "NATO Challenges and Opportunities: A Three-Track Aproach,"
speech to the DMS Symposium on Industrial Cooperation within NATO, April 13, 1987.

THE CURRENT SITUATION: A U.S. PERSPECTIVE

The current pressures in the United States to reduce defense expenditures will inevitably influence U.S. policy in Europe in some way. Exactly how remains a contentious issue. Real reductions in the level of defense exenditures have occurred over the past three years. Since FY 1985, defense expenditures have declined by 10 percent in real terms. More importantly, as indicated in Table 9.5, the FY 1986–90 defense plan has already been reduced by about 28 percent, or $550 billion. The FY 1989 defense budget alone is about $150 billion less than the level projected in early 1985.

TABLE 9.5 *Trends in Department of Defense Five-Year Plans (Budget Authority in Billions of Dollars)*

	FY 1986	FY 1987	FY 1988	FY 1989	FY 1990	Total 1986–90
Administration Request February 1985	$314	354	402	439	478	$1,986
Administration Request February 1986	$278	312	332	354	375	$1,651 (−335)
Administration Request January 1987	$281	285	303	323	344	$1,536 (−450)
Administration Request February 1988	$281	279	283	291	307	$1,441 (−545)

Because of the urgent need to reduce the federal deficit, defense spending is very unlikely to increase in the near future. If anything, it will continue to decline in real terms. Defense planners will have to adjust their programs accordingly. Some leaders see partial troop reductions as an attractive means of offsetting reduced defense spending, arguing that the United States already contributes more than its fair share to NATO. They also feel that an excessive American contribution causes the allies to lose incentive to increase their own efforts.

Other leaders see a U.S. troop withdrawal from Europe as beneficial for additional reasons. Some, like former Secretary of the Navy

John Lehman, assert that the U.S. economic interests are in the Pacific,[16] or, like Representative Patricia Schroeder, that a war in Europe is a most unlikely scenario. Henry Kissinger advocates a partial troop reduction with the argument that U.S. and European interests are no longer necessarily concurrent. Zbigniew Brzezinski wants 100,000 of the European troops to be earmarked for southwest Asia.[17]

In the last two years, some members of the House of Representatives have begun to link the U.S. trade deficit with its allies to the issue of NATO burdensharing. The European Economic Community is the largest trading partner of the United States. Some members of Congress feel that the United States should not make such a large contribution to the NATO alliance while carrying a $115 billion annual trade deficit with its military allies. In 1986 the U.S. trade imbalance with the NATO allies accounted for 44 percent or $50 billion of the overall U.S. trade deficit. Recognizing the concerns of Congress, Secretary of State Shultz called on our NATO allies to spur growth to attract American imports.[18]

Several House members supported troop reduction bills when discussing defense funding for FY 1988. Representatives Judd Gregg and John Bryant both advocated troop reductions if the allies did not increase their contributions. Representative Bryant introduced a resolution in April 1987 to prescribe an end-strength level of U.S. forces assigned to permanent duty in NATO countries and Japan and to provide for the reduction of U.S. forces in the countries under certain circumstances.[19] The initiatives were dropped, however, with the understanding that the burdensharing issue would be examined in detail in the future. A House Concurrent Resolution was then introduced in June 1987 to express the sense of Congress that the United States should enter into negotiations with countries that participate in a common defense alliance with the United States for the purpose of a more equitable apportionment of the burden of financial support for the alliance.[20]

In 1988, two proposed amendments to the FY 1989 defense authorization bill that would have linked U.S. troop levels in Europe to allied defense spending were overwhelmingly defeated on the House

[16] Benjamin F. Schemmer, "An Exclusive AFJ Interview with Phillip A. Karber," *Armed Forces Journal* (June 1987): 132.

[17] Morrison, "Sharing NATO's Burden," p. 1394.

[18] Elaine Sciolino, "Shultz Asks NATO to Raise Spending on Non Atom Arms," *New York Times*, December 13, 1987, p. 1.

[19] House Resolution 2231, April 30, 1987.

[20] House Concurrent Resolution 139, June 11, 1987.

floor.[21] Demonstrating the continuing congressional intent to promote shifts in defense burdens, however, the Defense Appropriations Subcommittee of the Senate Committee on Appropriations approved a substantial package of proposals and limitations designed to shift a number of defense expenditures from the United States to the European allies and Japan. The package, part of the proposed FY 1989 defense appropriations bill, called for the president to appoint a special burdensharing negotiator to lobby with the allies for increased defense efforts.[22]

Some Mitigating Factors

Although the United States does account for a large share of defense spending by NATO countries, a 69.85 percent,[23] some mitigating factors are not often noted in the current debate. West Germany, under the wartime Host Nation Support Treaty, has financial responsibilities that make a considerable contribution to NATO defenses. Most allied countries have host nation support arrangements with the United States for both peacetime and wartime. The arrangements vary, but they are a valuable contribution to burdensharing as they reduce requirements for U.S. combat service support forces, facilities, and supplies. Many of the host nations, particularly in central Europe, assist U.S. troops on their bases with rent-free or reduced-price real estate, including family housing, real property maintenance, facility improvements, utilities and other base-operating support, the use of test and training ranges, air traffic control, navigation aids, and the like at joint-use airfields and comparable services at other joint installations. West Germany alone provides free some 40,000 military installations and training areas for the use of U.S. and other allied forces. The host nation support agreements are even more extensive for wartime. Most of the different agreements provide for various services from lines-of-communication agreements to medical treatment.[24]

West Germany also has defense responsibilities for West Berlin. Its expenses in this area are not included in the estimates of its contribution to NATO, even though alliance doctrine is that the

---

[21] Tom Kenworthy, "House Defeats Proposals on Allies' Defense Spending," *Washington Post*, April 30, 1988, p. 8.

[22] Debra Polsky, "Senate Presses for Research Delay until Allies Agree to Share Costs," *Defense News*, June 27, 1988, p. 3.

[23] Caspar Weinberger, "Department of Defense, Report on Allied Contributions to the Common Defense" (Washington, D.C.: Government Printing Office, 1987), p. 7.

[24] Ibid., pp. 49-52. (See also Richard Burt, "The Allies' Fair Share of Defense," *Washington Post*, October 8, 1987, p. A-23.)

defense of West Berlin is a NATO commitment. If the funds West Germany spends in West Berlin (over $5.4 billion per annum) were included in its NATO total, Bonn's officially documented burden-sharing level would increase substantially.[25]

A look at NATO's commonly funded programs shows increasing allied efforts in recent years. Although the total U.S. defense expenditures continue to exceed those of all other NATO countries combined, U.S. contributions to all the common funded programs (i.e., infrastructure, military budget, and civil budget) now average less than 30 percent.

The infrastructure program in particular has been a vehicle for producing greater allied contributions to Western defense. The infrastructure program finances the capital costs of commonly funded military facilities and communications and/or electronic systems for wartime common use, for joint use by two or more countries, or by NATO-committed forces of one country. Although funding for a six-year period 1985–90 was increased to more than double the funding agreed in the previous five-year program, the share of these costs born by the United States has decreased from 43 percent originally to just over 27 percent today. U.S. troops are the beneficiaries of projects costing a significantly greater percentage of the total budget.[26]

Another indication that the allied contribution to NATO is not as small as it seems is the relative rise in their defense budgets over time. Between 1970 and 1986 the allies increased their defense spending in real terms by 35 percent while U.S. real defense spending increased by only 19 percent. As a result, the non-U.S. portion of total NATO defense expenditure has risen from 23 to 30 percent.

Moreover, there was a real decrease, both monetarily and military, in the U.S. contribution to NATO during the 1970s, with American troop levels dropping as low as 291,000. The substantial increases in U.S. defense expenditure in the early 1980s can be seen as an attempt to make up for the reduction in the ten years that President Reagan called the "decade of neglect." Cumulative real U.S. defense spending for the early 1970s through the mid-1980s was approximately what it would have been if U.S. defense spending had declined by a uniform annual rate of roughly 1 to 2 percent each year during that period.[27] Allied defense expenditures rose in the 1970s and slowed down in the 1980s, thus making the present differences appear larger than they in fact are.

---

[25] Ibid., p. 95.
[26] Ibid., pp. 2, 16, 41.
[27] Ibid., p. 37.

Between 1971 and 1985, U.S. manpower levels decreased by 17 percent, lowering its share of the NATO total from 45 percent to 37 percent. Allied manpower levels increased by 14.5 percent over this same period and now account for 63 percent of NATO active duty forces. If reserves are included in the totals for military and civilian staffing, then the allies account for 64 percent (7.9 million people) of the NATO total; the United States has 5.1 million people included in this category. When examining staffing levels as a percentage of the population, the non-U.S. level of 1.2 percent of their populations is very close to the U.S. level of 1.4 percent of its population.[28]

In addition, allied armies are based on conscription rather than on a volunteer program. Thus, their manpower costs are less, which lowers their overall defense-spending levels. The NATO allies field more division-equivalent firepower (a measure of effectiveness of ground forces based on the quantity and quality of their major weapons) and tactical combat aircraft in relation to their economic strength than does the United States. The allies supply 60 percent of division-equivalent firepower for the alliance, and the United States supplies only 40 percent. In addition, the holdings of all of the non-U.S. nations combined exceed those of the United States by 20 percent for tanks and by 108 percent for artillery.[29]

The allied powers supply only 34 percent of naval tonnage for NATO; the United States supplies the other 66 percent. Though the United States seems to bear the largest part of the naval burden, several allied countries are in the process of modernizing their navies. In terms of air force tactical combat aircraft, the United States provides about 47 percent with the allies providing 53 percent.[30] These allied contributions are summarized in Table 9.6.

Moreover, U.S. security is inextricably linked to the defense of Europe. U.S. defense strategy is to contain the Soviets through the use of deterrence and, if deterrence fails, to limit the resulting conflict. This strategy requires the forward deployment of U.S. troops and the maintenance of sufficient conventional forces to lower the risk of nuclear escalation.[31] Senator Nunn has pointed out that if NATO cannot fight and fight well with conventional forces for its own 30-day declared goal, we do not have a flexible response capability to match

---

[28] Ibid., p. 4.
[29] Ibid., pp. 4, 31.
[30] Ibid., p. 35.
[31] Barry R. Posen and Stephen van Evera, "Defense Policy and the Reagan Administration," *Conventional Forces and American Foreign Policy*, p. 25.

TABLE 9.6 *Allied Contributions*

Overall NATO Spending Share	Common-Funded Programs	Staffing (Military and Civilian)	Division-Equivalent Firepower
30 percent of NATO total	70 percent of NATO total	64 percent of NATO total	60 percent of NATO total
$101.3 billion (1985) $110.0 billion (1988 dollars)			

Naval Tonnage	Air Force	Special Contributions	
33 percent of NATO total	51 percent of NATO total	Host nation support agreement Defense of West Berlin	

our strategy, and U.S. forces serve primarily a psychological role rather than a conventional military role.[32]

Without a strong U.S. military presence in Europe, NATO's strategy of deterrence would lack credibility. Neither Great Britain with its continuing economic difficulties, West Germany with its shrinking manpower base, France with its emphasis on its own nuclear capability, nor the smaller NATO nations would be able to increase their national defense efforts sufficiently to fill the vacuum left by a large U.S. withdrawal.

Despite statements by some prominent public figures questioning the current U.S. role in NATO, most U.S. citizens are in favor of a strong commitment to the alliance. A recent poll conducted by the Chicago Council on Foreign Relations found that 70 percent of the respondents favor current or an even greater degree of military commitment to NATO.[33] The American public does not seem to believe that the U.S. trade deficit justifies altering the U.S. commitment to NATO.

Although the House of Representatives has debated U.S. troop withdrawals in 1987 and 1988, most members of Congress continue to support a strong U.S. contribution to NATO. In January of 1987, Representative Charles Bennett introduced House Resolution 15 as the sense of the Congress that the United States should place greater emphasis on the improvements of the capabilities of the U.S. conventional forces, particularly in cooperation with other member

---

[32] Senator Sam Nunn, "NATO Challenges and Opportunities," speech.
[33] Morrison, "Sharing NATO's Burden," p. 1498.

nations of NATO.[34] The one amendment dealing with burdensharing to pass in the first session of the 100th Congress was one by Representative Bill Richardson forbidding reductions in U.S. troops stationed in Europe during FY 1988.[35] Although Representative Richardson underlined the importance of deficit and burdensharing issues, he also wanted to reassure NATO allies that the United States will not abandon them.

The issue of U.S. contributions to NATO defenses will receive increased emphasis in the future due to the INF Treaty between the United States and the Soviet Union. The treaty has raised concerns among some West European military and political leaders that they would be left facing a far superior Soviet conventional force.[36] Although NATO Secretary General Lord Carrington admitted that the Warsaw Pact might gain an edge during the three years in which the intermediate-range missiles were being dismantled,[37] he also claimed that the tangible manifestation of the American commitment to the defense of Europe is not missiles in Europe, but the presence of some 326,000 troops and their dependents. The outgoing secretary general argued that flesh and blood count for more than abstract deterrent concepts.[38]

In spite of the defense budget constraints facing the United States, Defense Secretary Carlucci has declared that, although the U.S. armed services are being required to reduce military forces, these reductions will not diminish the 326,000 troops that are currently in Europe. He asserts that the strategy of forward deployment must be maintained and that it can be sustained only by keeping U.S. troops in Europe.[39] Nevertheless, the reduced U.S. defense budget cannot help but affect the NATO alliance. The United States can no longer afford to increase its defense budget as it did in the first part of the decade. Unfortunately, U.S. defense-spending constraints come at a time of fiscal austerity for most NATO countries as well.

---

[34] House Resolution 15, January 1987.

[35] Morrison, "Sharing NATO's Burden," p. 1397.

[36] Serge Schmemann, "A Cautious Europe Cheers U.S.–Soviet Moves on Arms," *New York Times*, September 20, 1987, p. 6.

[37] Ibid.

[38] Karen DeYoung, "NATO Official Warns against 'Euphoria' over Missiles Pact," *New York Times*, September 18, 1987, p. 20.

[39] John Cushman, "NATO Seeks New Strategies in Era of Shrinking Budgets," *New York Times*, December 1, 1987, p. 7.

To deal with this situation, Carlucci "has suggested that NATO use innovative approaches to stretching declining defense funds."[40] So-called low-cost or no-cost approaches include the use of natural barriers to deflect a Warsaw Pact attack. Barrier defenses could include mine fields or trenches. Although some forms of barriers might enhance NATO's defensive capabilities, the idea has been opposed in the past for political reasons, including a fear that a Europe behind superficially secure barriers would be perceived as not needing American troops or that these barriers would signify a degree of permanence in the separation of the Germanies. Others see such barriers as throwbacks to the tragic Maginot Line strategy.

Using conventional arms control to reduce the conventional imbalance has been seen by some as another way out of the defense-spending dilemma. The United States apparently will seek to limit Warsaw Pact and NATO tanks and artillery pieces at or around the present NATO levels in new "conventional stability talks." This would require substantial Warsaw Pact reductions. Mr. Gorbachev has promised to consider such an alternative when it is presented,[41] but an outcome to these difficult negotiations may be some way down the road.

A CONTINUING DEBATE

The appropriate U.S. role in NATO is sure to be a subject of continuing and intense debate on both sides of the Atlantic. Whether one uses absolute or relative measures, U.S. contributions to NATO are substantial; so too are those of our allies.

Understanding the complex assumptions that underlie those calculations of costs is important to the public debate on the issue. Ignoring the complexity of the assumptions leads more to dema-goguery than debating. Given the current U.S. budget deficit, the American trade imbalance, and the INF agreement, that debate is bound to intensify.

However, whether their costs are too much or too little depends not only on financial calculations but on broader judgments about our national interests and the appropriate strategies to protect those interests. Ignoring these important factors can make policy-making more of an accounting than a strategic exercise. For the best interests of the United States and its Western allies, this must not be allowed to happen.

---

[40] Molly Moore, "INF Treaty Raises Apprehensions within NATO," *Washington Post,* December 5, 1987, p. A-10.

[41] 41 Michael Gordon, "U.S. Plan Would Cut Arms in East Bloc to NATO," *New York Times,* December 1, 1987, p. 7.

10

European Defense Cooperation and NATO's Future

By FRANÇOIS HEISBOURG

European defense cooperation can be seen from the perspective of widely differing policy objectives. For analytical purposes, the aims can be defined as being either of a revolutionary character or of a gradual nature. In the first category would be included all plans based on the premise that the breakup of the Atlantic alliance is inevitable and/or desirable and that therefore Western Europe must provide for its defense independently of the United States. Such an analysis need not necessarily posit "Finlandization" (to use an unfortunate but well-understood word) because, in the abstract, one can conceive of, for instance, a West European nuclear force or a militarization of NATO Europe to match the Soviet conventional force structure. Indeed, history provides numerous examples of radical strategic realignments, and therefore caution forces one not to exclude completely the possibility of a dissolution and a replacement of the alliance. However, this consideration makes such an occurrence neither inevitable nor, indeed, desirable.

The following analysis is therefore based on the premise that the existing bases of European security are not, as yet, preordained to fundamental change and that such upheaval is not desirable per se, even if one wished to act on the assumption that the geopolitical status quo in Europe (i.e., division accompanied by protectorate status east of the Iron Curtain) calls for reordering.

An incremental or gradual approach is retained here, with European defense cooperation integrating several more or less converging aims in proportions that depend on time and circumstances. Such cooperation is seen as a supplement and a complement to the existing defense efforts of individual members of the alliance, particularly the United States. Such an addition to NATO's capabilities could result from:

NATO—H

- qualitative improvements in the force structure (interoperability and standardization of European defense material);
- reduced susceptibility to political Finlandization and possibly improved morale in the face of a military crisis (European togetherness, particularly the French-German combination, was a contributing factor, alongside broader alliance solidarity, in ensuring the deployment of the Pershing II and ground-launched cruise missiles in the early 1980s); and
- possibly a greater quantitative defense effort, because a measure of autonomy can lead to willingness by the taxpayer to invest in defense, as demonstrated by the fact that France spends 4.1 percent of its gross national product on defense, the Federal Republic spends 3.3 percent, and Italy but 2.4 percent.

European defense cooperation can also be seen as a precaution vis-à-vis a possible reduction of the U.S. commitment in Western Europe. This is not necessarily synonymous with preparations for a breakup of the Atlantic alliance; rather, the objective would be to fill the gaps left or limiting the damage done in the case of a reduction of the U.S. force presence or, indeed, the elimination of a class of American weapons. Such measures would respond to the same logic as that which is apparently contained in General John Galvin's first public statement as SACEUR: "If the negotiations at Geneva result in agreement on the 'zero-zero' option . . . NATO's strategy of flexible response will still be valid; however, the means to implement NATO strategy will require buttressing. Otherwise, there will be a higher risk than we in the West should accept."[1]

AN OLD DEBATE IN A FLUID CONTEXT

Consideration of European defense cooperation is not particularly new. Plans for a fully integrated European defense community (albeit under an American SACEUR) were first framed in October 1951 (the Pleven Plan) and only narrowly rejected in August 1954. The notion of a European pillar within the alliance was formulated during the Kennedy administration, at time when the United States was beginning to accommodate the consequences of its vulnerability to Soviet nuclear forces and moving from the simplicity of massive reprisals to the subtleties of controlled escalation. Although talk about European defense cooperation has never ceased, no quantum leap has taken place in this area in the past three decades. However, this may

---

[1] Speech by General John R. Galvin at C.E.P.S. Brussels, July 30, 1987 (as published in U.S. Embassy Paris "wireless file").

change with what is possibly the most fluid period in postwar history of East-West relations.

What makes the past few years and months remarkable is that new developments with significant shifts in attitudes and policies have been taking place, in different forms, simultaneously within the two superpowers and concurrently in the West European countries. Such a conjunction has not occurred previously, a period of relative instability within one superpower (e.g., the Khrushchev years or post-Vietnam America) not being accompanied by a similar movement within the other great power.

Perceptions of a Weakening U.S. Commitment in Europe

Several trends appear to be converging in the United States that would, if unchecked, lead to a more or less brutal, more or less disruptive, reduction of the U.S. commitment within the Atlantic alliance. A rapid and necessarily simplified enumeration of these developments would include the following.

Deterrence fatigue is the notion that continuing to rely, inter alia, on nuclear weapons to prevent the outbreak of war between the United States and the Soviet Union is immoral and/or foolhardy. Already apparent in the aftermath of President Reagan's Star Wars speech,[2] the desire to make nuclear weapons "impotent" and "obsolete"[3] has translated itself into the October 1986 proceedings at Reykjavik. The Reykjavik summit, where apparently abstract wishes nearly became the basis of a new Soviet-American relationship, has made a deep impression on West European decision makers.

Global unilateralism is the concept wherein consultations with allies are an unacceptable impediment to the successful use of U.S. military power and U.S. interests in Europe are not of special magnitude. This orientation not only makes light of the lessons of history,[4] but, more basically, ignores the particular economic and military weight of the

---

[2] March 23, 1983.

[3] Remarks by President Reagan on December 21, 1984.

[4] Successful overt U.S. interventions have usually been cooperative and have had wide political support: Korea (U.N. endorsement and command), Santo Domingo (endorsement and participation by the O.A.S. and its member nations), Grenada (involvement of Caribbean countries). The failures are: Vietnam (support limited to the Republic of Korea, Australia, and New Zealand) and Lebanon, where the United States' hasty withdrawal was certainly not incumbent upon the French and Italian allies present there.

West European area, which generates close to a fourth of the global gross economic product and hosts the world's largest concentration of military forces. Global unilateralism presents the danger of uniting strands of sentiment in both the Democratic and Republican parties in the United States. Zbigniew Brzezinski's plan to redeploy forces from Europe to the United States so that they may, against all geographical logic, more easily intervene in the Persian Gulf and Melvin Krauss's book[5] are examples of recent developments in this respect. The Krauss analysis applies market force macroeconomics ("reducing social security will make people work harder") to the particular complexities of international politics ("withdrawing U.S. troops from West Germany will lead the Federal Republic to take the necessary steps to counterbalance the Soviet Union").

Defense budget cuts are forcing reconsideration of U.S. defense priorities. In 1986 and 1987, U.S. defense budget authority fell by a total of around seven percent. If, as seems likely, defense spending were to remain under pressure, the axe might well hit the U.S. force structure in Europe, possibly during the next American administration, when military outlays themselves will begin to decline. This happened to a limited extent at the end of the 1960s, with a reduction of 28,000 slots in the U.S. force posture. The sacrifices could be more painful during the next round.[6]

To these pressures, one must add the constant risk that trade and financial issues will spill over into European-American security relations. Most of these factors are not wholly new, and they have been successfully countered in the past. But their combination can produce drastic measures of the sort that nearly befell the alliance during the Vietnam War with the recurring Mansfield Amendments. Similarly, several of these trends, such as deterrence fatigue, are stronger now than they were previously, and other trends, such as pressure for budget cuts, are likely to be more demanding in the next several years than they were earlier.

The Transformed Modus Operandi of Soviet Security Policy: The Primacy of Political Objectives

More than two years after Mikhail Gorbachev's accession to supremacy in the Soviet Union, many unknowns remain:

---

[5] Melvin Krauss, *How NATO Weakens the West* (New York: Simon and Schuster, 1987).

[6] For a more detailed exposition of the possible effect of budget cuts on U.S. forces in Europe, see: François Heisbourg, "Can the Atlantic Alliance Live out the Century?" *International Affairs* (London), Third Quarter, 1987, pp. 413–23.

- How solidly is he entrenched? Although many signs point to a successful consolidation of power, including the dismissal of Marshal Sokolov and the extensive renewal of the Politburo and the Central Committee, resistance is still indicated at the middle levels of the Party and even higher up.
- To what extent will Gorbachev come to grips with fundamental issues in economic reform (central planning, price-setting policies, collectivization of farms, etc.) and does the Soviet "social compact" face a risk of imploding under the pressure of resulting inflation and unemployment? As yet, Gorbachev has gone down only a fraction of the road that the Chinese have taken since 1978. For the time being, the promises of *glasnost* and *perestroika* have not produced the economic turnaround the Soviet leadership needs to accomplish if the Soviet Union is to retain in the long run its superpower status.

Such uncertainties notwithstanding, Gorbachev is displaying a high degree of creativity and appears to enjoy substantial domestic leeway as far as international security policy is concerned. The traditional objectives of the Soviet Union in this area do not seem to have changed during the past thirty years: the denuclearization of Europe (beginning with the withdrawal of U.S. weapons), U.S.-European strategic decoupling, and opposition to the emergence of a more coherent European identity in defense. The Soviet Union continues to devote an absolute priority to the European theater and the strategic U.S.–Soviet relationship: global unilateralism is not at present Soviet policy, even if Moscow is always ready to further its out-of-area interests. However, the pursuit of these aims has been radically changed in procedural and substantive terms.

The Soviets have put the professionals in charge of international security affairs and particularly the U.S.–Soviet relationship: Anatoly Dobrynin's move to Moscow and the role played by younger diplomats who have a good understanding of Western decision making are witnesses to this situation. Under their influence, the Soviets may have come to grips with the fact that, Irangate notwithstanding, U.S. policy leaders usually mean what they say. Soviet leaders may accept that the more useful course for them is to act on that premise rather than to continue reasoning in the conspiracy theory terms habitual for the Muscovite bureaucracy.

As for content, Gorbachev has turned traditional Brezhnev Soviet security policy on its head. Political considerations are now in the driver's seat, and military considerations are taken into account to the extent that they serve overall security objectives, which have as yet not deeply changed. Acceptance of the elimination of all SS-20s—relatively new "unamortized" weapons—is explicable in this new system of thought. Conversely, under Brezhnev and his immediate successors, military hardware took pride of place, even to the extent of running the risk of a major reverse, such as the deployment of the Pershing IIs, which represented a net improvement for the West. The logical conclusion to be drawn from this state of affairs, compounded by the probable desire of the present Soviet leadership to limit defense spending in favor of civilian investment, is that major conventional force reductions may well be ahead of us, either unilaterally (as under Khrushchev)[7] or, more probably, in the framework of the prospective conventional arms talks. Because force reductions may compel the alliance to rethink its own force structure, including U.S. forces in Europe, interallied consultations are likely; Europeans will feel a need to define their interests within European as well as alliance and national frameworks.

Discussions among the West European allies, alongside alliance debates, may also be called for in order to face the contingency of a more mobile Soviet policy toward the German question. Although the Soviet Union has not clearly shifted its position toward German unity,[8] a middle ground may be found between *Abgrenzung* at its harshest and overt self-determination. The Soviets may attempt to tap the popular sentiment of Germany for closer links between the two halves of that nation. European fora, particularly those dealing with primarily political and economic issues, such as the European Community, or societal issues, including the Council of Europe, have a potential to counter such moves.

Changing Attitudes in Western Europe: New Convergences and Uncertainties

In the absence of a distinct European pillar, the West European countries have been reacting to impetuses originating from their U.S. ally (e.g., SDI, Reykjavik) or from their potential Soviet adversary (the deployment of the SS-20s, for instance) rather than taking a collective proactive attitude.

Nevertheless, internal changes have been occurring that will influence the possibilities of establishing greater European defense cooperation. Some of the following developments constitute such endogenous evolutions that, independent of other factors, should facilitate progress toward a degree of European unity:

---

[7] See Albert Seaton and Joan Seaton, *The Soviet Army* (New York: New American Library, 1987).

[8] Gorbachev's public statements during Federal German President von Weizacker's official visit to the Soviet Union in July 1987 remain in line with previous Soviet declaratory policy on Germany unity.

1. The Europeanization of the United Kingdom is progressively adjusting to the political and strategic consequences of joining the European Community in the 1970s.
2. The normalization of France is reflected in more relaxed political attitudes toward NATO affairs. This easing is largely due to the general acceptance of the existence of the French nuclear force and of France's specific status within the alliance and the realization by France of the intrinsic limits to its own resources and independent power projection capabilities. France also shares with other countries and particularly the United Kingdom an interest in maintaining a broad-gauged defense industry, the long-term survival of which hinges on the creation of a European-wide market base.
3. Italy's potential has risen as its gross national product has surpassed that of the United Kingdom. Although Italian defense expenditures remain low (half of French and British levels), Italy may become a major player on par with the traditional "big three" European countries. Concurrently, Spain's entry into NATO and the European Community adds an important southern European partner to a prospective European pillar balanced between Mediterranean and Nordic countries.
4. The demographics in the Federal Republic of Germany will diminish personnel available for the *Bundeswehr's* standing forces by close to 50 percent between 1986 levels and 1994, assuming existing recruitment criteria. Countervailing measures, such as the extension of conscription from fifteen to eighteen months and more restrictive exemption decisions, will probably not be sufficient to avoid a reduction of on-duty military personnel, possibly affecting the standing frontline force structure itself. Combined with pressure on the U.S. defense spending, this situation may well call for a response from the European NATO partners, particularly in the absence of sufficiently asymmetrical Soviet force cuts.

Apart from these internal trends, events in the United States and the Soviet Union have compelled the Europeans to take a new and harder look at specifically European defense cooperation. Some of these pressures have already been mentioned. The shock waves of two recent occurrences have not yet expended themselves: the Reykjavik "presummit" and the decisionmaking that led to the second zero in the "double zero" on INF and short-range INF (SRINF).

Reykjavik created deep doubts about American reliability, not least in the United Kingdom, whose government had apparently established a trustworthy and confident relationship with the United States. That twenty-five years of joint NATO strategy could have been disregarded by the American partner, with no serious consultation with its allies, was maybe not entirely without precedent,[9] but for the first time this risk was actually on the brink of materializing in a relatively short (ten years) time span. As for the second zero, the damage done in West Germany, particularly within the traditionally pro-American CDU, has been significant. Whether these recent wounds will heal themselves, as others have in the past, without adverse long-term repercussions remains to be seen. For the time being, such are the immediate circumstances under which the European pillar idea has been given an ambiguous boost.

Before examining the construction material and the structure of such a pillar (or pillars), some consideration must be given to the contribution, positive or negative, that the other pillar, the United States, can make. American attitudes will, to a large degree, dictate the rate of growth and the nature of European defense cooperation.

THE ROLE OF U.S. POLICY IN DETERMINING THE EXTENT AND DIRECTION OF EUROPEAN DEFENSE COOPERATION

Three issues come to mind concerning U.S. attitudes and interests:

- The effects of a negative American stance on European defense co-operation
- The manner in which U.S. interests would be affected by the existence of a European pillar or conversely by the prolonged Balkanization of European defense efforts; and
- The possibility that American and European decision-making processes will interact to enhance evolutionary European defense cooperation

The impact of an American rejection of European efforts to coordinate policies alongside the alliance framework would be severe and probably complex. This would be the case not only if such a U.S. policy were of a negative variety ("no European cooperation") or highly qualified support ("European cooperation is all right if it does not deal with military affairs, armaments, arms control, and strategy"). It would also be the case if the United States advocated an "alliance-busting" formula of its own, such as the course advocated by Melvin Krauss,[10] seeing U.S. troop withdrawal as an "encouragement" to greater European defense cooperation, no longer alongside NATO but without NATO.

---

[9] The defense ministers of NATO countries in NATO's integrated command structure meeting in the Nuclear Planning Group in March 1985 were all caught short by President Reagan's Star Wars speech.

[10] Krauss, *How NATO Weakens the West.*

In all these hypotheses, European reactions would vary greatly from country to country, thus enhancing balkanization and weakening further the alliance. Some European countries would be cowed into submission, thereby increasing domestic radicalism and anti-Americanism, for nothing breeds resentment more than excessive dependence. Others would be tempted to steer their own course, which in theory would at best be of the Gaullist variety and at worst would lead to unarmed neutralism. The "best" outcome is also the least likely because it is based on the possession of a national nuclear deterrent, and all of Western Europe's nations except France have signed the Nuclear Non-Proliferation Treaty. In practice, therefore, a radical anti-European or anti-NATO policy in the United States would leave the West Europeans with few policy options, none as good for the alliance as the present ambiguous status quo and all worse for Europe than the possible results of a positive American attitude toward European defense cooperation.

Whether the United States, in terms of its own national interests, would gain more from the maintenance of the status quo—a fragmented Europe set within functioning alliance institutions—or whether encouragement of European defense cooperation would be a net "plus" remains to be seen. The immediate drawbacks for the United States of any reasonably ambitious European pillar can be summarized as follows:

1. The existence of a European-wide defense industry would represent greater competition for the American armaments firms than the existing, more narrowly based, national establishments in Europe.
2. Specifically European military cooperation (for example, French-German military units within a binational command structure) in liaison with NATO commands would reduce the de facto ascendancy of American military power within the alliance.
3. European arms control and defense policies elaborated upstream of the alliance would challenge or balance the traditional American pacesetting role within NATO. This development would be unpleasant politically and even more so bureaucratically for those U.S. agencies that are prime movers within NATO.

These elements must, however, be set against the wider long-term American interest:

1. A strong European defense industry will be a steady partner for cooperative transatlantic ventures and will help alleviate part of the overall spending burden by reducing waste due to duplication of effort and lack of interoperability. European defense consortia can also increase the efficiency of defense spending in the United States by competing actively within that market.

2. European military cooperation, a particularly delicate and difficult issue, if managed in close coordination with the Atlantic institutions could alleviate part of the American burden in Europe, notably by bringing French assets into play.

3. The alliance has never been as successful as when its policies have been the result of combined input. The greater the involvement of the Europeans in the decision-making process, the better the chances of implementation of policy, insofar as it touches the European theater. The Harmel Report in 1967 and the far-from-painless double-track INF decision in 1979 (originally a German initiative) are examples of this. In the very fluid period that has opened under Gorbachev, with major challenges in the field of arms control—including nuclear and conventional force reductions in Europe—the alliance as a whole would gain from seeing European input reinforced by more systematic intra-European cooperation. The unhappiness of diplomats in Washington and Brussels who would see their bureaucratic turf being encroached upon should not be a determining element.

Whether the American policy-making process will react, on average, favorably or unfavorably toward new European cooperative ventures remains to be seen. A look at the past thirty years would favor a degree of optimism. The United States, although understandably ambiguous about the creation and growth of a body such as the European Community, has, on balance, more often demonstrated benign neglect (or support) rather than malign concern, despite exceptions within this pattern. A look at some of the more recent trends in the United States, such as deterrence fatigue and bipartisan global unilateralism, do not, however, reinforce such an outcome.

Given the nature of the American political process and the contradictory forces at play vis-à-vis European defense cooperation, the answer to the question about future American attitudes will hinge to a significant extent on how European decisions and postures are viewed in the United States. The growing understanding of this in Europe is witnessed by the relatively prudent and subdued reactions by all of the European governments toward the extraordinary Soviet-American discussions in Reykjavik. More needs to be done, however. Systematic involvement by Europeans in congressional hearings would be useful in this respect, as would more frequent exchanges between American authorities (executive and legislative) and intra-European bodies in the field of defense and security policy, such as the Independent European Programme Group and the Western European Union.

Barring overt U.S. hostility and hoping for a degree of encouragement or benign neglect, what can the Europeans effectively do together, without weakening or compromising the Atlantic alliance? To what extent would alliance institutions have to adapt to accommodate European defense cooperation?

WHAT CAN BE DONE, HOW, AND WHERE?

As a rule, European defense cooperation is likely to progress most rapidly if it covers an area that is incompletely covered by existing alliance mechanisms. Arms cooperation would fit into such a category. Similarly, the European pillar can grow most readily when it does not need to oppose the basics that characterize the alliance: the maintenance of a degree of extended American deterrence and the existence of an integrated command structure (along with the absence of France from this structure). By combining these criteria, the following classification in terms of European leeway can be made.

1. Armaments cooperation, although peripheral in policy terms, lies essentially outside the competence of NATO, the Conference of National Armaments Directors notwithstanding. Although sectorial U.S. interests would be affected, this is clearly a field where Europe has a wide margin of maneuver for unification, while at the same time contributing to the greater overall efficiency of common defense spending.
2. Although greater intra-European operational military links may not necessarily call into question NATO strategy, they could create major difficulties in terms of earmarking resources and reconfiguring command structures. (Concurrent shifts in French defense doctrine and NATO strategy have probably brought the two close enough to make them compatible in a crisis or wartime situation, but peacetime cooperation still could pose problems.) Real limits here can be partially circumvented and, in time, alleviated. The area of nuclear cooperation also poses formidable obstacles, but practical steps could be taken even here as well.
3. In the area of policy cooperation, no theoretical or practical reason would prevent European bodies from engaging in defense and arms control policy formulation prior to deliberation within NATO councils; however, some institutional changes would be required to facilitate greater French input. Potential for conflict with the United States would be great in this area, and extreme caution is advisable on the part of Europeans.

These constraints being taken into account, some of the initiatives that would be part of the European defense cooperation can be outlined

220   *François Heisbourg*

by using the categories suggested here.[11] In every case, these proposals are pushed to the limit, within the framework of the gradual approach defined earlier.

Armaments Cooperation

Both transatlantic and European intragovernmental arms cooperation have known a fair number of successes, but their scope has been severely limited by a series of factors, such as the difficulty in defining common specifications and the desire of nation-states to procure armaments primarily from their own industries. However, the unit costs of major weapons systems and the rapidly escalating costs of research and development are giving new impetus to cooperative ventures. The contraction of traditional Third World markets, on which many European defense firms have relied to recoup some of the research and development costs and generate economies of scale, has a similar effect. Cooperation should and can be transatlantic whenever an alliance-wide requirement can be defined. Indeed, imaginative and useful mechanisms have been set in place by the United States, such as the 1985 Nunn-Roth and Quayle amendments. *Transatlantic* does not necessarily equal *American-led*, and European firms, in areas where they have particular proficiency, should have program leadership.

Nevertheless, cooperative procurement will probably remain essentially European-based for a number of technical military and political reasons, not least because the European taxpayer, like the American taxpayer, will want to have as much work done at home, both in the design and in the production phases. At present, the United States procures considerably less than five percent of its defense equipment from European sources (whether the criterion is the origin of program design or the source of production), whereas the proportion of U.S. armaments in European purchases is substantially greater than ten percent, the latter figure being a good indication of the relatively high degree of openness of European arms markets. Such an imbalance is not completely unnatural, given the disproportion of U.S. versus European procurement expenditures.[12] However, cooperative procurement does provide incentive for the Europeans to increase cooperation among themselves.

---

[11] Arms cooperation, military cooperation, and political-strategic cooperation are the three fields defined by the French-German Committee on Security and Defense set up at the end of 1982. In analytical and organizational terms, such a categorization has proven reasonably practical and comprehensive.

[12] The United States devotes more than $126 billion (1986 budget authority) to procurement (including research and development) versus roughly one-third of that amount in NATO Europe (at 1986 exchange rates).

To that one must add the fact that European defense firms are often fighting for survival, that is, attempting to retain their competence in a period of escalating investment and contracting export markets, whereas U.S. defense firms rely on a continent-sized domestic market that has grown by some 50 percent in the past five years. Even if U.S. defense spending tapers off, the absolute level of expenditure remains high. The question for European firms and countries is whether they shall respond in a competitive mode or be tempted by protectionist "remedies."

Toward a European defense market. In the area of weapons procurement, the European members of the alliance (except Iceland) have given an enhanced role to the Independent European Programme Group (IEPG). This body, created in 1976, was basically a talking shop for armament officials, with attempts made to discuss procurement schedules (with a view to harmonizing them) and to facilitate the launching of cooperative ventures. Since the end of 1984, the IEPG has been upgraded to the ministerial level, with ministers of defense and armament directors meeting at regular intervals. Such a body, alongside bilateral or multilateral ventures, has been involving itself notably in three major tasks:

- Facilitating intergovernmental armaments cooperation along the traditional lines of such initiatives but with a new twist, that is, setting "European staff targets" comparable to NATO staff targets;
- Promoting upstream cooperation on defense technologies (Duplication of efforts has been rife in military research in Europe, and the IEPG could serve as a framework for unifying such work. A first step has been taken in this direction with the setting up in 1985 of "cooperative technology programmes."); and
- Shaping an environment conducive to the development of a proficient European defense industry. A group of "Wise Men" has drafted a report for the IEPG[13] that notably advocates the gradual opening of national arms procurement to Europe-wide competition. This general approach was at least tentatively endorsed by the IEPG defense ministers in June 1987.[14] Such a marketplace would

---

[13] "Towards a Stronger Europe," a report by an independent study team established by the defense ministers of the IEPG to make proposals to improve the competitiveness of Europe's defense equipment industry, February 1987.

[14] Communiqué issued by the IEPG defense ministers meeting in Seville, June 22, 1987: "Ministers endorsed the general thrust of the report and expressed their determination to develop an action plan towards an open European market for defense equipment. They instructed National Armaments Directors to draw up an action plan. . . ." Recent French and British moves (September 1987) toward a reciprocal opening of armaments procurement to competitive bidding is also of note.

help ensure that Europe's defense firms would need to prove themselves in competition rather than becoming (or in some cases remaining) the costly wards of national governments. Such a European entity would not be of a different nature than the American one: a continental-scale marketplace. A high degree of openness of the American or the prospective European marketplace to outside international competition is in itself a desirable state of affairs, but it is not precluded (or preordained) by the prior existence of such continental entities.

If one pushed possible initiatives to their ultimate conclusion in the perspective of the European pillar, the following measures could be taken:

1. The IEPG would need to establish a military secretariat in order to coordinate the establishment of European staff targets, in liaison with national staffs and NATO military authorities.
2. Joint upstream technological ventures would call for joint funding and ultimately the creation of a European equivalent of DARPA, whether under the IEPG or between several European countries.[15]
3. Effective opening of competition for arms procurement between European countries could either be launched by the IEPG as a whole or by a group of its members (France and the United Kingdom have been particularly active in this regard). The establishment of comparable bidding rules and the regular publication of requests for proposals would be indispensable steps. Although some degree of centralization may become required, the creation of a centralized European armaments agency is not a necessary first or even second step. Such an opening to competition would have to be gradual in order to minimize domestic political and social tensions. Components, spares, subsystems, and munitions would be the logical places to begin, and they represent possibly more than half of procurement expenditure. In the long run, the requirements of competition would normally lead (1) to structural adjustments within the defense industry (creating European-wide consortia, phasing out lame ducks); (2) to a higher degree of defense cooperation (to win a bid in an industrialized market, you usually need to team up with a local firm); and (3) to more homogeneous force inventories.

The possible development of a European-scale defense market and its accompanying institutions, primarily the IEPG, would naturally

---

[15] An embryo of such an establishment has existed between France and West Germany since 1958 (Institut Franco-Allemand de Saint Louis).

affect transatlantic cooperation and notably the Conference of National Armaments Directors (CNAD) within NATO. Until now, relations between IEPG and CNAD have, on the whole, been informal and good. With new European initiatives on the one hand and the deserved success of the transatlantic ventures of the Nunn Amendment managed via CNAD on the other, now may be the time to establish a more formal relationship and systematic consultation, including the political dimension (at or above the level of the "reinforced Council" meetings established in 1984). This would serve both a general purpose—to reduce protectionist temptations in the armaments field both in the United States and in Europe—and reconcile possibly diverging programs. For example, the first phase of work is proceeding with IEPG on an ambitious European data distribution system (EDDS), while similar tasks are discussed within NATO agencies. These separate efforts will have to be coordinated at one stage or another.

On balance, the record of allied governments and, in the case of the United States, of Congress, on armaments cooperation has been encouraging over the past three to four years. Indeed, this is one of the few areas where U.S.–European relations have actually improved. In view of that achievement, the carefully managed building of a European pillar and a greater degree of transatlantic cooperation do not appear to be incompatible. Ministers and members of parliament on both shores of the Atlantic should feel encouraged to pursue armament policies that reject protectionism and to refuse to entertain the notion that greater European unity is incompatible with transatlantic armaments cooperation, notwithstanding occasional conflicts of interest.

Military Cooperation

Whereas NATO institutions as such do not pose major problems of coexistence with European bodies in the field of armament, the military operational area presents difficulties that are slightly less stark in practice than on paper.

Setting aside for an instant the particular circumstances created by the fact that France and Spain are not integrated within NATO's command structure, the status of the standing air and land forces in central Europe appears to be a black-and-white situation: either the SACEUR is in charge or he isn't. If he is, then the Europeans can establish very little between themselves, alongside NATO (although that *little* would be worth doing). If he isn't, then clearly we are talking about a different alliance and suggesting a revolutionary approach. However, some room for pragmatism is available, particularly if SACEUR demonstrates willingness to accommodate European cooperative ventures. The possibility of securing a higher degree of cooperation with French forces can serve as an incentive.

Pragmatism and ad hoc approaches: possibilities and limits. When French and German defense planners began their discussions within the newly created Commission on Security and Defense at the end of 1982, they did not expect breakthroughs in the strictly military field, whereas arms procurement and security policy seemed to offer more promising prospects. Five years later, somewhat paradoxically, significant military progress had been made. Some has been unilateral (e.g., the French decision in 1983 to create the *Force d'Action Rapide*—FAR, a rapid-action force capable of participating early on in forward defense), but bilateral moves have occurred and more are planned or can be expected in the future.

1. Large-scale bilateral French-German maneuvers have become a regular phenomenon (in Muensingen in 1985, *Frankischer Schild* in 1986, *Kecker Spatz* in 1987) and are growing in size.
2. French forces on maneuvers in Germany not only include those troops stationed in the Federal Republic (2nd Army Corps) but also draw on forces based in France, including three divisions of the Rapid Action Force for the September 1987 *Kecker Spatz* exercises.
3. Logistics, which are a national responsibility within the alliance, remain a subject of some confidentiality; the French and the Germans have improved arrangements to cooperate in this respect.
4. West German Chancellor Kohl has proposed a French-German brigade, tially under French command, which will probably be composed of active duty combat units from each country.
5. Possibly the most important changes have been induced by the habit of regular consultation at all levels, including twinning of French-German units, which involves large numbers of grass-roots military personnel. In case of crisis or war, French and German forces would be in a good position to interoperate, in particular if the long-standing Ailleret-Lemnitzer agreements between SACEUR and the French chief of staff (and the subsequent associated implementing plans) were applied.

Replicating what has been achieved between France and the Federal Republic of Germany should be possible in arrangements between France and other NATO partners. For example, trilateral exercises among the British Army on the Rhine (BAOR), France's Rapid Action Force, and the *Bundeswehr* should be possible, or among the Belgian Corps in Germany, the Rapid Action Force, and the *Bundeswehr*.

All of this requires some complicity from SACEUR and a good understanding by the different partners of their respective limits. Large-scale bilateral maneuvers imply that SACEUR (or his subordinate commanders) "de-earmark" the relevant integrated forces for the duration of such exercises. This has been accomplished without ado in previous French-German joint exercises. Command arrangements for joint units such as the future French-German brigade will require a high degree of pragmatism in order to reconcile command arrangements.

Such flexibility is necessary on both sides of the Rhine, because such a mixed unit will have to be under NATO, German, or French command in time of war. The question is left pending for the moment, as it can be allowed to do so given the currently limited numbers of forces involved. The implication, however, is that there wouldn't be serious debate about the French applying the Ailleret-Lemnitzer Agreements if push came to shove.

Several supplementary measures would both strengthen the French-German military relationship and broaden it to the other European allies.

1. Regular exercises between the French Rapid Action Force and those allied units alongside which it may need to deploy itself.
2. Bilateral military liaison missions within the General Staff (or equivalents) of the countries involved (France–Belgium, France–West Germany, France–U.K., etc.). These missions would be in addition to the existing French liaison missions within the NATO command structure (which take care of the U.S. element because SACEUR is also commander in chief of U.S. forces in Europe).
3. The earmarking of German territorial forces (*Land Heer*), which are not assigned to SACEUR, for cooperation with units tasked with comparable responsibilities within the French 1st Army (protection of lines of communication and sensitive installations). Such units could come under rotating French and German command.
4. Annual discussions among the chiefs of staff of the European countries whose forces are present in central Europe (Belgium, the Netherlands, the Federal Republic of Germany, France, and Great Britain). Such a body could not only serve as a forum for informal discussion but also examine questions that come under national responsibility; this could also be a way to improve peacetime preparation for logistical support at the theater level.

None of these proposals requires a major change in SACEUR's responsibilities and would indeed enhance overall defense capabilities by increasing France's European commitment. Such pragmatic approaches, however, would depend heavily on SACEUR's cooperation.

A European force structure alongside NATO institutions? Asking whether European force structures are possible alongside NATO institutions does not imply the author's willingness to envisage revolutionary change, which is probably undesirable in existing circumstances. In one contingency going beyond ad hoc solutions and envisaging *some* reform of NATO's integrated command structure may be necessary: if the United States and/or Germany reduce their force levels for budgetary or demographic reasons, gaps may emerge in the West's ability to implement a forward defense. Such gaps would have to be filled, and the most readily available forces for such a task would be those of France. Provided the gaps were relatively modest (comparable to the 48,000 men of the French 2nd Corps in Germany) and existing infrastructure were usable at acceptable cost, French troops could be relocated. However, the extent and location of such redeployments should take into account the usefulness of keeping French forces as an in-depth operational reserve for NATO.

Although forward defense does not carry the same stigma in Paris that was attached to it only a decade ago, France could probably envisage participating in the posture on terms compatible with her nonintegration within the NATO command structure. Yet forward defense would make little sense, for France as for its allies, if provisions were not established beforehand for operational control in times of crisis. The problems would not be as acute if French forces were placed in an operational reserve position, but even in that case, SACEUR would want to know when and to what extent he could draw on that reserve.

One move could help meet both French concerns and the requirements for a coherent command arrangement: the reaffirmation by France of the automatic commitment of her military forces in case of armed aggression. Such a commitment is contained within Article 4 of the Western European Union Treaty, that is, within a European pillar framework. Such a declaration, politically useful in its own right, should have as a rider that, if France were to permanently deploy forward-based forces, the Ailleret-Lemnitzer Agreements would be automatically implemented.

On the one hand, these suggestions do not resolve the question of earmarking and inclusion within NATO's command structure, which France would probably not accept. On the other hand, they stop short of proposing a rotating French-German command, for example, in the CENTAG region[16] and, a fortiori, of the bold suggestion by former Chancellor Schmidt to have all German and French forces come under French command. Some peacetime fuzziness is probably preferable to either of these stark choices, and half-way solutions are preferable to attempting to devise clear-cut but unacceptable proposals.

However, a frontline French military presence in peacetime, a reliable commitment if hostilities were to erupt, and the definition of clear provisions for operational control in wartime[17] would help limit the damage from a reduction in NATO's force structure.

Nuclear cooperation. Strictly intra-European nuclear cooperation, distinct from either NATO institutions, such as the Nuclear Planning Group (NPG), or the bilateral U.S.–U.K. agreements, could take two forms: nuclear consultations between France and its nonnuclear partners (particularly the Federal Republic of Germany) and bilateral French-British cooperation.

The groundwork for nuclear consultations between France and West Germany was laid on February 28, 1986, on the occasion of a French-German summit, when President Mitterrand stated that the use of France's prestrategic weapons would be envisaged in consultation with West Germany, time and circumstances permitting. Such a formula, quasi-identical to the unclassified description of NATO's Athens Guidelines, could lead the two countries to engage in coordination comparable to that conducted within the Nuclear Planning Group.

In theory, compatibility of plans may be a problem, particularly for the Federal Republic, because contingencies examined in the Nuclear Planning Group may differ substantially from those discussed in a bilateral French-German mode. In practice, however, the Federal German government is in a position to reconcile this matter, if it so decides, without impinging on France's ultimate control of release. The time-and-circumstances clause signifies that the nuclear power retains the ultimate capacity to use its delivery vehicles and warheads without veto power from the nonnuclear powers. U.S., U.K., and French nuclear weapons do not differ in this respect, even if employment doctrines may differ.

Another step for the French would be to deploy prestrategic weapons in the Federal Republic. Such a suggestion is no longer taboo in France, as recent statements by two former defense ministers

---

[16] CENTAG is NATO's designation for the central army group of the commander-in-chief central region covering Germany south of the line between Cologne and Harz.

[17] For example, along the lines of the Ailleret-Lemnitzer Agreements and the ensuing implementing plans.

indicate.[18] Here again, the European (French-German in this case) arrangements could be similar to those used within NATO, the problem of compatibility being a West German one, with the federal authorities in a position to reconcile or to choose. However, West Germany has shown no inclination to request the peacetime deployment of French airborne or ground-launched prestrategic missiles.

Even more ambitious would be a French-German agreement comparable to those applying to so-called double-key systems: warheads under French custody to be fitted on German delivery vehicles. No recent public expressions of interest of this sort have surfaced on either side of the Rhine, but theoretically the option exists. This concept could have been a way out of the problem posed by the modernization of the Pershing IIs in the context of the U.S.-Soviet double zero on intermediate nuclear force missiles and short-range INF missiles.

French-British nuclear cooperation is another possible variety of European cooperation, both powers possessing a strategic as well as a theater nuclear deterrent. Attempts have been made in the past (the Macmillan-de Gaulle talks in the early sixties, the Debre-Carrington discussions in the early seventies), without success. Some of the obstacles that existed then have attenuated. The United Kingdom's attachment to the "special relationship" has become less exclusive, and France's insistence on having partners choose between Paris and Washington has dissipated. However, the existence of the bilateral 1958 U.S.-U.K. nuclear agreements severely limits the scope of cooperation, because the United Kingdom cannot share with France information and technology generated in the United States, barring a general or case-by-case waiver by the United States of these restrictions. France and the United Kingdom can nevertheless work on subjects that are not covered or preempted under the special relationship, such as operational coordination of submarine-launched ballistic nuclear missiles (patrol and refit cycles) and modernization of theater nuclear weapons.

Nuclear modernization is an apparently promising field because the British will need to replace their nuclear gravity bombs (designed by Great Britain and assigned to the Royal Air Force Tornados), preferably with some sort of standoff weapons. Indeed, serious discussions have begun on this subject.[19]

---

[18] See statements by Messrs. Messmer and Hernu in July 1987.

[19] See statements by the French and British ministers of defense in London, December 1987.

This could occur without affecting NATO institutions because the British version of such nuclear weapons would presumably remain assigned to SACEUR. However, in the long run, jointly developed prestrategic weapons could form the nuclear core of a specifically European extended deterrent, alongside SACEUR-operated tactical nuclear weapons.

Potential French-British cooperation on nuclear hardware is consistent with an approach in which the European pillar could function both as a supplement to NATO, with minimum disruption of Atlantic institutions, and as a precaution if some degree of substitution became imperative.

European Formulation of Strategy and Policy

Cooperaton on software may seem simpler because it is essentially immaterial: on paper, the Europeans should be able to meet, in the venue of their choice, and agree on a wide range of issues before meeting their North American partners in the Atlantic councils. In practice, this is hardly the case. The sharp reactions that emanated from the U.S. Department of State when Western European Union political directors wished to discuss East-West negotiations in the absence of the Americans bears witness to this.[20]

To avoid damaging transatlantic decoupling, American sensitivities need to be taken into account. Bearing in mind this fundamental precaution, several steps suggest themselves:

- formulating a West European consensus on the fundamental bases of their security;
- facilitating common European positions on matters immediately relevant to their security, particularly in the area of arms control; and
- ensuring a wide and effective interface between European and alliance institutions.

Elaborating a West European consensus on security affairs is an exercise that can be a positive asset for the alliance. The belief in deterrence, including naturally its nuclear underpinning, is very unequally shared within the alliance. It is strongest within the seven countries of the Western European Union, which, with the understandable exception of Luxembourg, are host to nuclear weapons as owners and/or recipients. All of the intermediate nuclear force deployment countries are members of the WEU, as are the

---

[20] See Bridget Bloom, "U.S. Warns Europe on Independent Defence Stance," *The Financial Times*, April 2, 1985.

European possessors of national nuclear forces. The "security charter" that the WEU countries have elaborated can serve as a useful reminder of the alliance strategy. The Western European Union, despite its lackluster history and its weak institutions, has another advantage— the imperative nature of the military commitment that its members owe to each other in case of conflict, much beyond the corresponding clauses of the NATO treaty. Despite its past shortcomings, its attributes should allow it to play a pivotal role in the definition of security policy. The resumption of regular meetings of WEU foreign and defense ministers in 1984 demonstrates the increased potential for the organization.

The adoption by the WEU of a European Security Platform in October 1987 was a major step in such a direction. The clear and strong text adopted serves not only to reaffirm basic allied objectives of sustaining deterrence and preserving transatlantic links, but also serves to define the conditions for other countries to enter the WEU.

Beyond formulation of general principles, the Europeans could discuss between themselves issues that are likely to affect their security, without necessarily appearing to challenge the United States. If conventional arms control becomes a major topic, the alliance could thrash out only a limited set of options rather than having a free-for-all between sixteen member states with sixteen different views. Prior coordination between the European nations could indeed be helpful, particularly among the WEU countries.

A NATO-Europe political body could be called for in the long run. However, the creation of such a group would have a high potential for confrontation with the United States: if reinforcing an existing institution such as the WEU poses problems, all the more so for a completely new body.

Implementing the preceding ideas would require the establishment of more systematic and widely based cooperation between Atlantic and European organizations. Colocating these bodies in Brussels could help to achieve cooperation. The WEU Secretariat (based in London) committees and Assembly (located in Paris) could move to Brussels, given its growing role as de facto capital of both NATO and the European Community.[21] Similarly, if the Independent European Programme Group generates a cadre of its own, it could communicate more easily with the Conference of National Armaments Directors if it were established in Brussels. The advantage would not only be in proximity but also in ensuring that the permanent representations accredited to WEU would also be those attached to the North Atlantic

---

[21] Such a proposal to relocate WEU institutions has been made by Sir Geoffrey Howe.

Council; expertise and transparency in terms of information would be ensured because coordination would be organic. Alternatively, WEU could at least concentrate all its elements in a single location such as Paris.

A further step would call for a modification of alliance institutions. All moves toward a European pillar now involve France, for good political and geostrategic reasons. France's defense policies are shifting toward a higher degree of Europeanism in practical and procedural terms. For instance, French ministers of defense participate with their colleagues in the ministerial meetings of WEU and IEPG. There is no symmetrical presence of the French minister of defense within NATO meetings. In effect, the French viewpoint is expressed indirectly, which is probably not an optimal situation from either an alliance or a French viewpoint. As France has no strong domestic or foreign incentive to return to NATO's integrated institutions, and particularly no compelling reason to join bodies that were created in part as a consequence of France's withdrawal, some reordering would be called for. One solution would be to eliminate the Defense Planning Committee and hold defense ministers' meetings as part of the Atlantic Council's proceedings. This would accommodate French concerns about reintegration. Indeed, France, like Spain, would not need to join the integrated organization (the Military Committee and the military commands), and NATO would have the benefit of wider European input in defense policy deliberations.

Such a liquidation and reincarnation of the Defense Planning Committee may not be politically acceptable today, but in purely procedural terms it should be feasible. It would also be one good way to reduce the risk of a collision course between NATO institutions and European defense cooperation.

CONCLUDING OBSERVATIONS

In analyzing the potential for progressively greater European defense cooperation, the attempt has been made to make proposals going to the limit within the field left open by the set of existing constraints. From such an examination, several tentative conclusions can be drawn, and some questions posed:

1. Rather than as a single European pillar embodied in a single organization, European defense cooperation can manifest itself as a set of institutions (IEPG, WEU, the French-German Commission

on Security and Defense[22]) and initiatives. The absence of a
European political executive, along with the existence of alliance
institutions, leads to such a piecemeal, ad hoc approach.

2. U.S. attitudes will be of prime importance in speeding up or
slowing down European defense cooperation and in defining its
nature (as a positive addition to alliance capabilities or as a
potentially radical and possibly unfriendly substitute). The fear of
the self-fulfilling prophecy—the notion that the United States will
draw upon European initiatives to reduce transatlantic coupling—
acts in the short run as a powerful brake on European defense
cooperation. In the long run, undiminished dependence breeds
anti-American resentment and hence is ultimately decoupling. As a
corollary, European and American government officials and
lawmakers have a vested interest in making sure that moves toward
European defense cooperation are not misinterpreted.

3. Significant additions to European defense cooperation can be made
by working on the basis of existing bodies or ad hoc arrangements,
without calling into question the basic institutions of the Atlantic
alliance. This is particularly true of the tools of defense (armaments
cooperation). Scope for specifically European input is significantly
narrower in the area of military operational collaboration, if
damaging NATO's integrated command structure is to be avoided;
even there, more room is available for pragmatic intra-European
measures than appears at first glance.

4. In the long run, the question of the radical approach remains, that
is, the building of a European entity incompatible with or directed
against transatlantic coupling or, conversely, born from catastrophic
decoupling. Trends that lead to such a direction need to be carefully
monitored. They include not only some of the neo-isolationist
concepts in the United States but also anti-Americanism of parts of
the West European electorates. Heed must also be paid to the
manner in which the younger generations in Western Europe
consider a fundamental assumption underlying the Atlantic
coalition: that strategic stability, security, peace, and freedom in the
West imply a degree of acceptance of geopolitical stability for
Europe as a whole, and Germany in particular, that is, the division
of that continent and a corresponding lack of self-determination in
its eastern half. There is a de facto trade-off here, even if the West
has attempted to alleviate its consequences through detente,
Ostpolitik, or similar devices.

---

[22] The Commission was established in 1982 and chaired by the ministers of defense and
foreign affairs. The French-German Commission is being upgraded; the new Council (top
decision-making body of the Commission) will be headed by the president of France and the
chancellor of the Federal Republic of Germany.

The coexistence of these two forms of stability may or may not cease to be acceptable in the future. Containment and its successors (detente in its various guises) would then be contested in favor of more radical attitudes including neutralization (Finlandization) and the search for a "middle-European" order. One of the most compelling long-term political arguments in favor of European defense cooperation lies precisely in this as yet vague but high risk: the temptation that reunification be bought at the price of freedom.

West European defense cooperation, as the European Community in the political-economic area, has the effect of anchoring our countries more strongly in an environment ensuring freedom with peace and contains the potential for opening a perspective toward an undivided Europe. In today's circumstances, talk about policies for undoing the division of Europe and Germany would probably verge on the irresponsible, but the fact remains that no reason exists why that split should remain eternal; no geopolitical order has ever had that quality.

Therefore, working toward a European pillar ultimately serves the wider purpose of giving the European continent a future compatible with the aims and values of the Atlantic alliance.

11

Rebuild or Decay: The Future of the European Security System (A French Perspective)

By PIERRE LELLOUCHE

BEYOND THE DOUBLE ZERO

The Soviet-American treaty on the elimination of intermediate-range (INF) and short-range (SRINF) nuclear missiles based in Europe marks a crucial step in the ongoing process of change in the European security system.

Even those Europeans who, like former NATO Secretary-General Lord Carrington and former French President Giscard d'Estaing, have welcomed the INF Treaty nonetheless recognize a fundamental change on the strategic landscape in Europe. Lord Carrington, for example, thinks that the "substantial change" brought about by the treaty is the most "profound" in a generation.[1] Giscard d'Estaing, after defending the treaty at length, goes on to talk of the "end of the 40-year post-war period 1947–1987." During this period, he continues,

> the security of Europe has rested totally on American nuclear deterrence. With the sole exception of France, which has been partially protected by its own deterrent, all the continental states have rallied for their security on the United States' commitment to a nuclear response to any conventional or nuclear attack on our continent. This was the answer to the lack of conventional forces. This whole situation was managed and controlled by American commanders. The final decisions were taken by the President of the United States on his responsibility alone. We should be grateful to the United States for the 40 years of security they have thus obtained for us. But we must also be aware that such a situation was by its very nature impermanent and that as a united Europe emerged from the ruins of war, it became inevitable that it would

---

[1] Lord Carrington, "A World after Agreement: Picturing Soviets as Sirens over European Landscape," *Los Angeles Times*, September 27, 1987, p. E-1.

take on an increasing share of the burdens and responsibilities of its own defense. This process occurs quite naturally at the meeting point of history.[2]

Whether we like it or not, we Europeans will have to face the consequences of this treaty, from both the military standpoint (the future of the American deterrent) and the political one (the development of the situation in West Germany and the question of the presence of American forces in Europe).

But the challenge facing Europeans goes far beyond just the treaty on the double-zero option. The Euromissile accord is far from being a staging post along the road emerging from the confusion of the Reykjavik summit in October 1986 or a reaction to the masterly diplomacy of the Gorbachev team alone; it has to be seen as the culmination in practical terms, at the diplomatic level, of a whole series of significant trends—some going back a long way, others more recent—that have converged to bring about a fundamental questioning of the very basis of the European system of security.

The common denominator among all these different political, military, technological, and even social strands is none other than a denial of the basic concept of nuclear deterrence and the terms on which it is practiced in Europe by the United States. The essential point to be made here is that the entire system of European security established after World War II was specifically based, both from the military and the political points of view, on the maintenance of a credible nuclear deterrent capability by the United States and subsequently by the United Kingdom and France.

Seen alongside the national political developments in a number of key countries, particularly in the United States and West Germany, the current questioning of the role of nuclear arms in the defense of Europe—as evidenced in ordinary discussion as well as in the military and diplomatic processes conducted by Washington and Moscow—therefore threatens to overturn the very foundations of security and, by implication, the political and territorial order of postwar Europe. At the same time, it further weakens what remains of the public consensus on deterrence in the Western democracies.

In these circumstances, Europeans must squarely face the need to readapt their system of security to the changing conditions of the next few years. This also applies to France, whose defense policy, conceived as it was in the strategic context of 30 years ago, must as a matter of urgency be thoroughly reviewed and adjusted to the present realities of its strategic environment.

---

[2] Valery Giscard d'Estaing, "Un bon accord, une chance pour l'Europe," *Le Monde*, September 23, 1987, p. 2.

This chapter aims to provide a basis for such an overall review, without claiming to give all the answers to all the problems we face. To this end, I examine the following issues:

1. The military, political, and technological changes taking place, which taken together amount to nothing less than a strategic revolution;
2. The foreseeable impact of the INF Treaty from both the military and the political points of view; and
3. Finally, future developments: either the whole system will fall into more or less rapid decay, or—should Europeans find in themselves the necessary will—the political, military, and institutional framework of European security will be completely rebuilt.

THE END OF AN ERA

The system of security with which Europe has lived very comfortably for forty years is before our very eyes undergoing a fundamental and no doubt historic change.

This change is affecting not only the principal actors on the East-West stage but also the military and institutional machinery that has kept the peace and maintained stability in postwar Europe.

From the West's Perspective

Although the basic problem of security has not changed since 1945 in that no European power in the postwar period can stand alone against the Soviet Union, the conditions within which the alliance with the United States has operated have gradually changed over the years.

After World War II ended, Europeans realized that security in Europe would be collective or not at all. They first initiated regional arrangements (French-British Treaty of Dunkirk in 1947, Treaty of Brussels in 1948)[3] and then appealed to the United States to contain the Soviet Union and also to formalize the appearance of a new political entity in the western part of Germany, a birth that neither Paris nor London seemed capable of realizing without help.

Although the 1949 Atlantic Charter was to provide the diplomatic basis for what eventually became NATO, the return of American forces to European soil was mainly due to the Korean War and the establishment of the policy of containment. Nothing in its history (anti-European) or aspiration (as a seafaring nation) preordained the

---

[3] This was to give rise to the Western European Union (WEU).

United States to become a permanent European power (enshrined as such in the 1975 Helsinki Agreements) with a presence of more than 300,000 military personnel in mainland Europe 40 years after the war. This "historical anomaly," as Helmut Sonnenfeldt termed it, of an America catapulted into playing the part of Europe's long-term protector, is more readily understandable as a result of the vacuum created by the self-destruction of the former great European powers when confronted by the emerging empire of Eastern Europe, than in terms of deliberate policy by America's leaders immediately after the war. The United States had originally hoped that the West European countries would provide most of NATO's defensive forces in Europe. The U.S. Senate, in fact, approved the North Atlantic Treaty believing that this would be the case. The Lisbon force goals set by alliance defense ministers in 1952 provided for the buildup of conventional forces by Europeans to match those of the Red Army. Of course, these goals were never attained, partly because a solution had still not been found to the problem of German rearmament, but above all because the other European powers had other priorities (rebuilding, colonial wars, etc.) and were unwilling to embark on such a rearmament plan.

This touches on important constraints that were to have a profound influence on the development of the alliance: economic and social factors. From the beginning of the 1950s, neither the Americans (under Eisenhower) nor the Europeans were prepared to make the economic and social sacrifices needed to build up conventional forces to match those of the Soviet Union. Then the miracle solution arrived from America: the alliance would agree to continue in a state of military inferiority in Europe, but this acknowledged inferiority would be offset by the then-crushing nuclear superiority of the United States. In Washington, where Eisenhower had been elected on a platform of reductions in the defense effort (this had increased considerably during the Korean War), the current byword was "a bigger bang for the buck." In terms of European strategy, this axiom was translated into the doctrine of massive retaliation (MC 14/2 in NATO jargon). The United States undertook to respond by nuclear means to any Soviet attack on the European allies. The introduction of thousands of American tactical weapons on European soil dates from this time (weapons that will survive the withdrawal of cruise and Pershing missiles at the end of the INF Agreement).

Over the years, European dependence on America's nuclear capability was to increase as the conventional imbalance with the Red Army grew and economic and social constraints on the West's defense budgets became stronger. The trouble was that, at the same time, the credibility of the American nuclear umbrella and public acceptance of deterrence by the West were gradually decreasing, culminating in the present situation. Now Europe has never been so dependent on nuclear deterrence, yet never has it been so uncertain about nuclear deterrence in military terms and so reluctant to accept it at the social-political level.

Thus the Atlantic alliance, which started life as a partnership between the two sides of the Atlantic Ocean, was rapidly to change—as a result of the preeminence given to American deterrence—into a protectorate under the authority of Washington. The Europeans were happy to provide military personnel and resources required under the force goals and doctrine laid down by the Pentagon, and the Americans provided the leadership—military, political, and by implication economic—for the whole system.

Such a disparity became more and more difficult to sustain in the long term as the United States gradually lost its economic preeminence over Europe and Japan and its military supremacy over the Soviet Union. Today it is no longer capable of taking on the political, economic, and military leadership of Europe on its own, and still less of the West as a whole. At the same time, Europe was becoming more prosperous and more eager to proclaim its own political interests to the outside world. The result was growing tensions within the Atlantic alliance itself: the extreme dependence of the Europeans in matters of security was in stark contrast to the declaration of its own political and economic interests, which were often different from those of the Americans (particularly in Third World crises such as Afghanistan, Libya, or the Gulf). In America, meanwhile, the lack of "solidarity" shown by the allies produced growing exasperation and a strong current of unilateralism (protectionist pressure, toying with the idea of withdrawing troops from Europe). From this point forward, the burden of economic constraints in the United States itself was to enter the picture (budget deficit roughly equivalent to the defense budget, with nearly half of that budget devoted to NATO), and both leadership and public opinion became reluctant to allow the United States to be dragged into a major nuclear conflict with the Soviet Union in the European theater. These trends produced an increasingly direct repudiation of the U.S. nuclear commitment in Europe and the rise of a strong current of neo-isolationism aimed at the withdrawal of U.S. soldiers from Europe.

The other aspect of the alliance's internal development concerns Germany. Here, the fragility of the situation is at the same time military and political. It was military because, in contrast to France and the United Kingdom, a divided and conquered Germany lost in

1954 (Paris Agreements) the right to become a nuclear power[4] and therefore had no choice but to place itself under the nuclear protection of America, with all the uncertainties that were to ensue from such a position. The situation was also fragile politically because the question of reunification necessarily remained an open one for the Germans, despite their being anchored to the West as symbolized by the presence of American nuclear forces and weapons on German soil. As the two institutional frameworks that were supposed to have resolved the "German question"—NATO (for security) and the European Economic Community (for the economy and as a way of giving younger generations of Germans a spurious European identity)—became even more sterile, German policy was gradually to move away from NATO and Europe and to try as skillfully as possible to walk the tightrope between the three axes of Washington, Moscow, and Paris.

At the same time, the nuclear weapons in particular (and, by extension, the U.S. troops) that had previously guaranteed peace and freedom came for a growing fringe of the German population to symbolize the danger of a limited nuclear war and the preservation of the territorial and national split forevermore. From being the star pupil in the Atlantic class, entirely devoted to American deterrence in the 1950s and 1960s, the Germany of today has edged toward a deep-rooted rejection of everything nuclear (both civil and military), with a fear of again becoming the battleground for the superpowers (a new Versailles complex), and a confused national aspiration that sees in the permanence of the nuclear arsenals in Europe a fundamental obstacle to the reunification of the two parts of Europe. A deep split in the consensus on deterrence has opened up, and the vast majority of German public opinion now favors a strictly conventional defense posture.[5]

From the Soviet Perspective

The Soviet Union is obviously aware of and not averse to taking advantage of the internal developments in the Western alliance. Emerging from World War II as the biggest power on the Euroasian continent, the Soviet Union went on to dominate the center of Europe both politically and militarily. With its expansionist ideology (i.e., the desire to impose its own political structure on the rest of the world) and its gradual acquisition of the military attributes of a superpower with ambitions on a world scale (strategic nuclear capability on a par with the United States, an oceangoing navy, and superiority in all conventional means over all the countries on its periphery), the Soviet Union understandably considers Europe to be the center of its historic struggle with the United States. The Soviets have in this context shown total continuity in their long-term strategic goals for Europe, not ruling out (as remains the case today) tactical maneuvers.

Soviet leaders from Stalin right up to Gorbachev have believed that the political and territorial status quo in Europe is not set in concrete and that inevitably the Soviet Union will establish a "new order" in security, based in practice on the expulsion of the United States from the continent (turning America into an "island" strategically and economically cut off from its markets) and on its political and military preeminence over its West European neighbors.

In Europe, the Soviets are pursuing a strategy that is the opposite of Clausewitz's famous dictum, because diplomacy (called *peace*) is put forward as the continuation of war by other means. These means are:

- The maintenance of a local military capability much larger than that of the West, with the joint aim (other than the occupation of the central European satellite countries) of political intimidation and neutralizing the strategic doctrine of its adversaries. At the end of the 70s, the Soviet Union managed through strategic parity with the United States and its nuclear and conventional superiority in the so-called European theater to make the NATO doctrine of flexible response inoperable.
- Relying on this strategy of military decoupling, the Soviet Union intends gradually and by diplomatic means to transform the political and territorial status quo in the West. It has therefore insisted since the 1950s (even more evident under Gorbachev) on denuclearizing Western Europe, the surest way of getting the United States expelled from Europe and West Germany neutralized. Seen in this context, Gorbachev's various proposals (repeated at the Warsaw Pact meeting in Berlin in May 1987) speak volumes: no first use of nuclear weapons, denuclearized corridor between the two Germanies, massive withdrawal of Soviet and American forces from central Europe, elimination of all nuclear weapons from Europe (including tactical weapons).

Within such a historical perspective, Gorbachev's strategy seems totally consistent with the one followed by his predecessors. Compared to the past, however, the strategy has two significant differences:

- First, an infinitely more effective diplomatic style, as can be seen in the way Gorbachev has been able to make the West fall into the trap of its own rhetoric: Reagan with his theme of a denuclearized world when launching the concept of the Strategic Defense Initiative (SDI) in March 1983, and NATO with its zero-option proposal for INF in 1981;
- Second, Gorbachev's wish to pursue his ends by political and diplomatic means rather than just by exploiting the Soviet military buildup. His intention is to replace the militaristic expansionist policy of Brezhnev, which was far too costly for the national economy and did great damage to the image of the Soviet Union around the world (Afghanistan). Giving greater impetus to diplomatic and strategic activity will enable him to achieve the same goals by negotiation, at the same time as transferring for a while human and financial resources for the purposes of modernizing the whole of the economy with up-to-date technology, such modernization being regarded as a precondition for maintaining Soviet military power in the long term. A certain "modernist" fringe in the military (new defense minister Yazov, General Agaiev) appears to endorse this relative change in priorities.

In a relatively short time, Gorbachev has succeeded in setting his own agenda (denuclearization of Europe, massive American and Soviet troop withdrawals from central Europe) and in putting the West on the defensive, most frequently split down the middle. Such a situation could eventually give rise to the real danger of a major crisis in Europe, because the Soviet Union might be tempted to use its military power against a demoralized and militarily weakened West in order to speed up the course of "history."

The Decline of Nuclear Deterrence

Alongside these political developments, the most significant change for the future of the Atlantic alliance concerns the concept of nuclear deterrence, which, as has already been pointed out, has been the very backbone of the alliance. Although the role of nuclear arms in the defense of Europe has been the subject of constant debate within the alliance, what we are seeing today is a fundamental questioning of the very concept of deterrence in the Western democracies in the face of three sets of factors (some old, some of more recent vintage):

- a change in the balance of military forces between the two superpowers;
- a parallel decline in the public consensus on deterrence; and
- developments in armaments technology.

First, the changing balance of military forces between the two superpowers has over the decades led to their strategic arsenals being neutralized at the same time as the nuclear and conventional lead held by the Soviet Union in Europe became even greater. The result of this dual process has been a Europe obliged, through the growing imbalance in conventional forces, to depend more than ever on the first and earliest possible use of nuclear weapons by the United States at a time when the United States has become much more reluctant to risk an intercontinental nuclear war over a conflict in Europe. An apparent consensus has developed within America (spanning liberals and conservatives) that NATO's military posture and doctrine of flexible response should be redefined in favor of greater emphasis on conventional weapons and that America's nuclear commitment to Europe should be increasingly moderated (call for withdrawal of medium-range missiles, debate on "no first use"). These ominous tendencies in the strategic policy of the United States hark back to the very origins of the alliance (1952 Lisbon Conference, McNamara's policy of the early 1960s).

Second, questioning of deterrence is also apparent throughout public opinion in the West, except in France.

The breaking of the consensus on nuclear matters (as much civil as military, after all) is not only due to short-term factors arising at the end of the 1970s (neutron bomb affair, Afghanistan crisis, collapse of detente). It is more closely linked to a structural phenomenon arising from the passing of the generations and the declaration of differing security interests on both sides of the Atlantic, and even from one country to another. The antinuclear lobby in the United States thus reflects the tendency toward nuclear isolationism (fear of being drawn into a nuclear apocalypse by a European conflict). Conversely, in Europe, the antideterrence argument is at once a means of giving voice to the realization that the protection afforded by the American umbrella has weakened and a refusal to pay a price that suddenly became abundantly clear in the Pershing affair: nothing less than a "limited" nuclear war in Europe. This phenomenon of rejection is reinforced by the search for a national identity and national interests in Germany in particular, the most exposed of the Western nations and the one with the largest stockpile of nuclear weapons on its territory. The presence of such weapons in a way freezes the territorial status quo inherited from the war.[6]

---

[6] For a detailed analysis of the phenomenon of pacifism and antinuclear opposition, see Pierre Lellouche, ed., *Pacifisme et Dissuasion*, IFRI-Economica, 1984.

The way in which the counterargument has been expressed has changed dramatically in the last few years. Starting with the mass demonstrations, opposition has gradually penetrated the social and political fabric of a fair number of countries to the point of having a major influence on the security policy of several states. The double-zero option agreement, opposed by some European governments, was thus finally conceded under the pressure of public opinion.

The fact that Reagan (since announcing SDI in March 1983) and Gorbachev (since his speech on January 15, 1986) have personally, and subsequently in concert at Reykjavik, taken up the theme of denuclearization as a desirable basis for a future international strategic framework has played a major part in destabilizing the Western consensus on deterrence and, by implication, destabilizing the entire system of European security.

Third, the very rapid progress made in military technology, particularly in nonnuclear fields ("intelligent" conventional arms, space weapons), has fostered a worldwide questioning of deterrence by presenting alternatives to Western public opinion that are claimed to be less painful and without any danger to the present system of deterrence. Aside from the postnuclear world envisaged by Reagan and Gorbachev (the former laying stress on SDI and the latter on negotiation), the fashion now is for so-called conventional deterrence, which is put forward as a substitute for NATO's present policy in Europe.

However, the reality is quite different. More than four years after the idea of SDI was first raised, clearly even an antimissile defense system in space will not put an end to the business of deterrence between the two superpowers. At the very most, a system of deterrence based on a purely offensive posture will change to a mixed offensive-defensive system that will not under any circumstances "disinvent" nuclear weapons.

Likewise, the cost of the new conventional technologies, the uncertainty as to their operational performance, and the decreasing demographic resources constitute unavoidable obstacles on the path to the purely conventional defense of Europe that is so popular in certain quarters.

Indeed, the American faith in Western technological supremacy has already been channelled into the strategic thinking of liberals and a majority of conservatives in the form of the hazy concept of "conventional deterrence." The new technologies are supposed to enable Europe to defend itself without needing to risk nuclear war. In this way, the current "revolution" in military technology will have the effect of strengthening the other two strands of current antinuclear unease within public opinion.

The most worrying aspect is that the concept of conventional deterrence is given wide currency without the public ever being informed that its real implications include the increased risk of a conventional war in Europe, a steep rise in expenditure on weaponry, and conscription of human resources from a smaller base because of demographic changes.

The result is that the West, starting with the United States, is busy cutting off the nuclear branch on which it is perched while giving the impression to Western public opinion that other more economical, less dangerous solutions to the problem are now available, whereas in reality there are none. Losing a grip on reality in this way is all the more serious because Soviet military strategists are at the same time drawing the appropriate inferences from the neutralization of American nuclear power in Europe; aware of the potential of the new technologies, particularly in the conventional sector, they are themselves veering more toward a policy of "conventionalizing" war in Europe.

THE INF TREATY: STRATEGIC AND POLITICAL IMPACT

The Context

The extraordinary surge in the pace of East-West diplomatic activity in the last few years is impossible to understand without constantly bearing in mind the political and strategic background described above.

The October 1986 Reykjavik summit, the Soviet-American agreement on the double-zero option in April 1987, and the intense pressure exerted by Washington on the allies to accept it without further ado provide a faithful reflection of the new political and strategic realities of the alliance.

In Europe, a strong current of opposition to deterrence persists in Western public opinion (except in France), a current bolstered by Reagan's antinuclear rhetoric, so adroitly exploited by Gorbachev. This opposition has come to paralyze any will to act on the part of the West European policymakers. This goes hand-in-hand with an almost structural incapacity on the part of the Europeans to react as one in the face of these changes, which have been viewed with the same concern in Paris, London, and Bonn. Coming after the muddled European reactions in 1983–85 following the announcement of the SDI, Europe's discordant reaction to the post-Reykjavik events shows how crucial a role national slowness to respond and short-term electoral choices play in these affairs. That is another fundamental truth in today's Europe that must also be borne in mind when considering the prospects for reform of the present security system in a more "European" direction. Some have taken the view that Reykjavik or the double-zero option would eventually "wake up" the Europeans and oblige them in some way to join together and rethink their future system of security. For the time being, practically no evidence of this awakening has surfaced. (We shall be returning to this point in the last part of this chapter.)

Second, as regards the Americans, the most senior political and military leaders in Washington (except for a small minority fringe of "traditional Atlanticists") are convinced that strategic realities (parity) and new policies (unilateralism for the United States, German doubts) mean that the very structure of the alliance as well as its military posture must be redefined. Although the doctrine of flexible response remains for the time being sacrosanct (at least as a dictum), American strategic policy is tending strongly toward:

• Nuclear disengagement from Europe, except for a limited number of short-range tactical weapons, the aim being to contain all risk of escalation within the geographical area of Europe and ensure deterrence "from a distance" with the intercontinental arsenal of weapons;
• A more widespread military redeployment by the United States toward regions other than Europe (hence the Reagan 600-ship navy) and ever-growing pressure for withdrawal of a proportion of American troops from Europe, the economic argument being bolstered by strategic arguments in favor of a more global and less European-based role; and
• Finally, the conviction that the tide of public opinion and the dangers inherent in any crisis mean that the purely nuclear age is past and that the alliance must move toward an essentially conventional posture on a par in practical terms (but without saying so for the time being) with a policy of no first use of nuclear weapons. The developments in conventional and space technology are seen here as a way of remedying the quantitative imbalance between NATO and the Warsaw Pact, with the Europeans having henceforth to take more of the burden, that is, no longer stand easy but make up for the withdrawal of the U.S. troops and buy more high-tech weapons, preferably from the United States.

The Lessons to Be Drawn from Negotiation

Space prevents me from going into the very instructive details of the negotiations that have led the two superpowers to this agreement.[7]

---
[7] This area will be covered in the RAMSES report 1987–88 (IFRI, October 1987).

I shall therefore confine myself to comments on two specific areas of the bargaining involved: the respective roles played by the United States and the Soviet Union and the attitude of the Europeans.

First, the Reykjavik talks, as well as the diplomatic process that followed, were in reality dominated by the Soviet side, with the West being constantly surprised or caught on the hop.

Thus in Reykjavik, Mikhail Gorbachev, not Ronald Reagan, succeeded in imposing his agenda on the talks, an agenda that is written in capital letters all over his speech of January 15, 1986: zero-zero for INF in Europe, 50 percent reduction in strategic offensive weapons (the whole package being initially subject to abandonment of SDI), and finally a complete stop to nuclear testing.

From the outset at Reykjavik, that Euromissiles should be totally eliminated as the basis for a future agreement on INF was formally accepted, and the Americans therefore abandoned the idea of an agreement based on 100 warheads, which they had been advocating to their NATO allies.

The historical irony is that, having won this point of vital importance for Europe, the Soviets decided not to take the prize at Reykjavik because they thought that Europeans would, in their disappointment at being deprived of an agreement on Euromissiles, turn against Washington and SDI. In reality, the reverse occurred. The "failure" at Reykjavik was welcomed by the European governments, in private if not in public, as a breathing space. We therefore had to wait until February 28, 1987 for the Kremlin to decide to take the Reykjavik package off the shelf and propose a separate INF agreement on the basis of the zero option.

Second, the Europeans have once again shown their impotence. Although they had deep misgivings at the outcome of Reykjavik (both on the question of eliminating Euromissiles and at the American idea of eliminating all the ballistic missiles vital to NATO's American nuclear cover), the European governments, faithful to the Atlantic alliance and anxious not to divorce themselves from domestic public opinion, made a show of applauding the "progress" made at the summit in Iceland. What actually happened was that the failure of Reykjavik to settle the question of SDI was greeted with relief, with Europe hoping that it had avoided the elimination of the INF. However, this breathing space did not last long.

Caught in the trap of their own rhetoric on the zero option (this also applies to Mitterrand and his slogan "no Pershings and no SS-20s"), the European governments found it politically impossible to reject the Soviet "offer" of February 28, which they themselves had been advocating to their publics since 1981. The political situation in

Europe (success of the Liberal party and the Genscher line in the February elections in Germany, election year in the United Kingdom, cohabitation in France, fall of the Craxi government in Italy) effectively prevented anyone in Europe from being more Reaganite than Reagan on arms control. Reagan has been considerably weakened by the Irangate scandal (which broke on the morning after Reykjavik). From that moment on, he evidently wanted a summit in Washington in 1987, which made him more in a hurry than ever to conclude a "minimum" agreement with Moscow on Europe.

Rather than trying to stop the Reykjavik train, the Europeans committed the strategic error of fighting, with broken ranks, a rearguard action on the question of the shorter-range INF missiles, only to be once again outflanked by the second Gorbachev zero-option proposal of February 28, exactly one month after the Soviet offer of an INF agreement on a zero basis. Always one proposal ahead, the Soviet leader succeeded in removing European objections in advance. How could Europe refuse such an apparently generous offer: 1400 SS-20 missiles to be destroyed in exchange for 300 American systems, no restriction whatever on the French and British forces, plus 130 SS-22 and 23 rockets to be destroyed almost "free," as the United States had no equivalent systems deployed in Europe?[8] Dazzled by this avalanche of Soviet concessions, Secretary of State George Shultz, on his return from Moscow in April, generously gave the Europeans a fortnight to state their views—to be favorable, of course—while Ronald Reagan started talking of the imminent signing of a historic agreement with the Soviet Union.

Suddenly, without being at all prepared, Europe found itself pushed into a corner and having to resolve a whole series of fundamental problems from both the military and political standpoints.

The Strategic Impact on Europe

Although put forward in Washington and Moscow as a historic step on the road to disarmament, this agreement in fact represents a turning point that is potentially disastrous for the system of European security.

First of all, the double-zero option is not a step forward on the road to disarmament: the treaty covers only a tiny fraction of nuclear weapons in Europe (a twentieth in the case of the United States) and leaves intact from 10,000 to 15,000 Soviet nuclear weapons of all types capable of annihilating Europe, whereas Europe will be losing the

---

[8] The 72 Pershing 1A missiles, although fitted with American nuclear warheads, are the property of the *Bundeswehr*.

only American missiles capable of reaching the Soviet Union from European soil. If they had really been interested in disarmament, the superpowers could have begun—as they were committed to do before and after Reykjavik—by eliminating 50 percent of their strategic arsenals, which would have left them with arsenals three times in excess of the ceilings laid down in the 1972 SALT I agreement. Instead of adopting this line, the Americans and the Soviets chose to disarm Europe or, more accurately, to eliminate from the European theater any weapon (except for the F-111 bombers based in Britain) that could rapidly cause a European conflict to escalate into an intercontinental nuclear war.

The impact of the double-zero treaty should be seen from the military standpoint. The combination of the two zero options (on INF and SRINF) will, indeed, bring about a reduction of the Soviet nuclear threat. But this reduction is marginal compared with the enormous mass of Soviet tactical and strategic nuclear forces remaining (in particular, the 590 Scud-B missiles), all capable of striking Europe, not to mention the conventional and chemical power of the Soviet Union. On the other side of the coin, the departure of Pershing will mean that American nuclear cover rests on the two extreme pillars of short-range tactical weapons based in Europe and the intercontinental American arsenal, with just the F-111 bombers based in Britain as the sole intermediate support. The whole essence of the question first raised in 1977 during the preparatory discussions on deployment of the Euromissiles and again in 1987 in anticipation of their departure is whether, therefore, the extended American deterrent—as part of the NATO doctrine of graduated response—can or cannot continue in the circumstances, and if so, how. Should, as a number of American experts supported by the European left advise, the alliance opt for a straightforward conventional strategy in Europe, content to remain the background of the "existential" deterrence that will continue to be exerted by the core American systems? Should it consider deploying new sea- or bomber-based cruise-type missiles to take over the baton from the ground-to-ground Pershing and cruise missiles withdrawn from Europe? In the latter case, would the Soviets stand by in the face of what looked like an obvious breach of a freshly signed agreement? Would Congress finance new nuclear weapons, and would the Europeans deploy them at the very time when the existing ones were being withdrawn?

Consider the political corollary to this problem: where will the process of successive zero options end? More specifically, how will the Europeans, resigned to two zero options (INF, SRINF), be able to draw the final line beyond which no further zero options can be tolerated without resulting in the complete denuclearization of Europe? Aware of having started to slide (through their own fault, for the most part) down the slippery slope eroding NATO's nuclear posture, the Europeans, led by the Germans, were for a moment tempted to reject the second zero option or at least press for a right to match the number of Soviet SS-22s and 23s. That the *Luftwaffe's* Pershing IA missiles be modernized by using the guidance mechanism from the Pershing IIs about to be destroyed was proposed. However, political realities soon broke down this last-minute resistance. Intense American pressure, the sudden revival of the fortunes of Thatcher (who supported double zero), French uncertainties resulting from cohabitation, and finally, the CDU defeats in the May 1987 partial elections forced the Kohl government as well to endorse the U.S.–Soviet INF Treaty by reluctantly abandoning Pershing I. The attempt to place a "fireguard" around the SRINF had thus failed. Nevertheless, the political problem remained, made thornier, in fact, because the 500-kilometer lower limit will make Germany, as the main storehouse for the remaining 4,000 American tactical nuclear weapons, the prime target of a nuclear attack in peacetime as well as in a crisis. Thus, by focusing the main nuclear risk on the most exposed country, as well as the most insecure by virtue of its division and its antinuclear tendency, the position adopted by the alliance on double zero will have the direct effect of increasing German unease. How can German opinion, once the Pershing missiles have been withdrawn, accept a role as nuclear take-off pad for not only the Americans but also other Europeans? How are we going to justify to the Germans taking away the weapons capable of striking the Soviet Union while specifically keeping those which would kill Germans on both sides of the border?

To sum up, militarily speaking, the INF–SRINF Treaty is a swindle: even as a generous estimate, the withdrawal of the SS-20, 22, and 23 will cover some 1,500 Soviet nuclear warheads. That figure in reality represents only a twelfth or a fifteenth of the Soviet nuclear power remaining, which will continue to pose a threat to Europe. However, what the Europeans have agreed is to abandon all Pershing II and ground-to-ground cruise missiles, the only American missiles capable of making a strike on Soviet territory from European soil.

The incontrovertible strategic consequence of this trade-off is that Europe will from now on be an area of unequal security, open to nuclear, conventional, and chemical strike by the Soviets, and have no power to strike back at its adversary. The truth of the double-zero option is that the superpowers have, in fact, concluded an agreement on mutual sanctuary on the backs of the Europeans. Should by some misfortune a conflict break out on mainland Europe, it will be confined to the European battlefield. That is decoupling in the most basic sense.

However, the situation is more serious still. By agreeing to dismantle long-range weapons and keep only the systems with a range of under 500 kilometers, the Europeans have also deprived the policy of nuclear deterrence in Europe of all political and military legitimacy. How can the alliance explain to European public opinion that the zero option is ideal for weapons capable of striking the Soviet Union but out of the question for weapons that will kill Europeans alone—particularly the Germans?

The crux is that the double-zero option is tantamount to diverting the main nuclear risk onto the Federal Republic of Germany alone, as the storehouse for the vast majority of the remaining tactical weapons. The Italians, Belgians, British, and even some French have welcomed the double zero because Germany alone will pay the price, in peacetime as in a crisis. This "pass-the-buck" policy, which in the short term satisfies electoral anxieties on all sides, is in practice disastrous for Europe.

How can we imagine for one moment that a divided Germany, in the front line, obsessed by the specter of Chernobyl and plagued for ten years by a powerful neutralist-pacifist tendency, will be able to agree to act as the nuclear take-off pad for the rest of Europe?

If Germans have to choose between a nuclear Germany in order to protect the rest of Europe and a denuclearized neutral Germany to save their skins, then the Germans will, I fear, inevitably opt for the latter course. Who would act differently in their position? The result would be the unavoidable collapse of NATO and of the whole, forty-year European edifice.

Now is not too late to stop this infernal engine of successive zero—provided the Europeans pull themselves together, of course. Ten years after Helmut Schmidt began the whole business of Euromissiles, the intense diplomatic activity of recent months puts a Europe in disarray again on the spot with the same fundamental questions as to its future: what should the strategy for the future be and, above all, will security be structured by means of the alliance, in fact, or beyond?

REBUILD OR DECAY: THE FUTURE OF THE SECURITY SYSTEM IN EUROPE

In such a situation, Europeans now have a stark choice between resigning themselves to the slow, inevitable disintegration of the remains of the postwar security system—with the risk of being brutally awakened by a crisis—and finding the will to come together and rethink without delay the whole basis of their future security system.

The Risks

Three series of dangers directly threaten Europeans in the very short term (one to five years).

First, as regards the United States: during the coming months, the Europeans will have to discuss with Washington two fundamental problems on which fate of the Atlantic alliance will depend: the need to adapt the nuclear posture of the alliance immediately after the withdrawal of Pershing and cruise missiles, and the possible withdrawal of a substantial proportion (the figure of 100,000 is the one most commonly mentioned) of the American troops in Europe on the grounds of budgetary economy.

These problems will not solve themselves, and the alliance cannot count on muddling through as it has in the past. The nuclear dilemma of the alliance will not be resolved by U.S. agreement to deploy a few additional F-111s in Britain, any more than the removal of American troops will be avoided this time by the simple expedient of opening new negotiations on conventional arms, as occurred in 1973.

Neither of these two options, furthermore, is politically viable in view of the internal situation in the United States and the dynamism of Soviet diplomacy—a factor that has some influence in the matter.

As regards the U.S. troop presence, some members of Congress have made themselves clear that they have no intention of once again being ensnared by negotiations like those that started on Mutual and Balanced Force Reductions (MBFR) in 1973 and that they are banking on rapid results from the new "negotiations on conventional stability" specifically to enable American forces in central Europe to be reduced. Some American experts reckon that savings of $25,000 per soldier per year could be achieved, provided the soldier was demobilized and not transferred to another unit.

According to such estimates, a total of $25 billion could be saved if 100,000 U.S. troops were withdrawn, a sum that might seem modest to European eyes (a twelfth of the Pentagon's budget) when compared with its military consequences for NATO. However, it appears a considerable sum when seen from Capitol Hill, where the House of Representatives is faced with the prospect of raising taxes to make good the budget deficit. Because the Soviet team is aware of this situation down to the last detail, the Kremlin can be expected to propose a massive withdrawal of American and Soviet forces from the center of Europe, that is, from the two Germanies. Proposals of this kind have already been voiced at meetings of the Warsaw Pact in Budapest (June 1986) and Berlin (May 1987), with the Soviets going as far as to talk of withdrawals of 500,000 men on both sides.

As far as nuclear weapons are concerned, although NATO is contemplating replacing the Pershing II and cruise missiles with sea- or bomber-based systems (even converting the old B52Gs just assigned to the Pacific Command and bringing them back to Britain), Congress is unlikely to agree to such a course or to financing it, if only because deployment of such systems could be seen as a breach of the INF Treaty. The Soviets would have a field day accusing the Americans of bad faith and would at the very least demand that the forces concerned be taken account of in setting the ceiling for intercontinental strategic armaments. Because these ceilings are to be reduced by 50 percent (to 6,000 warheads), the United States is even less likely to agree to dismantle a substantial proportion of their sophisticated weapons to replace them with air-to-ground or sea-to-ground cruise missiles assigned to NATO. Even if such an arrangement were established, the political and strategic problem created by the withdrawal of Pershing would not be resolved because:

• The new systems (cruise, probably) would be based outside continental Europe and outside German soil in particular; they could not act as a "fireguard" against the current tendency toward denuclearizing central Europe. The problem of Germany's anchorage in the West and the retention of "its" tactical nuclear weapons would therefore remain unchanged.
• Militarily speaking, such systems would not help to reestablish coupling with Europe, specifically because they would be an integral part of the centralized American system.

Whatever the actual circumstances, the withdrawal of Pershing I and II and of the cruise missiles will therefore deal a fatal blow to the NATO doctrine of flexible response, which will then be resting on two equally incredible extreme scenarios:

• Either recourse to very short-range tactical weapons based in Germany, which would mean the destruction of Europe,
• Or recourse to American intercontinental rockets, which would mean suicide by the United States.

All this means that the Europeans can no longer expect any favors from the United States, at least on the nuclear protection front. Europeans really cannot expect their future to be resolved by an America tempted once again by isolationism and protectionism and prey to political and economic difficulties as a result of its new status as a semisuperpower. Europe no longer has the soft option of hiding the might of American power, because that no longer exists: not militarily, compared with the Soviet Union, nor economically, compared with Japan.

Only by demonstrating to American public opinion and to Congress that Europe is now prepared to take on a decisive role in its own defense can Europeans succeed in containing the very real risk of a massive and probably messy American disengagement from Europe. Force brings respect; weakness invites contempt and indifference. The era of the NATO protectorate is over, and so is that of America as the world's policeman. The Euro-American alliance, if it is to remain vital to both parties, must be fundamentally remodelled on the basis of a balance of responsibilities between the two sides of the Atlantic.

The second danger in continuing down the present path has nothing to do with Euro-American relations; it lies in Europe itself. Clearly, the impetus—already much weakened—of European construction will not long survive the balkanization of security policies by different European countries. We have already shown how the INF Treaty carries the seed of a possible split, at least at nuclear level, between Germany and rest of Europe. A Germany that felt betrayed by its American ally and abandoned by Europe would inevitably slip toward some kind of accommodation with the Soviet Union, bringing with it the neutralization of the smaller states, while France and Britain returned to splendid nuclear isolation. To believe that the edifice of Europe as it exists today could check, or even survive, such a process is a vain hope.

Rightly or wrongly, the "community" ideal as shaped by 30 years of agricultural marathons can no longer in its present form serve as a mobilizing force for a Germany intent on resolving its own future or as a focal point for its identity. Moreover, only the political and military anchorage of Germany in Europe can rescue Europe as a community. However, Germany's anchorage cannot be secured by economic and trade measures alone. Only a qualitative leap in cooperation on security can reestablish the retarded momentum of European unification and demonstrate to the Germans that the rest of Europe stands with them and shares the same fate. Thirty years after the Treaty of Rome, we must enlarge the scope of Europe beyond just economic and customs integration and thereby provide the goal of unifying the West European democracies to inspire the younger generations. Indeed, in the longer term, only the establishment of an axis of economic and political power in Western Europe that is capable of ensuring its own defense can provide the framework for possible reunification of the two parts of mainland Europe.

The third and last danger is from the Soviet Union. Much is now being made of the "changes taking place within the Soviet Union"; some observers (Hans Dietrich Genscher, no less, in Davos in February 1987) see in them the signs of a complete reform of the Soviet Union along Western lines. Nothing could be further from the truth. What Gorbachev is trying to do is make the Soviet Communist system work, because otherwise the Soviet Union is doomed to economic and technological decline. To achieve this, he is trying to modernize the whole fabric of economic production and planning by changing people's attitudes and keeping the structures. In foreign policy, Gorbachev needs for his purposes a period of stability in East-West relations, which he will take advantage of to change the military status quo in Europe by negotiation and reprime the pump of transfers of technology from the West. An examination of Gorbachev's diplomacy over the last few years makes clear that with the exception of the July 1986 Vladivostok speech, which was directed at Asia, he has concentrated his efforts on Europe and specifically on the disarmament of Europe.

The implication is as plain as day: in two or three years' time, the famous Gorbachev restructuring (*perestroika*) will probably have failed and Europe might well at the same time find itself militarily weakened (withdrawal of Pershing, possible removal of some of the American troops) and politically demoralized (by the effect of the separatist tendencies described above). The ingredients would be there for a potentially very serious crisis for which Europe could well pay dearly. Who would there be to prevent Gorbachev's successor or Gorbachev himself, should he decide to pursue a Stalinist line to stay in power, from triggering a crisis in Europe by exploiting the military weakness and political divisions of the Western powers to the full? The conditions that hitherto have deterred the Soviets from taking such a risk—American nuclear superiority, 300,000 U.S. soldiers in Europe, Germany's anchorage in the alliance and Europe—are all fast disappearing. A crisis (as opposed to war), with the threat of a swift and inevitable takeover (more and more feasible due to the Soviet conventional forces in central Europe), could therefore become a tempting option for a Soviet Union that is economically weak, still militarily powerful, and afraid of losing control over Eastern Europe. Safeguarding the alliance with the United States, preventing the danger of Balkanization in Europe, and deterring a serious crisis with the Soviet Union are reasons enough to push Europeans into rapidly taking the initiative and redefining their system of security by moving toward a policy of unified European defense. The aim of the closing arguments in this study is to show that such an initiative is possible, is

in no way illusory, and would in fact have a major stabilizing effect on
the strategic equation in Europe. The crucial point, of course, is
whether any politicians in Europe are capable of carrying through
such a policy.

The Options: The European Imperative

Regarded for a long time as a taboo subject after the failure of the
European Defense Community in 1954, European defense cooperation
has nonetheless developed in recent years, in particular as Europeans
realized that their strategic environment was rapidly changing.
Europe can therefore rely on a number of important achievements in
this area, even if these are still too fragmentary to constitute a
"European pillar" for NATO.

These achievements exist first of all at the institutional level, where
two frameworks—one multilateral, the Western European Union
(WEU); the other bilateral, the Franco-German Elysée Treaty of
1963—have been reactivated in recent years. Furthermore, a fabric of
cooperation within the European arms industry exists at both bilateral
(Franco-German, in particular) and multilateral levels (Tornado
consortium, for example).

More recently, more progress has been made toward greater
understanding and harmonization of the security policies of the major
European nations.

Probably the most significant progress, although as yet insufficiently
translated into practice, is in the state of mind of leaders and public
opinion on both sides of the Rhine. In France, the political parties
(except the Communists) are now all aware of the fundamental fact
that French security is in practice indivisible from that of Germany
and that France therefore does not have the option of nonaggression or
armed neutrality in the event of a serious crisis in central Europe. A
similar attitude has likewise developed in Germany. Given American
reluctance and a growing shortage of personnel in the *Bundeswehr,*
the contribution that conventional French forces would make as soon
as crisis broke is regarded as crucial. Finally, and despite the
persistence of a strong current of opposition to nuclear weapons in
Germany, Germans now have a greater understanding of the
importance of the French deterrent to European deterrence as a whole.

The initial application of this dual change of attitude in practical
terms has been greater military cooperation between the two countries,
the creation of the Rapid Action Force (FAR) in France, and the
opening of consultations at the most senior level in both countries on
how prestrategic weapons should be used. Recently we can point to
the "bold sparrow" maneuver of September 1987 and the joint

announcement by Kohl and Mitterrand on that occasion of a Franco-German Defense Council.

In parallel, recent months have seen the intensification of Franco-British talks on European defense matters, the laying of foundations for possible coordination by the two nuclear powers at the operational level (patrols, strike plans), and the joint planning of future nuclear systems. Likewise, bilateral cooperation has increased with other countries (France, Italy), particularly on the military application of space.

Nevertheless, the progress has been far too fragmentary, and it lacks overall consistency and a common political vision. Europe is in reality still far from having succeeded in coordinating its different national security policies, as evidenced by the European inability to arrive at a common attitude to the Soviet-American negotiations, which were of paramount importance to Europe (agreement on double-zero option). Evidence of this is also seen in the fact that the different defense budgets continue to reflect purely national priorities (nuclear and military space in France, conventional in Germany). Furthermore, without a common military strategy and hence clear political will on the part of governments, cooperation in the arms industry is tending to mark time—the victim of bureaucratic sluggishness as well as the intense industrial rivalry and protectionism that Europeans exhibit among themselves in the armament sector; naturally, in the final analysis this benefits American industry and helps to maintain the enormous imbalance (of the order of six to one) in favor of the United States in the arms trade across the Atlantic.

The dual realities of this situation—rapid change imposed from outside on their system of security, cooperation as yet too fragmentary between their different defense policies—means that Europeans have to accept that they must make a real qualitative leap in the area of defense. However, such a leap cannot succeed unless the recommended course of action remains in the realm of the possible and not in Utopia, which presupposes that a number of key principles should be accepted by all from the outset. Three principles are suggested.

1. The first principle concerns the actual objectives of the process of European military unification and especially the relationship between this process and the Atlantic alliance. Clearly, the aim of the effort that Europeans must make together is not to weaken their security, but to guarantee it in the best possible way. Therefore, the effect cannot encompass making or indeed conducting the effort to integrate Europe in such a way as to bring about the disintegration of the Atlantic alliance (by, for example, inducing the American troops to

leave more quickly) at a time when no European alternative would be ready to take over. Common sense indicates that conducting the process with the Americans is better than conducting it against them. The long-term objective is restoring the balance of the alliance rather than establishing some substitute in the form of a Europe supposedly equidistant between the two superpowers.

A clear distinction should be made here between the approach proposed in this chapter and certain propositions advanced in parts of Europe, particularly in the antinuclear and pacifist movements. Some have taken hold of the concept of a European defense as a means of preparing the ground for a kind of demilitarization and voluntary declaration of neutrality by the European nations themselves.

The whole difficulty of the exercise lies precisely in that area. The proposition is not that the military unification of Europe should amount to nothing other than a second pillar under Washington control. Such an arrangement would be tantamount to reintegrating France into the integrated NATO organization, which is neither politically desirable from the standpoint of the French internal consensus on defense, nor militarily useful to Europe in general. Nor would it have the slightest attraction for European public opinion. What indeed is the point of building a European defense if Europe has as before to place itself under the wing of the United States?

Between these two equally unsound solutions—a hypothetical third path between Moscow and Washington and a more European pendant within the existing alliance—Europeans should find a way of gradually unifying their defense. The path is a narrow one certainly, but such a course does enable the present to be safeguarded as well as the future. The process of intra-European cooperation would therefore evolve in parallel with NATO's existing structures, rather than instead of them. Arrangements for integrating European forces and military commands could be gradually introduced, performing a dialogue function with the American command in times of peace and operating under the authority of SACEUR in a crisis.

2. The second principle is that nuclear deterrence is and will remain an essential element in the security of Europe. Europeans should succumb neither to the illusion of negotiations on security with the Soviet Union nor to the mirage of sophisticated technology as a means of genuinely resolving their security problems. European politicians must grasp the nettle and explain to the public what is at stake and thus put a stop to the postnuclear rhetoric of Moscow and Washington. A Europe without nuclear weapons and devoid of an American military presence, as Moscow is proposing, is favorable neither to stability nor to peace in Europe. Likewise, the prospect of a

so-called conventional deterrent is neither acceptable in itself (as this type of "deterrence" has always failed in history and has twice already this century caused Europe to be destroyed), nor is it genuinely feasible. A purely conventional defense for Europe would involve a massive increase in defense budgets and the mobilization of vast numbers of human resources that Europe does not possess. The fact that the nuclear deterrent will remain the keystone of the future European security system necessarily implies that the problem of the Europeanization of Europe's only autonomous nuclear forces—those of France and Britain—must inevitably be the subject of the most detailed debate.

3. The third and final principle is that the Franco-German axis will be the kernel of the process of European integration at the military level. This does not mean that the process will be reduced to nothing but the Paris-Bonn axis. On the contrary, Britain in particular and also the other European powers should be closely and gradually associated with the concept of the sharing of tasks among the different states. Existing institutional machinery could play a valuable role in this respect.

Having set the principles, the following measures could be implemented without delay as a start to the unification process:

1. For the French, the long-postponed clarification of national strategic policy must be embarked on immediately, first with a declaration. France should announce that the defense of Germany is from now on one of its "vital interests." Survival and not just the defense of France would therefore begin on the Elbe and not the Rhine. Such a gesture would have a major psychological and political impact in the Federal Republic. It would also remove any temptation on the part of the Soviets to drive a wedge between the two countries, particularly in a crisis.

   Then such a commitment could be translated into practice by:
   - Strengthening the logistic ties between territorial France and the defense of the front, starting in peacetime (access to French ports and airbases, early positioning of equipment);
   - Moving some French conventional forces to the front line in proportion with requirements for the defense of central Europe (in the event of a number of American units being withdrawn); and
   - Adjusting France's nuclear posture and capacity so that it is the territory of the Soviet Union rather than that of the Federal Republic of Germany that is under direct threat should France use its nuclear weapons. This presupposes the purchase by

France of ground-to-ground long-range missiles (S-4) and the location on the front line of some of its prestrategic systems.

2. On the German side, this new commitment by France must be reciprocated by cooperation in the arms industry (an essential condition if the French field forces are to undergo necessary modernization), but German attitudes toward nuclear deterrence must be clarified. Neither Germany nor France would benefit by showing the Soviets that Europe would be unified in its defense only so as far as its conventional forces were concerned and that it would be content to give battle on its own soil, in other words, under the most favorable conditions for the Red Army.

3. The problem of nuclear cover for Germany (and the other European states) by the French and British deterrent forces must therefore be discussed at the same time as the strengthening of links between conventional forces. To resolve it would mean coordination between London and Paris on nuclear modernization programs and access by Germany, if not to decision making, at least to the planning and utilization of such forces. A European nuclear planning group could be set up, consisting initially of France, Britain, and the Federal Republic of Germany. The establishment of a common deterrent axis among the Europeans would be significant to the Soviet Union at a time when Soviet leaders may be tempted to think that they had succeeded in neutralizing the American nuclear cover in Europe. In practice, neither the French nor the British have the U.S. option of being able to lose their expeditionary forces in Germany in a conventional war without endangering their survival. A comprehensive European deterrent, based on the nuclear submarine ballistic missile forces (about a thousand warheads) belonging to France and Britain, is not only possible and credible but also the only way in which the nuclear deterrent can remain part of the European defense system in the long term.

4. At the same time as this series of military measures, the Europeans should aim to define jointly their position on the arms negotiations. Here again, the forum of the Western European Union could play a key role. This applies particularly to conventional arms as well as to the nuclear field.

The measures proposed here might be thought too fainthearted in the face of the challenges now confronting Europe. The modesty of the measures is only on the surface, however, for the European security system can be redefined and stabilized in the long term without an all-or-nothing approach or Utopian revolutions. The measures proposed here are politically realistic and militarily effective. Nothing and nobody can condemn 300 million Europeans to turning their backs and to Finlandization, except one thing: the very attitude of renunciation that unfortunately has been seen too often in recent years. However, that seems to me to be a problem of political psychology and therefore of political education or of the analysis of political leadership on the part of those at the helm, and not a matter of military strategy.

In other words, a deterrent to the Soviet Union will continue to be possible, provided that Europe wants it.

12

The Future of NATO's Deterrent Posture: Nuclear Weapons and Arms Control

By LAWRENCE FREEDMAN

When the negotiations on intermediate nuclear forces began in November 1981, the United States proposed the global elimination of all intermediate-range missiles with collateral constraints on shorter-range systems—the zero option. This the Soviet Union rejected; it proposed instead constraints on its own intermediate-range forces in return for the abandonment of the NATO proposals to introduce Tomahawk cruise and Pershing II ballistic missiles into Europe. The agreement would be confined to Europe, aircraft would be covered as well as missiles, and British and French systems would have to be taken into account.

Six years later the treaty was signed in Washington. It covers missiles but not aircraft; it includes Soviet systems based in Asia but excludes those of Britain and France. The ground-launched Tomahawks and Pershings will go but so will *all* comparable Soviet systems. The zero option is to be implemented. Indeed, the treaty goes further, as some shorter-range systems will be removed as well. As a result of all of this, the United States will be required to move a few hundred missiles that have only recently arrived, and West Germany will dismantle 72 elderly Pershing I missiles. For its part, the Soviet Union will need to remove well over a thousand warheads.

At first glance, this can be described only as a triumph for NATO. The alliance adopted a radical arms control proposal and backed it up with serious deployments until the Soviet Union agreed. Yet, the agreement has been criticized by many of the alliance's most thoughtful supporters, including members of the mainstream strategic studies community and opposed by a former SACEUR. We have no way of measuring the length of the faces in the higher military commands of the Warsaw Pact as they contemplate the proposed agreement, but we have seen many long faces among their Western counterparts.

The concern revolves around the proposition that whatever the short-term political advantages provided by the zero option, it was strategically ill-considered. The Warsaw Pact can afford to make the concessions in the nuclear area, the argument goes, so long as this helps undermine NATO's strategy of nuclear deterrence. If the alliance allows itself to be denuclearized, to use the current jargon, then the military competition will revert to the conventional sphere, where the Warsaw Pact enjoys all the advantages. The long faces result from this prospect. When the Reagan administration challenged the proponents of a policy of no first use of nuclear weapons early in the 1980s, it claimed that such a policy would make "Europe safe for conventional war." This is the charge also leveled against the Reagan administration.

My objective in this chapter is to assess the requirements for NATO strategy in the light of the INF agreement. Some of the adjustments required will be unfortunate, others long overdue. I will argue that although the posture that could emerge from the review process will not be optimal because of the INF constraints, it will not be disastrous. To develop this argument and to provide a sense of historical perspective to the current controversy, the chapter opens by identifying some of the considerations that influenced the 1979 double-track decision and then assesses them in the light of what has transpired since that date.

Although 1979 does provide a useful starting point for this analysis, this time frame is extremely narrow. A true historical perspective must assess current developments by reference to the whole postwar period. We have now passed the twentieth anniversary of the promulgation of the doctrine of flexible response—MC 14/3. The recent debates do not suggest a great movement in favor of a new MC 14/4. The very flexibility of flexible response and its lack of precision allow for a variety of interpretations. What it lacks in military guidance it makes up for in diplomatic convenience. However, there is a widespread feeling that the alliance is in some ways at a turning point in its development. In addition to the challenge to nuclear deterrence that influences opposition parties in Europe and is said to be posed by the INF agreement, the complex of political relations that has defined the European security system since the 1950s is now undergoing substantial change, which must affect the military relationship. Apart from the familiar questions of alliance unity and defense budgets, stirrings in the center of Europe and, most significantly, evidence of a movement in Soviet politics and policy open up a set of opportunities and risks that have still to be clarified.

This political uncertainty provides the context for this chapter, even if it cannot be addressed directly. Strategy is about the relationship of military means to political ends, and as the political circumstances that shape those ends evolve, our military means must also evolve. The political circumstances also shape the sort of military means that are available. Identifying exciting new military options with no prospect of being funded is pointless.

THE CONSIDERATIONS OF 1979

In 1979 the structure of long-range nuclear capabilities in Europe was deemed to be inadequate in a number of ways. First the United States could cover most of the important fixed military targets in the Warsaw Pact and western military districts of the Soviet Union by systems based either in continental United States or at sea. The 1974 Schlesinger doctrine had been designed to emphasize this capacity so as to reinforce the link between U.S. strategic assets and the defense of Western Europe. By the late 1970s, this doctrine was suffering from three criticisms:

1. The impact of the political commitment was diluted by distance. Psychologically it was not the same.
2. The buildup of Soviet missile strength that had begun in the 1960s was now creating an inferiority complex in Washington. This was, after all, the time when people who should have known better warned of an imminent Soviet "window of opportunity." The new "countervailing strategy," announced by Harold Brown in 1980, was seen as a continuation of the changes in targeting philosophy that had been set in motion by Schlesinger. However, as the name implied, the emphasis was on neutralizing the nuclear options of the Soviet Union rather than creating options for NATO to initiate nuclear hostilities.
3. The SALT II Treaty of June 1979 confirmed the nuclear status quo without doing much to address the concerns over the vulnerability of U.S. ICBMs that was driving concerns over the Soviet "window of opportunity." The treaty reinforced the sense that U.S. strategic systems derived their meaning and purpose in relation to those of the Soviet Union rather than through alliance commitments.

In addition, 400 Poseidon SLBM warheads (the contents of 2.5 submarines) were assigned to SACEUR. Their relative invulnerability meant that they would serve as an ideal reserve force, even if their relative inaccuracy meant that they would be less than ideal for attacking point targets. This formal link with the NATO command structure compensated for some of the problems of distance. However, as with other central strategic systems, the problem with these missiles was their political rather than their military quality. Crudely put, they could easily be withheld by an American president. Systems based in Europe might actually have less military quality because of their vulnerability, but politically they could not be so easily held back and therefore would be more likely to get entangled in a land battle.

Plenty of short-range nuclear systems, consisting of a great variety of types of weapons and, via the dual-key system, operated by a number of NATO armies, were deployed in Europe. By the end of the 1970s, the number of nuclear warheads based in Europe was put at some 7,000. Although NATO governments did not attach the same importance to this number as to the number of U.S. troops in Europe, it had taken on some political significance as a symbol of the American nuclear guarantee, so that any diminution in this number might be taken as a diminution in the U.S. guarantee. Nonetheless, this arsenal had a number of failings.

1. No clear military concept guided their use. In 1969, the Nuclear Planning Group had adopted proposals for initial use of nuclear weapons. Since then, guidelines had not been developed for follow-on use if the initial use failed to have the desired effect on the Warsaw Pact.
2. The guidelines for initial use stressed the importance of signaling a willingness to use nuclear weapons and contemplate further escalation. The use of nuclear weapons on the battlefield as part of general purpose forces was played down, despite the fact that the original weapons had been designed and integrated into the NATO force posture with such employment in mind. Studies of "nuclear war fighting" did not encourage confidence that any war in which these systems were used could be contained or that NATO could expect to gain a serious military advantage by initiating nuclear use at this level because of the comparable capabilities of the Soviet Union and its potentially greater staying power in a nuclear war of attrition. Others feared that the forward deployment of these systems and their integration with general purpose forces could result in premature use (use 'em or lose 'em) that could turn a possibly manageable conflict into a nuclear holocaust.
3. NATO's short-range systems were in need of modernization, but the muddle surrounding their rationale and employment concepts provided little guidance for planners. In 1978 NATO had failed miserably with the enhanced-radiation weapon (neutron bomb) as a result of this confusion. This failure provided a lot of the political impulse for getting things right regarding what were then known as long-range theater nuclear forces.

The only long-range theater nuclear forces were the American F-111s and British Vulcan aircraft. These were getting old. The demands to be placed on the dual-capable F-111 in the conventional area were substantial, and they could not be guaranteed to penetrate Soviet air defenses in sufficient numbers. They lacked an obvious successor. The 52 Vulcans were in fact removed in 1983. The Vulcan had a successor in the Tornado, but the Tornado lacked, to any serious extent, a capacity to attack targets in the Soviet Union.

Meanwhile, the Soviet Union was steadily expanding its nuclear options for use against European and Asian targets. Weapons at a variety of ranges were involved, but the most notorious examples were the Backfire bomber and the intermediate-range SS-20 missile. As worrisome for NATO was that the Soviet Union seemed to have developed a doctrine that matched its nuclear arsenal, provided guidance for weapons designers and force planners, and was more self-confident than the West's notion of nuclear use as a last resort with the expectation of a slide into mutual destruction. The Soviet approach stressed attacking NATO's nuclear assets by conventional means during the first, conventional stage of a conflict and then at the appropriate moment delivering the coup de grace by a nuclear strike, at whatever the necessary level, to eliminate remaining assets and put Western Europe at its mercy. This approach was critically dependent on keeping nuclear hostilities confined to central Europe and preserving Soviet territory as a sanctuary.

In the SALT II negotiations, the United States had shown apparent indifference to Soviet SS-20s and Backfire bombers except as part of a threat to the continental United States. Rather than seek to match these systems, either to neutralize their influence or to create the conditions for their eventual exclusion in an arms control deal, the Carter administration appeared prepared to bargain away the most interesting counter—the new cruise missiles. The way for their exclusion had been prepared in the protocol to the treaty. However, as concern grew over this question, the administration insisted that it saw no incompatibility between SALT II and eventual deployment of cruise missiles in NATO.

At the same time, as NATO addressed the question of long-range theater nuclear forces in December 1979, President Carter met with the new British Prime Minister Thatcher and agreed to make available Trident missiles to Britain to replace its aging Polaris force. At the time there could be no certainty that this program would ever be implemented. More certain was the French nuclear modernization program, with the new multiple-warhead M4 SLBM at its center.

NATO had determined in 1978 to reverse the trend toward lower defense budgets and the consequent deterioration in conventional forces. The three percent target was adopted for budgetary growth, and objectives for force improvements were endorsed in the long-term defense plan. By 1979, all this was expected to be honored more in the breach than in the observance. NATO was not expected to cease depending on nuclear deterrence.

On December 12, 1979, NATO decided to remedy the situation in its long-range theater nuclear forces. The decision was to introduce 464 cruise missiles into Britain, West Germany, Italy, Belgium, and the Netherlands, and 108 Pershing II into West Germany. Five important features of this deal were:

1. The Germany insistence on *nonsingularity*, which meant that it would not be alone in accepting new weapons on its soil; other NATO countries had to join in.
2. The belief that the new missiles had to be land-based to reinforce the U.S. nuclear guarantee; sea-launched cruise missiles were considered and rejected.
3. The missiles should be operated by a single American key; although the United States had no objections in principle to dual key arrangements, dual key normally means dual finance, and this was not of great interest to the Europeans.
4. The offer of arms control talks, hence the "dual-track"; the NATO offer wavered uneasily between a recognition that the alliance's requirement reflected its unique strategic position and therefore existed irrespective of the character of comparable Soviet systems, and the natural tendency when thinking about arms control to do so in terms of parity between comparable systems; any negotiations were to take place in the SALT context out of a recognition of the dangers of talking about a separate Eurobalance in isolation from the overall strategic balance.
5. Belgium and the Netherlands were less than wholehearted in their commitment to the program.

Two weeks after NATO had decided to remedy the deficiency in long-range theater nuclear forces, Soviet forces entered Afghanistan. This invasion immediately changed the political context in which the program would be implemented, if at all. The unequivocal end to detente combined with nuclear rearmament generated widespread public unease and the formation of protest movements opposed to the new missiles. President Carter removed SALT II from the Senate's consideration so that it was not ratified. The December 1979 commitment to a double track could now be met only by separate talks on these systems. These talks began with something of a false start in October 1980. They were never again merged into the strategic arms talks.

1979 TO 1988

What has changed since has been the improvement in East-West relations after the trough of the early 1980s. The INF agreement itself has been an important manifestation of this, as has a political climate in which deescalated military confrontation is expected. NATO's military spending rose in the first half of the 1980s, but no further growth is likely. If anything, a slight contraction in military spending may occur.

In strategic terms the most important development of the decade has been the shift in the American approach to nuclear issues. This shift has been particularly marked because of the early enthusiasm of the Reagan administration for a robust form of nuclear deterrence in which the Western position would be reinforced by a strategic modernization program that would provide a future president with a range of options, including the conduct of a protracted nuclear war, should deterrence fail.

This approach influenced attitudes toward U.S. systems based in Europe. Although the administration made INF a key test of alliance solidarity, in strategic terms, modernizing the short-range battlefield systems as a means of confusing Soviet plans drew more interest. The essentially political virtues of the INF deployments were of less interest. The inspiration for the zero option was not only the political advantages of such a radical position but also that many of the president's advisors felt that the INF program was unnecessary. If the United States could retrieve its former strength at the strategic nuclear level, then reassuring deployments at lower levels were not needed. The land-based systems were also considered to be too vulnerable.

Far more important for alliance nuclear strategy than the removal of some systems from Europe has been the declining confidence in the United States that the appropriate options could be developed. The long saga of the MX ICBM and the doubts over the capacity of command, control, communications, and intelligence systems to operate in the way required under any circumstances, and certainly not in a nuclear environment, undermined the approach. Politically it also ran into problems as it suggested an optimism over the prospects for nuclear war fighting that appeared sinister and reckless to many sections of public opinion. The more the *counter*vailing rather than the *pre*vailing aspects of strategy (that is the readiness to react to nuclear moves by the Soviet Union rather than to take the nuclear initiative) were stressed, the less the administration appeared to have any novel answers to the traditional dilemmas of NATO strategy.

The bipartisan Scowcroft Commission's report of April 1983 marked the end of the early confidence in an offensive nuclear strategy.

The previous month saw President Reagan's now notorious speech, which set in motion the Strategic Defense Initiative. The long-term practical impact of SDI will probably be slight. However, the philosophy surrounding the Initiative was clearly opposed to traditional forms of nuclear deterrence. From a technical fix designed to render nuclear weapons "impotent and obsolete," a political fix to achieve the same objective was only a short step. The obvious method for this was arms control, which was far less controversial than SDI and more likely to produce results. Again as exhibited most dramatically at the 1986 Reykjavik summit, the philosophy was opposed to nuclear deterrence. This evidence of a trend in American thinking was reinforced by revelations by such key figures as Robert McNamara and Henry Kissinger as to their own doubts over the U.S. nuclear commitment to Europe.

This trend caused evident unhappiness among West European governments. However, their ability to stand firm for the old orthodoxies was limited by the public support for reduced dependence upon nuclear weapons. When the antinuclear movement had been at its height in the early 1980s, governments had dissented from its methods (unilateralism) rather than its objectives (nuclear disarmament). When Chancellor Kohl and his defense minister expressed their doubts as to the wisdom of the double zero, they received little encouragement from their allies (Thatcher was facing a general election), their Free Democrat coalition, or the German electorate. Resistance soon evaporated.

The Soviet Union also appears to have reappraised strategy. One of the consequences of the arrival of cruise and Pershing is that they undermined Soviet hopes of keeping the Soviet Union a sanctuary in an East-West nuclear exchange. The Soviet Union did not share the antinuclear movements' concern that these missiles were part of preparations for a limited nuclear war. The Soviet concern was exactly the opposite: that they were instruments of escalation from a limited to a more general war because they were likely to get involved in a European land war *and* could hit Soviet territory. One perhaps should not underestimate the impact of the theories of nuclear winter and the very real experience of Chernobyl.

For whatever reasons, from the early 1980s the Soviet military seems to have been putting a steadily greater stress on the conventional stage in a conflict, envisaging now not so much that a successful campaign in this stage could create the conditions for a decisive nuclear strike but that victory might be achieved without any resort to nuclear weapons. In a sense many in NATO had long made this presumption about Soviet strategy because of the assumed Warsaw Pact advantages in the conventional area. Only now was it starting to become a reality, which explains why the Soviet leadership was more relaxed about nuclear disarmament.

Leaving aside their interest in the ultimate goal of nuclear disarmament, eliminating the direct threat to Soviet soil posed by the new intermediate-range missiles was still vital; threats to the soil of other Warsaw Pact countries were easier to tolerate. The zero option came to make sense because it meant trading alliance-threatening weapons (SS-20s) for superpower-threatening weapons (cruises and Pershings).

THE FUTURE OF NUCLEAR DETERRENCE

This chapter is not the place to seek to analyze or explain all these developments. For the current discussion, what is important to recognize is the secular decline in nuclear deterrence that is a trans-atlantic and East-West phenomenon and much more than a function of arms control agreements. The need to adjust NATO strategy would exist even without the INF Treaty.

The decline in nuclear deterrence has limits. No longer does anyone have the same sort of confidence that one side could emerge victorious in a nuclear war or that initiating nuclear hostilities would have great military value. However, there is still a long way to go before NATO will relinquish the first-use option. Leaving aside such matters as the actual value of no-first-use pronouncements (or whether one would want political leaders to take them seriously during a crisis and act as if a major war could be fought without nuclear use), NATO is unlikely to feel able to rely for some time on conventional strength alone to deter a Warsaw Pact conventional invasion. Furthermore, a broad consensus remains for the need to maintain nuclear weapons to deter nuclear use by an adversary. Moreover, the principle of deterrence through uncertainty still applies. So long as nuclear weapons exist, their use in war cannot be precluded, whatever the peacetime assumptions or even declarations that nuclear weapons will not be used first.

Therefore, NATO strategy still needs a nuclear component. Although the problems of extended deterrence appear in a particularly acute form when discussing whether the United States would put itself at nuclear risk when reacting to a *conventional* attack against its allies, the problems are still there when discussing an American nuclear response to a *nuclear* attack on its allies. Britain and France have their own means of retaliation. The other allies, including West Germany, must rely on another nuclear power, and they would still prefer to rely on the United States.

U.S. nuclear systems will be required to remain on European soil for some time. Although many will require that these systems provide no more than a retaliatory threat, others will expect that the risk of nuclear war remains inherent in any major conflict on the continent. The question is, therefore, to what extent has the INF agreement made this more difficult?

NATO'S NUCLEAR REQUIREMENTS

As a result of the agreement, NATO will not be denuclearized. It is giving up some 430 missiles and the plan for a further 140 intermediate-range missiles. None of these missiles were available before 1983, and no other systems of equivalent range have been removed to make way for them. What is being lost is a new capability rather than one that has long had a central place in NATO plans. In addition, 108 old Pershing IAs operated by the U.S. Army have been removed to make way for the Pershing IIs, and 72 Pershing IAs assigned to the Germany, and their American warheads, will also be removed. A possible replacement by a new short-range missile has not been closed off, but then the domestic political situation in West Germany made this less than a foregone conclusion.

Let us now examine the nuclear system that will remain in or assigned to Europe.

Battlefield Nuclear Weapons

The objections to the systems outlined above remain powerful. One of the advantages in the INF deployments was that it created the conditions to shift the emphasis in the NATO force structure away from the short to the longer range. In the Montebello agreement of 1983, the alliance moved in this direction. The decline in nuclear warheads was confirmed by a move down to 4,600. Much of the decline has been in obsolete systems and by such overdue moves as the shift from the nuclear Nike-Hercules to the conventional Patriot air defense missile.

What could be achieved by way of unilateral reductions had limits because of the importance many of those responsible attached to the need to ensure that those countries whose armed forces operated nuclear systems continued to do so, in order that nuclear risks continued to be shared. The Montebello Decision also left open the question of modernization. Although new nuclear artillery shells are under development, Congress has been less than enthusiastic about these programs.

The role of nuclear artillery and very short-range missiles will be controversial in future NATO planning. Given the concerns over denuclearization, NATO commanders will argue the need to hold on to what we have. There are, however, a number of contrary pressures. These weapons are likely to be raised as an arms control problem by the Soviet Union, even though far more Soviet systems are at stake than Western systems. (The Warsaw Pact has some 750 short-range Frog and SS-21 missiles to NATO's 90 Lance; the Warsaw Pact has over 6,000 nuclear-capable artillery pieces, of which about half might actually be available for use in the nuclear role; NATO has some 4,000, of which no more than 1,100 are available for nuclear use.) Many Western strategists remain unhappy about the destabilizing role these weapons might play in a conflict by encouraging premature nuclear escalation. Developing effective tactics and doctrine for nuclear artillery has never been easy, and many in NATO armies would prefer to dedicate the artillery pieces to conventional tasks. Furthermore, a deal by which the short-range missiles were removed (and not just their warheads) would also remove some of the conventional options for attacking NATO's forward air bases that have been of concern to NATO planners.

Perhaps most important, the West German government is unhappy about a class of weapons that can be used only on or against German soil. Having reluctantly agreed to the second zero, it now seems more enthusiastic about the third. One reflection of this attitude is their lack of enthusiasm for a replacement for Lance. This would essentially be a nuclear version of the MLRS.

Therefore, a triple zero to remove all the missiles and artillery pieces below the 500-kilometer-range may attract considerable attention. One of the concerns in NATO is the difficulty of confining the triple zero to these elements. Such a limitation might intrude into tactical air forces, which have now taken on a greater importance in the framework of nuclear deterrence as well as providing a key source of conventional strength.

In addition, many practical problems are connected with trying to negotiate arms control in this area. Dual capability and the need to control warheads rather than delivery systems pose peculiar problems of counting and verification, although with the increased willingness to contemplate on-site inspection such problems need not prove insuperable. The artillery pieces may turn out to be covered in an eventual conventional force agreement, and this might satisfy those who would prefer this issue to be deferred until more of a conventional balance has been obtained with the Soviet Union. However, the sort of attractive conventional disarmament deal offered by the Warsaw Pact, for example, dramatically reducing its armored divisions in Eastern Europe, may be conditional on NATO concessions in tactical air forces.

In the absence of arms control, NATO may still see an advantage in continuing its own rationalization of nuclear systems. The most logical development would be to maintain Lance and move to a follow-on system, while turning the artillery over to conventional use.

The only effective counter to nuclear missiles and artillery currently available is a preemptive attack and some hardening of critical installations. An antitactical ballistic missile has been discussed over the past few years. Discussion in NATO has largely been confined to defenses against conventional missiles; within the SDI program, defenses against nuclear missiles have been investigated. Although some technical possibilities exist and the Patriot air defense missile is being slightly improved to give some protection against missile attack, the consensus would appear to be that the resources required and the current state of the threat do not warrant a major investment in this area. The double-zero agreement is likely to reinforce this judgment.

Nuclear-Capable Aircraft

The main responsibility for nuclear roles will now pass to aircraft. NATO's tactical air forces have been strengthened in recent years, so it has no real problem with means of delivery, most notably with the F-15 and the Tornado. The exception to this is the longer-range category. Now only the F-111 poses a serious threat to Soviet territory.

NATO is likely to atempt to sustain the "vertical firebreak," dividing nuclear systems sharply between aircraft and missiles, rather than horizontally according to range. Every effort will now be made to protect nuclear-capable aircraft from arms control.

The credibility of nuclear deterrence in Europe is now bound up with aircraft. Their flexibility and versatility makes them more suited than artillery and short-range missiles to this task, as does their more straightforward command and control arrangements. However, an enhancement of their nuclear roles may prove difficult. They will still be needed in conventional roles. Whatever the attractions of dual capability in principle, in practice the tendency will be to devote aircraft to urgent conventional tasks even if doing so means using up a nuclear reserve. Furthermore, the forms of defense against aircraft are known. The prospect is an offense-defense duel that takes the form of a technological arms race, which could lead to considerable expense and uncertainty.

As with the earlier discussion of the appropriate structure for NATO's nuclear missiles, the optimum approach might be to put more emphasis on nuclear roles for longer-range aircraft and accept that shorter-range aircraft will be largely if not wholly dedicated to conventional tasks. The problem here is the lack of a successor to the

F-111. The best solution would probably be the development of a new standoff missile for use with the F-15. Britain and France also have some interest in a standoff missile to improve the effective range of their aircraft.

Submarine-Launched Ballistic Missiles

The commitment of SLBM warheads to SACEUR remains and is being improved with the replacement of Poseidon by Trident. In the course of the INF debate, this commitment was played down and is now often forgotten. However, it provides SACEUR with a considerable nuclear capability. The problem remains, as noted earlier, that politically they are not tied to Europe, as they could be withheld. If some declarations by the Reagan administration were pursued by a future U.S. administration, then these missiles could be removed as part of an overall elimination of all long-range ballistic missiles. As yet such a possibility does not appear to have excited much Soviet interest, but the same was said about the zero option. There would seem to be a strong argument for the West to forgo this approach. For Western Europe, a nuclear force posture dominated by short-range systems would raise fears of decoupling and limited nuclear war with a vengeance. For the United States, the confidence in the B-1 and new stealth technology may not outweigh the Soviet advantages in air defense, including geography (compare the access to Moscow with access to the U.S. eastern seaboard). As the elimination of ballistic missiles is part of the American position on SDI rather than START, it may be easy to abandon. The tentative START agreement outlined after the December 1987 Washington summit does not envisage the removal of all ballistic missiles, but it does suggest substantial cuts that will limit the number of SSBNs that the United States will be able to deploy (especially as the new Ohio-class carry 24 missiles each). This could lead to some competition over SSBN assets in the future between their NATO and central strategic roles.

British and French Nuclear Systems

The modernization of British and French strategic forces is now proceeding apace, leading to an eventual accumulation of warheads and a relative strengthening of their numerical position vis-à-vis the superpowers. As a result of the 1987 election, the British Trident program is almost certain to be completed, although this will take until the end of the century. Both countries also deploy substantial numbers of medium-range aircraft. In addition, France has 18 land-based missiles, which will soon be unique on the continent, and short-range missiles (Pluton/Hades). The dual-key artillery and Lance systems operated by the British Army raise no special issues beyond those raised for other NATO armies.

All these systems can be expected to draw increased political attention, which might take two forms.

If strategic arms control makes progress, then there will be pressure to include British and French missiles in a future arms control regime. Neither country precludes this possibility, although neither is enthusiastic. Both stress the need for substantial cuts in superpower offensive forces and no expansion of Soviet strategic defenses and would prefer that little is done before the conventional imbalance has been redressed. What they would do should their conditions be met is not altogether clear, as they cannot reduce their forces significantly without effectively abandoning nuclear status. In practice they will be unable to offer much other than a warhead ceiling. Britain's hand might be forced by the United States conceding the Trident program in a future START deal.

British and French nuclear forces could be seen by other European countries as the embryo of an alternative form of nuclear deterrence. Although doubts about the durability of the American nuclear guarantee help explain the attachment to these systems, neither Britain, France, nor their European allies have shown great enthusiasm for an alternative to the U.S. nuclear guarantee. Britain does deploy a substantial portion of its nuclear assets—the Tornado squadrons—on German soil, and this constitutes a significant commitment to West German security.

Britain and France might cooperate on a new air-launched standoff missile in the future, but cooperation is unlikely to extend much beyond that.

If France moves closer to NATO, the contrast between the two force postures, with French forces displaying a much more pronounced nuclear bias, could cause tension.

Compensation for the "Loss" of INF

Some have suggested that NATO should be compensated for the "loss" of INF systems through the introduction of alternatives not covered by the agreement. The two main options are extra long-range aircraft and submarine-launched cruise missiles.

Extra Long-Range Aircraft. The options here would be either introducing extra F-111s into countries other than Britain, bringing over the extended-range FB-111s that have always been based in the United States although they would be flown to Europe in a crisis, and basing some B-52s, the old strategic bombers, in Europe. The main difficulty with all these options, in addition to the cost of the extra facilities, would be political. To have a reassuring effect on Europeans concerned about decoupling, these new deployments would need to be given a high profile. However, such a profile would create considerable problems for the host country and would carry the risk of increasing the pressure for aircraft to be included in an arms control regime.

Submarine-Launched Cruise Missiles. This option was widely canvased as an alternative to GLCMs in the 1970s. If insufficient systems will now be available to threaten the whole of the Warsaw Pact target set (bearing in mind the number of targets now to be withdrawn), then a case might be made for looking again at SLCMs. However, whatever would be accomplished by such a step could be accomplished more simply by providing renewed emphasis to the SLBM warheads to SACEUR. Both SLBMs and SLCMs lack political presence, but SLBMs have the advantage of no problems in penetrating defenses and no problems of dual capability. Considerable difficulties could develop in the command of cruise missile–carrying submarines if they were required both to engage in their maritime roles and to remain available to SACEUR. Also, SLCMs are likely to be restricted in any future START treaty.

THE SHIFT TO CONVENTIONAL DETERRENCE

The logic of the whole trend of developments within the alliance (and not just the INF Treaty) is that NATO should rely more on conventional forces in the coming years. NATO strategy must be sensitive to political context, and no longer does a sufficient consensus back the threat to initiate nuclear hostilities as a deterrent to all war. Greater success in designing options that held out some hope of gaining military advantage through nuclear use might have enabled the threat to last longer with greater credibility. As it is, however, the most important nuclear requirements now are to ensure attention to the problems of providing a credible second-use threat and to remind that war moves in unexpected directions; we can never have full confidence that a major East-West conflict would not take on a nuclear character.

The unavoidable logic is that we should now attend to the conventional balance. Three problems are normally identified with the movement in this direction: the conventional balance finds NATO at a severe disadvantage; the resources will not be available to correct the balance; even if a balance were obtained, it would not constitute a sufficient deterrent.

The Military Balance

The political rhetoric with regard to the balance suggests that the situation is all but hopeless. Words like massive, huge and overwhelming are habitually used to describe Warsaw Pact superiority. The problem with interpreting the numerous facts and figures available to describe the conventional military balance is that they tell us absolutely nothing about the likely outcome of a conventional war. Facts and figures cannot include military factors such as quality, morale, training, leadership, tactics, disposition, supply lines, and stocks. They also cannot take account of the two key *political* factors that would in practice determine the impact of the military relationship at times of crisis or war.

First, a future war is unlikely to start with a set piece confrontation along all fronts and on all flanks, even though NATO tends to work on the assumption that none of its members could be safely ignored by the adversary. The opening stages of a war are highly political affairs, with each side seeking to undermine its opponent's alliance as much as its armed forces, while shoring up its own. The sort of crisis that would make war at all possible in Europe would be one that would see the existing alliance structure under enormous strain. Few countries will beg to be allowed to join in the fun; a number can be expected to renege on their obligations. Statecraft in these circumstances will be about the balance of alliance as much as the balance of military power.

Second, the balance of military power will itself be transformed through the processes of mobilization and preparation for war. Neither side could prepare for war without warning, but the available indicators that something is up might or might not be recognized and acted upon. Arguments within and between alliance countries are likely to occur over the meaning of these indicators and what should be the appropriate response. Political leaders will take a lot of convincing before they put their countries on a war footing. Even if a few accept the necessity, those who find the process too provocative will still raise objections. If the response is made and the threat subsides, will the doubters be convinced that the threat was real, and will those who were prepared to respond this time be prepared to do the same a second time, given all the expense and bother entailed?

In addition to these political factors, an important *military* factor needs to be remembered about attempting to draw strategic conclusions from an assessment of opposing inventories of forces.

How these systems will actually operate in practice is extremely difficult to predict, more so now than ever. We simply do not know how armies will fare under modern conditions—with weapons that can be used at any time of day and in any weather, with extraordinary surveillance combined with extraordinary precision, with the ever-present possibility of nuclear use, and with superb communications one moment and dead silence the next. Where will the soldiers take cover and when can they rest? Who will coordinate these massive armed forces? The "friction" of which Clausewitz wrote so eloquently is likely to be accentuated rather than eased by modern technology. ("Everything in war is very simple but the simplest thing is very difficult. . . . Countless minor incidents—the kind you can never really foresee—combine to lower the general level of performance, so that one always falls far short of the intended goal.")

VALUE FOR MONEY

The logic of improved conventional deterrence has not been followed by any noticeable increase in resource allocations to defense. In terms of force levels, the main issue for the coming few years at least and probably over the long term is not going to be how best to expand our conventional forces but how best to manage steady contraction. The climate created by a successful arms control deal on nuclear systems backed up by Warsaw Pact proposals for dramatic reductions in the conventional sphere will not seem to be the right time for major increases in defense spending. In the United States, the budget deficit is going to loom larger as the existing political mechanisms fail to grapple with it.

The Soviet Union cannot easily avoid these pressures, so in relative terms the position may not alter so much. However, at issue is not simply balance but the structure of armed forces. We will need ingenuity and new thinking to find ways to meet our existing commitments in the most cost-effective manner.

One possibility is a steady movement toward two- or even three-tier force structures. Distinctions will develop between units (squadrons, divisions, naval groups) fully equipped with the most sophisticated equipment and those that are making do with older and/or less capable equipment. This differentiation need not be bad if it is linked with new concepts of operations that do not rely on advanced technology systems for every task, for example, the use of light as against heavy divisions. However, the risk of a simple hierarchy is obvious. The armed forces of the various members of the alliance will become increasingly interdependent. The extent to which this is already taking place is obscured by the practical problems evident in drives towards "standardization" and "interoperability" of equipment, and institutional resistance to "specialization." In practice, the expansion of the areas within which individual operations may have to be conducted and their complexity mean that the forces of a single country can rarely be sufficient in themselves. They must therefore draw on the resources of other nations. Exercises, planning, and command structures must reflect this requirement. This tendency obviously undermines those who always prefer to think in terms of self-sufficiency either for an individual country or a group of countries, such as members of the Western European Union. In the long term, this interdependence may turn out to be a significant integrative force within the alliance itself.

For Western Europe the most important integrative factor remains the presence of substantial American forces on the continent. As a result of the INF Treaty, the "coupling" role of American forces may be given even greater prominence. However, at the same time, budgetary pressures are liable to encourage a contraction in American force levels. Therefore, the symbolism attached to a specific number should be diminished in the discussion of future force levels, and the possibility of some reduction in overall numbers should be accepted. A troop cut of 5,000 introduced to send a message to Europe would be more damaging than a troop cut of 50,000 as a result of the need for the sort of adjustments that budgetary pressures impose on all NATO countries at some time or other.

Arms control does not provide an easy way out of conventional force problems. The most promising developments may continue to be in the area of confidence- and security-building measures, as reductions will take a long time to arrange and to implement. On the evidence of the Mutual and Balanced Force Reduction negotiations, they may be impossible. Much will depend on whether the new Soviet leadership does have a different attitude toward its military power in Europe.

Lastly, too much cannot be expected from the West's technological superiority. Although in air and sea warfare, it will continue to be of critical importance, in land warfare the significance of a technical edge can easily be exaggerated. Furthermore, a lot depends on the speed with which technological advances can be exploited. In the future more stress should be placed on reliability and maintenance than on exacting performance characteristics, and the systems should be designed according to what *needs* to be done as opposed to what *could* be done if the designers were given their head. Indeed, where possible in the interests of economy, off-the-shelf purchases should be favored over "designer" equipment. However, a clear view of requirements depends on a clear strategic concept.

STRATEGIC CONCEPTS

For all these reasons, a general alliance debate on conventional strategy is needed. Two sets of questions appear to be of particular importance.

Mobility versus attrition. Military reformers on both sides of the Atlantic have been rediscovering the virtues of maneuver warfare. They see it as involving more of the "operational art" than the crude trading of casualties involved in attrition warfare. However, they are also rediscovering the political difficulties involved in not committing forces in peacetime to the forward defense of West Germany, as well as the command and control and logistics problems involved in managing maneuver warfare. Wars tend to be shorter in anticipation than in practice. The blitzkrieg exercises a powerful hold on the military imagination but as likely a prospect may be an offensive bogged down under its own weight and the problems of supply and facing a defender unable to muster the strength to expel the invader. In these circumstances, the fluidity on the battlefield may not be in the central engagement but in maneuvers designed to probe for weaknesses on the other side and counteract the other's probes.

The extent to which NATO forces will be expected to attack targets to the rear of the enemy lines rather than be confined to engagements on the forward edge of the battle area. This question is raised by those who are concerned that preparations for *any* military operations into the enemy rear is inherently provocative and destabilizing. It is raised in a different form by those who have no objections in principle but are concerned about a possible diversion of resources from the primary task of holding onto NATO's own territory. This issue has come to the fore with such schemes as Follow-on Forces Attack, which has been criticized by some as being of marginal value if NATO's front line has insufficient resources to cope with the first wave of the Warsaw Pact attack. Guaranteeing any adversary that its rear area will be respected as a sanctuary would seem unwise, for that will ease his military planning considerably. Posing a threat to the rear may be necessary to ensure that the adversary is obliged to take full defense precautions, without necessarily devoting a major share of resources to that task.

CONCLUSION

At issue is not whether conventional deterrence can or should substitute for nuclear deterrence. The question is the relative weight accorded the two. The thought that a future European war could go nuclear is still a sobering prospect, even if the fuse is getting a little longer. What is important is that the uninviting prospect of conventional war is given its due stress. A conventional war fought with modern weapons in the middle of Europe would result in terrible death and destruction. Its outcome would be uncertain, simply because the methods employed would not be tried and tested and the rules of this military game would have to be worked out as it was played. In this sense a truly "conventional" war is no longer possible if by that we mean it will follow "conventions" that are well known and understood. Once it began, its limits, including its geographical scope, could not be anticipated. Whatever NATO says now about the limits of its objectives, should a war start, these objectives are unlikely to be limited to a return to the status quo ante after a Soviet attempt to create a new status quo. Moreover, regimes that start and then lose wars do not tend to survive long.

East-West relations appear to be entering a new period that may introduce new uncertainties, may ease tensions, or may end up changing the political map of Europe. At the moment the pace of change and its direction remain unclear. As the situation becomes clearer, the consequent political adjustments will inevitably mean military adjustments. For those concerned with NATO's armed forces, this could become an uncomfortable process. However, in the final analysis the role of the military is to help meet political objectives. All that they can ask is that the political objectives are realistic and that their full ramifications have been considered, so that the military is not required at some later date to salvage a deteriorating situation.

13

The Future of NATO's Deterrent Posture: An American Perspective

By R. JAMES WOOLSEY

"I have heard much talk of moving from nuclear deterrence to conventional deterrence," said a French participant at a NATO conference several years ago, "and I wish to make an observation. A thousand years of European history teaches us one thing: conventional deterrence does not work."

But the double-zero agreement at the December 1987 Washington summit between the United States and the Soviet Union—covering long- and short-range intermediate nuclear forces (INF) and eliminating worldwide all land-based ballistic and cruise missiles with ranges between 300 and 3,000 miles—has taken the world a small step, militarily, and a rather larger step, philosophically, back toward the troubled millennia of warring European states that ended in 1945.

Viewed in isolation, this agreement might not seem to have such an effect. In order to understand the problems for NATO's deterrent that must now be solved, however, one must assess the INF agreement in the context of other developments that are affecting NATO's posture and deterrence in general. From that perspective, the current situation may be salvageable, but it is highly troubling.

The roots of the double-zero INF agreement lie in the events of a decade ago when, unexpectedly and against nearly unanimous advice, President Carter astounded West German Chancellor Schmidt and much of the rest of the world by effectively abandoning the deployment of the enhanced-radiation warhead (the "neutron bomb") and leaving Schmidt in an untenable political position. Schmidt's subsequent call for the United States to compensate for the speedy ongoing deployment of the new Soviet SS-20 medium-range nuclear missiles was echoed by other Europeans, and it grew directly out of the

283

neutron bomb imbroglio. Schmidt's request was answered by the Carter administration, after some initial reluctance, with an American commitment to the dual track: a deployment of Pershing II and ground-launched cruise missiles (GLCMs) in Western Europe and a simultaneous negotiation for a limit on those deployments in exchange for limits on the Soviet SS-20s.

The initial American reluctance to deploy was matched by initial European skepticism that the deployment would in fact occur. The skeptics' point was well-taken: a vigorous European antinuclear movement had developed, and it was growing in size and influence in many parts of Europe by the early 1980s. It soon gained influence in both the British Labour Party and the German Social Democrats and then effectively claimed both as adherents. As recently as the late 1970s both socialist parties had been committed to NATO's deterrent and, when in power, had made major contributions to maintaining it. Now Americans faced the unaccustomed sight of two sets of old friends— not merely demonstrators in the streets—telling them that their willingness to make financial sacrifices and to expose the United States to risk on Europe's behalf was not only the major current problem facing Europe but also, at best, morally equivalent to Soviet behavior. From the American side of the Atlantic, this set of events made many think that an overly nervous Europe, exaggerating its need for American assurance that it would not be abandoned, had suddenly become neurotically hesitant to accept the assurance for which it itself had called.

Neither the intranational nor the international diversity within Europe is well appreciated in the United States. In the early 1980s political developments that were underway in any event and the understandably different European reactions to two quite different American presidential styles became fused in American minds. In any case, in the United States a strong impression arose that the Europeans were perversely seeking simultaneously to lure their reluctant Yankee cousins into a militarily unnecessary deployment and to punish them for being responsive. Europeans seem to have been driven by equally distorted views: first, that President Carter was a hopeless weakling, and then later, that his successor was a dangerous and uncontrollable cowboy. Although under neither Carter nor Reagan were American policies toward NATO vacillating and unstable, as many European observers had feared, a disturbing trend nonetheless was being set in motion on both sides of the Atlantic—a deterioration in the willingness to maintain a nuclear deterrent.

Part of the American response to the vigorous European opposition to NATO's INF deployment was the zero-option proposal of 1981. This was the Reagan administration's first effort to steal the clothes of an antinuclear movement, a pattern of attempted larceny that was later to be repeated with sufficient frequency and zeal that on occasion distinguishing between the thief and the victim became difficult. In 1981, however, it seemed to be a sound tactical move. The political point made by the offer of a zero option seemed attractive: we are the ones who are opposed to nuclear weapons; the Soviets are the ones who are nuclearizing the continent. Moreover, the result, if the offer were by some chance accepted, would have been to trade potential (and at that time highly uncertain) American INF deployments for existing Soviet ones. If some philosophical difficulties loomed in the distance, some small weakening of the principle of flexible response, there seemed in 1981 to be little risk that the Soviets would accept the proposal in any case—indeed, little risk that they would do more than fume. The zero option's troubling long-range implications for deterrence were appreciated at the time by only a prescient few.

In 1982 the administration's allegiance to the zero option held firm. A potential agreement—"the Walk in the Woods" between the veteran U.S. statesman and INF negotiator in Geneva, Paul Nitze, and his negotiating counterpart, Ambassador Kvitsinsky—was rejected by the Soviets, and subsequently support deteriorated in the U.S. government as well. This tentative agreement would have significantly reduced Soviet SS-20s in Europe to 75 (to 225 warheads), cancelled the Pershing II, and permitted 300 single-warhead U.S. GLCMs— essential INF equivalence in warhead numbers at a relatively low level, but a Soviet advantage in time of flight.

This agreement in 1982 would not have eliminated "a whole class" of weapons, the proud claim of the supporters of the current INF accord, but it would have come half a decade earlier. At the expense, admittedly, of completeness and ready verifiability and with some adjustments in deployment location doubtless made necessary, such an agreement would have left intact the coupling provided by NATO INF forces in Europe between the U.S. deterrent and the defense of the continent. Who can say what share of the alliance's confusion and disarray in the years 1982-87 might have been forestalled by the acceptance in 1982 of an agreement permitting a modest number of SS-20s and GLCM warheads? Clio never reveals the consequences of the paths she does not take, but the nagging thought remains that the twin causes of strategic stability and alliance solidarity, together with some modest complementary progress in arms control, might have been well served by pressing hard for a different decision in 1982. In any case, the zero option for INF had taken the giant step from ploy to doctrine.

What followed in the United States in late 1982 and early 1983 was striking indeed. In short order, deterrence was no longer a boring theoretical subject. The Reagan administration had indulged in an early delay in resuming strategic arms talks, in part because it could not decide what to do about the U.S. ICBM force, and had permitted several of its members some curious rhetoric about nuclear war. It began to pay the price. During the 1982 elections it saw the nuclear freeze movement triumph almost everywhere it was on the ballot; the American antinuclear movement was becoming as active as the European one. In the same elections, the administration's party lost 26 seats in Congress and consequently its working majority (Republicans together with conservative Democrats) in the House of Representatives —the majority that had enabled it to work its will in the government as a whole in 1981–82. The National Conference of Catholic Bishops issued a pastoral letter that ultimately offered conditional support for nuclear deterrence, but only by "a centimeter of uncertainty," according to its principal draftsman. Indeed, the letter came close to repudiating the morality even of maintaining an American nuclear deterrent, not to speak of using it, against Soviet aggression.

Then, shortly after the 1982 election, the lame-duck Congress which was presumably at least 50 votes or so more favorable to the administration and its programs than the Congress that would be arriving in January, overwhelmingly rejected the new dense-pack basing mode for the MX ICBM. The administration had brought this problem on itself by cancelling, in part because of its political concerns about public reaction in Utah and Nevada, the complex but fairly survivable shell-game basing mode for the MX ICBM (multiple protective shelters, or MPS) that had been developed by the Carter administration. However, the Reagan administration had endorsed the MX missile itself, leading many to worry that it was only interested in a first-strike use for the U.S. ICBM force. The administration's new dense-pack basing mode in 1982 was complex, a radical departure from the past, and unacceptable to Congress.

Many in the administration felt that this rejection by Congress, in the context of all the other shocking developments of late 1982, meant that Congress would be highly likely in the future to reject any other MX deployment as well and thus ICBM modernization of any kind; some feared that it was also likely to reject other important modernization of offensive nuclear forces. A presidential commission (the Scowcroft Commission) was convened in early 1983 to assess the problem of what to do about U.S. strategic forces. The commission's recommended approach toward maintaining an offensive deterrent and making progress in arms control was not formally reported until April 1983, but its central features were well known in the executive branch and Congress by February. By late March, the specifics of the commission's compromise program—which later in the spring turned out to give some renewed life to both U.S. ICBM modernization and arms control—had been brokered between the key players in both branches of government.

In the meantime, in the prevailing environment of executive branch despair about the prospects of offensive force modernization, the president had been preparing his March 23 speech that launched the Strategic Defense Initiative (SDI) with its now-famous paragraph calling for nuclear weapons to be made "impotent and obsolete." Thus this vague but exuberant call to redirect American strategy away from deterrence and toward what the secretary of defense later came to call "thoroughly reliable" defenses became a third and much larger step along the antinuclear road—a road on which the first steps had been taken by adopting the zero option and then by turning away from the walk in the woods.

The March 23 speech was, however, the Reagan administration's first real venture into the rhetoric of nuclear eschatology. The Democratic left on both sides of the Atlantic had wandered from time to time into this verbal fog. Now it was joined by the president of the United States. The strategic worldview of some on the left had become that the West no longer needed nuclear deterrence because the Soviet Union was a threat neither to its neighbors nor to freedom. The worldview of some on the right now became that the left was correct about the West's not needing offensive deterrence but for a different reason: American technology in space could free the world, they said, from the fear of nuclear weapons.

During 1983-86, the administration seemed to lapse into several simultaneous states of mind on these nuclear questions; its laissez-faire economic principles were seemingly applied to nuclear policy within the government. Parts of the air force and several prominent Democrats in Congress—Representatives Aspin, Gore, and Dicks, for example—worked hard to maintain the survivability of an offensive deterrent, the central issue being whether to continue to implement the Scowcroft Commission recommendation to move forward both with a small, mobile ICBM and, for the near future, with MX. Much of the Office of the Secretary of Defense tried to undermine this approach and to spend the money on SDI or other programs instead. The State Department went its own way and focused on what would succeed in negotiations. The White House was unpredictable—an interagency group approved a proposal at Geneva to ban mobile ICBMs, for example. During these years the president seemed to smile tolerantly upon all of this; from time to time he would reiterate his antinuclear vision.

The administration's infatuation with antinuclear sentiment bloomed into true romance in the autumn of 1986 at the Reykjavik summit. With the president's proposal there to abandon ballistic missiles, to deploy SDI, and to provide SDI technology to the Soviets, some hoped that antinuclear sentiment in the Reagan administration had crested and would subsequently recede. However, the proposal to ban ballistic missiles reverberated in 1987 into the campaign for the Democratic presidential nomination. There a majority of candidates—with an eye toward pleasing the antinuclear groups in the first event of the Democratic election-year calendar, the Iowa caucuses—endorsed a total ballistic missile flight test ban, an approach seemingly designed to enforce the president's Reykjavik proposal. Only Senator Gore and former Governor Babbitt resisted the antinuclear groups' pressure.

From NATO's perspective the key point about such efforts to ban ballistic missiles is that neither during the now-famous proposals in Reykjavik's reputedly haunted house where Reagan and Gorbachev met nor in the more recent Democratic candidates' endorsement of a ballistic missile flight test ban did any shred of appreciation surface for the importance of nuclear weapons in deterring conventional war. Although some American commentators have recently sought to minimize proposals such as the one at Reykjavik to ban ballistic missiles as mere "loose talk" and to ignore the context and many of the broader antinuclear implications of the double-zero agreement, this lack of appreciation about the core of NATO doctrine is disturbing.

The problems of relying solely on air-breathing systems to maintain an offensive deterrent have been airily dismissed by too many who should know better. Radical proposals to scrap the bulk of the nuclear deterrent are lightly tossed into both the diplomatic and political hoppers by Republicans and Democrats alike, including presidents and presidential aspirants, without any apparent concern for the consequences. The serious problems—how to maintain a credible deterrent if the United States had no ballistic missiles and if all of its nuclear systems had to penetrate the Soviet Union's massive air defenses, how to maintain the survivability of our own aircraft on their bases, how much making our own air defenses comparable to the Soviets' would cost—are apparently beneath discussion.

Key parts of the rhetoric of the antinuclear movement about a nuclear-free world have been bought wholesale by important figures in both parties. One side posits a Soviet change of heart as its deus ex machina; the other posits a successful space-based SDI. For both the White House and the Iowa caucus wings of the American strategic debate today, the central notion seems to be that nuclear weapons are not an instrument of state power, dangerous because they are possessed by a dangerous state, but that they are, in essence, a virus that we and the Soviets can and should work together to cure and for which we may soon develop an inoculation by a friendly sharing of technology and effort. Once wedged into this framework of thinking, nuclear weapons will be routinely viewed and assessed in isolation from the principal reason that gave rise to their deployment by NATO, the reason that has sustained their importance to the West for four decades—the conventional imbalance favoring the Soviets in Europe and the consequences of Soviet domination of the European continent.

If the only purpose of American nuclear weapons were to deter Soviet nuclear attack on the United States, then radical nuclear arms reductions—perhaps to zero—logically await only one thing: Soviet acceptance of adequate verification. This problem is far from simple but intellectually neater than the morass of interactions between political will, conventional force imbalances, and nuclear deterrence that represent the messy reality underlying the strategic debate. For forty years, however, Western Europe has prospered and remained at peace because the leaders of NATO nations on both sides of the Atlantic have been willing to deal with this reality and have not fled from it. We now face the problem that, both on the right and on the left, some American political leaders have grown weary of this complexity and of nuclear weapons. Neither deus ex machina that would resolve these dilemmas—neither "thoroughly reliable" defenses nor the political transformation of the Soviet state—has yet descended to the stage.

To its credit, the Reagan administration made an effort in the early 1980s to take an important step toward redressing the conventional imbalance by adding heavily to the U.S. defense budget. The funds were used principally to acquire larger numbers of existing types of weapons and weapon platforms—ships, aircraft, tanks, and the like. However, too small a share was used in those years, when funds were readily available, to pursue seriously the types of technology that could lead to NATO's being able to put Soviet armor at risk and thus to deter a Soviet blitzkrieg with innovative technology rather than with massive expenditures.

The problem was made even more difficult by the huge cut in the nation's revenue base that was made by the 1981 tax law. A few farsighted Americans, among them Senators Nunn and Moynihan, Congressman Aspin, and James Schlesinger, said at the time that such cuts would put a heavy strain on defense. The administration's response was of a piece with the worldview of Dickens's financially troubled Mr. Micawber: "Something will turn up."

What in fact subsequently turned up was an increasingly strident and politically vigorous antinuclear movement in the United States and then several consecutive years of real decline in the U.S. defense budget. Although taken aback by the SDI proposal, the antinuclear movement has recently seemed to become heartened, not disillusioned, by the points of agreement between it and the Reagan administration, for example, the aversion to ballistic missiles.

But a general public desire in the United States to retreat from foreign, especially European, entanglements is not what has driven the defense budget cuts and produced the groping for a simple, single answer to nuclear complexities. It is faulty decisions by American political leaders. Some types of isolationism are indeed small clouds on the American horizon, but withdrawal from Europe is not one of them. Trade difficulties, burdensharing arguments, and the normal noise caused by an alliance of free nations bartering with one another all do exist, but they should not be exaggerated. One or two conservative intellectuals—most prominently Irving Kristol—have called for withdrawal of forces from NATO and, essentially, reliance on SDI instead, but at this point they are strategic curiosities, not trendsetters. The understandable concern in the United States about the NATO allies' (and, even more so, Japan's) failing to spend a share of the GNP on defense comparable to that spent by the United States creates continuing political difficulty for Americans who argue for strongly supporting our alliance structure. Nevertheless, very little grass-roots pressure exists in the United States today for any pullback from the American commitment to NATO.

NATO has, for many years, been the American military commitment to which almost all American politicians have repaired. It continues to be so. Even during the Carter administration when Korea, for example, understandably grew nervous about proposed American troop pullouts and when those who saw the need for adequate funds for the U.S. defense budget understandably grew despondent, real growth for NATO improvements still had wide support in the administration and in Congress.

The risk today is not that American political leaders may be driven to retreat from NATO due to a surge of isolationist sentiment in the American heartland. The risk is rather that American leaders will fritter away the time that they have been given by the American people's strong commitment to the alliance and to the freedom of Western Europe by engaging in fitful pursuits of romantic illusions. American and European leaders might use this time to place greater emphasis on the technologies needed to deter and defeat armored attacks without nuclear weapons. They might use it to redeploy NATO's conventional forces more effectively. They might use it to modernize nuclear forces with smaller numbers of highly accurate low-yield weapons. They might use it to deploy an effective antitactical ballistic missile defense. They might use it to undertake a major effort, with both arms control proposals and public education, to highlight the threat to peace caused by Soviet forward deployment of large numbers of armored units and to help the nations of central Europe find further ways to assert their independence from Moscow.

They must use the time, not waste it. They cannot be permitted to forget that this Indian summer of reform in Moscow can—like the varied reform periods of Peter the Great, Alexander II, Lenin's New Economic Policy, and Khrushchev's early years—quickly be followed by a cold Russian winter. They cannot be permitted to forget that many slips occur between the dream of technological wonders and the reality of operationally sound and secure defense systems. While they use the time, an alliance version of the Hippocratic oath should be observed: *primum non nocere*, especially do no harm by removing NATO's nuclear umbrella while working for positive changes to take place.

The INF agreement alone can be managed if we take the right steps. The agreement's military effect, which is relatively small, is not the problem, but rather the illusion that today, or at least very soon, NATO's deterrent will not be needed—an illusion that the INF agreement both symbolizes and can further encourage. The risk is not principally that isolationist sentiment will lead the United States to withdraw from its commitments to the alliance, but rather that the curious antinuclear double-envelopment now being undertaken by the right and the left in U.S. politics, augmented by fiscal worries, will succeed against those laboring to maintain both a deterrent and the alliance.

The rush toward a separate INF agreement should be seen in this context. Certainly a U.S. reversal of its 1981 position to abolish INF systems would have created problems. The people of democratic countries can tolerate only so many sharp reverses from their national leaders on matters of this importance and substance. What is regrettable is that a *separate* INF agreement was struck and that the negotiations were conducted in such a way as to put those European leaders, especially in the Federal Republic, who are favorably disposed toward NATO in a very difficult political position. As part of an agreement on strategic forces, the Europeans would have been likely to understand that an agreement withdrawing the hard-won NATO deployments was an understandable part of some wide-ranging bargaining. Taken alone and in the present context, it presents some serious potential problems.

The heart of NATO's combined military and political strategy has to be the continued integration of a free Federal Republic of Germany into the West's political fabric and its central military alliance. The separate INF agreement now foreseen thus takes on a dim hue when one realizes that under the double-zero formulation, the preponderance of nuclear weapons left in central Europe are those that would detonate on German territory during any hostilities. West German leaders understandably observe that "the shorter ranged the missiles, the deader the Germans."

Thus antinuclear sentiment in Germany and elsewhere is bound to produce a push for the elimination of short-range nuclear weapons in the aftermath of a separate INF accord that seems to go out of its way to offend West German sensibilities for no particular strategic or military advantage. The nuclear systems below the INF threshold should rather be modernized with an eye not on numbers, but on survivability and effectiveness. A relatively few land-based launchers, for example, carrying a longer-ranged successor to Lance, could be effectively augmented by nuclear and nonnuclear sea-based cruise missiles, as long as these are not unwisely bargained away in START. Some reductions in battlefield nuclear weapons may be negotiated as part of a broader agreement, but dealing with them separately or eliminating them would only enhance even further the Soviet predominance in conventional, particularly armored, power.

Deterring a Soviet blitzkrieg was the purpose of the deployment of NATO's short-range nuclear weapons in the first place. The Soviets, with their newfound skills in public relations, might well parlay this antinuclear sentiment into accommodation to their objectives — dangling the hope of German reunification tantalizingly just out of reach. In the face of these sorts of concerns, the administration ordinarily changes the subject and responds that the separate INF agreement will eliminate many more Soviet warheads than American ones.

If one has sold the pass, pointing out that it was sold on favorable terms is no answer, especially if it turns out to have been the pass to Rapallo. In subsequent arms control negotiations, resisting any such single-minded concentration on nuclear weapons alone, especially European-based ones, is extraordinarily important, for the ultimate price may be the Federal Republic's drifting away from the alliance.

The foremost objective of any future arms control with the Soviets should be to use what leverage the West has to bargain for something that will not undercut the Atlanticists in the Federal Republic, as the separate INF agreement does, but help them: not just a reduction in manpower, the focus of the talks on Mutual and Balanced Force Reductions, but a major withdrawal of Soviet armor from East Germany. These Soviet armored deployments must become the central public and arms control issue now and must replace denuclearization of the continent, the number one item on the Soviet agenda. NATO may never be militarily ready for such denuclearization unless and until a fundamental change in the nature of the Soviet state occurs. It is certainly not ready now. Although armored units withdrawn to the Soviet Union or even beyond the Urals could be brought back to East Germany with relative ease, the mobilization and warning that would occur would at least give NATO far more time than it has now to take compensating action, if its own deployments were not heavily crippled by any such agreement. One, perhaps the only, positive feature of the prospective INF agreement is that it established the principle of disproportionate Soviet reductions. Such disproportionality is essential if conventional arms control is to have any utility.

There is one bright spot on the horizon. The growing cooperation between the Federal Republic and France in military matters may give the West added strength and cohesion in the difficult years ahead. This could make possible more effective conventional forces, backed by French (and British and American) nuclear forces, than would have been imaginable a few years ago. Some redeployments of NATO forces, for example, could help NATO's conventional defenses significantly. France's current role in the structure of Werstern defense is positive in another way as well. French intellectuals have not only led the rest of the world in the now-rampant rejection of the philosophical underpinnings of communism, but France is the only major Western power in which the leaders of both principal political parties have kept their heads about them in the political storms over nuclear weapons in the 1980s. A gradual reintegration of French forces into NATO's military command may be a romantic illusion, but from the point of view of preserving peace and freedom for Western Europe it is a far more attractive illusion to pursue than at least two of its competitors.

Some have suggested that negotiators must move immediately beyond the INF accord to strategic arms control to obtain reductions in long-range strategic offensive forces, perhaps coupled with limitations of some sort on defensive systems, for example, a reaffirmation of the 1972 ABM Treaty or a pledge to abide by the narrower of the two currently competing interpretations of that treaty. Strategic offensive arms control would have the logical effect of making the task of covering the same targets by increasing warheads on ICBMs or SLBMs more difficult for the Soviets, or for either side, for that matter. Because the INF agreement covers only three to four percent of the nuclear weapons on each side, both the United States and the Soviet Union could feasibly retarget some current strategic assets to cover targets originally covered by INF missiles.

This possibility raises the general issue of the overall utility of strategic offensive arms control or arms reductions in today's circumstances and particularly of the impact either would have on NATO's deterrent.

For much of the eighteen years in which the United States has been involved with the Soviet Union in negotiations to limit strategic offensive arms, our primary purpose has been to limit or reduce large, fixed MIRVed Soviet ICBMs, the objective being to preserve the survivability of U.S. silo-based ICBMs. The United States has been willing to accept such limitations, the theory being that a mutual enhancement in survivability would improve the stability of the strategic balance and that such a mutual step would in any case be preferable to either unilateral American ICBM vulnerability or to mutual vulnerability of such systems. For this entire time, however, the Soviets have sought to establish or perpetuate a unilateral advantage in ICBM survivability while resolutely making the U.S. problem worse by themselves deploying larger, more highly MIRVed, more accurate ICBMs. Many of the notions that pass for arms control proposals today still seem to try to deal with this ICBM survivability problem, although in practice they would lock in a unilateral Soviet advantage. Under such proposals the United States would still have to take steps other than arms control measures, such as deploying the small, mobile ICBM (mobile Midgetman), to reduce the problem of disproportionate ICBM vulnerability.

The SS-18 has become both the centerpiece and the symbol of this Soviet effort to maintain a unilateral advantage in ICBM survivability. Moreover, much of the American SDI program, at least its space-based weapon portions, has been concentrated against the SS-18, which is large, MIRVed, and liquid-fueled, with a slow-burning booster.

If silo-based U.S. ICBMs, the targets against which the SS-18 is uniquely capable, were replaced in the American force structure by a weapon that is not uniquely vulnerable to Soviet SS-18s, such as a small, mobile ICBM on a hardened launcher, three groups of people would tend to become discomfited, or at least disoriented.

First, Soviet strategic planners would then face the problem of targeting mobile and survivable, not vulnerable, American ICBMs.

Second, those supporting the early deployment of SDI—especially early versions of space-based, boost-phase interceptors and exoatmospheric, ground-based interceptors—would have to cope with the argument that SS-18s were now no more militarily useful to the Soviets against the remaining American nonsilo targets than any of a whole range of other Soviet nuclear systems. In that case, why deploy a space-based, boost-phase portion of a defensive system that either has no special leverage or has no capability at all against the rest of the potential Soviet offensive forces, for example, solid-fueled (and hence faster-burning), single-warhead ICBMs and depressed-trajectory SLBMs?

Third, those who are eager to make arms control or reductions the primary tool of ensuring American security would be surprised to find that an important part of the rationale for the *military* importance of such limitations or reductions has been undercut. This point requires some explanation.

If the survivability of the U.S. ICBM force is preserved through the mobility of small ICBMs on hardened mobile launchers—a force that is not uniquely vulnerable to MIRVed Soviet ICBMs or even to barrage attack by large amounts of Soviet throw weight—what are we trying to accomplish with limitations on or cuts in Soviet strategic offensive arms? Such limitations or cuts may reduce the damage if war occurs, but the cuts would have to be extraordinarily deep to do that. Limitations or cuts may save some of the costs of strategic forces, but the budgetary impact is not likely to be what is advertised. The vast preponderance of military expenditures are in conventional forces, which may have to be increased.

The principal rationale for arms control has traditionally been to reduce the risk of war by reducing vulnerability. Even if our own forces can be made sufficiently survivable without such controls or reductions—or if controls or reductions contribute nothing to survivability because of the nature of our forces—we may still want to negotiate for Soviet arms reductions. In such a case, however, we need not pay in the coin of otherwise undesirable limits on our own forces, for example, in agreements that restrict our own survivability. Indeed, Soviet willingness to negotiate large reductions in their own strategic offensive forces is likely to exist only if they see that the United States has, by its chosen modernization program (that is, one with small mobiles), already begun to make the SS-18 a wasting asset. In such a case, we may be far freer to use our negotiating leverage to pursue other objectives more important than the reduction for reduction's sake of strategic offensive weapons—Soviet armor withdrawals from Eastern Europe.

If the United States moves forward with a properly designed and deployed small, mobile ICBM (and possibly with MX in rail garrisons as an adjunct), its strategic forces do not require control or reduction of Soviet nuclear arms for survivability; indeed, the U.S. forces, including the traditional survivable triad of ICBMs, SLBMs, and bombers are relatively indifferent to the numbers of Soviet nuclear weapons deployed.

To be specific, our submarine-based ballistic missile force has never depended on limitations on or reductions in Soviet offensive weapons to preserve its survivability; the submarines rely on their quietness, the range of the missiles they carry, and the technology of antisubmarine warfare as applied to ensuring ballistic missile submarine survivability.

Our bomber force and the cruise missiles it carries have also never depended on negotiated limitations on or reductions in Soviet strategic offensive weapons for survivability. The sorts of Soviet systems that threaten the bombers—Soviet submarines carrying SLCMs or depressed-trajectory SLBMs and pulled close to American shores—have never been effectively limited by any of the proposals in strategic offensive arms control agreements. SLCM-carrying submarines have had no limitations, and limits on submarines carrying ballistic missiles have never been even close to low enough to hinder a few submarines from being available for such an attack. The same is true of our strategic command, control, and communications (C^3). We depend on warning, operational techniques, and improved built-in survivability for our bombers and C^3 systems in order to limit the effectiveness of any Soviet strike against them, and not on negotiated limitations or reductions. Use of arms control or arms reductions to improve the survivability of these systems is either not necessary or would so enmesh one in limitations on complex and pervasive conventional forces (e.g., antisubmarine warfare capabilities) as to be wholly impractical.

Thus strategic offensive arms limitations or even substantial reductions are not likely to be particularly important in the future in preserving the survivability of U.S. strategic forces, as long as we move forward with a force of small ICBMs in hardened mobile launchers deployed on the large military bases in the southwestern United States. MX ICBMs parked on trains in rail garrisons (roundhouses, essentially), ready to be moved out on the U.S. railroad systems in peacetime, are not survivable without a number of hours of warning previous to any Soviet attack. So whereas arms control is not really needed to preserve the survivability of mobile Midgetman, it can do virtually nothing to help the survivability of rail-garrison MX against a surprise attack. We have tried for twenty years to use arms limitation and reductions to preserve the survivability of one part of our deterrent—silo-based ICBMs—and we have failed. Now is the time to move on to other approaches. Mobility, if we pick the right kind, is available to do the job instead.

Such a conclusion undercuts much of the military and strategic rationale for arms limitation and even for substantial arms reduction. Support for the process is thus thrown back on the political and economic reasons for it. These may well provide important spurs to action, but the objectives have changed.

Although much enthusiasm is expressed from time to time about the potential for the world's economies if we could all be freed of the burden of developing and deploying nuclear weapons, the root cause of the military expenditures in the West continues to be the hegemonic ambitions of the Soviet state. If *glasnost* and *perestroika* portend a real desire in Moscow to cut Soviet weapons programs and to reverse efforts to dominate the Soviet Union's neighbors, and are not just tokenism and a skillful public relations campaign, then in time some economic savings and real progress toward reduced reliance on nuclear weapons might be realized. However, jumping to conclusions about this is silly and dangerous. In spite of some American observers' optimism, *glasnost* is very far from being so powerful a movement that Soviet public opinion and intellectual critiques in the West are already determining Soviet weapon-deployment decisions. We will know that we are beginning to make some progress only after real changes occur in the Soviet empire: once Afghanistan is free of Soviet troops and dominance, once the Soviet armored units in East Germany are withdrawn, once the leaders of Solidarity or modern-day Dubceks can be part of government rather than prisoners or internal exiles. Although we should do what we can to encourage these sorts of positive developments in the Soviet Union and its neighbors, the time to begin to dream is after they begin to occur, not now.

To the end of Reagan's presidency, the administration continued to put denuclearization very high on the list of conscious objectives and struggled along this path paying heavily in the coin of reduced survivability (as in the American START proposal to ban mobile ICBMs), foregone opportunities (such as neglecting to press for cuts in Soviet armor), naive efforts to ban ballistic missiles (using one gimmick or another), and general confusion. In following such paths, American administrations deal clumsy, backhanded, unintentional blows at American nuclear forces and thus at NATO's shield, cohesion, and deterrent. Along this route lies greater difficulty for NATO, a less easy maintenance of the peace, and less stability than if the United States concentrated on solving the vulnerabilities of its strategic offensive forces on its own, applying its technological genius to preventing blitzkriegs, and using its bargaining leverage to reduce the Soviet conventional threat to the West and the Soviet dominance of central Europe.

In the meantime, work is necessary, in NATO's interest, to ensure that the ghosts that haunted the Reykjavik negotiations do not reappear at subsequent U.S.–Soviet summits, that fogs such as ballistic missile test bans slowly dissipate after the 1988 election, and that the common sense of the American people and the checks and balances of our Constitutional processes prevail over present and future rhetorical enthusiasms. Such an effort can and must enable the United States to continue to help prevent the states of Europe from drifting again into the sort of tragic turbulence that dominated their existence for a thousand years.

14

Conventional Arms Control and NATO's Future

By KARL KAISER

THE POLITICAL CONTEXT

Many diverse elements will come into play when East and West attempt to increase conventional stability in Europe and to decrease the cost of armaments for both sides in a new round of negotiations. These elements include the improvement of the West's conventional force structure, the future of NATO's doctrine of flexible response, the internal structure of West European cooperation, the Franco-German relationship, the role of the Soviet Union within the Warsaw Pact and hence the internal structure of the socialist system, the establishment of new links between Eastern and Western Europe, and the future of Gorbachev's reform policy within the Soviet Union. More than ever Western policy on arms control will have to consider the wider political and security implications of actions in the field of conventional arms control. Politicians and experts will consequently face a difficult problem: on the one hand, they must not let the complexity of the problems at hand paralyze their capacity for concrete action; on the other hand, they must constantly consider the wider implications of their steps and explain them to their publics.

In the course of the postwar period, arms control negotiations have taken on an increasingly public character. To a growing extent, the secret diplomacy of the negotiating table is complemented by a public discussion meant to put pressure on other governments by mobilizing public opinion and parliaments. The most recent and most intensive form of such an interaction of diplomacy and public debate could be observed during the NATO double-track decision up to its most recent developments leading to the double-zero solution. The next round of negotiations on conventional disarmament is likely to give further impetus to this trend toward increasingly "public" arms control

negotiations because the numerous links with various political areas
are likely to produce much mobilization and public articulation of
divergent interests. Moreover, Gorbachev's new and dynamic style is
characterized by a significant shift toward public diplomacy calculated
to mobilize support both in his own and in Western publics.

The new "Atlantic-to-the-Urals" conventional arms control negotiations will consist of a complicated process that is likely to be stretched
out over a number of years. The complexity of the problems will make
partial solutions easier and grand solutions highly unlikely. Progress
in this area will conceivably take the form of isolated steps in certain
sectors that may form a mosaic of change that increases stability in
Europe and reduces the cost of armament.

In earlier years, attempts by East and West to influence each other's
publics were asymmetric in structure: the governments of the Soviet
Union and its allies could use the possibilities of free and independent
media in the West to mobilize individual groups or parties within the
pluralistic structure of Western democracies in favor of its arguments
and initiatives. Given the closed character of socialist countries, their
monolithic political structures, and state control of the media,
Western countries did not have the same instruments at their disposal
in trying to influence the East.

However, new developments increasingly upset this asymmetry.
Public communication no longer takes place as a one-way street from
East to West; Eastern societies are undergoing changes that are
resulting in an increasingly lively discussion of different points of
views within their systems. In particular, within the Soviet Union the
beginnings of genuine debate can be observed. Yet, *glasnost* represents
not only the goal of Gorbachev's policy but also the more or less
inevitable consequence of technological and societal changes within
the East. Given the growing volume of transfer of facts and
information through television, radio, printed media, or direct-
broadcasting satellites, a process of public discussion of facts and
arguments in arms control and disarmament is likely to evolve even
within socialist societies.

Conventional disarmament negotiations are likely to last for many
years. In that time, further technological developments and breakthroughs are likely to intensify the structure of communication
between East and West. In the course of this process, the dynamics of
mutual influencing in a public process of communication will
probably intensify and characterize the future conventional arms
control negotiations. Such a growing parallelism between diplomacy
at the negotiating table and the public process of mutual influencing
and communication is nothing new for the West, but the increasing
participation of East European societies will offer Western democracies

a growing opportunity that they can use creatively in the forthcoming round of conventional arms control.

NUCLEAR CONDITIONS OF
CONVENTIONAL DISARMAMENT

Within NATO's strategy of flexible response, nuclear and conventional weapons form an organized whole with each component occupying a clearly defined place in relationship to the other. This syst of interaction will cause changes in the conventional sector to spill back into the nuclear sector. Put simply, changes of the conventional balance to the West's disadvantage will increase the relevance of its nuclear weapons. This concept is also applicable to the forthcoming negotiations on conventional weapons and would, in fact, work against the tendency in many Western societies to reduce the relevance of nuclear weapons, and vice versa, a reduction of the nuclear component in flexible response would increase the relevance of the conventional sector. In the hypothetical case of nuclear disarmament at the expense of the West, the conventional superiority of the Warsaw Pact would become an even greater threat to European stability than it is today. In such a case, a change of the conventional force ratio in favor of the West would become even more urgent.

Nuclear arms control and disarmament therefore circumscribe the conditions for conventional disarmament. The separation of the two areas, sometimes propagated by politicians and experts, can have fatal consequences. If NATO governments do not recognize this close interaction and consequently begin to neglect the nuclear component, wrong moves or inaction within the nuclear area could worsen the conditions for conventional disarmament.

A Western policy of conventional disarmament must take into account several problems of the nuclear component of flexible response and act accordingly.

1. Within the United States, one can observe a growing malaise about the nuclear commitments involved in extended deterrence to protect Western Europe. Because limited conflicts can lead to nuclear escalation and potentially reach the United States, the desire to create guarantees or constraints to avoid the use of tactical nuclear weapons is growing there. The proposal for an East-West agreement on the no first use of nuclear weapons, formulated first in the United States and supported by a number of political forces in Europe, would create a zone of guaranteed nonnuclear war fighting. Consequently, the risks of a conventional war would become relatively calculable and therefore increase the likelihood of

war. Because conventional war continues to be the most important—
if not only—likely trigger of nuclear war, a no-first-use proposal
would, in fact, increase the probability of the nuclear war it claims
to decrease. A total removal of tactical nuclear weapons or the
acceptance of a no-first-use posture would threaten European
stability and turn conventional disparity into an even greater
problem of conventional arms control policy.

2. The delegitimization of nuclear deterrence has been going on for
several years. The political forces working in this direction span the
entire political spectrum from President Ronald Reagan (in
justifying SDI) to the Catholic bishops of America to the
antinuclear protest movements of Western Europe. A reversal of
priority replaces the priority of war prevention as a consequence of
the incalculable risk of nuclear weapons by the priority of damage
limitation dictated by the enormous destructiveness of modern
nuclear weapons. In this context, a more probable conventional
war becomes more acceptable than an improbable nuclear war. The
lesson to be drawn for a policy of conventional arms control is that
delegitimization of nuclear deterrence makes the conventional field
—the very area where the West suffers a structural disadvantage—
the decisive arena for stability in Europe. For this reason, such a
delegitimization is not in the West's interests.

3. The theoretical option to respond to the Warsaw Pact's conventional
superiority by using tactical nuclear weapons in case of aggression
can be annulled by the Warsaw Pact at the beginning of a conflict if
by superior conventional means it succeeds in destroying the
tactical nuclear potential of NATO. Such a scenario is constantly
drilled in Warsaw Pact maneuvers. If successful, such an action
would reduce a nuclear response to strategic means, which the
United States can hardly use for limited conflicts. In such a case, the
strategy of flexible response would be rendered ineffective. To be
sure, this danger is only theoretical danger, but it must be taken
seriously. A lesson can be deduced for a policy of conventional arms
control: it must avoid agreements that increase the capability of the
Warsaw Pact to undermine flexible response at the tactical nuclear
level and must, if possible, attempt to reduce the existing
conventional superiority of the Warsaw Pact.

4. A further problem of flexible response derives from the considerable
superiority of tactical nuclear weapons with a reach of less than five
hundred kilometers, which will remain after a double-zero
agreement on INF weapons has been implemented. The Warsaw
Pact maintains a superiority of roughly ten to one in the field of
short-range missiles. In view of this superiority, Western decision
makers are likely to suffer from "self-deterrence" because they will

face the prospect of triggering an immensely destructive strike with superior tactical weapons if they make the first escalatory step. If their reluctance to escalate were to become a reasonable certainty, a zone of nonnuclear war fighting would be created that would allow the Warsaw Pact to bring its conventional superiority into play and in which relatively calculable risks would make war more probable.

This means that, given the disparity of tactical nuclear weapons with a range of less than 500 kilometers, both conventional reductions with the aim of parity and the creation of a balance of ground-based tactical weapons are of crucial relevance for European stability.

5. Since the 1950s, Western policy has been not to try to match the conventional armament of the Warsaw Pact. As a result the East armed itself to a status of conventional military superiority and relative economic poverty. The West, however, relied on the deterrence value of nuclear weapons and thereby bought social and economic progress. The Western dependence on nuclear weapons for maintaining stability has therefore always remained considerable. That dependence is actually increasing as Western military budgets stagnate or diminish and because the conventional share is indeed being reduced in the case of the nuclear powers. Throughout the 1970s and 1980s, NATO arms production of decisive weapons systems represented only a fraction of the Warsaw Pact production; for example, all of NATO produced only 40 percent of the main battle tanks produced by the Warsaw Pact between 1984 and 1986. The deployment of *Speznaz* troops for offensive purposes goes on. The Western lead in technology and the growing unreliability of the military forces of the Soviet Union's allies for aggressive purposes moderate but do not compensate for this disadvantageous trend for the West.

The simple fact remains that as a consequence of the new INF agreement nuclear weapons are being eliminated at the very moment when the West's reliance on nuclear weapons has increased as a result of the deterioration of the conventional balance. Contrary to the public presentation of flexible response, such a reliance is real. The prevailing rhetoric of NATO governments has put a growing stress on no early use of nuclear weapons that reflects, not as many politicians and military would have liked growing conventional options to repel aggression by nonnuclear means, but simply a political response to increasing antinuclear feelings in Europe and a growing malaise in the United States about being implicated early in tactical nuclear war.

The obvious conclusion to be drawn is that as NATO prepares for a new round of conventional arms control it must undertake concomitant steps to preserve and improve the minimum structure of flexible response. Without such policies, conventional arms control will either be rendered extremely difficult or be likely to undermine stability.

The most important imperative consists of preventing the ongoing nuclear disarmament from slipping into a triple zero: total denuclearization of central and Western Europe. The double-zero agreement on INF weapons does not end flexible response as some argue, but it could endanger the strategy if various pressures combine to produce a total denuclearization. To some extent, such pressure may result from the momentum that could evolve from a desirable solution to achieve balance in the field of nuclear weapons under a range of 500 kilometers. After the conclusion of an INF agreement, certain political forces in West Germany are likely to argue that this country alone carries the risk of tactical nuclear warfare. To be sure, this argument is incorrect because other European countries (Norway, Denmark, Britain, Benelux, France, Italy, Greece, Turkey) are within reach of Soviet tactical nuclear weapons, and all European countries can be hit by Soviet strategic weapons in a tactical mode.

Nevertheless, such an argument can easily be combined with existing antinuclear sentiments to argue in favor of a total elimination of all nuclear weapons from central Europe. This course would find the support of those Americans who feel uneasy about extended deterrence and would confine the American nuclear posture to a purely strategic one. Naturally such an outcome would be vigorously sought and favored by the Soviet Union, whose strategic goal has always been to eliminate nuclear weapons from central and Western Europe. Such an outcome would bring to bear its conventional superiority and geopolitical advantage without in any way relinquishing the threat of its own strategic nuclear weapons, which can be directed at any point in Western Europe (even in a tactical mode). A triple-zero solution would therefore fundamentally undermine West European security.

At the beginning of a new round of conventional arms control negotiations and in the midst of successful attempts at nuclear disarmament, the West must now define the bottom line of flexible response. Such an attempt could consist of three elements.

1. A vigorous effort should be made to convince Western democratic publics that even under conditions of nuclear and conventional disarmament a minimum deterrence remains imperative. To be sure, successful conventional disarmament would decrease dependence on the use of nuclear weapons, but contrary to some assertions in Europe's political debate, even a conventional balance does not eliminate the need for nuclear deterrence; the function of nuclear

deterrence is to prevent war, whereas a purely conventional constellation makes war more likely because of the relatively calculable risk. The disappearance of nuclear deterrence is imaginable only where the political conflict at its root has been resolved.

2. The minimum elements of a tactical posture in Europe should be defined now and pursued in future decisions on procurement and modernization: an adequate aircraft capacity with sufficient range and modern penetration technology in combination with standoff weapons that can reach targets within the Soviet Union, the assignation of sea-based systems to SACEUR, and a sufficient number of short-range nuclear missiles with a range below five hundred kilometers (possibly in a package combining a total elimination of all nuclear artillery with a modernization of Lance in numbers roughly equal to the Soviet counterparts at present Wesern levels).

3. A stronger cooperation between the British and French nuclear deterrents in combination with a European consultation process (but without shared decision) could strengthen the role of these nuclear forces in a European mode.

THE CENTRAL PROBLEMS OF
CONVENTIONAL ARMS CONTROL

East-West Asymmetries

Four asymmetries will have to be dealt with in the forthcoming round of arms control negotiations. The first is an asymmetry of military doctrine. NATO's military doctrine is defensive both in intention and capabilities. The basic philosophy of the NATO Treaty is defensive. None of the participating democracies underwrite anything but a defensive policy; West Germany has even stated this purpose as a principle in its constitution. The military posture of the alliance is organized around the principle of forward defense in Europe in order to defend itself against an attack on Western soil. Although NATO has a limited tactical ability to move forward a few kilometers or to make selective strikes deep into the territory of an aggressor, it has no capacity to move forward into and hold the aggressor's territory. Its military incapacity to attack is complemented by a political inability to attack, because NATO as an alliance of democracies would never agree to do so, even in the unlikely event of a member trying to find support for such a policy.

The military doctrine of the Warsaw Pact is defensive in intention but offensive in capability. Starting from the premise that a war must be fought on the territory of an aggressor, the Warsaw Pact proclaims itself to be merely defensive in purpose but capable of launching an attack into the territory of the aggressor. It has acquired a massive capacity to move into Western territory and to hold it even under conditions of short warning and/or limited reinforcement. Consequently, East Germany is defended by fighting in West Germany. The force structure (with its emphasis on a combination of mobility and firepower), the training of officers and soldiers, and the constant practice of maneuvers prepare the Warsaw Pact for offense in case of war. The moment the offensive capability is no longer constrained by a defensive intent (as it is constrained under present Soviet leadership), the Western alliance would be threatened.

A second problem consists of the asymmetry of options between the two pacts. This asymmetry derives from differences in doctrine. In a long process of arms procurement and training, the Soviet Union has acquired options of attack with relatively short warning and a capacity to invade. These options are due to significant inequalities of forces in areas crucial for offense, such as main battletanks, armored vehicles, self-propelled artillery, bridging equipment, multiple rocket launchers, or special units such as *Speznaz* troops. Depending on how one counts, the West would face inequalities on an order of magnitude of around 1:2 and 1:3.

A third problem lies in the asymmetry of geography. Whereas the Soviet Union is a superpower located in Europe and consequently able to bring in reinforcements from a relatively limited distance, the opposing United States is situated across the Atlantic and has to move its reinforcements across the Atlantic Ocean. Stability can therefore be achieved only by compensating for this inequality. Moreover, the alliances are not comparable with regard to their hinterland as long as France remains outside NATO integration and projects that posture into conventional arms control measures.

The fourth inequality is due to the asymmetric share of American and Soviet forces within their respective alliances. Whereas American troops represent only 11 percent (16 percent without Spain and Turkey) of NATO land forces (army and air force) in Europe, the Soviet share of Warsaw Pact forces west of the Urals is 46 percent. From a Western perspective, Soviet forces represent the primary threat. Consequently, attempts to increase stability would have to deal primarily with them.

The criteria for conventional arms control on which Western consensus is beginning to evolve reflect the lesson of MBFR that reductions per se must not be the goal of Western policy. Because stability is the yardstick, the main target of arms control must be to reduce existing capacities for short-warning attack and invasion. Such a goal can be pursued through a variety of methods. They range from increased transparency (which increases warning time) to changes of the structure of the armed forces (e.g., removal of offensive elements or changes in the state of combat readiness), reductions with ensuing destruction of weapons, or redeployment of units or weapons to rear areas.

Given the substantial conventional superiority of the Warsaw Pact in central Europe, reductions would have to be asymmetrical. According to a RAND study[1] a 3:1 reduction in division equivalents in favor of NATO would still substantially worsen NATO's situation, and only a reduction of 4:1 would slightly improve it. These strikingly unequal ratios are no surprise because they reflect the long years of Soviet armament efforts that led to a significant superiority in a number of fields. In all likelihood, the Soviet Union will denounce such ratios as unfair or excessive, sometimes even quoting from Western studies that might support its case. An obvious conclusion to be drawn for a negotiating strategy would be to avoid ratios in case of reductions and to return to the concept of common ceilings, which is a well-established and acceptable concept, even though common ceilings require unequal reductions in case of asymmetries.

Whether the Soviet Union will accept sufficiently asymmetrical reductions remains to be seen. Although the principle has been accepted by Gorbachev in a speech on April 10, 1987 and at the Warsaw Pact summit in May 1987, the long history of MBFR gives no clue whatsoever as to a willingness to proceed seriously in that direction. What reasons could induce the Soviet Union to give up a significant military and political advantage? The list is only moderately convincing: first, such asymmetric reductions would lead to savings of resources, but that is true only in the very long run, because initially conventional disarmament will absorb additional funds for the redirection of personnel as well as investments for the conversion of armaments industry. Second, such a movement would no doubt have a positive impact on the world and improve the standing of the Soviet Union. Third, such asymmetric reductions could be pursued in connection with Western concessions in the field of economic relations and a freeze on conventional technology. Although the first is by no means excluded, it is difficult to operationalize. A freeze on conventional technology is highly problematical because it would close the most important avenue to compensate for existing East-West inequalities.

---

[1] James A. Thomson and Nanette C. Gantz, "Conventional Arms Control Revisited: Objectives in the New Phase," in Uwe Nerlich and James A. Thomson, eds., *Conventional Arms and the Security of Europe* (Boulder, Colo.: Westview Press, 1987), pp. 108–120.

Intra-Western Problems

The intra-Western disagreements concerning negotiating method (i.e., the problem of the interalliance and the CSCE framework of negotiations), are likely to appear trivial in comparison with the divergencies that are likely to emerge once NATO moves beyond the present agreement on general principles, such as stability and invasion capacity, and attempts to work out practical proposals that translate them into reductions, force redeployments, geographical zones, verification, and the like.

Differences of opinion could quickly come into the open if the Soviet Union were to seize the initiative and present proposals before the West has worked out a clear negotiating strategy. In such a case, a superficially attractive offer with an asymmetric reduction that is presented as fair and possibly even accepted as such by many groups in the Western public could reduce the chances for working out sensible solutions that could increase stability.

Consensus on reducing the invasion capacity of the Warsaw Pact has to be translated into agreement on what types of weapons should be reduced first and in what order of priority. Even the East has agreed to the principle that defense should be "nonoffensive," but the packages to be worked out have to combine many different elements, including quantity and quality of weapons, training, and combat readiness. Many weapons can be used both for offense and defense, and whether they can be used in one or the other mode depends on numerous other factors that have to be taken into account.

The disaggregation in geographic zones will no doubt represent another difficult problem. Such a disaggregation is a prerequisite for restructuring the military postures of both sides according to agreed criteria in order to maintain adequate defense without providing capacities for offense and invasion. However, any geographic disaggregation creates differences in the status of those zones and therefore raises delicate political problems for a country that has to reduce (like West Germany) and for countries that might have to receive redeployed units or materiel (like the Benelux or France).

Verification will be another difficult problem. Because the formulas of reduction, restructuring, or redeployment of forces will inevitably be complex, they require an intensity of verification that will be without precedent in the history of arms control. How far one should go is by no means an East-West problem alone but will have to be settled first among Western countries.

France will have the special problem of being forced to make up its mind about the status of its territory if redeployment schemes in negotiations require the availability of French territory for units or weapons. Moreover, both France and the Federal Republic of Germany will no doubt want to avoid measures in the field of conventional arms control that might impede their effort to build a stronger mutual security relationship.

Intra-Eastern Problems

Soviet troops have always had a double function in Eastern Europe. They were a factor of defense and offense opposing the forces of NATO as well as a policing factor guaranteeing Soviet influence in central Europe. Significant reductions, which are bound to affect Soviet troops more than those of its allies, are likely to affect the internal policing role. Although the West has an interest in seeing that role reduced, this factor cannot be introduced explicitly into the East-West arms control negotiations. The evolution of the internal structure of the Warsaw Pact will greatly determine the relevance of this question. Moreover, as the 1981 Polish crisis has shown, Soviet troops can play their hegemonial role within the Warsaw Pact system without being inside the territory of the country in question. In the last analysis, the relevance of this factor in forthcoming negotiations on conventional arms control can be decided only by the Soviets themselves.

TOWARD A FEASIBLE APPROACH TO CONVENTIONAL ARMS CONTROL

Even a superficial look at the issues of the forthcoming round of conventional arms control reveals the extraordinary complexity of the issues to be negotiated, even if they are broken down into smaller components of negotiation, such as reduction packages, verification measures, and thinning-out moves. Moreover, each item is interconnected with many other sensitive areas. Within the West, views differ on many important issues. The first substantial agreements between East and West in this field will probably take a long time. Perhaps an approach to negotiations could be organized according to feasibility and practicability of progress, and negotiations would then proceed accordingly in succeeding phases.

A Discussion of Military Doctrine

A first phase of negotiations could consist of a thorough discussion of the military doctrines of both alliances. Several practical reasons commend such an approach. A discussion of doctrine involving both military officers and diplomats could lay the groundwork for later negotiations on specifics by analyzing thoroughly which threats each side perceives with regard to the military posture, procedures, and doctrine of the other. By identifying the central elements of threats, important criteria and priorities for the ensuing negotiations could be identified. Furthermore, such discussions could be started without being forced to overcome the numerous divergencies of views within the West and can, therefore, begin reasonably soon.

Moreover, such discussions can play an important political role for the West. A review of the military doctrine offers the opportunity to bring into relief for Western publics the striking disparity between the defensive claim of the Warsaw Pact's doctrine and the offensive reality of force ratios, force structure, training, and readiness. A review of these issues will lay the groundwork for a better understanding by Western publics not only of the general issues but in particular of the necessity for asymmetric reductions.

Second, such a discussion is likely to have an impact on the East as well. Not only are some of the public arguments carried into the East with the potential of a moderate though not insignificant impact, but more important, the participating elites will be exposed to a critical analysis of their own doctrine and posture. Conceivably such a process may help those forces in the Soviet bureaucracy willing to challenge military orthodoxy and its tremendous political and economic burden for the Soviet Union.

Some argue against such a discussion of doctrine on the grounds either that it will be used by Soviet propaganda to denounce NATO's policies about the follow-on-forces attack (FOFA) concept and no first use of nuclear weapons, or that it will result in a confrontation of irreconcilable views on military data worse than that experienced during MBFR. However, NATO has nothing to fear from such a debate. By now the alliance is used to controversy about its policies, which, after all, enjoy clear political support by the participating countries. NATO has a good case in comparing Eastern and Western military doctrine. Finally, only a test will show whether or not a discussion will get bogged down in disagreements on data and whether or not Gorbachev's *glasnost* policy will have its impact here as well.

The Priority of Confidence Building

Even if East-West measures on military hardware or troops are difficult and time-consuming to agree upon, a lack of success in this area need not prevent progress in the realm of confidence building. New measures of confidence building could superimpose greater transparency on the existing military setup in East and West with all its asymmetries so that both sides can become confident that they will not be the object of surprise moves or disadvantageous' changes in military strength.

Such confidence-building measures could consist of a further intensification in scope of the measures agreed upon at the Stockholm Conference in 1986 by creating a dense network of observation on both sides of the East-West border, notably in central Europe. Such measures could cover both maneuvers and all movements of troops and materiel. Moreover, they would have to include the perhaps most important element that the Stockholm Agreement failed to cover, alert exercises of military units; from the point of view of crisis stability, such exercises deserve prior notification and some degree of observation even more than maneuvers do.

Confidence-building measures as an opening of a new round of conventional arms control in Europe would have the net effect of increasing stability even without reductions, would lay the groundwork for the relatively dense network of verification that has to accompany later reductions or redeployment measures, and would hopefully create a politcal atmosphere conducive to more far-reaching measures of conventional arms control.

An Agreement on Equal Levels of Arms Production

Agreement on military data, not to mention reduction and redeployment formulas, will be difficult and time-consuming. If the asymmetries that the West is rightly concerned about cannot be reduced quickly, negotiations can at least try to prevent them from getting worse in a parallel action.

Taking the average of 1984–86 production by both alliances of military equipment particularly relevant for the conventional posture in Europe and consequently for stability, the picture in Table 14.1 emerges.[2]

An agreement to reduce—possibly in phases—the production of military equipment to roughly equal levels would circumvent the inevitably controversial discussion on what forces exist and where (although that has to take place when reductions and redeployments are negotiated) and instead focuses on *future* outcomes. Verification is relatively easy because it need not cover large areas but only the exit points of production facilities.

---

[2] Source for the material is Department of Defense, *Soviet Military Power* (Washington, D.C.: U.S. Government Printing Office, 1987), p. 122.

TABLE 14.1 *Conventional Arms Production*

Category	NATO as a percent of Warsaw Pact
Tanks	40
Other Armored Fighting Vehicles	55
Towed Field Artillery	21
Self-Propelled Artillery	19
Multiple Rocket Launchers	27
Self-Propelled Antiaircraft Artillery	24
Towed Antiaircraft Artillery	4
Bombers	18
Fighters	79

The fact that Soviet production has to go down substantially not only underscores the Western point about the excessive military overinsurance of the Soviet Union in the past but may be attractive to those forces in the Soviet elites who want to liberate themselves from the tremendous economic cost of that unnecessary overinsurance.

Key Measures

A discussion of military doctrine, new confidence-building measures, and an agreement to scale down asymmetries in production could be the elements of a first phase of conventional arms control to be followed by carefully worked-out and inevitably complex packages of reductions, redeployments, and associated measures. Nevertheless, an attempt could be made to identify approaches that are simple and feasible and affect conventional stability favorably. Such measures could be initiated relatively early. They could include proposals such as that of Senator Sam Nunn to reduce equal percentages of American and Soviet troops in Germany or Phil Karber's suggestions to phase out tanks to roughly equal levels in the central front area.[3]

CONCLUSION

As the West enters a new phase of conventional arms control, it will have to reconcile its activities in three complex areas: the preservation and possible restructuring of the nuclear prerequisites for conventional arms control proper by beginning with a debate on military doctrine and confidence-building measures, and at the same time, the improvement of its own force structure and internal alliance arrangements. Even some progress in conventional arms control will not remove the

[3] Phillip A. Karber, "Conventional Arms Control Options," in Nerlich and Thomson, eds., *Conventional Arms*, pp. 158–181.

necessity to engage in such improvements, in strengthening the European pillar of NATO, and in preserving the American-European links. Needless to say, Western policy should encourage reform and change of military policies in the Soviet Union. However, Western concessions further reducing its already inadequate conventional posture can come only as a consequence of significant Soviet moves, not as their precursor. Nevertheless, many signs in the Soviet Union suggest that for the first time a genuine chance exists to pursue successful conventional arms control between East and West.

15

NATO's Future: The Out-of-Area Problem

By ROBERT E. HUNTER

During recent years, the term *out of area* has gained currency in debate within the North Atlantic Treaty Organization. At one level, the term is capable of precise definition. It refers to anything that happens beyond the boundaries set by the North Atlantic Treaty of 1949, as amended to add Greece, Turkey, West Germany, and now Spain, and to delete the Algerian departments of France.[1] The NATO boundaries encompass a good deal of land and sea, including all of allied national territory, the Mediterranean Sea, and the Atlantic Ocean north of the Tropic of Cancer. At another level, however, the term *out of area* has also come to mean those locales and activities where common agreement does not exist among the allies that the treaty can or should be invoked. Thus the Gulf of Sidra, formed by two arms of Libyan territory but still part of the Mediterranean Sea, is technically "in area," but it surely is not so regarded by the European allies. Nor has the United States pressed the point during its military confrontations with the Libyan regime of Col. Muamar Qaddafi.

These definitions have become important because of the rise of circumstances in which one or another ally as sought help from the others, or from the alliance as a whole, to cope with contingencies outside of Europe. The ally asking for help generally represents its viewpoint and actions as contributing to the broader security of the

---

[1] Article 5 of the North Atlantic Treaty provides that "an armed attack against one or more of [the allies] in Europe or North America shall be considered an atack against them all. . . ." Article 6, as modified by the protocol on the accession of Greece and Turkey, defines the application as "i. the territory of any of the Parties in Europe or North America, on the Algerian Departments of France, on the territory of Turkey or on the islands under the jurisdiction of any of the Parties in the North Atlantic area north of the Tropic of Cancer; ii. on the forces, vessels, or aircraft of any of the Parties, when in or over these territories or any other area in Europe in which occupation forces of any of the Parties were stationed on the date when the Treaty entered into force or the Mediterranean Sea or the North Atlantic area north of the Tropic of Cancer."

alliance, or at least to the protection of interests of some allies in addition to itself. In recent years, the United States has most often been in the position of asking for help, and discussions about out-of-area problems usually pit U.S. views against those of most if not all of its European and Canadian allies.

That approach is not always true of the allies. France, for instance, is scrupulous about not asking for help, within the NATO framework, in its military activities beyond the treaty area; on the basis of its clear reading of the treaty, it denies that right to any other ally. Yet, it does believe that its actions—say, in Chad—serve purposes shared by other allied states, and it would surely take amiss any direct action to counter its efforts. Britain did not formally apply to the North Atlantic Council or to any of the joint military commands for assistance during the Falklands War. Bilaterally, however, it sought and received U.S. logistical assistance, and it sought diplomatic support from its NATO allies, as well as their forbearance in aiding Argentina. In addition, France, Belgium, and the United States were engaged in Shaba Province in Zaire in the late 1970s, although this cooperation was kept strictly separate from NATO.

Despite today's impressions, historically the United States has not been the only nation to seek help or forbearance from its allies out of area, either bilaterally or formally within NATO. Indeed, the treaty lines were drawn tightly largely at the behest of the United States, which did not want either itself or the fledgling Western alliance to be drawn into the colonial conflicts or other foreign quarrels of its European partners. The many applications included France in Vietnam and Algeria (the latter then technically within the scope of the alliance), Britain and France at Suez, Portugal in southern Africa, Belgium in the Congo, and the Netherlands in the East Indies. In none of these cases did NATO as an institution become involved in the actions of its individual members.

NATO'S CENTRAL PURPOSE

In the early days of alliance, strictures against acting beyond the treaty area were seen as critical precisely to preserve the central elements of common purpose, namely, the security of Western Europe against aggression or other forms of encroachment by the Soviet Union and its East European allies. Anything that detracted from this effort, such as a colonial war, had to be resisted by the institution. Where the United States, as key organizer of Western security, sought formal support from European states in other parts of the world, it did so through separate treaty organizations (SEATO, CENTO) or—in the Korean War—through action in the United Nations.

This point is instructive because it relates directly to current and, no doubt, future debate: how do efforts to invoke the NATO alliance or the support of its individual members to act out of area conform to or conflict with the central purposes of the North Atlantic Treaty Organization? This question has acquired greater relevance than at any other time in the alliance's history for many reasons, but three stand out.

1. The West has succeeded in containing Soviet expansion in Europe, military and political stability have both increased, little risk of a European war is apparent, and political tensions have been substantially reduced.
2. A number of threats to the interests of individual allied states, or to all of them, have emerged outside the treaty area. These threats now appear relatively more pressing than European security concerns. The Middle East from North Africa to southwest Asia is clearly most prominent.
3. The United States, the ally most often concerned about out-of-area threats and most inclined to act, no longer has the margins of power sufficient to permit it, in many circumstances, to act both alone and successfully. Bearing in mind the qualifications already cited, it is the ally most likely to ask for help from others.

In the absence of events that lead the allies singly and severally to refocus their attention on the security of Western Europe, these trends are likely to persist for the foreseeable future, at least through the period covered by this study: the end of the century. The out-of-area problem is likely to have a subtle impact on basic questions concerning the central purposes of alliance. What allies do elsewhere may not lead to a serious weakening of West European military security, except in the instance of a serious and sustained diversion of forces that was not offset by the actions of other allies. The alliance has already weathered the (long-term) diversion of U.S. military power to Indochina and the (short-term) diversion of British naval power to the South Atlantic. What allies do or do not do out of area can in some circumstances help to undermine key political understandings within the alliance and thus erode Western security in its largest sense. Success so far in Western Europe cannot be an excuse for ignoring the challenge from the out-of-area problem.

LIMITS ON THE USE OF THE NATO STRUCTURE

One issue is worth discussing and settling at the outset: the possibility of using NATO institutions formally for out-of-area purposes. In theory, occasions such as an interruption in the flow of oil from the Persian Gulf could occur in which every ally would have a stake, indeed a vital stake, in meeting an out-of-area threat. Those with military forces and the physical and legal capacity to project them might all agree to act, even to act in common. That common action does not mean that NATO itself should be the vehicle, through one or more of its three principal military commands.

So far, France's position has been stoutly to resist any such action by NATO. This position is likely to continue, although circumstances can be imagined in which it would change. Even so, any appreciable benefit to the allies in invoking formal military procedures within the alliance would be questionable, even to meet a challenge that all agreed upon. At the simplest level of explanation, the military commands are not configured—either in command structure or military forces—for operation beyond the areas within which they now act. That they could be reconfigured without placing undue stress on their ability to perform their central purposes under current mandates is not clear. In some circumstances, this might be less true with regard to Allied Command Atlantic (SACLANT) than of Allied Command Europe (ACE) or the Channel Command, because for steaming ships limits on areas of action are often just lines drawn in water. Nevertheless, preparing to deal with far-flung contingencies would impose added costs—political as well as military—and whether the price is worth paying is questionable.

Conceivably, NATO could develop an out-of-area analogue to the ACE Mobile Force that provides some degree of mobility for special units in central Europe, but the practicable development of such a force would require more allied agreement more of the time on possible threats and responses than is likely.

The same objections do not apply to the possible use of the North Atlantic Council as a focus of discussion and debate about out-of-area issues and activities. The French veto would likely still apply to any decision within this framework, but that is not particularly significant. The point of using the Council is not to gain unanimity on some course of action but to permit a thorough discussion of points of view, especially discussion well in advance of any action by one or more allies. The Council can be a sounding board for the multilateral, informal exchange of ideas and political signals.

The Council has already become the focus of discussions about problems in the Middle East and occasionally elsewhere. This role can and should be extended to cover each non-European region. Different allies will want to talk about different subjects and regions. Some, especially those that have inhibitions on the use of force beyond Europe, might want on occasions to absent themselves and be able, plausibly, to deny that they had discussed any contingency planning. The existence of the forum provides an opportunity for what has been termed a *variable geometry* for considering different out-of-area problems: different configurations of allies, depending on the subject.[2] That "geometry" also has value beyond discussions in Brussels, for example, allied involvement in the Multinational Force and Observers (Sinai), the Multi-Lateral Force (Lebanon), in the Persian Gulf in 1987–88, or diplomatically in the Contact Group for southern Africa. In these cases, too, limits should be imposed in terms of the risk that out-of-area topics could encroach upon the central purpose of the alliance, namely, to preserve European security.

DEFINING THE PROBLEM

That NATO must have an out-of-area problem is not self-evident. In theory, this topic should present no difficulty, provided that each ally goes about its own business in the outside world, that activities external to Europe do not impinge adversely on security in its broadest sense on the continent, and that no ally calls for active support on the part of other allies. Fulfilling these conditions is becoming increasingly difficult, however, especially in view of attitudes and actions on the part of successive U.S. administrations, plus European responses, for reasons that have already been mentioned.

Until quite recently, the most important aspect of NATO's out-of-area problem stemmed from reactions by West European allies to activities of the United States. This European reaction has been in tacit, sometimes explicit, recognition of the leading role that the United States plays in the alliance, politically as much as militarily. For example, many of the West European states have been troubled by U.S. policy toward Central America and, in particular, toward Nicaragua. This area is far from the locus of alliance, and as an out-of-area problem it is dwarfed by the Middle East. At times, however, it has still produced four concerns:

- that the United States would do something that could lead to a direct military engagement;
- that U.S. preoccupation with Central America could distract America's attention from Western Europe;
- that the U.S. focus on the Soviet and Cuban involvement in Nicaragua could affect prospects for East-West detente in Europe; and

---

[2] See Robert E. Hunter, "Safeguarding Western Interests Outside the NATO area," in *Ditchley Conference Report No. 11/1982* (Ditchley Park, England, 1983).

- that U.S. policy toward Nicaragua could have a negative impact on West European public opinion and thus weaken the bonds of alliance.[3]

Agreeing with these observations about West European attitudes—which vary in importance and intensity from country to country—is not necessary to recognize in them a process of relating U.S. actions far afield from NATO to the core of alliance. The Central America issue doe not stand alone. These four concerns or variants of them have long been evident in West European perceptions of the U.S. role beyond Europe. Indeed, they figured prominently during the Vietnam War.

This method of looking at the activities and other behavior of allied states has become a two-way street, however. In the example of Central America, the U.S. government has been concerned about the role played in the region by individual West European governments and by quasi-official bodies like the West German political foundations. Few Americans are aware of this activity, however, and many might support it. Where evident, however, it has been an irritant in transatlantic relations.

In the same vein, during the late 1970s the U.S. government often took exception to positions advanced from within the European Community toward the Arab-Israeli peace process, in particular, to the Venice Declaration of 1980. Many U.S. government officials saw the declaration as undercutting U.S. efforts to promote the Camp David Accords by backing demands made by one party to the conflict, in this case the Palestinians.[4]

The European position on Arab-Israeli peacemaking was developed within what is called European Political Cooperation, the fledgling effort to devise means for the gradual elaboration of a foreign policy within the community. Part of that effort has, indeed, been to devise positions that can be differentiated from those of the United States.[5] This motive has been important for some European states and relatively insignificant for others, but it has caught the attention of

---

[3] See *Report of the National Bipartisan Commission on Central America* (the Kissinger Commission) (Washington, D.C.: U.S. Government Printing Office, January 1984) for an exposition of these points.

[4] In January 1988, the European Community issued a declaration similar to that in 1980. Also see Robert Hunter and Geoffrey Kemp, "Western Interests and U.S. Policy Options in the Middle East," a Joint Policy Project of the Atlantic Council of the United States and the Middle East Institute (Washington, DC., February 1988), pp. 18–19.

[5] Thus European Political Cooperation has long debated the extent to which there can be consultations with the United States about Community deliberations in this area. The so called Gymnich Formula, named after a meeting held at the West German government retreat, provided that the state holding the presidency of the European Community could brief the United States government on what had transpired.

U.S. officials. Also involved are questions of potential European defense cooperation and greater independence from the United States; a larger role for Europeans can stimulate U.S. pressure for a smaller role for itself, not just in Europe but in various places out of area.

Far more important, however, has been the revival of a classic allied debate about the relative sharing of defense burdens. However, this time there is a difference. Debate is not only about the relative contribution of resources that each ally makes to promote security directly within Europe. This debate is a time-honored process with rules and conventions of its own. Now, however, the theme of burdensharing has been extended beyond NATO's traditional boundaries. Debate now includes what the allies will do to help the United States accomplish its declared purposes elsewhere. It extends to occasional American pique at not even being able to use U.S. forces, deployed in Western Europe for European defense, for U.S. purposes out of area. This aspect of the burdensharing issue became most intense during the U.S. bombing of Libya in April 1986. In the view of many observers in the United States, it was being hampered in the use of U.S. forces, which were deployed abroad at least in part to protect European lives, when they were needed to protect American lives.

Assessing the accuracy or fairness of these attitudes is not necessary to acknowledge the force of the problem they represent. That problem will likely grow more serious in the years ahead, as more challenges to the interests of individual Western states emerge, as the margins of U.S. power decline further, and as the United States seeks followers for its lead. This will be particularly true regarding the possible use of European bases for U.S. actions out of area, especially when these relate to Middle East terrorism. Recent U.S. difficulties in retaining base access in Spain and Greece, plus questioning in Portugal about the terms of U.S. access to the Azores, portend more problems ahead.

At the same time, West European governments have considerable concern that their contributions to common security are not adequately appreciated in the United States. This includes recurring charges in the U.S. Congress that the allies do not pull their weight in terms of European security. The charges are regularly refuted, by the U.S. Defense Department among others, but they persist.[6] Furthermore, the allies note that they make a considerable contribution to common

---

[6] See, for instance, Frank C. Carlucci, Secretary of Defense, *Fiscal Year 1989 Annual Report to the Congress* (Washington, D.C.: U.S. Government Printing Office, 1988), p. 74, and "Report on Allied Contributions to the Common Defense," A Report to the United States Congress by Caspar W. Weinberger, Secretary of Defense, Washington, D.C., April 1987. See also Robert E. Hunter, "Allies Point Beyond Budgets to Find 'Fair Share,'" *Navy Times*, March 14, 1988; "After the INF Treaty: Keeping America in Europe," *SAIS Review* (Summer 1988); and "Will the United States Remain a European Power?" *Survival* (May-June 1988).

security through their foreign aid programs. That of the United States is still the largest in the world, by volume, but in terms of percentage of gross national product, U.S. foreign aid regularly lags behind that of virtually all of its allies.[7] In any debate about out-of-area issues, these allied contributions must be given their full weight.

The easy argument is that the out-of-area problem could be solved if each ally decided to look the other way. With demands for action or restraint, however, this solution will rarely be valid. The contemporary out-of-area problem can be dealt with only if it is broken down into its individual parts.

DEFINING INTERESTS, THREATS, RESPONSES, AND RESPONSIBILITY INTERESTS

The first element in structuring a reasonable and responsible out-of-area policy for NATO and its member states is to decide what matters are most important. Thus regarding three sets of Middle East problems already alluded to—Arab-Israeli peacemaking, terrorism, and the flow of oil—U.S. complaints about West European attitudes and actions have taken three forms: impediments to U.S. actions on behalf of all the allies (peacemaking); failure to understand U.S. needs and the imposition of constraints on unilateral U.S. efforts to meet those needs (terrorism); and reluctance to provide much assistance, as defined in the United States, as it tries to protect interests that are of equal or greater importance to the European allies (the flow of oil). In this last area, however, the deployment of ships in the Persian Gulf by five allied states during 1987–88, organized in part through consultations in the Western European Union, represented significant support for U.S. policy. Notably, concerns expressed in the U.S. Congress about allied participation quickly subsided.

The common thread that runs through these three examples is the issue of defining interests, threats, responses, and responsibility. Most important is the need to define interests more precisely than has often been done in the Western alliance. A key element of NATO security

---

[7] According to the Development Assistance Committee (DAC) of the Organization for Economic Cooperation and Development (OECD), the United States in 1985 ranked last out of 10 NATO countries that belong to the 18-nation DAC, in terms of percentage of gross national prodouct provided for Official Development Assistance (ODA). In addition, the other 17 DAC countries (which also include eight non-NATO countries) together contributed more than twice as much ODA as did the United States. By contrast, the United States spends about two and a half times as much on defense as do the other members of NATO. See *Growth, Exports, & Jobs in a Changing World Economy: Agenda 1988* (New Brunswick, NJ: Transaction Books (for the Overseas Development Council), 1988, p. 240, and Weinberger, "Report on Allied Contributions to the Common Defense (1987)," p. 71.

has been the principle of "an armed attack against one...shall be considered an attack against them all."[8] This commitment is not differentiated. The implication is that NATO security is a seamless web and that Iceland, the Outer Hebrides, and Greek islands in the Aegean are, at least in principle, as important as the central front in Germany.

Out of area, however, not even a principle or signed agreement covers the fiction of equal interests and equal importance. Differentiation is the rule even with something as critical as a complete stoppage of Persial Gulf oil. Even there, the impact would not be spread equally throughout the alliance, although all the allies, including those with North Sea oil and gas, would be seriously affected.

In the first instance, the burden must lie with the state that asks its allies for some positive action in support of a defined out-of-area interest. It must be prepared to bear the bulk of responsibility and also to make a convincing case that lending a hand will profit one or another of its North Atlantic allies. The state seeking to act has less to prove if it is asking its allies only for forbearance, such as not selling weapons or not undercutting diplomacy. It should have even less to prove if it is primarily seeking leave to act on its own behalf, as the United States was doing in seeking to use its European-based forces to attack Libya.

Every member of the North Atlantic Treaty Organization owes its allies the benefit of its best advice and counsel. Thus U.S. actions against terrorism in 1986 might not have represented the best tactics to achieve agreed objectives, and allies have a right and often a duty to make their viewpoints known. Furthermore, the actions of one ally may impose costs on others. These costs need not be limited to the ones adduced earlier as part of traditional West European fears about U.S. out-of-area activities: distraction of U.S. attention, concerns about possible U.S. error, threats to detente in Europe, and opposition from European publics. Thus, some U.S. antiterrorist actions have been viewed in Western Europe not just as the wrong approach but also as increasing the risks of more terrorism in Europe against Europeans.[9] In this particular case, both facts and interpretations can be disputed, but the point is valid that out-of-area actions by one ally can impose costs on others, and these must be accounted for.

---

[8] Article 5, North Atlantic Treaty.

[9] Middle East-born terrorism against both Americans and West Europeans has decreased significantly in the past two years. It is not possible to say for certain why this is so. It could be because of the U.S. attack on Libya, or it could stem from more complex factors. As a result, however, West European pressure on the United States to deal with the causes of terrorism has also declined.

In some circumstances, one ally will insist on its own course of action, even when that course is disputed, if it judges that its national interests are overriding. It might judge that it must act or face the possibility of being unable to sustain, in its domestic public opinion, support for core commitments to the central purposes of alliance. No doubt, the British government acceded to U.S. requests regarding the Libyan bombing in large part because it feared repercussions in U.S. domestic opinion if all Europeans withheld all assistance. The popular reaction in the United States to the behavior of other allies underscores the point. Similarly, five allied states sent ships to the Persian Gulf in late 1987 in major part for the same reason. This reason is not invalid. Yet within the structure of a transatlantic alliance that can continue to provide for core elements of security, should not as a rule be put in this position for less than compelling reasons.

This rule can be amplified as follows: allies on both sides of a dispute about the importance of particular interests out of area need to take fully into account the costs that are involved. These are costs, on the one hand, of not accepting an interest as important or, on the other hand, of risking damage to European security by insisting that something elsewhere should take priority. Making such decisions requires both judgment and statesmanship.

Threats

Even when more than one ally can agree that they share interests in common, this does not dispose of several other key factors. Most important is the nature of threats. Thus there has long been dispute across the Atlantic about the most important source of threats to Western interests in a number of areas, such as Central America, parts of southern Africa, and the Middle East. Generally, the disputes have pitted the United States against many of its allies, although not all the allies have accepted France's judgments about its activities in parts of Africa, and not all agreed with Britain's emphasis on recovering the Falkland Islands.

Prominent in allied debate about the nature of threat has been the role of the Soviet Union versus other potential sources of challenge for Western interests. In general, the United States has put more emphasis on Soviet activities in various Third World areas, and most West European states—where they agree upon the existence of a "threat"— place emphasis either on regional conflict or internal instability.

The tendency of individual allies to place different degrees of emphasis on the role of the Soviet Union also reflects two other factors: the general concern of most West Europeans that detente on the continent not be jeopardized and a U.S. purview that is more global than that of any of its allies. The debate does not have to be settled whether East-West competition must be viewed as worldwide in scope, whether Soviet involvement in particular Third World situations is the cause or the result of local instability, or whether circumstances can exist in East-West competition where one side does not have to "win" while the other "loses." In terms of alliance issues, what is more important is understanding that divergence of opinion is common among the allies on these points, and that this divergence both conditions attitudes toward out-of-area problems for the alliance and makes their resolution more difficult.

Clear predictions about the course of East-West relations during the 1990s are not possible. Soviet leadership under Mikhail S. Gorbachev has been posing a challenge quite different from that which NATO faced during most of its history. However, a reasonable surmise is that East-West (and particularly U.S.–Soviet) competition will continue in the Third World, even if the methods change and become less confrontational. The tactical flexibility that Gorbachev has shown so far seems to portend a more subtle but by no means less assertive approach to competition with the West in areas beyond Europe.

The Soviet factor is not alone in providing a source of disagreement within the alliance concerning the nature of out-of-area threats. Thus in 1987 many Europeans questioned U.S. actions in the Persian Gulf in terms of the source and nature of threats to Western interests in the region. In general, most West European states pay greater attention than does the United States to instability and threats to allied interests emanating from developments within Third World countries, especially to problems due to a lack of political, economic, and social development.

Responses

Divergence of opinion about the nature of threats to Western interests and about the importance of those interests to individual allies make broad-scale support unlikely for out-of-area action by any ally.

Independent actions will tend to cause friction within the alliance. Bargaining for support will be difficult, especially when a link is apparent between events in Third World areas and Western Europe. This difficulty was evident, for instance, in West European reluctance to follow the U.S. lead in imposing sanctions on the Soviet Union following its invasion of Afghanistan and in imposing sanctions against Iran during the hostage crisis of 1979-81.

Division within the alliance regarding the use of military force has tended to place the United States on one side and most of its allies on the other. This division has been true even when the nature of the threat has not been in dispute. Thus virtually every European ally questioned the efficacy of the use of force against terrorism originating in the Middle East in the mid-1980s. The clear West European preference has been to try doing something about the causes of terrorism. In Europe, the primary cause is seen to be the unresolved Arab-Israeli conflict, particularly the Palestinian problem. The U.S. government has not agreed with that view, and this divergence of opinion helped create the serious tensions within the alliance at the time of the U.S. bombing of Libya. Indeed, the United States regularly comes under pressure from its allies to play an active role in Arab-Israeli peacemaking, and it is often severely criticized when its abstention is perceived in Western Europe—rightly or wrongly—as exacerbating problems, from the zone of Arab-Israeli conflict to the Persian Gulf to terrorism.

American attitudes toward the use of force, as opposed to other instruments designed to achieve U.S. and allied interests out of area, are hard to forecast. Attitudes have been evolving along the lines of the so-called Weinberger Doctrine, reflecting the views of the former U.S. secretary of defense about requirements that must be fulfilled before the United States should employ military force abroad.[10] Indeed, the strictures he urged regarding the use of force probably represent an accurate accounting of basic, historical American attitudes to war.

That the rest of the allies, with the exception of France and possibly Britain, will continue to be more inclined to seek nonmilitary means of securing out-of-area interests is easier to forecast. These means include diplomacy and economic instruments, as befits the basic West European theory of threat that centers on difficulties within individual Third World states more than on cross-border or Soviet-inspired destabilization. This generalization about European attitudes toward the use of military force out of area has already stood a test of several years, and it is underscored by the inhibitions under which several allied governments operate in their politics and law. In the future, West Germany might be progressively less inhibited about using force beyond the continent, but that does not mean that it would give preference to military actions if viable alternatives were available.

---

[10] In summary, the former defense secretary argued that the United States must have important interests, and that these should be clearly understood by the American people; that there must be popular backing for the use of force; that it should be used in sufficient strength, with the lowest possible cost, with dispatch, with allies if that can be done—and with victory as the outcome.

During 1987, terrorism originating in the Middle East against Americans declined, and in no such incident was the United States inclined to use military force and risk serious disagreement within the alliance. In general, however, current wisdom predicts low-intensity conflict in various parts of the world, with the Middle East being the most likely locus. Allies on both sides of the Atlantic can expect that their differing attitudes toward such situations will continue to pose problems for relations among allies.

Responsibility

Finally, even where and when agreement develops within the alliance about the nature of allied interests, threats to them, and appropriate responses, deciding who should act will be difficult. No doubt, the United States will seek a greater role for its allies. To the degree that that role is defined in military terms, most if not all of the allies will likely continue to hold back. The question is whether the United States has enough to gain by seeking reluctant military support from allies out of area. As argued above, failure by allies to act can have consequences in U.S. domestic opinion, but the opposite is also true regarding domestic attitudes in most West European countries toward the United States.

However, various allies can increase their involvement in peace-keeping activities, whether those undertaken by the United Nations or those that could be undertaken by allies working together, as has happened in the Sinai and Lebanon. Individual allies, such as Britain and France, may be motivated to provide support for U.S. military actions on behalf of other allies in order to reduce the risk that the U.S. government, the Congress, or the American people would conclude that the allies were not sufficiently responsive to U.S. definitions of threat to Western interests. This matter must be subjected to the most searching inquiry and debate within the alliance.

European Political Cooperation or cooperation in the Western European Union could develop to the point that Europeans will consider some form of peacekeeping force of their own. Any form of joint military force for out-of-area action is unlikely, however, unless and until sufficient progress is made on security cooperation and supranational decision making for defense within Europe.

The allies should revive the concept of a division of labor within the alliance. Put forward by West German Chancellor Helmut Schmidt in 1979 at U.S. suggestion, this concept focused on gaining West European economic aid for distressed countries, primarily Turkey. The concept should now be extended to areas of the Third World with important allied interests, for example, Egypt, Pakistan, and the

Philippines.[11] Focusing on major increases in foreign aid has an advantage over conventional force increases in NATO Europe because it is consonant with a political ethic that has widespread appeal. Many Europeans who, for a variety of reasons, would resist spending extra money for military buildup might be prepared to see the same "security" funds devoted to economic development in Third World nations. In some circumstances, these funds would help deal with situations that could otherwise become threats to Western interests. Organized formally, such a division of labor would also ensure that the European allies get proper credit for the efforts they are now undertaking.

Division of labor is also possible in other nonmilitary ways, including peacemaking diplomacy. However, few of the non-U.S. allies have shown much inclination for assuming responsibility for peacemaking out of area.[12] Some form of joint European peacemaking might become possible within European Political Cooperation, especially if it begins to develop in parallel with increasing defense cooperation in Western Europe. But the limits will continue, however, especially in terms of standing and stature. In the Arab-Israeli conflict, for instance, no West European country or collection of them has so far gained the standing to negotiate between Israel and its neighbors. In some circumstances, the power, presence, and prestige of the United States are still required for the effort to be effective. The exceptions have included the special role Britain played in Rhodesia/Zimbabwe and the activities of the five-nation Contact Group in regard to Namibia.

During the next several years, stimulating a larger role for European states in peacemaking and similar diplomatic activities would have considerable value. This value is particularly great in dealing with countries and situations where one or more allied countries could have greater access than the United States; Iran has been a case in point during the 1980s. At the same time, for West European states to be more active diplomatically on behalf of their own or allied interests out of area, in many instances the United States would have to be prepared to cede some pride of place.

---

[11] This division of labor should include Japan, which also gains benefits from Western security efforts by its allies. Indeed, Japan and other nations that are not part of NATO will increasingly be faced with an out-of-area problem of their own in regard to U.S. definitions of the common security problem.

[12] A number of European states are involved in United Nations peacekeeping efforts which, by their nature, also entail some elements of peacemaking.

NATO AS A REGIONAL ALLIANCE: THE LOWEST COMMON DENOMINATOR

This brief discussion of possible conflicts of viewpoint among the allies—as well as potential for cooperation—is intended to demonstrate a range of factors that will be important during the next several years as the alliance develops policies and procedures toward out-of-area issues. Several guidelines emerge from this discussion.

1. Whether or not allies will accede to requests for assistance out of area will depend very much on circumstances. Hard-and-fast rules will be hard to derive. Bargaining over each issue will be extensive, with different factors in play on each occasion.

2. For the foreseeable future, the United States will remain the country most likely to request assistance—from European states and perhaps also from other countries—in meeting out-of-area challenges. Increasingly, resistance on the part of its allies is likely to have a negative impact on U.S. domestic opinion. This will be added to other irritations, including classic concerns about burdensharing and newer concerns about trade deficits and growing economic competition from European Community countries.

3. Thus the United States should accept, to the degree possible, that individual allies will be more likely to take part if they can tailor their responses to what they can and will do, both materially and politically. The concept of security should be broad, with room for economic, diplomatic, political, and peacekeeping activities as contributions to protecting Western interests. The deep involvement of other states, particularly Japan, should be encouraged by a division of labor that assigns economic tasks to them.

4. Some common action can be possible—if primarily through parallel action—as demonstrated by the patrolling of the Persian Gulf in 1987–88. Specific circumstances will likely prevail in each instance, but at least the precedent has been set.

5. Most joint activity by allies will have to be organized on a bilateral basis, usually with the lead of the United States. In general, the United States should try to work with a few allies that are willing to help, rather than trying to garner greater support from reluctant allies.

6. Any ally, particularly the United States, will have to weigh the importance of gaining help out of area against potential difficulties in preserving cohesion regarding the core purposes of the alliance.

7. NATO should receive increasing emphasis as a regional alliance with regional responsibilities, rather than as a collection of states called upon to respond to the U.S. lead in other parts of the globe.

330   *Robert E. Hunter*

8. The allies should focus on the core elements of security in Europe, even if that means recognizing that NATO remains a lowest-common-denominator alliance, rather than risking these elements through too much effort to broaden the NATO mandate.

At the same time, however, the attitudes of recent U.S. administrations have been moving in the opposite direction. Ironically, the tendency in the United States is to view NATO as an alliance with broader, though not global, responsibilities (as opposed to the initial American view of NATO as a regional alliance) at the precise time when the West European allies increasingly think regionally, not globally.

Following these guidelines will not be easy. In particular, U.S. administrations will have an increasingly difficult time arguing for a continued high level of military expenditure on European defense in the face of other demands elsewhere. Allied participation in out-of-area activities can help to offset the growing trend in the United States to favor troop cuts, but it may not be sufficient. If American out-of-area activities and demands for European support increase resentment in Europe about U.S. policies and pressures, in many circumstances the effort may not be worthwhile.

A VARIABLE GEOMETRY OF U.S. INVOLVEMENT

Several suggestions have been made regarding changes in the pattern of U.S. force deployments on the European continent. One school of thought argues that U.S. forces should be reduced in order to be available for contingencies elsewhere, such as the Persian Gulf or Central America.[13] This idea introduces both a problem and a partial solution. The problem has three key parts:

• the need to find a means of reinforcing—politically and psychologically—the U.S. commitment to Europe at a time when few observers predict war;
• the need to deal with U.S. trade deficits and a growing popular feeling of discontent in the United States about the level of U.S. financial contribution to European security; and
• the need, perceived in many quarters in the United States, to be able to deal effectively with low-intensity conflict and other threats to U.S. security, even where this sense of threat is not shared by European allies.

---

[13] See, for instance, Zbigniew Brzezinski, *Game Plan* (Boston: Atlantic Monthly Press, 1986).

For some time, the use of U.S. forces based in Western Europe for out-of-area contingencies has been debated. This is not just a burdensharing question. Indeed, many analysts argue that moving U.S. forces from Europe to the United States and keeping them in being might save on foreign exchange, but it would impose greater budget costs for the United States, such as loss of so-called Host Nation Support and the added expense of sealift and airlift to move these forces abroad from the continental United States.[14] Critics note, however, that forces brought home would likely be disbanded for reasons of economy, not kept ready for overseas contingencies.

Beyond burdensharing is a key question about the structure of U.S. forces for different contingencies. An army division that could be effective on the European central front is not necessarily the same force that a military commander would need for action in many areas of the Third World. These other forces can be created, but at a price.

The partial answer lies in using U.S. forces stationed in Western Europe, as well as some based in the United States that are earmarked for European service, to do double duty. Thus they could be on the NATO roster for most of their useful service life, but be subject to diversion to some other part of the world—especially the volatile Middle East and southwest Asia—if events warranted diversion. However, configuration of forces for one task may not be compatible with the configuration required for another task.

Among the alternative solutions, three stand out. One would be to emphasize, for some U.S. forces in NATO Europe, those tasks that would prepare them to do double duty. It is not clear how far this could go in helping to provide combat-ready and -trained U.S. forces in the European theater that could operate effectively elsewhere. At the very least, a separate logistics base would be necessary, just as the possibility of low-intensity conflict will require the U.S. Navy to place increasing emphasis on being able to move forces for limited action, if need be at the expense of some preparations for a hypothetical U.S.-Soviet clash at sea in the opening stages of World War III.

Another possible solution would be for the West Europeans to be prepared to take up the slack. This could be particularly relevant for West Germany and its sizable reserve units. These forces could be called up at a time of U.S. involvement elsewhere, and they could make use of U.S. equipment left behind by diverted U.S. forces, especially as much of it either could not or should not be transshipped to an out-of-area location. This solution implies a political agreement

---

[14] See Carlucci, *1989 Annual Report to the Congress.*

between the United States and the Federal Republic on the nature of out-of-area contingencies and the appropriate response.

A third possible solution is to recognize the realities of U.S. force deployments in Western Europe. They are there essentially to fulfill four major purposes. Three are directly military and political-military: to help sustain a strategy of flexible response by contributing to a robust conventional defense; to provide some possibility for implementing the forward strategy that is politically important to the Federal Republic; and to obscure politically the fact that the *Bundeswehr* is the largest land army on NATO's central front. The fourth purpose is strategic: the hostage role played by U.S. forces and their dependents that helps to ensure the credibility of the U.S. nuclear commitment. In fulfilling this function, however, no specific number of U.S. forces is required. If the United States diverted some of its capability to out-of-area contingencies for a limited time—with the clear understanding of its allies and especially West Germany—the allies would not need to compensate fully for these reductions. Because NATO security ultimately depends on the U.S. nuclear commitment, a logical basis does not exist for arguing that such diversion of limited U.S. military resources would leave the central front vulnerable to Warsaw Pact aggression. Indeed, the demonstration of U.S. willingness to take military action in defense of Western interests should reinforce, not reduce, deterrence of any Soviet adventure.

In practice, committing some U.S. forces in Europe to possible double duty can be sustained politically only if it clearly comports with the interests and approval of the European allies, if they are prepared to make the financial investments necessary to make this a viable option, and if they are prepared to be politically and economically committed in some way to U.S. actions out of area that are plausibly in the common allied interest. Both sides must be prepared to compromise if the core elements of alliance are to be preserved.

CONTINGENCIES IN CHANGE

This discussion has been very much rooted in today, but imponderables are likely tomorrow. From the point of view of out-of-area issues, three possibilities stand out:

- a major reduction of U.S. forces deployed in Europe, perhaps accompanied by a weakening of transatlantic political ties; or
- advances in East-West understanding and arms control, or even significant political accommodation on the continent, that would

lead to a thinning out of forces on both sides of the central European front, even if this did not lead to a lessening of U.S.-Soviet competition out of area; or

- a radical increase in intra-West European political and defense cooperation that would lead to a strong European pillar in NATO and perhaps also to much greater independence for the West European states.

But none of these cases suggests an appreciable diminishing of low-intensity conflict in various parts of the Third World that could affect Western interests. A prime example is the Middle East, where East-West competition is only one factor among many making for instability.

Even if any or all of these three possibilities came to pass, different states would be likely to continue having different views about what is important out of area, and they would make their independent calculations about interests, threats, responses, and sharing of responsibility. Indeed, a loosening of ties across the Atlantic would be likely to lead to less comity about what should be done out of area and to a greater emphasis by the United States on gaining the support of major European countries.

The alliance does not define the context for out-of-area contingencies. They exist on their own, and the alliance is a mechanism for attempting to rally support, to give advice, and to bargain about priorities, contributions, and cooperation. Unless the United States also truncated its sense of interest in many parts of the Third World as it reduced its troops in, and ties to, Western Europe, an out-of-area problem would continue. To the extent that interests were at stake for more than one country that is now an ally, the problem would continue.

In sum, NATO's out-of-area problem will likely grow in importance. No simple answer is possible. Certainly, it does not lie in reducing transatlantic ties and mutual obligations. An answer lies primarily in each ally's understanding that nothing out of area has yet been proved to be so important as to warrant taking military or political risks that could jeopardize core elements of alliance. If that lesson is learned thoroughly, then bargaining can take place about individual developments in a way that is consistent with NATO's essential purposes. In the final analysis, the bargaining will produce valid results, provided everyone who is engaged in it constantly, clearly, and correctly judges the priorities for security.

Index

Aircraft: B-1 bomber, 275; Backfire bomber, 267; F-15, 274–75; F-111 bombers, 249, 252, 267, 273–75; Tornado, 97, 228, 274–76; Vulcan, 267

Afghanistan, Soviet invasion of: European response to, 88, 117, 268; exaggerate alliance differences, 108, 120, 145–46, 239, 243, 325; and Gorbachev's foreign policy, 135–36, 242; increase East–West tensions, 58, 69, 150; and nuclear weapons in Europe, 268; Soviet troop withdrawal, 130–32, 296

Allied Command Atlantic (SACLANT), 318

Allied Command Europe (ACE), 186, 318

America First movement, 90, 120

Anti-ballistic Missile (ABM) Treaty, 131, 293

Antinuclear weapons movements, 161–62, 258, 270, 284–87, 292, 302–304

Arms control, 33, 36, 116, 168, 261–62, 273–74; conventional weapons, 34, 101, 189, 208, 214, 252, 304–13; East–West, 14, 82, 97, 126; nuclear weapons, 7, 119, 267; Reykjavik Summit, 175, 270; strategic weapons, 276, 286, 293–96. *See also* Report of the Independent Commission on Disarmament and Security

Austria, 56, 110

Balkanization of European defense efforts, 216–17, 254–55

Baltic waterways, 28, 190

Belgium, 225; burdensharing, 181, 190; commitment to nuclear deployment, 251, 268; and NATO, 32, 57, 170; out-of-area issues, 316

Benelux, 304, 308

Bulgaria, 50, 56

Burdensharing: "All-around security comparisons," 176; analysis of national effort, 125–26, 176, 193–200; calculations of, 176–91; collective planning process, 190, 210; D/GDP, 177–78; defense expenditures, 183, 185, 195–98, 204–205, 330; Defense Planning Questionnaire (DPQ), 194–96, 198; division of labor within the alliance, 66, 108, 125, 176, 189–90,

210, 280, 328–39; domestic public financing (taxation), 177–79, 181–82, 210, 220; foreign aid, 328; and GDP, 92, 177–179, 181, 184; and GNP, 92, 177–78, 193–94, 197–98, 210, 290, 322; national audits, 184; national force subscriptions, 188–91, 205; offset payments issue, 198–200; out-of-area issues, 315–33; prosperity index (PI), 179, 181; role specialization, 189–91, 280; U.S. congressional amendment on, 207; U.S. interests and Europeans' interests, 98–100, 118, 120; U.S. negotiator, 203

Canada, 18, 31; burdensharing, 175–191; and NATO, 1, 9, 109, 119

Carter administration, 147, 266, 283–84, 290

CENTO, 66, 316

Chernobyl, 162, 251, 270. *See also* Civilian uses of nuclear power

Chicago Council on Foreign Relations, 150–52, 158–59, 206

Civilian uses of nuclear power, 162, 251. *See also* Chernobyl

Command, control, and communications systems (C^3), 296

Command, control, communications, and intelligence (C^3I) systems, 269

Commission on Integrated Long-Term Strategy, and *Discriminate Deterrence*, 88–89

Commission on Security and Defense, 224

Conference of National Armaments Directors (CNAD), 219, 223, 230, 299

Conference on Confidence- and Security-Building Measures and Disarmament in Europe, 8, 35–36

Containment doctrine, 102, 106. *See also* United States: Containment of Soviet expansionism

Conventional Defense Improvement (CDI), 4, 28

Conventional forces imbalance, 22, 243, 293

Conventional stability talks, 7, 208, 252. *See also* Arms control

Conventional weapons, 243, 264; asymmetrical cuts in, 131, 140, 215, 293; freeze on technology, 307–308

335

About the Editor

Stanley R. Sloan is the specialist in U.S. Alliance Relations for the Congressional Research Service, Washington, D.C. Previously he served as head of the Europe/Middle East/Africa Section, Congressional Research Service; as Deputy National Intelligence Officer for Western Europe (CIA); and as a member of the U.S. delegation to the MBFR negotiations. He is the author of *NATO's Future: Toward a New Transatlantic Bargain*, as well as numerous studies on NATO, arms control, and other international security topics.

About the Contributors

A. W. DePorte is a visiting scholar at the Institute of French Studies, New York University. He previously served as a career official of the U.S. Department of State during which, among other positions, he was a member of the Policy Planning Staff and Director of the Office of Research on Western Europe. He is the author of *Europe Between the Superpowers: The Enduring Balance* and of many scholarly studies of U.S.–European relations and French foreign policy.

Lawrence Freedman is professor and head of the Department of War Studies at Kings College, University of London. He previously served as head of Policy Studies at the Royal Institute of International Affairs, Chatham House, and held research positions at Nuffield College, Oxford University, and the International Institute for Strategic Studies. He is the author of *The Price of Peace* and numerous other books and scholarly works on defense strategy, arms control, and alliance issues.

David Greenwood is Director of the Centre for Defence Studies at the University of Aberdeen, Scotland. An established expert on defense spending and burdensharing issues, he is the author of numerous research reports, contributions to symposia, and journal and newspaper articles on the economic aspects of British and European defense.

François Heisbourg is Director of the International Institute for Strategic Studies, London. He has served as Vice-President of Thomson S.A., responsible for cooperative U.S.–European defense programs; International Security Advisor to the French Minister of Defense; First Secretary at the French Mission to the United Nations;

member of the Foreign Ministry's Policy Planning Staff; and assistant to the director of the Economics Department of the Foreign Ministry. He has published widely on defense cooperation and other security issues.

Robert E. Hunter is Director of European Studies at the Center for Strategic and International Studies in Washington, D.C. During the Carter administration, he was Director of European Affairs at the National Security Council (1977–79). He is author of *Security in Europe* and editor of *NATO: The Next Generation*.

Karl Kaiser is professor of political science at the University of Cologne and Director of the Research Institute for the German Society of Foreign Affairs, Bonn. He has taught at the University of Bonn, Johns Hopkins University in Bologna, and at the Saarland. He has served as a member of the Council of Environmental Advisors of the Federal Republic of Germany and of the Government Commission for the Reform of the Armed Services. He has published extensively on transatlantic and European security issues.

Catherine McArdle Kelleher is professor at the School of Public Affairs and Director of the Center for International Security Studies at the University of Maryland. She served on the staff of the Carter National Security Council and is a member of the Council on Foreign Relations and the International Institute of Strategic Studies. She has written extensively on European security issues and is the author, coauthor, or editor of *Germany and the Politics of Nuclear Weapons, American Arms and a Changing Europe, Wealth, Welfare, and Security,* and *Evolving European Defense Policies.*

Lawrence Korb is Director of the Center for Public Policy Education at the Brookings Institution, Washington, D.C. He formerly served as Dean of the Graduate School of Public and International Affairs at the University of Pittsburgh, as Vice-President for Corporate Operations for the Raytheon Corporation, and as Assistant Secretary of Defense for Management, Reserve Affairs, Installations and Logistics. He is author of numerous books, monographs, and articles on national security issues.

Pierre Lellouche is Deputy Director of the French Institute for International Relations (IFRI), Paris. He has served as a consultant to the Government of France, international organizations, and corporate enterprises and is a frequent media commentator on security policy issues. He is the author of *The Future of War* and of numerous publications on French national security policy, arms control, and Western alliance issues.

Dimitri K. Simes is Senior Associate at the Carnegie Endowment for International Peace in Washington, D.C. He formerly served as a

Senior Research Fellow and Director of Soviet Studies at the Center for Strategic and International Studies. He lectures at the Johns Hopkins School of Advanced International Studies and has taught at the University of California (Berkeley) and at Columbia University. He is the author of *Detente and Conflict: Soviet Foreign Policy 1972-77* and of numerous scholarly works, articles, and commentaries on Soviet foreign policy and U.S.-Soviet relations.

Michael Stuermer is Director of the Stiftung Wissenschaft und Politik in Ebenhausen, Germany. He has written and lectured extensively on East-West issues and intra-German relations.

Stephen F. Szabo is Professor, National Security Affairs at the National War College in Washington, D.D., and Professorial Lecturer in European Studies, The School of Advanced International Studies, The Johns Hopkins University. His publications include *The Successor Generation: International Perspectives of Postwar Europeans* and numerous articles on public opinion and the politics of European security.

R. James Woolsey is a partner in the Washington, D.C., law firm of Shea and Gardner. He formerly served as Under Secretary of the Navy and as Delegate-at-Large to the U.S.-Soviet Nuclear and Space Arms Talks, Geneva. He is a member of the Board of Directors of the Atlantic Council of the United States and has written and commented extensively on strategic force posture and arms control issues.